ANNUAL EDITIONS

Educational Psychology 09/10
Twenty-Fourth Edition

EDITORS

Kathleen M. Cauley
Virginia Commonwealth University

Kathleen M. Cauley received her PhD in Educational Studies/Human Development from the University of Delaware in 1985. Her current research interests are student transitions to a new school, and the influence of assessment practices on motivation.

Gina M. Pannozzo
Virginia Commonwealth University

Gina M. Pannozzo received her PhD in Educational Psychology from the University of Buffalo in 2005. Her current research examines the relationships among student engagement patterns in school and dropping out.

 **Higher Education**

Boston   Burr Ridge, IL   Dubuque, IA   New York   San Francisco   St. Louis
Bangkok   Bogotá   Caracas   Kuala Lumpur   Lisbon   London   Madrid   Mexico City
Milan   Montreal   New Delhi   Santiago   Seoul   Singapore   Sydney   Taipei   Toronto

The McGraw·Hill Companies

Mc Graw Hill Higher Education

ANNUAL EDITIONS: EDUCATIONAL PSYCHOLOGY, TWENTY-FOURTH EDITION

Annual Editions® is a registered trademark of The McGraw-Hill Companies, Inc.
Annual Editions is published by the **Contemporary Learning Series** group within the McGraw-Hill Higher Education division.

1 2 3 4 5 6 7 8 9 0 QPD/QPD 0 9

ISBN 978–0–07–351640–0
MHID 0–07–351640–6
ISSN 0731–1141

Managing Editor: *Larry Loeppke*
Senior Managing Editor: *Faye Schilling*
Developmental Editor: *Dave Welsh*
Editorial Coordinator: *Mary Foust*
Editorial Assistant: *Nancy Meissner*
Production Service Assistant: *Rita Hingtgen*
Permissions Coordinator: *DeAnna Dausener*
Senior Marketing Manager: *Julie Keck*
Marketing Communications Specialist: *Mary Klein*
Marketing Coordinator: *Alice Link*
Project Manager: *Sandy Wille*
Design Specialist: *Tara McDermott*
Senior Production Supervisor: *Laura Fuller*
Cover Graphics: *Kristine Jubeck*

Compositor: Laserwords Private Limited
Cover Images: © Photodisc Collection/Getty Images/RF (inset); © Getty Images/RF (background)

Library in Congress Cataloging-in-Publication Data
Main entry under title: Annual Editions: Educational Psychology, 24/e
  1. Educational Psychology—Periodicals by Kathleen M. Cauley, Gina M. Pannozzo, *comp.* II. Title: Educational Psychology
658'.05

www.mhhe.com

Editors/Advisory Board

Members of the Advisory Board are instrumental in the final selection of articles for each edition of ANNUAL EDITIONS. Their review of articles for content, level, currentness, and appropriateness provides critical direction to the editor and staff. We think that you will find their careful consideration well reflected in this volume.

Preface

In publishing ANNUAL EDITIONS we recognize the enormous role played by the magazines, newspapers, and journals of the public press in providing current, first-rate educational information in a broad spectrum of interest areas. Many of these articles are appropriate for students, researchers, and professionals seeking accurate, current material to help bridge the gap between principles and theories and the real world. These articles, however, become more useful for study when those of lasting value are carefully collected, organized, indexed, and reproduced in a low-cost format, which provides easy and permanent access when the material is needed. That is the role played by ANNUAL EDITIONS.

Educational psychology is an interdisciplinary subject that includes human development, learning, intelligence, motivation, assessment, instructional strategies, and classroom management. The articles in this volume give special attention to the application of this knowledge to teaching.

Annual Editions: Educational Psychology 09/10 is divided into six units, and an overview precedes each unit, which explains how the unit articles are related to the broader issues within educational psychology.

The first unit, *Perspectives on Teaching,* presents issues that are central to the role of teaching. The articles' authors provide perspectives on being an effective teacher and the issues facing teachers in the twenty-first century.

The second unit, entitled *Development,* is concerned with child and adolescent development. It covers the biological, cognitive, social, and emotional processes of development. The essays in this unit examine the ways in which developmental factors prepare students to do well in school, as well as the impact of school on child and adolescent development.

The third unit, *Individual Differences among Learners,* considers the individual differences among learners and how to meet those needs. It focuses on inclusive teaching, serving students who are gifted, gender issues, and multicultural education. Diverse students require an individualized approach to education. The articles in this unit review the characteristics of these children and suggest programs and strategies to meet their needs.

In the fourth unit, *Learning and Instruction,* articles about theories of learning and instructional strategies are presented. The selections on learning and cognition provide a broad view of different aspects of learning, covering areas such as constructivist learning, critical thinking, differentiation, and cooperative learning. Although they cover a broad variety of topics, the common thread is that learning is an active process and involves construction of meaning. In the instructional strategies section of the unit, the articles provide a range of strategies for improving student learning, covering such topics as instructional technology, differentiating instruction, and the use of questioning.

The topic of motivation is perhaps one of the most important aspects of school learning. Effective teachers need to motivate their students both to learn and to behave responsibly. How to manage children and what forms of discipline to use are issues that concern parents as well as teachers and administrators. In addition, the climate or environment of the classroom greatly impacts their motivation, influencing how and in what ways students engage in activities. The articles in the fifth unit, *Motivation and Classroom Management,* present a variety of perspectives on motivating students and discuss both general approaches to classroom management, as well as more challenging behaviors. The articles in the sixth unit review assessment approaches that can be used to diagnose learning and improve instruction. The focus here is twofold, providing perspective with regard to how standards and high stakes assessments influence students, as well as effective strategies for classroom assessment such as involving students in the assessment process, the use of feedback in formative assessment, and how students' perceive assessment. Throughout this unit, the theme is integrating assessment with instruction to enhance student learning.

This edition also features selected *World Wide Web* sites, which can be used to further explore the articles' topics. These sites are cross-referenced by number in the *topic guide.*

This twenty-fourth *Annual Editions: Educational Psychology* has been revised in order to present articles that are current and useful. Your responses to the selection and organization of materials are appreciated. Please complete and return the postage-paid *article rating form* on the last page of the book.

Kathleen M. Cauley
Editor

Gina M. Pannozzo
Editor

Contents

UNIT 1
Perspectives on Teaching

UNIT 2
Development

The concepts in bold italics are developed in the article. For further expansion, please refer to the Topic Guide.

UNIT 3
Individual Differences among Learners

Unit Overview 44

The concepts in bold italics are developed in the article. For further expansion, please refer to the Topic Guide.

UNIT 4
Learning and Instruction

The concepts in bold italics are developed in the article. For further expansion, please refer to the Topic Guide.

UNIT 5
Motivation and Classroom Management

The concepts in bold italics are developed in the article. For further expansion, please refer to the Topic Guide.

The concepts in bold italics are developed in the article. For further expansion, please refer to the Topic Guide.

UNIT 6
Assessment

The concepts in bold italics are developed in the article. For further expansion, please refer to the Topic Guide.

Correlation Guide

The *Annual Editions* series provides students with convenient, inexpensive access to current, carefully selected articles from the public press. **Annual Editions: Educational Psychology 09/10** is an easy-to-use reader that presents articles on important topics such as *teaching perspectives, individual differences, motivation,* and many more. For more information on *Annual Editions* and other *McGraw-Hill Contemporary Learning Series* titles, visit www.mhcls.com.

This convenient guide matches the units in **Annual Editions: Educational Psychology 09/10** with the corresponding chapters in one of our best-selling McGraw-Hill Educational Psychology textbooks by Santrock.

Annual Editions: Educational Psychology 09/10	Educational Psychology, 4/e by Santrock
Unit 1: Perspectives on Teaching	**Chapter 1:** Educational Psychology: A Tool for Effective Teaching
Unit 2: Development	**Chapter 2:** Cognitive and Language Development **Chapter 3:** Social Contexts and Socioemotional Development
Unit 3: Individual Differences Among Learners	**Chapter 3:** Social Contexts and Socioemotional Development **Chapter 4:** Individual Variations **Chapter 5:** Sociocultural Diversity
Unit 4: Learning and Instructions	**Chapter 6:** Learners Who Are Exceptional **Chapter 7:** Behavioral and Social Cognitive Approaches **Chapter 11:** Learning and Cognition in the Content Areas **Chapter 12:** Planning, Instruction, and Technology **Chapter 13:** Motivation, Teaching, and Learning
Unit 5: Motivation and Classroom Management	**Chapter 14:** Managing the Classroom
Unit 6: Assessment	**Chapter 15:** Standardized Tests and Teaching **Chapter 16:** Classroom Assessment

Topic Guide

This topic guide suggests how the selections in this book relate to the subjects covered in your course. You may want to use the topics listed on these pages to search the Web more easily.

On the following pages a number of Web sites have been gathered specifically for this book. They are arranged to reflect the units of this Annual Editions reader. You can link to these sites by going to *http://www.mhcls.com*.

All the articles that relate to each topic are listed below the bold-faced term.

Internet References

The following Internet sites have been selected to support the articles found in this reader. These sites were available at the time of publication. However, because Web sites often change their structure and content, the information listed may no longer be available. We invite you to visit http://www.mhcls.com for easy access to these sites.

Annual Editions: Educational Psychology, 09/10

General Sources

American Psychological Association
http://www.apa.org/topics/homepage.html

By exploring the APA's "PsycNET," you will be able to find links to an abundance of articles and other resources that are useful in the field of educational psychology.

Educational Resources Information Center
http://www.eric.ed.gov

This invaluable site provides links to all ERIC sites: clearinghouses, support components, and publishers of ERIC materials. Search the ERIC database for what is new.

National Education Association
http://www.nea.org

Something—and often quite a lot—about virtually every education-related topic can be accessed at or through this site of the 2.3-million-strong National Education Association.

National Parent Information Network/ERIC
http://npin.org

This is a clearinghouse of information on elementary and early childhood education as well as urban education. Browse through its links for information for parents.

U.S. Department of Education
http://www.ed.gov/pubs/TeachersGuide/

Government goals, projects, and grants are listed here, plus many links to teacher services and resources.

UNIT 1: Perspectives on Teaching

The Center for Innovation in Education
http://www.center.edu

The Center for Innovation in Education, self-described as a "not-for-profit, non-partisan research organization," focuses on K–12 education reform strategies. Click on its links about school privatization.

Classroom Connect
http://www.classroom.net

This is a major Web site for K–12 teachers and students, with links to schools, teachers, and resources online. It includes discussion of the use of technology in the classroom.

Education World
http://www.education-world.com

Education World provides a database of literally thousands of sites that can be searched by grade level, plus education news, lesson plans, and professional-development resources.

Goals 2000: A Progress Report
http://www.ed.gov/pubs/goals/progrpt/index.html

Open this site to survey a progress report by the U.S. Department of Education on the Goals 2000 reform initiative. It provides a sense of the goals that educators are reaching for as they look toward the future.

Teacher Talk Forum
http://education.indiana.edu/cas/tt/tthmpg.html

Visit this site for access to a variety of articles discussing life in the classroom. Clicking on the various links will lead you to electronic lesson plans, covering a variety of topic areas, from Indiana University's Center for Adolescent Studies.

UNIT 2: Development

Association for Moral Education
http://www.amenetwork.org/

AME is dedicated to fostering communication, cooperation, training, curriculum development, and research that link moral theory with educational practices. From here it is possible to connect to several sites on moral development.

Center for Adolescent and Families Studies
http://www.indiana.edu/~cafs

This site provides information on research practices of instruction. Also included is a link to other resources.

Child Welfare League of America
http://www.cwla.org

The CWLA is the United States' oldest and largest organization devoted entirely to the well-being of vulnerable children and their families. This site provides links to information about issues related to morality and values in education.

The National Association for Child Development
http://www.nacd.org/

This international organization is dedicated to helping children and adults reach their full potential. Its home page presents links to various programs, research, and resources into such topics as ADD/ADHD.

National Association of School Psychologists (NASP)
http://www.nasponline.org/

The NASP offers advice to teachers about how to help children cope with the many issues they face in today's world. The site includes tips for school personnel as well as parents.

Scholastic News Zone
http://www.scholasticnews.com

At this site, Scholastic Classroom magazines provide up-to-date information to children, teachers, and parents online to help explain timely issues.

UNIT 3: Individual Differences among Learners

The Council for Exceptional Children
http://www.cec.sped.org/index.html

This page will give you access to information on identifying and teaching gifted children, attention-deficit disorders, and other topics in gifted education.

Global SchoolNet Foundation
http://www.gsn.org

Access this site for multicultural education information. The site includes news for teachers, students, and parents, as well as chat rooms, links to educational resources, programs, and contests and competitions.

International Project: Multicultural Pavilion
http://curry.edschool.virginia.edu/curry/centers/multicultural/papers.html

Here is a forum, sponsored by the Curry School of Education at the University of Virginia, for sharing stories and resources and for learning from the stories and resources of others. These articles on the Internet cover every possible racial, gender, and multicultural issue that could arise in the field of multicultural education.

Internet References

Let 100 Flowers Bloom/Kristen Nicholson-Nelson
http://teacher.scholastic.com/professional/assessment/100flowers.htm

Open this page for Kristen Nicholson-Nelson's discussion of ways in which teachers can help to nurture children's multiple intelligences. She provides a useful bibliography and resources.

National Association for Multicultural Education
http://www.nameorg.org

NAME is a major organization in the field of multicultural education. The Web site provides conference information and resources including lesson plans, advice for handling touchy issues, and grant information.

National Attention Deficit Disorder Association
http://www.add.org

This site, some of which is under construction, will lead you to information about ADD/ADHD. It has links to self-help and support groups, outlines behaviors and diagnostics, answers FAQs, and suggests books and other resources.

National MultiCultural Institute (NMCI)
http://www.nmci.org

NMCI is one of the major organizations in the field of diversity training. At this Web site, NMCI offers conference data, resource materials, diversity training and consulting service information, and links to other related sites.

Tolerance.org
http://www.tolerance.org

This site promotes and supports anti-bias activism in every venue of life. The site contains resources, a collection of print materials, and downloadable public service announcements.

UNIT 4: Learning and Instruction

The Critical Thinking Community
http://criticalthinking.org

This site promotes educational reform through fair-minded critical thinking. The site also provides information and resources on critical thinking.

Education Week on the Web
http://www.edweek.org

At this page you can open archives, read special reports, keep up on current events, and access a variety of articles in educational psychology. A great deal of this material is helpful in learning and instruction.

Online Internet Institute
http://www.oii.org

A collaborative project among Internet-using educators, proponents of systemic reform, content-area experts, and teachers who desire professional growth, this site provides a learning environment for integrating the Internet into educators' individual teaching styles.

Teachers Helping Teachers
http://www.pacificnet.net/~mandel/

This site provides basic teaching tips, new teaching-methodology ideas, and forums for teachers to share their experiences. It features educational resources on the Web, with new ones added each week.

The Teachers' Network
http://www.teachers.net/

Bulletin boards, classroom projects, online forums, and Web mentors are featured on this site, as well as the book *Teachers' Guide to Cyberspace* and an online, 4-week course on how to use the Internet.

UNIT 5: Motivation and Classroom Management

I Love Teaching
http://www.iloveteaching.com

This site is a resource for new and veteran teachers as well as preservice teachers and student teachers. Information is broken out into various links such as "Encouraging Words," and "Classroom Management."

The Jigsaw Classroom
http://jigsaw.org

The jigsaw classroom is a cooperate learning technique that reduces racial conflict among school children, promotes better learning, improves student motivation, and increases enjoyment of the learning experience. The site includes history, implementation tips, and more.

North Central Educational Regional Laboratory
http://www.ncrel.org/sdrs/

This site provides research, policy, and best practices on issues critical to educators engaged in school improvement. A number of critical issues are covered.

Teaching Helping Teachers
http://www.pacificnet.net/~mandel/

This site is a resource tool for all teachers. It includes links to "Classroom Management," "Special Education," and more.

UNIT 6: Assessment

Awesome Library for Teachers
http://www.neat-schoolhouse.org/teacher.html

Open this page for links and access to teacher information on everything from assessments to child development topics.

FairTest
http://fairtest.org

This site is the homepage for the National Center for Fair and Open Testing. The main objective of this group is to end the misuses and flaws of standardized testing and to ensure that evaluation of students, teachers, and schools is fair, open, valid, and educationally beneficial.

Kathy Schrocks's Guide for Educators: Assessment
http://school.discovery.com/schrockguide/assess.html

Sponsored by Discovery School.com, this webpage has a comprehensive compilation of sites about classroom assessment and rubrics.

Phi Delta Kappa International
http://www.pdkintl.org

This important organization publishes articles about all facets of education. You can check out the online archive of the journal, *Phi Delta Kappan,* which has resources such as articles having to do with assessment.

Washington (State) Center for the Improvement of Student Learning
http://www.k12.wa.us/

This Washington State site is designed to provide access to information about the state's new academic standards, assessments, and accountability system. Many resources and Web links are included.

UNIT 1
Perspectives on Teaching

Unit Selections

1. **Character and Academics: What Good Schools Do,** Jacques S. Benninga et al.
2. **Memories from the 'Other': Lessons in Connecting with Students,** Thomas David Knestrict
3. **A National Tragedy: Helping Children Cope,** *National Association of School Psychologists*

Key Points to Consider

- What questions would you like to see educational psychologists study?

- Describe several characteristics of effective teachers.

- As we move into the twenty-first century, what new expectations should be placed on teachers and schools? What expectations will fade?

Student Web Site
www.mhcls.com

Internet References

The Center for Innovation in Education
 http://www.center.edu
Classroom Connect
 http://www.classroom.net
Education World
 http://www.education-world.com
Goals 2000: A Progress Report
 http://www.ed.gov/pubs/goals/progrpt/index.html
Teacher Talk Forum
 http://education.indiana.edu/cas/tt/tthmpg.html

The teaching-learning process in school is enormously complex. Many factors influence pupil learning—such as family background, developmental level, prior knowledge, motivation, and, of course, effective teachers. Educational psychology investigates these factors to better understand and explain student learning. We begin our exploration of the teaching-learning process by considering the characteristics of effective teaching.

In the first article, a new teacher received advice from an experienced educator. The second article dramatically shows how important it is for teachers to believe that each student can learn. The third article discusses the skill set that graduates will need to compete in a global society.

Finally, the fourth article discusses the range of reactions that children and adolescents have experienced in response to tragedies such as the terrorist attacks of September 11, 2001 or the recent hurricanes, and suggests ways in which educators can help them to cope and continue their schooling.

Educational psychology is a resource for teachers that emphasizes disciplined inquiry, a systematic and objective analysis of information, and a scientific attitude toward decision making. The field provides information for decisions that are based on quantitative and qualitative studies of learning and teaching rather than on intuition, tradition, authority, or subjective feelings. It is our hope that this aspect of educational psychology is communicated throughout these readings, and that, as a student, you will adopt the analytic, probing attitude that is part of the discipline.

While educational psychologists have helped to establish a knowledge base about teaching and learning, the unpredictable, spontaneous, evolving nature of teaching suggests that the best they will ever do is to provide concepts and skills that teachers can adapt for use in their classrooms. The issues raised in these articles about effective teaching, and the issues facing teachers in the twenty-first century, help us understand the teaching role

© Laurence Mouton/Photoalto/PictureQuest

and its demands. As you read articles in other chapters, consider the demands they place on the teaching role as well.

Character and Academics

What Good Schools Do

Though there has been increasing interest in character education among policy makers and education professionals, many schools hesitate to do anything that might detract from their focus on increasing academic performance. The authors present evidence indicating that this may be misguided.

JACQUES S. BENNINGA ET AL.

The growth of character education programs in the United States has coincided with the rise in high-stakes testing of student achievement. The No Child Left Behind Act asks schools to contribute not to students' academic performance but also to their character. Both the federal government and the National Education Association (NEA) agree that schools have this dual responsibility. In a statement introducing a new U.S. Department of Education character education website, then Secretary of Education Rod Paige outlined the need for such programs:

> Sadly, we live in a culture without role models, where millions of students are taught the wrong values—or no values at all. This culture of callousness has led to a staggering achievement gap, poor health status, overweight students, crime, violence, teenage pregnancy, and tobacco and alcohol abuse. . . . Good character is the product of good judgments made every day.[1]

And Bob Chase, the former president of the NEA, issued his own forceful call to action:

> We must make an explicit commitment to formal character education. We must integrate character education into the fabric of the curriculum and into extracurricular activities. We must train teachers in character education—both preservice and inservice. And we must consciously set about creating a moral climate within our schools.[2]

Despite the clear national interest in character education, many schools are leery of engaging in supplementary initiatives that, although worthy, might detract from what they see as their primary focus: increasing academic achievement. Moreover, many schools lack the resources to create new curricular initiatives. Yet the enhancement of student character is a bipartisan mandate that derives from the very core of public education.

The purpose of public schooling requires that schools seek to improve both academic and character education.

If it could be demonstrated that implementing character education programs is compatible with efforts to improve school achievement, then perhaps more schools would accept the challenge of doing both. But until now there has been little solid evidence of such successful coexistence.

Definitions and Research

Character education is the responsibility of adults. While the term *character education* has historically referred to the duty of the older generation to form the character of the young through experiences affecting their attitudes, knowledge, and behaviors, more recent definitions include such developmental outcomes as a positive perception of school, emotional literacy, and social justice activism.[3]

There are sweeping definitions of character education (e.g., Character Counts' six pillars, Community of Caring's five values, or the Character Education Partnership's 11 principles) and more narrow ones. Character education can be defined in terms of relationship virtues (e.g., respect, fairness, civility, tolerance), self-oriented virtues (e.g., fortitude, self-discipline, effort, perseverance) or a combination of the two. The state of California has incorporated character education criteria into the application process for its statewide distinguished school recognition program and, in the process, has created its own definition of character education. Each definition directs the practice of character education somewhat differently, so that programs calling themselves "character education" vary in purpose and scope.

There is some research evidence that character education programs enhance academic achievement. For example, an evaluation of the Peaceful Schools Project and research on the Responsive Classroom found that students in schools that implemented these programs had greater gains on standardized test scores than did students in comparison schools.[4] The Child Development Project (CDP) conducted follow-up studies of middle school students (through eighth grade) who had attended CDP elementary schools and found that they had higher course grades and higher achievement test scores than comparison middle school students.[5] Longitudinal studies have reported similar effects for middle school and high school students who had participated as elementary school students in the Seattle Social Development Project.[6]

A growing body of research supports the notion that high-quality character education can promote academic achievement. For example, Marvin Berkowitz and Melinda Bier have identified character education programs for elementary, middle, and high school students that enhance academic achievement.[7] These findings, however, are based on prepackaged curricular programs, and most schools do not rely on such programs. Instead, they create their own customized character education initiatives. It remains to be seen whether such initiatives also lead to academic gains.

Toward an Operational Definition of Character Education

We decided to see if we could determine a relationship between character education and academic achievement across a range of elementary schools. For our sample we used the elementary schools that applied in 2000 to the California Department of Education for recognition as distinguished elementary schools, California's highest level of school attainment. Eligibility to submit an application for the California School Recognition Program (CSRP) in 2000 was based on the previous year's academic performance index (API) results.

However, 1999 was the first year for California's Public School Accountability Act (PSAA), which created the API. Thus, while the state department stated that growth on the API was the central focus of the PSAA, schools applying for the CSRP in 1999–2000 did not receive their 1999 API scores until January 2000, after they had already written and submitted their award applications. Approximately 12.7% of California elementary schools (681 of 5,368 schools) submitted a full application for the award in 2000. The average API of these schools was higher than the average for the schools that did not apply, but both were below the state expectancy score of 800. The mean API for applicant schools was 751; for non-applicant schools, 612. The API range for applicant schools was 365–957; for non-applicant schools, 302–958. Hence the sample for this study is not representative of all California elementary schools. It is a sample of more academically successful schools, but it does represent a broad range of achievement from quite low to very high.

Specific wording related to character education was included for the first time in the CSRP application in 2000. Schools were asked to describe what they were doing to meet a set of nine standards. Of these, the one that most clearly pertained to character education was Standard 1 (Vision and Standards). For this standard, schools were required to include "specific examples and other evidence" of "expectations that promote positive character traits in students."[8] Other standards could also be seen as related to character education. For these, schools were asked to document activities and programs that ensured opportunities for students to contribute to the school, to others, and to the community.

We chose for our study a stratified random sample of 120 elementary schools that submitted applications. These 120 schools were not significantly different from the other 561 applicant schools on a variety of academic and demographic indicators. For the schools in our sample, we correlated the extent of their character education implementation with their API and SAT-9 scores—the academic scale and test used by California at that time.[9]

The first problem we needed to grapple with was how to define a character education program. We spent considerable time discussing an operational definition to use for this project. After conferring with experts, we chose our final set of character education criteria, drawn from both the standards used by the California Department of Education and the *Character Education Quality Standards* developed by the Character Education Partnership.[10] Six criteria emerged from this process:

- This school promotes core ethical values as the basis of good character.
- In this school, parents and other community members are active participants in the character education initiative.
- In this school, character education entails intentional promotion of core values in all phases of school life.
- Staff members share responsibility for and attempt to model character education.
- This school fosters an overall caring community.
- This school provides opportunities for most students to practice moral action.

Each of the six criteria addresses one important component of character education. We created a rubric encompassing these six criteria and listing indicators for each, along with a scoring scale.

Character Education and Academic Achievement

Our study of these high-performing California schools added further evidence of a relationship between academic achievement and the implementation of specific character education programs. In our sample, elementary schools with solid character education programs showed positive relationships between the extent of character education implementation and academic achievement not in a single year but also across the next two academic years. Over a multi-year period from 1999 to 2002, higher rankings on the API and higher scores on the SAT-9 were significantly and positively correlated with four of our character education indicators: a school's ability to ensure a clean and safe physical environment; evidence that a school's parents and teachers modeled and promoted good character; high-quality opportunities at the school for students to contribute in meaningful ways to the school and its community; and promoting a caring community and positive social relationships.

These are promising results, particularly because the *total character education score* for the year of the school's application was significantly correlated with every language and mathematics achievement score on the SAT-9 for a period of three years. In two of those years, the same was true for reading achievement scores. In other words, good-quality character education was positively associated with academic achievement, both across academic domains and over time.

What Good Schools Do

From our research we derived principles—the four indicators mentioned above—that are common across schools with both thoughtful character education programs and high levels of academic achievement.

- *Good schools ensure a clean and secure physical environment.* Although all schools in our sample fit this description, the higher-scoring character education schools expressed great pride in keeping their buildings and grounds in good shape. This is consistent with what is reported about the virtues of clean and safe learning environments. For example, the Center for Prevention of School Violence notes that "the physical appearance of a school and its campus communicates a lot about the school and its people. Paying attention to appearance so that the facilities are inviting can create a sense of security."[11]
- One school in our sample reported that its buildings "are maintained well above district standards. . . . The custodial crew prides themselves in achieving a monthly cleaning score that has exceeded standards in 9 out of 12 months." And another noted, "A daily grounds check is performed to ensure continual safety and cleanliness." Each of the higher-scoring schools in our sample explicitly noted its success in keeping its campus in top shape and mentioned that parents were satisfied that their children were attending school in a physically and psychologically safe environment.
- All schools in California are required to have on file a written Safe School Plan, but the emphases in these plans vary. While some schools limited their safety plans to regulations controlling access to the building and defined procedures for violations and intrusions, the schools with better character education programs defined "safety" more broadly and deeply. For example, one school scoring high on our character education rubric explained that the mission of its Safe School Plan was "to provide all students with educational and personal opportunities in a positive and nurturing environment which will enable them to achieve current and future goals, and for all students to be accepted at their own social, emotional, and academic level of development." Another high-scoring school addressed three concerns in its Safe School Plan: identification of visitors on campus, cultural/ethnic harmony, and safe ingress and egress from school. To support these areas of focus, this school's teachers were all trained to conduct classroom meetings, to implement the Community of Caring core values, and to handle issues related to cultural diversity and communication.
- *Good schools promote and model fairness, equity, caring, and respect.* In schools with good character education programs and high academic achievement, adults model and promote the values and attitudes they wish the students to embrace, and they infuse character education throughout the school and across the curriculum. Rick Weissbourd drove home this point in a recent essay: "The moral development of students does not depend primarily on explicit character education efforts but on the maturity and ethical capacities of the adults with whom they interact. . . . Educators influence students' moral development not simply by being good role models— important as that is—but also by what they bring to their relationships with students day to day."[12] The staff of excellent character education schools in our sample tended to see themselves as involved, concerned professional educators, and others see them that way as well.
- Thus one school described its teachers as "pivotal in the [curriculum] development process; there is a high level of [teacher] ownership in the curriculum. . . . Fifty percent of our staff currently serves on district curriculum committees." Another school stated that it "fosters the belief that it takes an entire community pulling together to provide the best education for every child; that is best accomplished through communication, trust, and collaboration on ideas that reflect the needs of our school and the community. . . . Teachers are continually empowered and given opportunities to voice their convictions and shape the outcome of what the school represents." A third school described its teachers as "continually encouraged" to grow professionally and to use best practices based on research. In the best character education schools, teachers are recognized by their peers, by district personnel, and by professional organizations for their instructional prowess and their professionalism. They model the academic and prosocial characteristics that show their deep concern for the well-being of children.
- *In good schools students contribute in meaningful ways.* We found that academically excellent character education schools provided opportunities for students to contribute to their school and their community. These schools encouraged students to participate in volunteer activities, such as cross-age tutoring, recycling, fundraising for charities, community clean-up programs, food drives, visitations to local senior centers, and so on.
- One elementary school required 20 hours of community service, a program coordinated entirely by parent volunteers. Students in that school volunteered in community gardens and at convalescent hospitals, and they took part in community clean-up days. Such

activities, while not directly connected to students' academic programs, were viewed as mechanisms to promote the development of healthy moral character. According to William Damon, a crucial component of moral education is engaging children in positive activities—community service, sports, music, theater, or anything else that inspires them and gives them a sense of purpose.[13]

- *Good schools promote a caring community and positive social relationships.* One school in our sample that exemplified this principle was a school of choice in its community. The district had opened enrollment to students outside district boundaries, and this school not provided an excellent academic program for its multilingual student population but also worked hard to include parents and community members in significant ways. Its Family Math Night attracted 250 family members, and its Family Literacy Night educated parents about read-aloud methods. Parents, grandparents, and friends were recruited to become classroom volunteers and donated thousands of hours.

- This particular school also rented its classrooms to an after-school Chinese educational program. The two sets of teachers have become professional colleagues, and insights from such cultural interaction have led both groups to a better understanding of the Chinese and American systems of education. One result has been that more English-speaking students are enrolling in the Chinese after-school program. And teachers in both programs now engage in dialogue about the specific needs of children. One parent wrote a letter to the principal that said in part, "It seems you are anxious to build up our young generation more healthy and successful. . . . I am so proud you are not our children's principal, but also parents' principal."

- Other schools with strong social relationship programs provide meaningful opportunities for parent involvement and establish significant partnerships with local businesses. They encourage parents and teachers to work alongside students in service projects, to incorporate diverse communities into the school curriculum, and to partner with high school students who serve as physical education and academic mentors. As one such school put it, all stakeholders "must play an important and active role in the education of the child to ensure the future success of that child."

Conclusion

It is clear that well-conceived programs of character education can and should exist side by side with strong academic programs. It is no surprise that students need physically secure and psychologically safe schools, staffed by teachers who model professionalism and caring behaviors and who ask students to demonstrate caring for others. That students who attend such schools achieve academically makes intuitive sense as well. It is in schools with this dual emphasis that adults understand their

role in preparing students for future citizenship in a democratic and diverse society. The behaviors and attitudes they model communicate important messages to the young people in their charge. Future research on the relationship between character education and academic achievement should include a greater representation of schools in the average and below-average achievement categories. In particular, a study of the extent of the implementation of character education in schools that may have test scores at the low end of the spectrum—but are nevertheless performing higher than their socioeconomic characteristics would predict—would be an important contribution to our understanding of the relationship between character education and academic achievement.

While this was our initial attempt to explore the relationship between these two important school purposes, we learned a good deal about what makes up a good character education curriculum in academically strong schools. We know that such a curriculum in such schools is positively related to academic outcomes over time and across content areas. We also know that, to be effective, character education requires adults to act like adults in an environment where children are respected and feel physically and psychologically safe to engage in the academic and social activities that prepare them best for later adult decision making.

At a time when resources are scarce, we see schools cutting programs and narrowing curricula to concentrate on skills measured by standardized tests. Our research suggests that school goals and activities that are associated with good character education programs are also associated with academic achievement. Thus our results argue for maintaining a rich curriculum with support for all aspects of student development and growth.

Notes

1. U.S. Department of Education, "ED Launches Character Education Web Site," www.thechallenge.org/15-v12no4/v12n4-communitiesandschools.htm.

2. Bob Chase, quoted in "Is Character Education the Answer?," *Education World,* 1999, www.education-world.com/a_admin/admin097.shtml.

3. Marvin W. Berkowitz, "The Science of Character Education," in William Damon, ed., *Bringing in a New Era in Character Education* (Stanford, Calif.: Hoover Institution Press, 2002), pp. 43–63.

4. Stuart W. Twemlow et al., "Creating a Peaceful School Learning Environment: A Controlled Study of an Elementary School Intervention to Reduce Violence," *American Journal of Psychiatry,* vol. 158, 2001, pp. 808–10; and Stephen N. Elliott, "Does a Classroom Promoting Social Skills Development Enable Higher Academic Functioning Among Its Students Over Time?," Northeast Foundation for Children, Greenfield, Mass., 1998.

5. Victor Battistich and Sehee Hong, "Enduring Effects of the Child Development Project: Second-Order Latent Linear Growth Modeling of Students' 'Connectedness' to School, Academic Performance, and Social Adjustment During Middle School," unpublished manuscript, Developmental Studies Center, Oakland, Calif., 2003.

6. J. David Hawkins et al., "Long-Term Effects of the Seattle Social Development Intervention on School Bonding Trajectories," *Applied Developmental Science,* vol. 5, 2001, pp. 225–36.

7. Marvin W. Berkowitz and Melinda C. Bier, *What Works in Character Education?* (Washington, D.C.: Character Education Partnership, 2005).

8. "California School Recognition Program, 2000 Elementary Schools Program, Elementary School Rubric," California Department of Education, 2001. (Data are available from Jacques Benninga.)

9. For more detail on the design of the study, see Jacques S. Benninga, Marvin W. Berkowitz, Phyllis Kuehn, and Karen Smith, "The Relationship of Character Education Implementation and Academic Achievement in Elementary Schools," *Journal of Research in Character Education,* vol. 1, 2003, pp. 17–30.

10. *Character Education Quality Standards: A Self-Assessment Tool for Schools and Districts* (Washington, D.C.: Character Education Partnership, 2001).

11. "What Is Character Education?," Center for the Fourth and Fifth Rs, 2003, www.cortland.edu/c4n5rs/ce_iv.asp.

12. Rick Weissbourd, "Moral Teachers, Moral Students," *Educational Leadership,* March 2003, pp. 6–7.

13. Damon is quoted in Susan Gilbert, "Scientists Explore the Molding of Children's Morals," *New York Times,* 18 March 2003.

JACQUES S. BENNINGA is a professor of education and director of the Bonner Center for Character Education, California State University, Fresno. **MARVIN W. BERKOWITZ** is Sanford N. McDonnell Professor of Character Education, University of Missouri, St. Louis. **PHYLLIS KUEHN** is a professor of educational research, California State University, Fresno. **KAREN SMITH** is principal of Mark Twain Elementary School, Brentwood, Mo. The research described in this article was funded by a grant from the John Templeton Foundation, but the opinions expressed are those of the authors.

From *Phi Delta Kappan,* February 2006, pp. 448–452. Copyright © 2006 by Phi Delta Kappan. Reprinted by permission of Phi Delta Kappan and Jacques S. Bennings et al.

Memories from the 'Other'

Lessons in Connecting with Students

Thanks to the good work of some significant teachers, Mr. Knestrict learned an important lesson: all children deserve to feel lovable and capable.

THOMAS DAVID KNESTRICT

I hated school. I struggled with it from the moment I started kindergarten. Before that, I had been so happy as a young child. I can remember when I was 4 years old, coloring with my mom at home. I can still hear her telling me how smart I was and how much she loved me. I remember quite vividly entering Hayes Elementary School in September of 1964 and walking into the large kindergarten room. I came into the room excited about school and eager to learn. I had perfect attendance the first semester of that year and received a certificate for my achievement.

But as the year progressed, things changed. My memories of that year have faded somewhat over time, but there are certain recurrent themes that stay with me today. The first is that I very clearly was different from most of the other children. I had trouble sitting on the floor "Indian style." I needed to get up and move. The next theme I clearly recall is that I wasn't as smart as the other boys and girls. Learning to read was difficult; learning to write was even harder. In fact, anything that required me to focus for an extended period of time or to use fine motor skills was lost on me. The final general recollection I have is discovering that I was a "problem" in class. I remember being sent to the "cloak room" several times that year for "not playing nice" or "disrupting the class."

Mrs. L. came over to me and took the paper fire truck I had just completed. She peeled the wheels off of the fire truck and told me that she knew I could do better. I had tried to cut out round wheels but was unable to create anything better than octagon shapes. Obviously this was not good enough.

In first grade I was placed in a class with an almost entirely new group of children. The only student I already knew was a boy named Tommy. We had been in kindergarten together, he came to first grade with me, and he was with me until my senior year of high school. But the rest of the students we had been with the previous year were placed in the two other classrooms. The children I met in first grade were to be my classmates for the next five years. Students were tracked back then, and I was in the "slow class." This was the term that Mr. P., our principal, used on more than one occasion. It was true. All of us had trouble reading, witting, and behaving. I can't imagine what the teacher must have been thinking when she received her class list in August. This might explain why many of the teachers we had did not return the following year.

Class was so boring. The print made no sense to me. So I found ways to entertain myself, especially during reading. I can remember looking for Tommy during reading group. I knew if I could catch his eye, I could make him laugh. I was always searching for a way to escape the monotony. When I got his attention I turned both of my eyelids inside out and stared at him. Pretty soon every boy in the reading group was doing the same thing. Mrs. S. became very angry and made all of us stay in for recess.

The overwhelming message I received every day was that I was different, not as good, and defective. I had different books. I completed different assignments. I was not asked to join in any of the extra activities my fellow students in the other classes participated in. There were only a few kids in our class each year who excelled. The next year they would be moved to one of the other classrooms. Their spot was always taken by a new kid—usually a kid like me or a new student who couldn't speak

English. The funny thing is that after a new kid learned to speak English, he usually excelled and left our class. My grades were horrible. The school used to trust me to bring my report card home for my parents to sign. But it never found its way home. Every year my mom would have to call about the whereabouts of my report card.

I dreaded oral reading groups. My handwriting was illegible, and the teachers always claimed that I was very smart but lazy. By third grade I had discovered some "truths" about myself. The first truth was that I was stupid. This was reinforced daily by teacher comments and by the eventual absence of teacher concern—a kind of teaching boycott put into effect because of my perceived bad attitude. Second, I was different from the "cool" kids in the other classes. I was viewed by my peers and my teachers as different, and because of this I had a very limited group of people around me from whom to draw friends. Last, I did possess a significant talent. I was one funny guy. I could make people laugh. Turning my eyelids inside out was just one trick. I had a million of them. But it worked only within the context of school. Outside of the classroom, the group were even more rigidly defined, and I had no capital.

The middle grades of elementary school were very tough. These years were marked by a tremendous lack of accomplishment. I never read a book. I never completed a book report. I rarely passed a test. I never completed any homework. But I continued to be passed to the next grade with little or no assistance for my increasing academic deficits.

In fourth grade I had Ms. S. for a teacher. She was determined to whip me into shape. I remember turning in some kind of written assignment to her and having her hand it back to me to be recopied. It was far too messy, and there were too many misspelled words. I recopied it, and she handed it back to me again. I handed it in a third time, and again she handed it back to me. I was not allowed to go to recess or gym that day. I stayed after school until 4:00. I started to cry, and she told me that if I continued to cry I would have to stay in the next day as well. I stayed inside for three consecutive days. She finally gave up. I did, too.

In fifth grade I had Mr. H. for math. It was in this class that I really learned my place in school. The pain and humiliation I and my fellow students suffered in this class were remarkable. By fifth grade you should be learning fractions, long division, pre-algebra, equations, probability. We were still on two-digit times two-digit multiplication. One day, Mr. H. caught me clowning around in class.

As punishment he had me get up in front of the class to complete the following problem:

$$23 \times 13$$

Mr. H. knew that I could complete this problem only to the point of putting the place-holding zeros down. I got lost and could not go any further. As I froze and tried to climb inside of the chalkboard, Mr. H. said these words: "Mr. Knestrict, I could teach and teach and teach, and you still would not get this. I give up." What I heard was, "You're stupid, Mr. Knestrict. You can't do math, Mr. Knestrict. You are not a capable student, Mr. Knestrict." This is a moment I would relive many times in my academic career. His is a voice I still hear today. I hear it when I bounce a check. I heard it when I took my first statistics course in college. I hear it when I am at the grocery store figuring my bill or when I am figuring the tip at a restaurant. Like so many kids with learning differences, I had these words burned into my heart, into my brain. At that moment Mr. H. verbalized 10 years of my internal dialogue. When he voiced this condemnation, it made it so for me, for my peers, and for him. At that moment I was defined.

Beth was a smart girl. She attended the same elementary school I did but was always in the "smart class." In junior high, members of my class were mixed in with the "smart kids" for art, music, and industrial arts. I sat next to Beth in music. We had to do a report together about a famous musician. We picked John Denver. We began reading some books on him, and Beth started taking notes on index cards. I asked her what she was doing, and she showed me how she would read a fact about John Denver that she thought was interesting and write it down on the card. "A different card for every fact. Then when it's time to write, we can just copy down what we wrote on the cards." I was stunned. I could do this. It took a 12-year-old girl to show me that I could complete a meaningful academic task.

In junior high, things changed a bit for me. I was still tracked with the same kids. However, several elementary schools merged, and all the "dumb kids" from each school were grouped together. At least there were some new faces. And there were the "mixed-ability" groups for some subjects. Beth was the first "smart girl" I had ever made friends with. She helped me get my first A in any class . . . ever! Our paper on John Denver was a thing of beauty. During the writing process, Beth told me that it was okay that I had trouble writing. "I'll carry us, Tom." And she did. But she also taught me that I could do a few things myself. During the research part of the assignment, she could not find some basic biographical data on Mr. Denver. I had all of his albums at home, and on one of them there was a John Denver biography. I brought this in and wrote out five fact cards to contribute to the effort. Beth was so pleased. I felt like Einstein.

I remember sitting in Mrs. A.'s English class. We were diagramming sentences. I could not figure out the appropriate lines to draw for the various parts of speech. So I invented my own. I brought my paper up to Mrs. A., and she looked at it and told me to sit down and reread the assignment because I had done it completely wrong. She handed the paper back to me and continued to work at her desk. She did not know I could barely read the book we were using.

I had to go to other classes in junior high. I had to take Spanish in sixth grade. I never could figure out how a kid who couldn't master English was supposed to learn Spanish. I failed. In fact, I took Spanish I three years in a row. I think it still stands as a record at Harding Junior High School. Math was still a mystery. Physical education, an enjoyable class for me in elementary school, became a daily nightmare in junior high. Taking your clothes off in front of others? Taking showers? All of the "smart" boys and all of the "dumb" boys were in gym together. In one respect, the playing field was leveled in gym class. Luckily, intelligence had little to do with the tasks in Mr. S.'s gym class. It was all about testosterone. Who could withstand pain, tumble, run, jump, and wrestle? I was a good athlete, and I went into this class feeling good.

But that wouldn't last. Mr. S. had a rule. If you did not remember to bring your uniform, you had to wear the "community clothes": a pair of very dirty shorts that smelled funny and had brown stains in the seat and a smelly tank-style top with the words "Lakewood" on the front. It was a well known fact that the girls wore the shirts that said "Lakewood" and the boys wore the shirts that said "Rangers." Because I sometimes forgot my uniform, I was now clearly a girl. I missed a record number of days during my sixth-grade year. Thirty-four to be exact.

There was a spelling bee in sixth grade. The entire sixth grade participated. I can remember standing in line, on stage, in front of all of the seventh-and eighth-graders, waiting for my word. The first round was usually seen as a practice round, and the students were given a simple word to spell in order to get comfortable. It came to me. My word was "Lakewood." Simple enough, my hometown. "L...a...k...w...o...o...d, Lakewood." Silence.

"Incorrect." The auditorium erupted. I laughed and joked, but I was dying inside. I then had to sit down in the front row for the next 30 minutes until another speller made a mistake and left the competition.

In high school I attempted to take Spanish again. I failed again. But my Spanish teacher, Ms. D., referred me to the school counselor, telling me, "Thomas, you must first learn the English language before learning Spanish." She referred me for academic testing. The year was 1975, and P.L. 94-142 had just been passed. I sometimes think I was the first child identified after its ratification. I was given a tutor and had to attend certain classes in the resource room for extra help. I made sure nobody saw me go into that room. It would be social suicide. Although, given my social status, I had very little to lose.

I was told that I was learning disabled and that I had to go to special education classes. The school psychologist told me this as if it were cause for celebration. "Hooray, we finally know what is wrong with Tom." But I wasn't ready to celebrate the fact that there was yet another thing that made me different.

Sometime during my sophomore year, a counselor met with me and talked to me about vocational school. "Tom," she said, "it's clear you are not on the college track here at LHS. So I would like you to start thinking about vocational school or even the military." I was devastated. My entire family had attended Bowling Green State University. I was going to go, too. But now, it looked like I would barely get out of high school. I finished that year in special education. I was 16, low on the social ladder, attending school on the special education track. I'd been told I couldn't attend the "regular" (read "normal") high school the next year, and I could barely read and write. I became very depressed. I started to cut class and feign illness to avoid going to school. There were days I came to school just for homeroom, so I could be counted as present, and then I would leave for home. I did this easily 50% of the time and never got caught. Still, I passed to the 11th grade. Remarkable!

In my junior year, I was required to take the ACT exam. I posted a total score of 7. I have been told that you could guess and score higher than this. I didn't guess.

At the end of my senior year, I had a grade-point average of 1.7. I read at about the fourth-grade level, still had not mastered my multiplication facts, had never read a book, had developed a consistent pattern of starting and then quitting new activities, thought of myself as stupid, could not write a coherent paragraph, had few friends, and in June was handed a diploma and graduated with my class from high school. It still ranks as the most inexplicable moment of my life. I kept thinking that my fellow classmates would attack if they knew that I was getting the same piece of paper they were that stated that I, too, had completed all the requisite coursework to graduate. No, I had not!

I woke up after graduation and wondered what had just happened. School was over—they let me graduate? Huh?

Somewhere between my graduation and the following school year, I had an epiphany. During that summer I worked at a gas station and a pizza place. I was very aware of how the people I was working with had been working these jobs for most of their adult lives and didn't seem real happy. I went home that night and talked to my father, and he convinced me to try taking a class at Cuyahoga Community College, also known as Tri C. I signed up for a series of high school-level reading and writing classes affectionately known as the 0900 courses. There were adults in these classes older than I was, and somehow that fact made me feel better about myself.

I signed up for all the high school-level courses I could that year, and in my first writing course I had a professor who saved my life. He taught me how to write and how to love to read. We read *Death of a Salesman* and books by Hemingway and Poe, and then we talked and wrote about the books. It would take me forever to finish a book, and sometimes it would be a combination of reading the book, watching the movie, and using the Cliff notes that got me through the assignments, but I loved every minute of it. It was the most amazing thing I had ever experienced. I was learning about metaphor and simile, seeing how the literature gave me insight into my life, writing reflections on my feelings about these books. It was wonderful. It was life changing. I learned more in that one year at Tri C than I had learned in the previous 12 years of school.

What was different was that I was seen as capable. The professors knew I could do it and expected me to do it. Also, they wanted me to enjoy the process and worry about the products later. One professor I had during this time stated, "Process over product. If you learn the process of reading and writing, the products will follow." But most important, they knew me and I knew them. We had a relationship. They cared about me. I had never, in 12 years of school, had that before.

As I was leaving my last writing and reading class at Tri C, the professor looked at me and said, "Make sure you read the comments I wrote on your last paper." When I got to my car, I pulled the paper out and read, "Thomas, this paper was one of the most insightful and inspired papers I have ever received from a student. I am so pleased with your progress this year. Grade for the quarter: A." I cried.

Later that year I ended up being accepted "conditionally" to Kent State University. During that year I met a man who ran a camp for children with learning disabilities and behavior problems. He was at Kent to hire counselors for the summer. I started talking to him a bit about my school experience. He hired me on the spot. I worked that summer leading hikes, camping, doing crafts, and canoeing with children who were experiencing some of the same things I had gone through in school. I found I had a real talent for working with children. From that point on, I knew I would teach.

That summer, the director of the camp, Jerry Dunlap, taught me something that has become a fundamental part of my teaching philosophy: he told me that all children deserve to feel lovable and capable. He then asked me if I felt lovable and capable. And for the first time in my life, I could say yes. I had spent most of my school years believing that I was not lovable and not capable. The system had beaten me up. But thanks to the good work of some significant teachers in my life, I was on the mend, with a focus on teaching and helping kids.

During my first year of teaching in the classroom, I had a student named Dante. He was 7 years old, could not read or write, and spoke only sparingly. As I introduced myself to Dante and his parents on the first day of school, I laughed at the joke God had played on me. Dante was me, and I was quite possibly the only person able to help him. We had a wonderful year, filled with lots of loving and learning. In June I asked Dante if he felt lovable and capable. He looked at me and smiled and said, "I know you love me, Mr. Knestrict, but what does 'capable' mean?"

Postscript

As I reflect on my life in school, I am struck by the times teachers failed to connect with me on any real human level. I am a professor of education now, and I am still struck by the lack of emphasis on this human connection in education. We spend so much of our time as teachers worrying about the standards, giving tests, and focusing entirely on content that the child as a person seems to disappear. One of the fundamental theories we teach undergraduates in our education programs is Abraham Maslow's hierarchy of needs. We know that human connection is crucial to child development, but our schools fail to manifest this knowledge in practice. Classes get bigger and bigger, and test scores matter more and more. Our cultural obsession with measurement and testing often serves to sort students, not help them. These values define students very early in life. Once defined, individuals begin to see themselves that way, and the perception becomes a self-fulfilling prophecy. In fact, when a child is identified with a special need and placed on an Individualized Education Plan, he or she will actually have that label for a minimum of three years—and, as research suggests, much longer emotionally.[2]

I can tell you firsthand that I still hold internalized notions of myself as a child. I still have trouble seeing myself as smart, lovable, and capable. I believe that this difficulty is a result of the damage caused by my experience in schools and in particular our education system's notion of how to help children with different needs. I am not advocating de-emphasizing content.

However, it is not unreasonable to assume that we can teach a solid curriculum and at the same time treat students with dignity and care.

Notes

1. Joan Wink and Dawn Wink, *Teaching Passionately: What's Love Got to Do with It?* (Boston: Pearson/Allyn and Bacon, 2004).

2. John R. Weisz et al., "Cognitive Development, Helpless Behavior, and Labeling Effects in the Lives of the Mentally Retarded," *Applied Developmental Psychology,* vol. 24, 1985, pp. 672–83.

Thomas David Knestrict is an assistant professor of education at Xavier University, Cincinnati. He taught in the public schools for 15 years.

A National Tragedy: Helping Children Cope

Tips for Parents and Teachers

Whenever a national tragedy occurs, such as terrorist attacks or natural disasters, children, like many people, may be confused or frightened. Most likely they will look to adults for information and guidance on how to react. Parents and school personnel can help children cope first and foremost by establishing a sense of safety and security. As more information becomes available, adults can continue to help children work through their emotions and perhaps even use the process as learning experience.

All Adults Should:

1. **Model calm and control**. Children take their emotional cues from the significant adults in their lives. Avoid appearing anxious or frightened.

2. **Reassure children that they are safe** and (if true) so are the other important adults in their lives. Depending on the situation, point out factors that help insure their immediate safety and that of their community.

3. **Remind them that trustworthy people are in charge**. Explain that the government emergency workers, police, firefighters, doctors, and the military are helping people who are hurt and are working to ensure that no further tragedies occur.

4. **Let children know that it is okay to feel upset**. Explain that all feelings are okay when a tragedy like this occurs. Let children talk about their feelings and help put them into perspective. Even anger is okay, but children may need help and patience from adults to assist them in expressing these feelings appropriately.

5. **Observe children's emotional state**. Depending on their age, children may not express their concerns verbally. Changes in behavior, appetite, and sleep patterns can also indicate a child's level of grief, anxiety or discomfort. Children will express their emotions differently. There is no right or wrong way to feel or express grief.

6. **Look for children at greater risk**. Children who have had a past traumatic experience or personal loss, suffer from depression or other mental illness, or with special needs may be at greater risk for severe reactions than others. Be particularly observant for those who may be at risk of suicide. Seek the help of mental health professionals if you are at all concerned.

7. **Tell children the truth**. Don't try to pretend the event has not occurred or that it is not serious. Children are smart. They will be more worried if they think you are too afraid to tell them what is happening.

8. **Stick to the facts**. Don't embellish or speculate about what has happened and what might happen. Don't dwell on the scale or scope of the tragedy, particularly with young children.

9. **Keep your explanations developmentally appropriate**. *Early elementary school* children need brief, simple information that should be balanced with reassurances that the daily structures of their lives will not change. *Upper elementary and early middle school* children will be more vocal in asking questions about whether they truly are safe and what is being done at their school. They may need assistance separating reality from fantasy. *Upper middle school and high school* students will have strong and varying opinions about the causes of violence in schools and society. They will share concrete suggestions about how to make school safer and how to prevent tragedies in society. They will be more committed to doing something to help the victims and affected community. *For all children, encourage them to verbalize their thoughts and feelings. Be a good listener!*

10. **Monitor Your Own Stress Level.** Don't ignore your own feelings of anxiety, grief, and anger. Talking to friends, family members, religious leaders, and mental health counselors can help. It is okay to let your children know that you are sad, but that you believe things will get better. You will be better able to support your children if you can express your own emotions in a productive manner. Get appropriate sleep, nutrition, and exercise.

What Parents Can Do

1. **Focus on your children over the next week following the tragedy**. Tell them you love them and everything will be okay. Try to help them understand what has happened, keeping in mind their developmental level.

2. **Make time to talk with your children**. Remember if you do not talk to your children about this incident someone else will. Take some time and determine what you wish to say.

3. **Stay close to your children**. Your physical presence will reassure them and give you the opportunity to monitor their reaction. Many children will want actual physical contact. Give plenty of hugs. Let them sit close to you, and make sure to take extra time at bedtime to cuddle and to reassure them that they are loved and safe.

4. **Limit your child's television viewing of these events**. If they must watch, watch with them for a brief time; then turn the set off. Don't sit mesmerized re-watching the same events over and over again.

5. **Maintain a "normal" routine**. To the extent possible stick to your family's normal routine for dinner, homework, chores, bedtime, etc., *but don't be inflexible*. Children may have a hard time concentrating on schoolwork or falling asleep at night.

6. **Spend extra time reading or playing quiet games with your children before bed**. These activities are calming, foster a sense of closeness and security, and reinforce a sense of normalcy. Spend more time tucking them in. Let them sleep with a light on if they ask for it.

7. **Safeguard your children's physical health**. Stress can take a physical toll on children as well as adults. Make sure your children get appropriate sleep, exercise, and nutrition.

8. **Consider praying or thinking hopeful thoughts for the victims and their families**. It may be a good time to take your children to your house of worship, write a poem, or draw a picture to help your child express their feelings and feel that they are somehow supporting the victims and their families.

9. **Find out what resources your school has in place to help children cope**. Most schools are likely to be open and often are a good place for children to regain a sense of normalcy. Being with their friends and teachers can help. Schools should also have a plan for making counseling available to children and adults who need it.

What Schools Can Do

1. **Assure children that they are safe** and that schools are well prepared to take care of all children at all times.

2. **Maintain structure and stability within the schools**. It would be best, however, not to have tests or major projects within the next few days.

3. **Have a plan for the first few days back at school**. Include school psychologists, counselors, and crisis team members in planning the school's response.

4. **Provide teachers and parents with information** about what to say and do for children in school and at home.

5. **Have teachers provide information directly to their students**, not during the public address announcements.

6. **Have school psychologists and counselors available** to talk to student and staff who may need or want extra support.

7. **Be aware of students who may have recently experienced a personal tragedy** or a have personal connection to victims or their families. Even a child who has been to visit the Pentagon or the World Trade Center may feel a personal loss. Provide these students extra support and leniency if necessary.

8. **Know what community resources are available** for children who may need extra counseling. School psychologists can be very helpful in directing families to the right community resources.

9. **Allow time for age appropriate classroom discussion and activities**. Do not expect teachers to provide all of the answers. They should ask questions and guide the discussion, but not dominate it. Other activities can include art and writing projects, play acting, and physical games.

10. **Be careful not to stereotype people or countries that might be home to the terrorists**. Children can easily generalize negative statements and develop prejudice. Talk about tolerance and justice versus vengeance. *Stop any bullying or teasing of students immediately*.

11. **Refer children who exhibit extreme anxiety, fear or anger to mental health counselors** in the school. Inform their parents.

12. **Provide an outlet for students' desire to help**. Consider making get well cards or sending letters to the families and survivors of the tragedy, or writing thank you letters to doctors, nurses, and other health care professionals as well as emergency rescue workers, firefighters and police.

13. **Monitor or restrict viewing scenes** of this horrendous event as well as the aftermath.

For information on helping children and youth with this crisis, contact NASP at (301) 657-0270 or visit NASP's website at www.nasponline.org.

UNIT 2
Development

Unit Selections

Key Points to Consider

- How can schools and teachers provide an environment that is conducive to child and adolescent development?

- Why should play be a significant part of an early childhood classroom?

- How can schools help adolescents manage risk-taking behavior?

Student Web Site
www.mhcls.com

Internet References

Association for Moral Education
http://www.amenetwork.org/
Center for Adolescent and Families Studies
http://www.indiana.edu/~cafs
Child Welfare League of America
http://www.cwla.org
The National Association for Child Development
http://www.nacd.org
National Association of School Psychologists (NASP)
http://www.nasponline.org/
Scholastic News Zone
http://www.scholasticnews.com

The study of human development provides us with knowledge of how children and adolescents mature and learn within the family, community, and school environments. Educational psychology focuses on description and explanation of the developmental processes that make it possible for children to become intelligent and socially competent adults. Psychologists and educators are presently studying the idea that biology as well as the environment influence cognitive, personal, social, and emotional development and involve predictable patterns of behavior.

The perceptions and thoughts that young children have about the world are often quite different when compared to those of adolescents and adults. That is, children may think about moral and social issues in a unique way. Children need to acquire cognitive, moral, and social skills in order to interact effectively with parents, teachers, and peers. Human development encompasses all of the above skills and reflects the child's intelligent adaptation to the environment.

Today the cognitive, moral, social, and emotional development of children takes place in a rapidly changing society. The article "Play: Ten Power Boosts for Children's Early Learning" discusses the importance of play for supporting all areas of the development of young children. The article titled "Sustaining Resilient Families for Children in Primary Grades," shows how teachers can support children and their families as they cope with tough times. Finally, "The Curriculum Super Highway" argues that as schools promote academic achievement, they also need to approach curriculum in a way that respects the needs of students at different stages of development.

Adolescence brings with it the ability to think abstractly and hypothetically and to see the world from many perspectives. Adolescents strive to achieve a sense of identity by questioning their beliefs and tentatively committing to self-chosen goals. Their ideas about the kind of adults they want to become and the ideals they want to believe in sometimes lead to conflicts with parents and teachers. Adolescents are also sensitive about espoused adult values versus adult behavior. The first article in

© Lars Niki

this section addresses how the school environment can humilate students, and the adverse developmental impact it can have. The second article addresses adolescent risk-taking.

Play: Ten Power Boosts for Children's Early Learning

ALICE STERLING HONIG

Many adults think of play and learning as separate domains. Indeed, some people believe that academic school work is learning but that play is just what young children do to get rid of lots of energy. The truth learned from research is that rich, varied play experiences strongly boost children's early learning (Kaplan 1978; Bergen 1998; Johnson, Christie, & Yawkey 1999).

Children gain powerful knowledge and useful social skills through play.

Children gain powerful knowledge and useful social skills through play. This article offers 10 ideas about what children learn through play.

Play Enhances Dexterity and Grace

Preschoolers learn eye-hand coordination and skillful toy manipulation through play. They spin a top, stack blocks, wind up a jack-in-the-box, and try out ways to solve the chain bolt or buttoning activity on a busy board. The variety of hand motions required to latch, lace, or twirl a top enhances hand dexterity. As they eat with a spoon, infants and toddlers are learning wrist coordination. Teachers support this control learning when they provide interesting activities, such as tossing a beanbag or throwing a soft yarn ball into baskets placed nearer or farther away. Babies adore filling and dumping games and will try to work a windup toy over and over again.

Place babies on their tummies on safe, warm surfaces. This gives them opportunities to stretch and reach for favorite chew toys. As they push up on their arms, infants practice coordination of their shoulder and chest muscles. Such body games are particularly important today because infants are habitually placed on their backs for safe sleeping in cribs.

Learning how to ride a tricycle or scooter enhances the coordination of muscles in legs and feet for toddlers and preschoolers.

Older children learn to play sports. They kick and throw basketballs, baseballs, and soccer balls. These games help children coordinate use of both sides of the body. Sports help children develop confidence and pride in their control over body movement in space.

"Hold-operate" skills in play are important for later learning. For example, a preschooler holds an eggbeater with one hand and turns the handle vigorously to make lots of bubbles during water play. A school-age child holds a book page open with one hand and writes notes with the other. Making a pop-it bead necklace is a challenging activity allowing toddlers to push and pull with their fingers. To promote whole body gracefulness, play soft, slow music, such as the "Skater's Waltz," and invite children to move their bodies.

Peer Play Promotes Social Skills

With admirable patience, teachers help children gradually learn how to take turns riding a tricycle, to share materials, and to work and build together. Soon they learn the pleasures of playing with peers (Smilansky & Shefatya 1990). As buddies, older infants giggle and take turns crawling or running into the cardboard house in the play area and popping their heads through the play-house window to shout "Hi" to a grinning peer peeking in. Toddlers might help put a train track together on the floor and play at being engineers. Preschoolers collaborate on lugging a wagon full of blocks or filling it with a heap of scooped up snow for building a snowman together.

Some children need a teacher's encouraging words to ask a peer for permission to join in a game (Honig & Thompson 1994). Henry pulls his wagon, and Jerry wants his pet cat to go for a ride too. Giving words to such longings boosts a child's ability to learn a variety of ways to get to play with a peer, instead of standing on the sidelines. In a warmly encouraging voice, the adult suggests, "Tell Jerry, 'I want to put my cat in the wagon.'

Children sometimes need an adult's unobtrusive arrangement of props to encourage more advanced sociodramatic play. Others need innovative, adult suggestions to encourage more *inclusive* play. Overhearing some preschoolers tell Kao he cannot play house with them because they already have a mommy, a daddy, and children in their play scenario, the teacher comments, "Suppose there is going to be a birthday party. Kao can be the mail carrier delivering birthday presents to your home." The children take over from there.

In a tussle over a toy, an adult may need to model prosocial solutions for children who struggle to come up with social problem-solving ideas on their own. Shure's (1994) ICPS (I Can Problem Solve) techniques can be helpful. "Julio wants to play blocks, and you want him to play Batman dress-up. Can the two of you find a way to play what you want some of the time and what Julio wants the rest of the time? If you each get a turn choosing an activity, both of you can get your wish and have fun together." Getting children to think through the consequences of interactions is a daily challenge. Teachers can help boost children's ability to figure out how to make and keep a play pal by role-playing helpful scenarios: "Howie, if you go on the seesaw with me awhile, then we can play in the sandbox together." Children learn social skills combined with body coordination in games such as Hokey Pokey and London Bridge Is Falling Down.

Teaching social skills in play is crucially important for children with neurological or developmental disabilities.

Not excluding other children from play is a noble task for which Vivian Paley has instituted a classroom rule: You can't say you can't play. Her book (1992) by this name describes the day-to-day struggles of children to gain empathy and lessen the hurt others feel when they are excluded from peer play. Teaching social skills in play is crucially important for children with neurological or developmental disabilities such as autism spectrum disorders, who may need help decoding the emotions of others and responding in socially effective ways.

Children's Play Sharpens Cognitive and Language Skills

Teachers who carefully prepare materials for sensory motor activities are helping children learn tasks that involve what Piaget ([1951] 1962) calls "means-ends separations" and "causal relationships." When a baby pulls a toy on a string to move it closer or shakes a bell to hear it ring, she is delightedly learning that from certain actions, she gets a specific effect. The toddler banging a stick on a xylophone and miraculously producing musical notes also learns that those specific actions cause interesting results. Scientists use these same early life lessons in their laboratories every day.

Singing with young children creates a pleasurable form of play that enhances brain development and learning.

Infants who play with syllables in their cribs are practicing coordination of lips, tongue, palate, and vocal chords. Singing with young children creates a pleasurable form of play that enhances brain development and learning. Some young toddlers stretch their language abilities amazingly as they try to sing along with the words (Honig 1995). This learning counters theories that play is purely for sensory, personal, or social pleasure. Musical play involves lots of word learning; listen as an enthusiastic group of toddlers tries hard to copy the teacher's words as she sings "Frère Jacques."

Teachers can play rhyming games with toddlers and preschoolers. Start out with easy syllables: "I have a little gray mouse, and he lives in a little gray _____!" If children have trouble at first hearing the sounds, give them the answers and start the rhyming couplet game again. The ability to enjoy and participate in rhyming games is one predictor of success in learning to read.

Play promotes language mastery. Children talk together as they build houses with blocks, piece puzzles together, or construct a space tower using Legos. They talk excitedly as they pretend to get "hurt people" from a car crash scene into ambulances. Social play strengthens language interactions, and teachers may provide a word here and there as catalysts for language interchanges (Honig 1982). Housekeeping corners with dress-up clothes and workbenches and tables with safety goggles and woodworking tools promote feelings of efficacy and self-esteem as well as purposeful, harmonious peer interactions and accomplishments.

Preschoolers Acquire Number and Time Concepts

The Piagetian concept of *conservation of number* is difficult learning during the preschool years (Piaget [1951] 1962). By playing with toys with large, separate parts (that cannot be swallowed!), a preschooler begins to find out that whether he stacks the pieces, lays them out in a circle, or sets them out in one long row, he will still count the same number if he puts his finger carefully on each item while counting. Learning that the sum total does not depend on configuration may be easier if children feel encouraged to experiment with different arrangements of small animals, cars, or blocks.

Concepts such as *soon* or *later* and *before* or *after* are hard for young children to understand. To make the child's construction work, inserting one special piece *before* adding another piece may be the secret. Lego blocks that fit together into three-dimensional space require learning which parts to put together first and which ones to add on later to make the structure stable.

Using a digital camera helps children become more aware of different spatial aspects and directions and viewpoints in space. Will Giana's picture of a small ball rolling really fast (or even slowly) down a chute into a basin capture the ball's action? Preschoolers will enjoy taking real pictures of favorite activity areas. A child might take a photograph while peering down from a raised reading loft or one at eye level while lying on her tummy.

Cooking activities offer rich possibilities for math learning. Children learn varieties of colors and textures of foods and first-before-next scientific procedures, such as measuring just one-half teaspoon of oil for each muffin pan before filling it with three tablespoons of batter.

When music play is embedded in the daily curriculum, children learn "sequences of time" as rhymes and rhythms of chants and songs vary in their patterns and progressions. Even eight-month-old babies can bounce to the musical syllables you emphasize as you chant or sing songs, such as "Hickory dickory dock! The mouse ran up the clock!" Offer play experiences with wrist bells, maracas, tambourines, and keyboards, and sing the same songs over and over. As children move their bodies to musical syllables, especially if they clap out rhythms, they learn one-to-one correspondence between a syllable and a clap of the hands.

Play Areas Promote Children's Spatial Understanding

Learning space concepts occurs gradually through the early years. Toddlers gain understanding of spatial extents, boundaries, and pathways as they develop the surety to run, twirl, jump, career around corners, or stop to bend down and pick up something with ease while galloping past an interesting toy. Preschoolers hop, jump, slide, swing from hanging bars, and climb up rope ladders—exploring spatial dimensions ever more bravely.

Some items, like a cardboard box tunnel, allow infants to crawl through and learn about *forward* and *backward*. Such toys as a car or truck with a front and back or a set of wooden toy trains connected by magnets at each end help babies and toddlers learn *front* and *back, longer* and *shorter, first* and *last*. As a toddler steers herself forward, cheerfully mindful of the wonderfully satisfying noise of the Corn Popper toy she pulls behind her, she is maneuvering and navigating through space, sometimes solving the problem of how to continue forward under the legs of a play table.

After three years of age, many children still have not learned to consider bounded space over their heads while getting out from under a table where they have crept to retrieve a toy. To promote spatial learning, a toy barn, house, or fire station is a fine prop. Children learn that the height of the door makes it easy or difficult to bring in a toy horse, stroller, or fire engine.

Play Prompts Children's Reasoning of Cause and Effect

From early infancy, play with various materials supports children's learning of *if-then* reasoning required for early experimentation and scientific thinking. Play with materials can introduce basic concepts in physics and in chemistry. Children learn how liquids mixed together form solutions with different properties, such as a change in color. A spinning gyroscope overcomes gravity, a lever lifts or moves something

heavy, balances measure weights, and an eyedropper sucks in a liquid. As the preschoolers enjoy seesaw (spring-loaded for safety) rides with friends, they learn how important weight and balance are in keeping the seesaw going.

Teachers' preparation of materials for science play arouses intense curiosity and leads to creative play experiments.

Water play is a particularly wondrous activity for experimenting. As children play with wooden and plastic cups, sifters and strainers, and eggbeaters at the water table, they learn that objects float or sink, pour or sprinkle. Teachers' preparation of materials for science play arouses intense curiosity and leads to creative play experiments. Block building is particularly fine for learning causal and space concepts. Smaller blocks seem to balance on bigger ones but not vice versa, no matter how many times a toddler determinedly tries. Toddlers often walk their toy animals down a slide and are not aware of how gravity could help. A preschooler easily depends on the awesome power of gravity as he launches himself down the playground slide. At play, children learn that things can roll if they have rounded sides but not if they have square sides or bumpy sides, like a not-quite-round potato!

Other science concepts learned in play are how to group objects together because of color, shape, size, or pattern design. Children learn too that things exist within larger groups: knives and forks are silverware, sofas and chairs are furniture.

Sociodramatic Play Clarifies the World of *Pretend* versus *Real*

Young children are not too certain what is *real*. For years, some children fervently believe in the tooth fairy and monsters under the bed. Remember the shepherd boy in Menotti's opera, *Amahl and the Night Visitors,* and the three kings on their way to Bethlehem? Amahl comes into the hut and exclaims excitedly to his mother that he has seen a "star with a tail as long as the sky!" A child may not be telling a lie; but imagination does fuel fantasy.

TV programs also encourage belief in fantasy and propel imaginative flights of pretense. After the Mars landing of an exploring robot, one preschooler gave his teacher a toy car, saying, "We are going to Mars, and we can drive our cars on Mars." His teacher nodded agreeably but was quiet. The child added reassuringly, "We just pretending!"

Imagination and pretend play are important giant steps forward in learning how to create dramatic scenarios in complex play with peers. Three-year-olds stirring pop-it beads in a pot pretend to make popcorn to eat. Play promotes the use of a rich imagination. An adult may be nonplussed when a preschooler objects to her sitting down on the couch, explaining that his imaginary playmate is already sitting there. When Talya proclaims she is a superhero and grabs Terry's toy, Terry's firm "My toy!" helps Talya learn the difference between the seemingly unlimited power of a TV fantasy character and the real needs and preferences of a playmate.

Play Enriches Children's Sensory and Aesthetic Appreciation

Listening to music of various genres or exploring color combinations with finger paints can arouse different feelings in children and their appreciation of beauty. Watch the glow on their faces as children carefully add drops of color to a small pan of water and then rejoice in the subtle color-patterned swirls they have created.

Teachers support aesthetic appreciation when they hang up colorful Kente cloth, tape large posters of Monet's *Water Lilies* on the wall, and play fast-paced salsa tunes for dancing. Providing squares of rainbow-colored nylon gauze adds aesthetic pleasure as well as bodily grace to children's dancing. Toddlers blowing and chasing bubbles to catch them in cupped hands is a game that combines aesthetic pleasure with increasing hand dexterity. It also enhances toddlers' abilities to estimate how far and how fast to run to catch a bubble before it pops.

Children delight in watching the unfolding of a fern's graceful fronds or the production of giant flowers by a big, brown amaryllis bulb they have planted. Their eyes widen in awe at the goldfish's graceful flick of its tail while swimming across the aquarium. Children seem primed early on to become lovers of beauty.

Play Extends Children's Attention Span, Persistence, and Sense of Mastery

Some children are cautious and slow in temperament, while others tend to be more impulsive. When children become absorbed in play, even children with shorter attention spans often stretch out their playtimes. Skillful, adult play partners can help children with short attention spans to extend their play. By providing intriguing toys and experiences and encouragement geared to the unique interests of each child, teachers help strengthen children's abilities to prolong play. This ability to focus attention and to persist at challenging learning tasks is a crucial component for later academic success in school.

When play is child initiated, children control the play themes and feel empowered. They come to realize their capabilities of mastering the roles, scenarios, and logistical problems that may arise in the course of sociodramatic play. No kennel for the stuffed puppy? OK, what can we use as a substitute kennel? As playmates arrange props and environments, teachers are superb helpers in facilitating child mastery of play themes.

Play Helps Children Release Emotions and Relieves Separation Anxiety

Learning to express and regulate emotions appropriately is a major challenge for young children. Sometimes they repetitively play out the central emotional concerns in their lives (Honig 1998).

Some children suffer anxious feelings from repeated separations and tearful parting from playmates who have become good friends. Children in military families may have already moved quite a few times, and if parents are deployed, the children may move again to stay with relatives they do not know. Hearing scary talk on the radio and TV may increase children's fears and lead to sadness and distress, bed-wetting, nail-biting, or fighting with peers instead of playing harmoniously. Caring teachers may notice a child's compulsive war play with toys and wisely give the child space, time, and acceptance to act out separation anxieties and fantasies in play, along with extra hugs, lap time, and soothing supportive actions.

Pretend play, even scary war play, provides a deep release for emotions. A toddler may soothingly feed a bottle to a baby doll or put a baby bear to bed in a toy crib. Teachers can build on this tender play to reassure the child how much an absent parent loves the child. Toddlers love telephone talk and gain opportunities to practice social interaction skills. Pretend telephone talk also comforts young children experiencing separation anxieties and lets them feel connected to their families, especially with ones far away.

Teachers need to be attuned to the sometimes worrisome messages that children's play can reveal. By observing how children express troubled feelings in play, teachers may better figure out ways to help young children feel nurtured and safe. After the events of 9/11, many preschoolers built block towers and crashed toy airplanes into them. Children's play provides a valuable window for tuning in to the worries, fears, angers, and happiness in their emotional lives.

Play deepens a child's sense of serenity and joy.

In closing, play deepens a child's sense of serenity and joy. Children digging in the sand at a neighborhood pocket park resemble scruffy cherubs, their faces and arms covered with sand or dirt. Their bodies look so relaxed. One rarely hears them crying.

Tuned-in teachers can shape almost any play experience into an opportunity for children to learn more about the world and how it works. Water play, sand play, block play, ball play, searching for signs with different shapes and colors on a neighborhood walk—all become grist for early learning as well as early pleasure in play.

As teachers promote and encourage play, they enhance children's feelings of security, of being deeply acceptable, of being a welcomed friend. In carving out safe, leisurely, and generous times for children's play, teachers provide the cognitive and social groundwork for children's future learning.

References

Bergen, D., ed. 1998. *Play as a medium for learning and development: A handbook of theory and practice.* Portsmouth, NH: Heinemann.

Honig, A.S. 1982. *Playtime learning games for young children.* Syracuse, NY: Syracuse University Press.

Honig, A.S. 1995. Singing with infants and toddlers. *Young Children* 50(5): 72–78.

Honig, A.S. 1998. Sociocultural influences on sexual meanings embedded in playful experiences. In *Play from birth to twelve and beyond: Contents, perspectives, and meanings,* eds. P. Fromberg & D. Bergen, 338–47. New York: Garland Press.

Honig, A.S., & A. Thompson 1994. Helping toddlers with peer group entry skills. *Zero to Three* 14(5): 15–19.

Johnson, J.E., J.F. Christie, & T.D. Yawkey. 1999. *Play and early childhood development.* 2nd ed. Upper Saddle River, NJ: Allyn & Bacon/Longman/Pearson Education.

Kaplan, L. 1978. *Oneness and separateness.* New York: Simon & Schuster.

Paley, V. 1992. *You can't say you can't play.* Cambridge, MA: Harvard University Press.

Piaget, J. [1951] 1962. *play, dreams, and imitation in childhood.* New York: Norton.

Shure, M. 1994. *Raising a thinking child: Help your young child to resolve everyday conflicts and get along with others.* New York: Henry Holt.

Smilansky, S., & L. Shefatya. 1990. *Facilitating play: A medium for promoting cognitive, socio-emotional and academic development in young children.* Gaithersburg, MD: Psychosocial and Educational Publications.

ALICE STERLING HONIG, PhD, professor emerita of child development, Syracuse University, New York, has authored more than 450 chapters and articles and more than a dozen books. She teaches annually the National Quality Infant/Toddler Workshop and lectures widely on prosocial and language development and gender patterns in play.

Sustaining Resilient Families for Children in Primary Grades

Janice Patterson and Lynn Kirkland

The adversities that today's families face are well-documented and staggering (Children's Defense Fund, 2004). Even in the midst of tough times, however, many families are able to display resilience. Family resilience refers to the coping mechanisms the family uses as a functional unit to recover from life's setbacks. The purpose of this article is to provide parents and teachers with guidelines for creating resilient families, thereby helping primary-grade children withstand the challenges in their lives. In this article, we will consider what is known about family resilience, examine the role of protective factors and recovery processes, and suggest specific strategies that families and teachers can use to support resilience.

Family Resilience

Much of the work on family resilience is anchored in studies about the resilience of children. Werner and Smith (1982, 1992; Werner, 1984), authors of arguably the most important study on childhood resilience, spent 40 years studying children on the island of Kauai who were judged to be at risk of living in hardship. The children were born into poor, unskilled families, and were judged to be at risk based on their exposure before age 2 to at least four risk factors, such as serious health problems, familial alcoholism, mental illness, violence, and divorce. By age 18, about two-thirds of the children had fared poorly, as predicted by their at-risk status. The remaining one-third had developed into competent, confident, and caring young adults living productive lives, as rated on a variety of measures. In a follow-up study, the overwhelming majority of this group, now at age 40, were still living successful lives. In fact, many of them had outperformed Kauai citizens from more advantageous backgrounds. They were more likely to be stable in their marriages and fewer were unemployed. The key factors that promoted individual resilience were:

- Caring and support were provided by at least one adult who knew the child well and cared deeply about that child's well-being
- Positive expectations were articulated clearly for the child, and the support necessary to meet those expectations was provided

- Meaningful involvement and participation provided the child the opportunity to become involved in something she cared about and to contribute to the well-being of others

Although it is not impossible for an individual child from a non-resilient family to bounce back from adversity, the child's health and well-being is best supported if the family functions as a resilient unit. When a crisis upsets the life of a primary-grade child, the impact of that crisis on the child is determined largely by the extent to which the family's normal functioning is disrupted. Even when the child is not directly affected by a situation, he or she is touched by the changes in relationships that result from the changes or crises for others in the family.

As we reflect on the image of a resilient family, note how changes in society contribute to that image. Traditionally, the model of a resilient family, those who successfully navigated the ups and downs of life, was the image of a white, affluent, nuclear family led by the breadwinning father and a mother working as full-time homemaker. Enormous social changes in recent decades highlight the fact that resilient families can be non-white, upper or lower income, represent a variety of ethnic and cultural traditions, and include single parents, non-custodial parents, grandparents, stepparents, and same-gender parents. Changes in the definition of family are dynamic. In one landmark court decision supporting the rights of gay parents, the judge recognized changing definitions of "family" by acknowledging, "It is the totality of the relationship, as evidenced by the dedication, caring and self-sacrifice of the parties, which should, in the final analysis, control the definition of family" (quoted in Stacey, 1990, p. 4).

Protective and Recovery Factors

An understanding of family resilience incorporates research on *protective factors* and *recovery factors* (Cowan, Cowan, & Schultz, 1996; Garmezy & Rutter, 1983; Hawley & DeHaan, 1996; McCubbin, Thompson, Thompson, & McCubbin, 1992). Protective factors are behaviors that help give people strength in times of stress (Patterson, Patterson, & Collins, 2003). Examples of such factors include family celebrations, planned family time, consistent routines, and family traditions. In addition, family resilience can be sustained by maintaining open communication within the family and building a solid support network beyond the family.

Recovery factors refer to the family's ability to develop and use adaptation strategies when confronted with a crisis. Families can and do bounce back and adapt by changing their habits, their patterns of functioning, or the situation that has created the problem. Some evidence exists that there may be variation in the nature of the needed recovery factors, depending upon the situation. For instance, families having to deal with chronically ill children (e.g., cystic fibrosis) made use of the following strategies:

- *Family integration.* The mother's and father's optimism and efforts to keep the family together were important to the child's health.
- *Family support and esteem building.* The parents made concerted efforts to reach out to family, friends, and the larger community, thereby helping them to develop their self-esteem and self-confidence.
- *Family recreation orientation, control, and organization.* A family emphasis on active involvement in recreational and sporting activities is positively associated with improvements in the child's health. The greater the family's emphasis on control and family organization, rules, and procedures, the greater the improvement in the child's health.
- *Family optimism and mastery.* The greater the family's efforts to maintain a sense of optimism and order, the greater the improvement in the child's health. Furthering one's understanding and mastery of the health regimen necessary to promote the child's health helps the adaptation process (McCubbin & McCubbin, 1996).

During any family crisis, disruption in the daily routine exacerbates the chaos and confusion. Within the context of divorce, for instance, it is important for the family to establish and maintain routines that provide continuity of family connections, such as Sunday brunch with Dad. Research on children's positive adjustment following their parents' divorce shows that predictability and reliability of contact with the non-custodial parent is as important as the amount of contact (Hetherington & Kelly, 2002; Walsh, 1991). It is also clear that authoritative parenting, which combines warmth and control, is a significant positive protection against family stress that children may encounter (Hetherington & Kelly, 2002).

Strategies to Strengthen Family Resilience

Effective communication, including problem solving and affirmation, is a critical variable for family success in facing routine and extraordinary challenges. Contemporary lifestyles may allow little time for really listening to children, discussing their problems, and affirming their value to the family. A growing number of parents and teachers realize that communication is not something that can be left to chance; they plan for it.

One family reported on the "talk" that took place each night at the dinner table (Feiler, 2004). First, dinner was designated as a sacred time and attendance was mandatory. No television was allowed. Instead, they played a game, "Bad and Good," which began with a moderator asking each person, "What happened to you today that was bad?" Everyone had to respond; respect for others was supported by not allowing anyone to criticize, interrupt, or refute another person's bad experience. It was important that parents participated, to demonstrate that bad things happen to all of us on a daily basis and how we cope is what matters. Next, the rotating moderator asked each person, "What happened to you today that was good?" As family members reported their good stories, others affirmed them and good news begot good news. Primary-grade children in the family learned to celebrate successes. Of course, some events had both good and bad elements; as the family discussed what happened, children learned that everything doesn't fit neatly into good or bad categories. Variations on the theme might be such questions as, "What are you most afraid will happen to you?" or "If you could have one wish, what would it be?" or "What makes you feel really special?"

Problem solving can be nurtured in this context by asking everyone for thoughts on solving family problems. Our daily lives are inundated by e-mail, voice mail, computers, video games, iPods, and other diversions that can replace face-to-face communication, and so we must take conscious steps to let children know we are listening and care about them and their ideas.

These strategies are easily adapted to the classroom. Teachers routinely listen to children during community time, at meals, and in small groups, and can pose questions for all to answer. Class meetings also can provide many venues for children to discuss issues related to their lives and the lives of their families. As part of a class meeting, carefully selected articles from the newspaper can be used to initiate conversation about issues that relate to the lives of the children in the class. For example, children can consider alternative ways of dealing with problems other than those exhibited by individuals acting unlawfully within the local community. As part of routine class meetings, children utilize problems that arise throughout the day in play situations in the classroom, coming up with appropriate resolutions. For example, if a problem has arisen on the playground between children, offering the opportunity for children to defend their position, as well as hear the positions of others, helps them to consider other people and become less egocentric in their reasoning. Hearing others' perspectives encourages the moral development of the child (Piaget, 1997) and encourages flexible thinking, which builds a child's resilience, both individually and within the family.

It is also important that parents and teachers teach children how to ask for help when they need it. One of the biggest predictors of resilience in the Kauai study mentioned earlier in this article was that children knew how to ask for help. We cannot assume that every child (or adult) will, or knows how to, ask for needed help. Today's society places a high value on independent action and neglects teaching collaboration. Parents and teachers can guide children in forming questions and in practicing their help-seeking skills (e.g., "Where would you go if no one was home when you came home after school?").

Within the classroom, teachers can use the writing workshop process to help children write about issues that trouble them. For instance, one teacher found it helpful to encourage a student, from a military family about to relocate, to draft a paper about her fears of moving to a new school. Through the writing and subsequent conferencing that preceded the final draft, the teacher and parent learned that the child's greatest fear was not having someone to sit with at lunch. The parent and teacher in the new school were able to find a "lunch mate" and thus eased the transition. A variation on the writing conference is to establish dialogue journals so that the student is writing to the teacher or parent and the adult responds in writing. Some children will write about fears that are difficult to verbalize.

Another important strategy is to strive to maintain an optimistic outlook, even when the going gets rough. The family that expects to prevail in times of crisis very often will prevail. An orientation toward such hardiness is reflected in the work of Steve and Sybil Wolin, who speak of "survivor's pride"—the deep self-respect that comes from knowing you were challenged and that you prevailed. Children who grew up in families that were *not* resilient and later compared notes reported very similar family experiences, as identified below:

- We rarely celebrated holidays.
- They [parents] hardly ever came to a soccer game, a school play, or a community picnic.
- There were no regular mealtimes.
- They forgot my birthday.
- The house was a pigsty.
- No one had a good word for me; nothing I ever did was right.
- They were always fighting with each other, tearing each other apart in front of us, as if we didn't exist. (Wolin & Wolin, 1993, p. 27)

If we turn this list around, we can see the practices of resilient families for primary-grade children. They *do* celebrate holidays and attend soccer games, school plays, and community picnics as a family. They make time for regular mealtimes and birthday celebrations. The house is clean enough to be functional and pleasant. Love and affirmation are given freely and parental conflict is minimized in front of children. Within the classroom, through conversations, parent meetings, and written communication, teachers can emphasize to parents the importance of participation in these activities as resilience-building strategies.

Importance of Family Traditions and Routines

A family that promotes its own resilience with these strategies takes deliberate steps in building the resilience of the family unit for all members, including the primary-grade child.

The family values traditions, saves mementos, and tells stories about family heroes. Conducting these activities within the family promotes pride in the family heritage and also can provide a link to the present. If the family reflects on the struggles immigrant parents faced in coming to a new country and the strategies they used to survive, the current move across town takes on a different perspective. Children in resilient families see themselves as part of the family unit and take pride in finding ways to contribute to the family's strength. Effective communication and family optimism work to create a resilient family that considers itself to be healthy and is reflected in such statements as:

- We are a good family.
- Home is a safe, welcoming place.
- We have a past that is a source of strength and we have good, sound values that guide our future.
- We are known and respected in the community.
- We like each other.
- Our blood runs thick; we will always be there for one another. (Wolin & Wolin, 1993, p. 40)

Without a doubt, a variety of challenges and crises can tax even the strongest family. Such situations call for all family members to pull together and use their collective strength (all of us are stronger than one of us) to weather the challenge. An attitude of family resilience gives the family a sense of its own competence and control over the outcome.

Deliberately structuring family time and rituals is another important strategy for strengthening resilience in families. Every family has a routine, even if it is one of chaos. Resilient families take control of the routine for the purpose of establishing predictability and stability—critical elements to family balance. Although sometimes difficult to establish, this strategy can make a difference in how the child copes with new events. For instance, a 7-year-old girl was confused by where she was to go each day after school and began crying every morning, saying, "I don't know where to go today." The mother and teacher combined forces to develop a routine in which the mother sent the teacher each Monday a list of where the child was to go every day of the week. She also tucked a note in the child's lunch box that said, "Today, you go to Brownies in the gym after school." The mother used a combination of words and picture symbols to be sure the child understood the message; thus, a stabilizing routine was established.

Family Communication with Children's Literature

Family mealtimes are important venues for communication, as mentioned earlier. They also serve the function of reinforcing family routine. Spending quality time together, including just "hanging out," is important for building family resilience. Family time together does not need to involve money or extensive time commitments. Playing board games or reading together can provide routine and meaning to family relationships.

Children's literature can be used at home or as part of classroom curricula to initiate caring and conversation related to issues that children and families face. When parents and teachers sit and read with children, caring for that child is reinforced and the child feels valued. Discussions of book characters and plots provide meaningful and relevant ways for children to consider the lives of others and begin to look at ways of dealing with problems they face. Resilience in children is promoted through time spent with a caring adult and their participation in retellings and creative dramatizations of story plots.

Table 1 lists examples of good books that promote resilience in primary-grade children. These books were selected because they address, either directly or indirectly, elements of resilience or strategies for strengthening the skills of resilience. For instance, in *Wemberly Worried* (2000), Henkes writes of Wemberly, the little mouse, who worries about everything, especially her first day of school. As Wemberly struggles not to worry, she taps into some basic resilience-building strategies (e.g., telling adults you're worried, finding a friend to share your worries, and building on your strengths by successfully navigating the first day of school and returning for another day). In Faith Ringgold's *Tar Beach* (1991), Cassie Louise Lightfoot, an African American 8-year-old growing up in Harlem in 1939, demonstrates how believing good things will happen and drawing on the love of friends and family can promote a feeling of pride. Critical elements in building resilience include a belief in a positive future and support from a loving community.

Another example of the power of these books is drawn from *Amazing Grace* (Hoffman, 1991). Grace is an African American girl who loves stories and regularly adopts the roles and identities of strong, problem-solving characters, such as Joan of Arc, Hiawatha, and Anansi the Spider, in the plays she writes herself. Grace's grandmother takes her to see a famous black ballerina to encourage her to do "anything she can imagine." That role model encourages Grace to work hard and ultimately achieve her dream of performing the role of Peter Pan in the class play. Grace demonstrates problem-solving skills, emulates successful positive role models, and maintains perseverance—all foundational traits in building resilience.

The literature on individual and family resilience underscores the importance of building strategies to secure a network of social support. Such support begins with a loving relationship between one child and one adult (generally, a parent). Family therapists have likened the resilient family to open systems with clear, yet permeable boundaries, similar to a living cell (Beavers & Hampson, 1993; Satir, 1988; Walsh, 1998; Whitaker & Keith, 1981).

Boundaries are important for the child and an authoritative parent earns the respect that comes from predictability; "no" means no. Inconsistent reinforcement of family rules undermines trust within the family and is not healthy. In fact, Hetherington and Kelly (2002, p. 130), in their studies of divorcing families, reported that "children of authoritative parents emerged from divorce as the most socially responsible, least troubled and highest-achieving children." Parents building resilient families ask their children for help in maintaining the household.

Examples include setting the table, mowing the lawn, washing dishes, and caring for a younger sibling, all of which can contribute to the resilience, maturity, and competency of a child. Age-appropriate chores are an important aspect of building children's resilience and sense of self-worth.

Family and Community

Resilient families have strength and integrity in their interactions within the family and also know when to reach outside the family circle for satisfying relationships. In an ideal world, the family of a primary-grade child is actively engaged in the broader community and relates to the community and each other with hope and optimism. Family members go out into the community and bring strength and new learnings back into the family circle.

There is a practical element to having relationships outside the family. Other connections can provide information, concrete services, support, companionship, and even respite from difficult situations. A family's sense of security can be enhanced by meaningful relationships with others. Community activities, including involvement in school and extracurricular activities, foster family well-being. Regular participation in sports leagues, faith-based activities, and parent-teacher organizations can bolster protective and recovery processes for the family. Research suggests that there is a highly protective element in belonging to a group and having regular social activity. This is particularly true for those in isolation and depression (Walsh, 1998b).

Because extended family is too often far away or unavailable for other reasons, it is important that families establish connections to meet their life circumstances. In the armed forces, families regularly share meals and child care in support of each other. Some families turn to older people in the community to provide "family" contact and meaningful activities with children at home or school. Both children and elders benefit in these situations. Also, multifamily groups band together in other ways to support single parents or families coping with a chronic illness, and such support can be vital in managing chronic stress or crises.

Conclusion

In this article, we have presented guidelines for creating and sustaining resilient families for primary-grade children and offered strategies for developing effective communication and building an attitude of family hardiness or resilience. We suggested promoting the value of family time, authoritative parenting, routine, and the importance of social support. We offer this work with the caveat that family resilience is an emerging field and we have only touched the surface.

Yet, our research and conversations with teachers, parents, and other child care providers have convinced us that teachers can take particular steps to support children and their families. Work with school administrators to develop sessions for parents on building family resilience during the critical primary-grade years. Invite children to talk about their experiences and say

Table 1 Resilience-Building Books for Primary-Grade Children

Andreae, G. (1999). *Giraffes Can't Dance.* New York: Orchard Books.

Bottner, B. (1992). *Bootsie Barker Bites.* New York: G. P. Putnam Sons.

Bradby, M. (1995). *More Than Anything Else.* New York: Orchard Books.

Brimner, L. D. (2002). *The Littlest Wolf.* New York: HarperCollins.

Burningham, J. (1987). *John Patrick Norman McHennessy—the boy who was always late.* New York: The Trumpet Club.

Burton, V. L. (1943). *Katy and the Big Snow.* Boston: Houghton Mifflin.

Cannon, J. (1993). *Stellaluna.* Orlando, FL: Harcourt Brace & Company.

Cannon, J. (2000). *Crickwing.* San Diego, CA: Harcourt.

Carle, E. (1999). *The Very Clumsy Click Beetle.* New York: Philomel Books.

Clifton, L. (1983). *Everett Anderson's Goodbye.* New York: Henry Holt and Company.

Couric, K. (2000). *The Brand New Kid.* New York: Doubleday.

Giovanni, N. (2005). *Rosa.* New York: Henry Holt & Co.

Havill, J. (1995). *Jamaica's Blue Marker.* New York: Houghton Mifflin.

Heard, G. (2002). *This Place I Know: Poems of Comfort.* Cambridge, MA: Candlewick Press.

Henkes, K. (2000). *Wemberly Worried.* Hong Kong: Greenwillow Books.

Hoffman, M. (1991). *Amazing Grace.* Boston: Houghton Mifflin.

Juster, N. (2005). *The Hello, Goodbye Window.* New York: Hyperion Books for Children.

Kraus, R. (1971). *Leo, the Late Bloomer.* New York: Windmill Books.

Kroll, V. (1997). *Butterfly Boy.* Honesdale, PA: Boyds Mills Press.

Lester, H. (1999). *Hooway for Wodney Wat.* New York: Scholastic Books.

Lithgow, J. (2000). *The Remarkable Farkle McBride.* New York: Simon & Schuster.

McKissack, P. (1986). *Flossie and the Fox.* New York: Scholastic Books.

Mora, P. (2005). *Doña Flor: A Tall Tale about a Giant Woman with a Great Big Heart.* New York: Alfred A. Knopf.

Moss, S. (1995). *Peter's painting.* Greenvale, NY: MONDO Publishing.

Piper, W. (1986). *The little Engine That Could.* New York: Platt & Munk.

Puttock, S. (2001). *A story for Hippo: A Book about Loss.* New York: Scholastic Press.

Ringgold, F. (1991). *Tar Beach.* New York: Scholastic Books.

Salley, C. (2002). *Epossumondas.* San Diego, CA: Harcourt.

Seskin, S., & Shamblin, A. (2002). *Don't Laugh at Me.* Berkeley, CA: Tricycle Press.

Taback, S. (1999). *Joseph had a Little Overcoat.* New York: Scholastic.

Tafuri, N. (2000). *Will You Be My Friend?* New York: Scholastic.

Tompert, A. (1993). *Just a Little Bit.* Boston: Houghton Mifflin.

Wyeth, S. D. (1998). *Something Beautiful.* New York: Dragonfly Books.

what they believe makes them "bounce back" when bad things happen. Get parents and others involved by creating informational programs and materials about the importance of family resilience. Together, we must do all we can to help families and their children develop and nourish their resilience.

References

Beavers, W. R., & Hampson, R. B. (1990). *Successful families: Assessment and intervention.* New York: Norton.

Children's Defense Fund. (2004). *The state of America's children 2004: A continuing portrait of inequality fifty years after Brown v. Board of Education.* Retrieved August 14, 2004, from www.childrensdefense.org/pressreleases/040713.asp

Cowan, P. A., Cowan, C. P., & Schulz, M. S. (1996). Thinking about risk and resilience in families. In M. Hetherington & E. A. Blechman (Eds.), *Stress, coping and resilience in children and families.* Mahwah, NJ: Erlbaum.

Feiler, B. (2004, August 15). A game that gets parents and kids talking. *Parade.*

Garmezy, N., & Rutter, M. (Eds.). (1983). *Stress, coping and development in children.* New York: McGraw-Hill.

Hawley, D. R., & DeHaan, L. (1996). Toward a definition of family resilience: Integrating life-span and family perspectives. *Family Process, 35,* 283–298.

Hetherington, E., & Kelly, J. (2002). *For better or for worse: Divorce reconsidered.* New York: W. W. Norton & Co.

McCubbin, H. I., & McCubbin, M. A. (1996). Resilient families, competencies, supports and coping over the life cycle. In L. Sawyers (Ed.), *Faith and families.* Philadelphia: Geneva Press.

McCubbin, H. I., Thompson, E. A., Thompson, A. I., & McCubbin, M. A. (1992). Family schema, paradigms, and paradigm shifts: Components and processes of appraisal in family adaptation to crises. In A. P. Turnbull, J. M. Patterson, S. K. Bahr, D. L. Murphy, J. Marquis, & M. Blue-Banning (Eds.), *Cognitive coping research in developmental disabilities.* Baltimore: Paul H. Brookes.

Patterson, J. L., Patterson, J. H., & Collins, L. (2002). *Bouncing back: How your school can succeed in the face of adversity.* Larchmont, NY: Eye on Education Press.

Piaget, J. (1997). *The moral judgment of the child.* New York: Simon & Schuster.

Satir, V. (1988). *Within our reach: Breaking the cycle of disadvantage.* New York: Anchor.

Stacey, J. (1990). *Brave new families: Stories of domestic upheaval in late twentieth century America.* New York: Basic Books.

Walsh, F. (1991). Promoting healthy functioning in divorced and remarried families. In A. Gurman & D. Kniskern (Eds.), *Handbook of family therapy.* New York: Brunner/Mazel.

Walsh, F. (1998a). *Strengthening family resilience.* New York: The Guilford Press.

Walsh, F. (1998b). Families in later life: Challenges and opportunities. In B. Carter & M. McGoldrick (Eds.), *The expanded family life cycle.* Needham Heights, MA: Allyn & Bacon.

Werner, E. (1984). Resilient children. *Young Children, 68*(72).

Werner, E. E., & Smith, R. S. (1982). *Vulnerable but invincible: A longitudinal study of resilient children and youth.* New York: Adams, Bannister, Cox.

Werner, E. E., & Smith, R. S. (1992). *Overcoming the odds: High risk children from birth to adulthood.* New York: Cornell University Press.

Whitaker, C., & Keith, D. (1981). Symbolic-experiential family therapy. In A. S. Gurman & D. Kniskern (Eds.), *Handbook of family therapy.* New York: Brunner/Mazel.

Wolin, S., & Wolin, S. (1993). *The resilient self: How survivors of troubled families rise above adversity.* New York: Villard.

JANICE PATTERSON is Associate Professor, Education Department, and **LYNN KIRKLAND** is Associate Professor, Education Department, University of Alabama-Birmingham.

From *Childhood Education,* Fall 2007, pp. 2–7. Copyright © 2007 by the Association for Childhood Education International. Reprinted by permission of Janice Patterson & Lynn Kirkland and the Association for Childhood Education International, 17904 Georgia Avenue, Suite 215, Olney, MD 20832.

The Curriculum Superhighway

In the race to get kids to the finish line, let's not bypass their developmental needs.

THOMAS ARMSTRONG

A superhighway is being built across today's education landscape. It has been under construction for some time. Initially, this project focused on connecting kindergarten to the elementary grades. Gradually, it has broadened its vision until now it extends from preschool to graduate school.[1] All the byways, narrow routes, and winding paths that have traditionally filled the journey from early childhood to early adulthood are now being "aligned" so that the curriculum (a Latin word meaning "a lap around a racetrack") can move along at breakneck speed.

So far, this project has received the approbation of most educators and policymakers. Such a colossal undertaking, however, extracts a great cost.

An Environmental Impact Report

Educators today are almost entirely engaged in *academic achievement discourse* (Armstrong, 2006). The topics of this discourse—test scores, benchmarks, data, accountability, and adequate yearly progress—are the bulldozers, backhoes, cement mixers, and asphalt pavers that are constructing the curriculum superhighway. A more appropriate focus of educators' dialogue would be *human development discourse,* which recognizes that human beings travel through different stages of life, each with its own requirements for optimal growth.

The curriculum superhighway is carving an asphalt swath through several distinct areas of the human development countryside, threatening to damage or destroy their delicate ecosystems. Let's consider some of the eco-disasters likely to ensue from this multi-billion-dollar road project.

Human beings travel through different stages of life, each with its own requirements for optimal growth.

Early Childhood

In early childhood, the developmental bottom line is *play.* When I say play, I'm not talking about playing checkers or soccer; I'm referring to open-ended play in a rich, multimodal environment, with supportive facilitators and a minimum of adult interference. Between the ages of 2 and 6, children's brains go through an incredible process of development. Metabolism is twice that of an adult, and brain connections are formed or discarded in response to the kinds of stimulation the child does or doesn't receive.

At this time of life, it makes the most sense to encourage open-ended engagement with the world in an environment like that of Habibi's Hutch, a preschool in Austin, Texas, that calls itself a "natural childlife preserve." Children spend most of their day playing on swing sets, in sand piles, in playhouses, and with art materials and toys. They perform their own plays and participate in a cooking class (Osborne, 2007). The preschool's Web site (http://habibishutch.com/philosophy.html) explains, "Our kids leave the Hutch with so much more than their ABCs and 123s. They all leave with a sense of themselves and a wonder and drive to know more about themselves and their surroundings."

This approach to early childhood education is a good example of a developmentally appropriate program. Unfortunately, the curriculum superhighway is delivering academic goods and materials as well as formal teaching lessons from the higher grades down to the preschool level—a trend that could ultimately destroy this precious ecology.

Middle Childhood

In middle childhood, the developmental bottom line is *learning how the world works.* Naturally, children of all ages are constantly learning about the world. But from age 7 to 10, this need becomes especially important. Kids are becoming a more significant part of the broader society, and they want to understand the rules of this more complex world. Their brains have matured to the point where they can begin to learn the formal rules of reading, writing, and math; but they also need to satisfy their insatiable curiosity by learning how governments work, how butterflies grow, how their community developed, and countless other things.

The "children's museum" model of learning, recommended by Howard Gardner (1994) among others, is a good example of how we can preserve this developmental ecology. "In a children's museum," Gardner explains, "kids have an opportunity to work with very interesting kinds of things, at their own pace, in their own way, using the kinds of intelligence which they're strong in." In a unit developed by the Minnesota Children's Museum, for example, 1st grade students spend six weeks studying insects using the museum's Insect Discovery Kit and then take a trip to the museum's anthill exhibit (Association of Children's Museums, 2003).

"In all the world there is no other child exactly like you. In the millions of years that have passed, there has never been another child exactly like you. You may become a Shakespeare, a Michelangelo, a Beethoven. You have the capacity for anything. Yes, you are a marvel."

—Pablo Casals

Because schools today are spending more and more class time preparing students for academic tests that are part of the superhighway scheme (a project aptly called "No Child Left Behind"), students have fewer opportunities to engage in a rich exploration of our incredible world. As a result, this ecosystem could eventually decay and disappear.

Early Adolescence

The developmental needs of early adolescence consist primarily of *social, emotional, and metacognitive growth*. Surges of testosterone at puberty swell the amygdala, especially in boys, generating strong emotions (Giedd et al., 1996). For girls, estrogen levels appear to affect serotonin levels, leading to high rates of depression (Born, Shea, & Steiner, 2002). The curriculum needs to reflect young adolescents' greater sensitivity to emotional and social issues. For example, at Benjamin Franklin Middle School in Ridgewood, New Jersey, students read about the Warsaw ghetto and then discuss how they can combat injustices that they see in their own lives (Curtis, 2001).

Just before puberty, children's brains experience a surge in the growth of gray matter in the frontal, parietal, and temporal lobes, which may be related to what Piaget called *formal operational thinking*—the ability to "think about thinking." This new capacity represents an incredible resource, enabling young teens to begin to reflect at a more abstract level—not only to gain perspective on their own emotional responses, but also to engage intellectually with such universal issues as justice and individual rights.

Unfortunately, the project managers of the curriculum superhighway appear to regard this newly acquired metacognitive capacity as merely an opportunity to teach algebra and reading comprehension. The components of the superhighway's infrastructure—tougher requirements, more homework, and harder tests—leave teachers little chance to engage students' emotions, social needs, and metacognitive thinking in any substantial way. The resulting deterioration in this ecosystem may lead to environmental hazards such as gangs, violence, and mental disorders.

Late Adolescence

In late adolescence, the developmental bottom line is *preparing to live independently in the real world*. At this age, neural pathways in the brain are becoming increasingly sheathed, or myelinated, so that nerve impulses travel more quickly—especially in the frontal lobes, which control planning and decision making (National Institute of Mental Health, 2001). At this age, young people in many states are legally empowered to set up their own individual retirement accounts, drive a car, marry, vote, and engage in other adult responsibilities. But in a typical high school classroom, these same adolescents have to raise their hand for permission to go to the bathroom.

At this stage of life, kids need less classroom time and more time out in the real world, in apprenticeships, internships, job shadowing, career-based work experiences, and other situations in which they can experience themselves as incipient adults. The traffic on the curriculum superhighway, however, is especially intense at this point. High school students are deluged with pressures to pass high-stakes tests, meet strict graduation requirements, and take advanced courses that will prepare them for four-year academic colleges. Many of them aren't even allowed to dip their toes into the currents of the real world, because to take this time would mean falling behind their peers in an increasingly competitive society The curriculum superhighway's attack on this ecosystem may erode students' ability to think for themselves, reflect on their futures, and make responsible choices that mirror their own proclivities and interests.

Restoring a Human Development Curriculum

Schools need to approach curriculum in a way that is environmentally sensitive to the ecologies of different developmental stages of life. Let's start with literacy. In early childhood, literacy needs to take place in the context of play. According to developmental psychologist David Elkind (2001), children aren't even cognitively ready to learn formal reading and math skills until they reach Piaget's operational stage of cognitive development around age 6 or 7. In early childhood, literacy should be just another part of the child's rich multisensory environment. A playhouse area, for example, should include books and magazines along with dolls and furniture. If a child wants to play at being mommy reading a story to baby, that's up to her (experts call this process *emergent literacy*).

At the elementary school level, we can appropriately teach formal reading and writing skills, because the symbol systems of literacy are an important component of how the world works. Literacy will develop best, however, not with boring worksheets and sterile reading programs, but with reading and writing experiences that give students a chance to learn about all aspects of the world, from science to history to social relationships. In such programs, students may read historical narratives, guidebooks on science topics, and other reading materials (such as reference sources, Internet text, or high-quality fiction) that whet their curiosity to find out more about the world. Likewise, they may take field notes on nature hikes, write letters to people of influence, and create reports based on what they've discovered about their community's history.

In middle school, literacy needs to take place in the context of a young teen's social, emotional, and metacognitive growth. Journal writing, therefore, is developmentally more important than book report writing. Reading material should include emotional themes that speak to the adolescent's inner turmoil. Teachers should assign collaborative and cooperative reading and writing assignments to honor the social needs of early adolescence. They need to teach students how to use metacognitive strategies to monitor their own reading and writing habits.

Finally, in high school, literacy needs to serve the interests of the student becoming an independent person in the real world. Here, college preparation reading lists are appropriate for some students. But all students should learn more practical literacy skills, including how to write a résumé, how to skim for essential information on the Internet, and how to develop a lifelong interest in reading as a hobby.

Math and science instruction should also evolve as children move through each developmental ecosystem. In early childhood, math and science are an integral part of daily play activities as kids build with blocks, examine insects, and dangle from the jungle gym. In elementary school, kids are developmentally ready to learn the formal systems of mathematics and the use of science to answer questions about the world, from why the sky is blue to how a car works.

In middle school, math and science become vehicles for exploring the biology of life, the ultimate nature of the cosmos, the consequences of a nuclear war, and other emotionally laden and thought-provoking topics. Students need to work on high-interest, group-oriented math and science projects (for example, preserving a bird habitat or monitoring junk food habits) and communicate their findings to others through the Internet, science fairs, and other means.

At the high school level, students need to study for preparatory exams in math and science to help them apply for college or technical schools. They also need to learn the practical math and technical skills necessary for living independently (for example, financial planning and using computer software) and develop the science and math literacy necessary to vote intelligently on such issues as taxation, global warming, and the costs of war.

Schools need to approach curriculum in a way that is environmentally sensitive to the ecologies of different developmental stages of life.

A human development curriculum also extends beyond literacy, math, and science to other subjects, including the arts, physical education, social skills training, and imaginative, moral, and spiritual development. In far too many schools, these subjects have been crushed beneath the heavy weight of the concrete (benchmarks), asphalt (standardized tests), and steel (adequate yearly progress) that make up the bulk of the curriculum superhighway.

As educators, we need to rescue these important components of person-building from the rubble of the superhighway construction site and preserve the delicate ecologies that make up our students' stages of human growth and development. By dismantling the curriculum superhighway, we can ensure that our students will not stress out in traffic jams, keel over from road fatigue, or be maimed or killed in collisions along the way. By focusing on the whole child, we can prepare our students to meet the challenges of the real world in the years to come.

Note

1. See, for example, the 2004 publication of the California Alliance of PreK–18 Partnerships, *Raising Student Achievement Through Effective Education Partnerships: Policy and Practice* (available at www.ced.csulb.edu/California-alliance/documents/AllianceReport-printversion.pdf).

References

Armstrong, T. (2006). *The best schools: How human development research should inform educational practice.* Alexandria, VA: ASCD.

Association of Children's Museums. (2003, May 2). *Whether with public schools, childcare providers, or transit authorities, children's museums partner creatively with their communities* [Online news release]. Available: www.childrensmuseums.org/press_releases/5_2_03.htm

Born, L., Shea, A., & Steiner, M. (2002). The roots of depression in adolescent girls: Is menarche the key? *Current Psychiatry Reports, 4,* 449–460.

Curtis, D. (2001, Spring). We're here to raise kids. *Edutopia,* 8–9. Available: www.edutopia.org/EdutopiaPDF/Spring01.pdf

Elkind, D. (2001). Much too early. *Education Next, 1*(2), 9–15.

Gardner, H. (1994). *Reinventing our schools: A conversation with Howard Gardner.* [Videotape]. Bloomington, IN: AIT & Phi Delta Kappa.

Giedd, J. N., Vaituzis, A. C., Hamburger, S. D., Lange, N., Rajapakse, J. C., Kaysen, D., et al. (1996). Quantitative MRI of the temporal lobe, amygdala, and hippocampus in normal human development: Ages 4–18 years. *Journal of Comparative Neurology, 366*(2), 223–230.

National Institute of Mental Health. (2001). *Teenage brain: A work in progress* (NIH Publication No. 01-4929). Washington, DC: Department of Health and Human Services. Available: www.nimh.nih.gov/Publicat/teenbrain.cfm

Osborne, C. (2007, January 22). South Austin preschool doesn't make children learn their ABCs, *Austin American-Statesman.* Available: www.statesman.com/news/content/news/stories/local/01/22/22preschool.html

THOMAS ARMSTRONG (Thomas@thomasarmstrong.com; www.thomasarmstrong.com) is a speaker with more than 30 years of teaching experience from the primary through the doctoral level. He is the author of 13 books, including *The Best Schools: How Human Development Research Should Inform Educational Practice* (ASCD, 2006).

The Under-Appreciated Role of Humiliation in the Middle School

Nancy Frey and Douglas Fisher

In his book *The World Is Flat,* Friedman (2005) argued that we have under-appreciated the role that humiliation plays in terrorism. He notes that the reaction humans have when they are humiliated is significant and often severe. If it is true, that humiliation plays a role in terrorism, what role might this under-appreciated emotion play in middle school? If terrorists act, in part, based on humiliation, how do middle school students act when they experience this emotion?

To answer these questions, we interviewed 10 middle school teachers and 10 students. We asked them about times they (or their students or peers) were humiliated and what happened. In each case, they were surprised to be asked about this emotion. They said things like "It just happens; you gotta deal with it" and "You know how kids are, they can be mean." The responses from the teachers and students about the ways that students are humiliated clustered into three major areas: bullying, teacher behavior, and remedial reading. In addition, we searched the ERIC database for documentation about the impact humiliation has on middle school students. In this article, we will begin by discussing the findings from our interviews and surveys, then we will describe the effects of humiliation on middle school learners.

Types of Humiliation

The 10 teachers and 10 students we interviewed worked or attended one of three large urban middle schools in two southwestern states. These schools fit the profile of many schools across America—large (more than 1,000 students), located in major metropolitan communities, with diverse demographic profiles among students and teachers. None of the schools had a formal anti-bullying or character education program. We sought a representative sample of teachers based on experience, gender, and subject area. We chose students who represented different

grade levels, genders, and achievement levels. The names of students and teachers are pseudonyms. We conducted individual interviews with each teacher and each student to ensure privacy and promote candor in their disclosures. Based on an analysis of their responses, we identified three themes.

Bullying

Student voices. The most common topic raised in the conversation for both teachers and students was bullying. Many students believed that bullying was part of life, something that was unavoidable. It need not be. "Being bullied is neither a 'part of growing up' nor a 'rite of passage'" (Barone, 1997, p. 80). Every student participant recounted a time in which he or she had been bullied or had witnessed it occurring with other students. Marcus, a sixth grader, described an incident that occurred earlier that school year.

> There're these older guys [eighth grade] who think they're the kings of the school. They talk loud, swear, shove people in the halls. I see them comin' and I bounce [leave]. My first month at this school, they walked behind me, talkin' loud about how I was a little faggot. I tried to ignore them, but they knocked my stuff out of my hand.

Marcus's experience is perhaps the most common type associated with bullying. There was an age and size differential between perpetrators and victim, accompanied by verbal abuse associated with sexual orientation, and some physical contact (Nishina & Juvonen, 2005; Olweus, 1993). This is also consistent with Bjorklund and Pellegrini's (2000) dominance theory of increased bullying directed at those entering a new social group.

Martha, a seventh grader, described a more subtle kind of bullying.

There's this girl, and she used to be our friend [named several girls] . . . but she's just so weird. What happened to her? We were all friends since second grade, but when she came back to school [entering middle school] she still dressed and talked like such a baby. It's embarrassing to be around her. So, we stopped talking to her.

Martha described relational bullying, memorably chronicled in a number of studies (Bjoerkqvist, Lagerspetz, & Kaukianen, 1992; Crick, Bigbee, & Howe, 1996; Simmons, 2002). Although Martha did not describe herself as a bully, she exhibited prevalent forms of female aggression: relational bullying and avoidance (Crick, Bigbee, & Howe, 1996). The transition from elementary to middle school appears to play a role as well. Pelligrini and Bartini's (2000) study of bullying across fifth and sixth grade noted that the move to larger, more impersonal school environments often interfered with the maintenance of peer affiliations.

We also sought students' perspectives on the reasons bullying exists. Their comments suggest that they accept bullying as a given, a common part of middle school life. "Everyone gets made fun of," remarked seventh grade student Juan. "If you can't take it . . . if you let anyone see it bothers you, you just get it even worse." Martha echoed this sentiment. "It's how girls are. One day you're friends, and the next day you're not. Better not be caught lookin' at someone else's man. That'll get you quicker than anything." Beliefs about the normative presence of bullying, verbal taunts, and teasing are prevalent among adolescents, who view these as *de facto* elements of the secondary school experience (Shakeshaft et al., 1997).

We also asked students about their reactions to being humiliated by their peers. Most described deep levels of shame and responses that could be categorized as either violent or avoidant. Students told us they "snapped," "pounded his face in," "blew," or "got my bitch on" to describe verbal or physical retaliation. In other cases, students described attempts to avoid a situation. Similar to Marcus's attempts to "bounce" when bullies were spotted, Al, an eighth grader, reported that he did not use certain restrooms or hallways, because he anticipated that his tormentor would be there. Adriana, an eighth grade student, poignantly recounted the following incident.

When I was in seventh, I made up a boyfriend to my friends. It was stupid. . . . Everyone had a boyfriend and I wanted one, too. I told them I had a boyfriend at [nearby middle school]. When Cindy found out that it wasn't true, she told everybody. They laughed at me, left notes . . . told some of the boys. I told my mom I was sick, and I didn't go to school for two weeks.

Adriana's avoidance of the situation is a common response to the humiliation resulting from bullying. According to the American Psychological Association and the National Education Association, 7% of eighth graders stay home from school at least once a month to avoid a bullying situation (cited in Vail, 1999). Other middle school students, like Marcus and Al, alter their paths in school to avoid encountering bullies (Wessler, 2003).

Teacher voices. The 10 teachers who participated in this study were conflicted about the role of bullying in middle school. All 10 participants expressed concern over the amount of bullying in their schools (i.e., responding positively to the queries, "Bullying occurs frequently at this school," and "Bullying negatively impacts the learning of students at this school"). All were aware of the deleterious effects of bullying on both the victims and the perpetrators. Mr. Lee, a seventh and eighth grade mathematics instructor, noted, "We have to worry about the kid who's doing the bullying as well as the one who's getting it. Those kids that are bullies now end up in trouble in school and in life." In addition, 8 of the 10 instructors reported that they "always" responded to incidents of bullying. Mr. Harper, a music teacher, said, "I had it happen last week. I was outside my class [during passing period] and saw a group of bigger students descend on this smaller boy. You could just see this kid brace himself for what was going to happen. It was like slow motion. . . . I stepped in and made the kids leave him alone." Five other teachers offered anecdotal reports of their personal responses to bullying incidents, although, in all cases, it was related to the threat of physical harm perpetrated by either boys or girls.

Verbal abuse did not prompt such swift responses. "I won't put up with profanity, name-calling. If I hear it, I stop it. I write a referral if I have to," stated Ms. Indria, a sixth grade social studies teacher. However, when probed, all 10 teachers stated that they did not get involved in "personal relationships, friendship stuff." Ms. Indria offered, "Girls just seem to treat each other badly. It's a part of adolescence. . . . I certainly remember doing it when I was that age." Seventh grade science teacher Ms. Anthony echoed a similar response. "I can't keep up with it. One week they're friends; the next week they aren't. Way too much drama. I find that when I have tried to mediate, it ends by consuming too much instructional time." Four other teachers made statements consistent with the belief that negotiating a verbally, or even physically, abusive landscape was a part of growing up. Physical education teacher Ms. Hartford noted,

> You really have to be careful when you choose to interfere. It [teacher involvement] can really make it worse. The kids will just pick more—"teacher's pet." If it looks like the kid is holding his own, I don't get directly involved. I keep an eye on it.

It is also likely that Ms. Hartford and the other teachers interviewed were not cognizant of their relationships with the aggressors. Elias and Zins (2003) found that bullies often hold high social capital with their teachers and are perceived positively, while victims are often perceived as less likable.

Statements like the one offered by the physical education and science teachers illuminate a commonly held belief among middle school educators—that the ability to "take it" is a necessary rite of adolescent passage. Computer instructor Ms. Andersen evoked her own junior high memories to defend this position.

> Face it, being able to dish it out and take it gets you ready for the real world. What's that old commercial? "Never let 'em see you sweat." Teenagers have to learn that you don't wear your emotions on your sleeve. People'll use it against you. I know, I went through it, but I survived. You have to toughen up.

When asked about the role of humiliation in bullying, she replied,

> Yeah, they're good at humiliating each other. I keep an ear on what's going on. But I have to say . . . a lot of times they use it to keep each other in line. In a funny way, they regulate each other's behavior.

Ms. Anderson's beliefs are not entirely misplaced. Tapper and Bolton (2005) used wireless recording equipment to analyze bullying interactions among 77 students. They found that direct aggression (without physical violence) often inspired peer support for the aggressor. The reaction of the victim is a factor in whether the bullying will continue. Perry, Williard, and Perry (1990) determined that displays of distress by the victim increased the likelihood that bullying would occur again. "Never let 'em see you sweat" appears to be accurate.

Teacher Behavior

Student voices. Students had strong feelings about the use of humiliation by teachers. Nine of the 10 student participants could recount times when a teacher had used sarcasm or humiliation to embarrass a student in front of the class. In some cases it was directed at them, while in others they had witnessed it in their classes.

> We had this one teacher in seventh grade; man, she was rough. She had a nickname for every kid in the class. Like, she called this one girl "Funeral," because she said she always looked like she was coming from one.

This story, told by Al, is admittedly an extreme example and not typical of the incidences that were shared by students. However, three students told of times when teachers had "busted someone" in front of the entire class for failing a quiz or test, using insulting language. "I don't know why they do it," said Gail, a sixth grader. "It's not like it makes a difference. Who wants to work harder for someone who embarrasses you that way?"

Other students admitted that the use of humiliation might have a positive effect, at least in the short term.

> My [seventh grade] math teacher reads everyone's quiz grades to the whole class. I failed one, and he said, "Spending too much time looking at girls?" It made me kinda mad . . . but I made sure I didn't fail another math quiz. (Juan, eighth grade)

Veronica, an eighth grade student, said,

> Ms. _____ likes to catch you doing something wrong. Like, we were reading our social studies book out loud and I missed my turn. She goes, "Wake up, Veronica! We're all waiting," in this really stupid way she has [imitates a sarcastic tone]. Everyone laughed as though it never happened to them. I don't let her catch me.

Veronica then used profanity to describe her teacher, evidence of the anger she felt toward this adult and perhaps school in general.

When asked what they thought these teachers hoped to gain with the use of humiliation, their insights were surprising. "They want to be cool, like it's funny," remarked sixth grade student Marcus. Seventh grader Harlan responded similarly. "They don't treat you like little kids. My dad talks the same way. Making fun of kids in the class is just what they do."

The use of sarcasm and humiliation by teachers has been less well documented in the literature than the prevalence and effects of bullying. It is certainly long understood in the teaching profession, as evidenced by Briggs's (1928) article on the prevalence of the use of sarcasm by young secondary teachers. Martin's (1987) study of secondary students' perspectives on this phenomenon was derived from surveys of more than 20,000 Canadian students. Students reported that the use of sarcasm resulted in dislike for the teacher and even anger toward the teacher. Martin also reported that some students described "anticipatory embarrassment," the dread associated with the belief that the teacher would humiliate them again. In addition, this created learning problems, including decreased motivation to study and complete homework, increased cutting of classes, and thoughts of dropping out. Turner and associates (2002) studied the classroom learning environments of 65 sixth grade mathematics classrooms to study factors that promoted or reduced help-seeking behaviors and found that the teacher's classroom discourse, including use of sarcasm, influenced the likelihood that students would seek academic help when needed. Classrooms featuring more negative teacher talk, including sarcasm, were associated with high levels of avoidance in asking for assistance.

Teacher voices. Six of the 10 teachers in the study named colleagues who regularly used sarcasm and humiliation with students. Ms. Robertson, a seventh grade language arts teacher, described a colleague as "us[ing] words like a knife. He just cuts kids down to size." Mr. Lee, the math teacher, described an experience when he was a student teacher.

> [The master teacher] was just vicious with students. Everything was a big joke, but kind of mean-spirited, you know? He'd single out kids because of a quirk, like they talked funny, or they had a big nose, or they wore clothes that were kind of different. Kids would laugh, but I saw the cringes, too.

Five of the participating teachers discussed the fine line between humor and sarcasm. Ms. Andersen offered,

> You have to take into account that they're really very fragile, in spite of all their bluster. We all remember what it was like. Worried all the time about sticking out. They're already sensitive to the need for conformity. As teachers, we have to make sure that we don't make them feel different.

Ms. Hartford noted, "It's great to keep it light and fun, but not at someone else's expense." Sarcasm is typically used for three purposes: to soften a criticism, especially through feigned politeness; to mitigate verbal aggressiveness; or to create humor (Dews & Winner, 1995). However, the use of sarcasm in social discourse assumes an equal relationship between parties. This is never the case in the classroom, where the teacher holds the power in the relationship. Therefore, the student cannot respond with a sarcastic reply without consequences. The use of sarcasm with middle school students is ineffective as well, as evidenced by a study of 13-year-olds by the Harvard Zero Project. They found that 71% of the students studied

misinterpreted sarcasm as deception. In other words, the majority had not yet reached a linguistically sophisticated developmental level that would allow them to accurately discern the speaker's purpose, even when it was accompanied by a gestural cue (Demorest, Meyer, Phelps, Gardner, & Winner, 1984).

Remedial Reading and Mathematics

Bullying and sarcasm are age-old tools of humiliation, but a more recent (and inadvertent) tool is that of the remedial class created for students who fail to achieve in reading and mathematics. Commonly referred to as "double dosing," it is the practice of increasing the number of instructional hours spent in remediation, at the expense of electives or core classes such as science and social studies (Cavanaugh, 2006). Though well-intended, our student participants were vocal about the negative effects on the lives of adolescents.

Student voices. "Everyone knows who the dumb kids are," explained Martha, a seventh grade student. "All you have to do is look around at who's not on the wheel [elective class rotation]. They're all in reading mastery." At Martha's school, students who score below a cut point on the state language arts and mathematics examinations are automatically enrolled in another section of instruction. Jessika, an eighth grader, is one of those students. "I hate it. We're all the stupid kids. Everyone knows it." Carol, another eighth grade student, described her classmates this way:

> Nobody even tries in my [remedial] reading class. It's like, if you do, you're trying to make yourself look better than you really are. No offense, but it's "acting white." People just sleep in class. You know, pull their [sweatshirt] hood up. If you look like you're trying, you'll catch it from [classmates.]

Marcus and Al are also enrolled in similar classes for mathematics. When asked what others said to them and about them in regard to their participation in these courses, we heard, "retard," "SPED" [special education], "loser," "tard," "spaz," and "window licker." These labels are quite troubling for students with disabilities, because they suggest an accepted intolerance for students in need of academic supports.

Slavin's (1993) review of the literature on remedial classes in middle school found a zero effect size for academic gains. While it is too soon to gauge the long-term effectiveness of double-dosing academic achievement, the voices of middle school students provide a bellwether for assessing the social and emotional repercussions of such practices. In a few short years, these students will have reached an age at which they can voluntarily exit school. There is further evidence that low-achieving students are more likely to use so-called "self-handicapping strategies" such as giving up and refusing to study (Midgely & Urdan, 1995; Turner et al., 2002). In particular, they are more likely to associate with other negative-thinking students. The remediation classroom, it would seem, from Carol's and Jessika's comments, is a perfect environment for breeding this sort of attitude toward school and learning.

Teachers' voices. We were particularly interested in the views of Mr. Lee and Ms. Robertson, both of whom teach a section of remedial math or reading. "No one wants those classes," remarked Mr. Lee. "I got it because I'm new here. They stick the new teachers with these classes. Wouldn't you think that they should be taught by people with lots of experience?" he asked. Mrs. Robertson described her classroom learning environment. "I'm ashamed to say that I dread fourth [period] because of the students. I feel like all the energy gets sucked out of the room, and me. I can't seem to inspire them, and it affects the way I teach." When asked to elaborate, she said, "I know I'm stricter, and I feel like I can't even smile or make a joke. I'm grim, and it makes for a grim period."

Two other teachers explained that, while they saw the logic in double dosing, they worried about the detrimental effects on their students. Mr. Espinosa, a seventh grade social studies teacher, said,

We're organized in houses here [a cohort model]. But every time we excuse students to go to another class, one that's different from everyone else, it chops away at the concept of a family of students and teachers. I can see the light go right out of their eyes when they have to pass up computer class to go for extra reading or math class.

Ms. Andersen, the computer teacher, expressed concern about the content students were missing. "If I'm not teaching literacy and math, then what am I doing? They'll just get further behind."

The Effects of Humiliation

In addition to the ways in which middle school students experience humiliation, we discussed the impact that humiliation has on young adolescents. Both students and teachers identified a number of outcomes from humiliation, including drug and alcohol use, attendance problems, dropping out of school, pregnancy, and suicide. Let us examine the perspectives of teachers and students on each of these issues.

Drug and Alcohol Use

Most educators recognize that experimentation with alcohol and drugs during adolescence is common. The Youth Risk Behavior Survey (www.cdc.gov/Healthy Youth/yrbs/index.htm) indicated that more than two-thirds of middle school students report ever having had a drink of alcohol and that 26% report ever having used marijuana. However, several students commented on the regular use of drugs and alcohol by students who feel humiliated at school. In the words of Marcus, "I know a kid who drinks every night. He hates school and says they make him feel stupid." One of the teachers noted that the rate of drug and alcohol use was highest for students who were enrolled in remedial reading classes. Mooney (Mooney & Cole, 2000), a student with a disability who subsequently graduated from an Ivy League college, discussed his use of drugs and alcohol to "turn off the shockers" at school.

Attendance Problems

Another outcome of humiliation that both students and teachers discussed was poor school attendance. Mr. Harper, the music teacher, put it eloquently—"They vote with their feet"—meaning that students tell us, by their physical presence in school, whether or not it is a comfortable place to be. Again, most educators acknowledge that there are patterns of problematic attendance, such as is typically seen in urban schools. More important, for our purpose here, is the difference of attendance patterns within the school. It is clear from an analysis of attendance patterns—both tardiness and absence—that students are communicating with which teachers they feel comfortable and with which they do not. While there are many reasons for students feeling comfortable with teachers, one reason is the climate that is created in class. Veronica reported, "Lots of us cut class with Mr._____ because he makes you feel bad when you try to answer."

Dropping Out

While calculating an accurate drop-out rate has been exceedingly difficult to do, it is important to note that in many states there is no mechanism for capturing middle school drop-outs. It seems that when the data systems were created, people assumed that middle school students either would not or could not drop out of school. Unfortunately, that is not the reality; middle school students are dropping out. In-grade retention (an indicator of either poor academic performance or poor attendance) is the single strongest school-related predictor of dropping out in middle school (Rumberger, 1995). As Ms. Indria reported, "There are students who just leave us. They don't find school fulfilling and are ashamed of their performance, and they stop coming. No one really knows where they go." Turner and associates' (2002) study on the relationship between classroom climate and help-seeking offers further evidence of the role of humiliation. There is also evidence that the overall school climate—the degree that students feel safe to learn and are not threatened by peers or teachers—is directly related to the drop-out problem (Wehlage, 1991). As Al indicated, "If I had to deal with the crap that Jeremy does, I'd just quit. I wouldn't come to this place."

School institutions related to humiliation play a factor as well. According to Goldschmidt and Wang (1999), "Two school policy and practice variables affect the middle school dropout rate significantly: the percentage of students held back one grade, and the percentage of students misbehaving" (p. 728). Here we see the snowballing effects of humiliation. Students retained in grade, attending remedial classes, surrounded by misbehavior (including bullying), with lower rates of attendance and less inclination to seek help from sarcastic teachers appear to be at great risk for dropping out, and humiliation plays a role in each.

Pregnancy

Another issue associated with humiliation, identified primarily by the teachers we interviewed, was teenage pregnancy. While less common at the middle school level than at the secondary level, teen pregnancy is still an issue with this age group. According to the Centers for Disease Control and Prevention, national data suggests that between six and seven of every 1,000 middle school girls become pregnant (Klien, 2005). While there are a number of theories about the causes of teenage pregnancy, including too much free time, poverty, access to alcohol, and physical maturity, Ms. Hartford had another take on the situation. She said, "In this community, pregnancy is one of the acceptable reasons to leave school. If school is a toxic environment for you, you can get pregnant and leave school. Nobody will question your decision."

Suicide

A final outcome of humiliation identified by the participants was suicide and suicidal thoughts. Public health officials have noted a significant increase in youth suicide—more than 300% since 1950 (Bloch, 1999). Suicide is now the third leading cause of death for youth ages 10 to 19 (following accidents and homicides) (Centers for Disease Control and Prevention, 2000). While the suicide rate for high school students has remained fairly stable over the past decade, the suicide rate for middle school students (ages 10 through 14), increased more than 100%

during the decade of the 1990s (Bloch, 1999). A haunting thought was shared by Adriana, who said, "Everybody I know has thought about suicide, but the one who did it was bothered all the time by other kids and no one did anything." As Fisher (2005) noted, teachers have to understand the signs and symptoms of suicide and ensure that students feel honored and respected at school. One of the teachers suggested, "I think that they're under a great deal of pressure to perform. If you add humiliation to that, they don't see a way out and might consider taking their own life."

Recommendations for Reducing Humiliation in Middle School

Some of the problems members of our profession discuss about the challenges to achievement in middle school might be explained by students' experiences with humiliation. When students experience humiliation, as these data suggest they do, a series of negative outcomes can be triggered. We recommend that educators make a commitment to reduce the needless opportunities for humiliation that creep into the daily experiences of their students.

Recommendation #1: Assess the School Climate

The first step to reducing humiliation is to recognize that it might, in fact, be present. Schools routinely administer annual school climate surveys, and this can provide an excellent starting point for analysis. For example, the California Healthy Kids Survey contains questions that can shed light on the issue of humiliation. The survey asks respondents to assess the extent to which adults "treat all students fairly" and "listen to what students have to say" and contains several queries about bullying and bully prevention programs (California Department of Education, 2005).

Recommendation #2: Observe and Analyze Curricular and Instructional Interactions

The middle school reform report entitled *Breaking Ranks in the Middle* (National Association of Secondary School Principals, 2006) strongly recommends heterogeneous grouping of students in small learning communities to improve achievement and personalize learning. This requires schools to abandon outdated ability grouping and tracking, which result in lowered expectations and missed opportunities for rigorous curriculum. Some schools cling to tracking and remedial classes because they do not possess the capacity to differentiate instruction for all learners. Building this capacity is not a matter of scattershot inservices, but rather targeted peer coaching, professional development, and administrative accountability. A first step toward realizing this goal is to conduct classroom observations for the purposes of data collection and analysis of needs. The Instructional Practices Inventory developed by the Middle Level Leadership Center is a useful tool for developing a school-wide profile of the instructional practices occurring at the school, including the amount of teacher-led instruction, student-led discussions, and levels of disengagement (www.mllc.org).[1] Classrooms with high levels of student disengagement should be targeted for further analysis to determine contributing factors, especially teacher behaviors and interaction styles. Teachers struggling with disengagement can participate in the Teacher Expectations and Student Achievement (TESA) professional development program developed by the Los Angeles County Office of Education (www.lacoe.edu/orgs/165/index.cfm). This is a five-month experience that involves peer observations and coaching focused on 15 specific instructional behaviors that increase positive student perceptions about learning. Other teachers who are having difficulty with curriculum design for heterogeneously grouped students can benefit from focused professional development and planning on differentiating instruction at the unit level. A beginning step may include the formation of book study groups using materials such as *Differentiation in Practice for Grades 5–9* (Tomlinson & Eidson, 2003). By collecting and sharing data to develop targeted professional development, teachers are able to move beyond "I've heard/read this before" to take specific action. This is further reinforced through administrative accountability and ongoing data collection to measure improvement at the curricular and instructional levels.

Recommendation #3: Make an Anti-bullying Curriculum Part of the School Culture

Much has been written in the past decade about anti-bullying curricula, especially in the wake of high-profile school shootings throughout the nation. Many fine programs exist, and the Olweus Bullying Prevention Program is among the most respected (www.clemson.edu/olweus/content.html). The multi-layered design of this program targets school-wide, classroom, and individual interventions for both bullies and victims. However, anti-bullying curricula are only effective if there is long-term commitment. Perhaps the most common mistake is that after a period of enthusiastic introduction and implementation, programs such as these fall to the

wayside as other initiatives command attention. A multi-year plan that includes refreshers for existing staff as well as training for teachers new to the school is essential for sustainability. The anti-bullying program should be written into the school's accountability plan, the new teacher induction program, and as part of the curriculum for each grade level.

Conclusion

The recommendations made are all costly in terms of time, money, and resources. However, the unintended costs of humiliation are much higher for our students. It is time to take another look at the anti-bullying curricula being developed by groups across the country and how they can be sustained for more than one school year. It might also be time to notice our own behaviors and to have hard conversations with our colleagues about appropriate interactions with students—interactions that clearly demonstrate care, honesty, and high expectations. And finally, it may be time to reconsider the ways in which we group students and provide supplemental instructional interventions such that groups of students do not experience school as telling them they are stupid, incompetent, and not worthy. In doing so, we might just see increases in student achievement as well as youth who are more engaged in their educational experience.

Note

1. For a comprehensive assessment of middle school programs, procedures, and processes, readers might want to consider using the School Improvement Toolkit, available from National Middle School Association at www.nmsa.org/ ProfessionalDevelopment/ SchoolImprovementToolkit/ tabid/654/Default.aspx

References

Barone, F. J. (1997). Bullying in school. *Phi Delta Kappan, 79,* 80–82.

Bjoerkqvist, K., Lagerspetz, K. M. J., & Kaukianen, A. (1992). Do girls manipulate and boys fight? Developmental trends in regard to direct and indirect aggression. *Aggressive Behavior, 18,* 117–127.

Bjorklund, D. F., & Pellegrini, A. D. (2000). Child development and evolutionary psychology. *Child Development, 71,* 1687–1708.

Bloch, D. (1999). Adolescent suicide as a public health threat. *Journal of Child and Adolescent Psychiatric Nursing, 12,* 26–38.

Briggs, T. H. (1928). Sarcasm. *The School Review, 36*(9), 685–695.

California Department of Education. (2005). *California healthy kids school climate survey.* Retrieved February 18, 2007, from http:// www.wested.org/chks/pdf/scs_05_alpha.pdf

Cavanaugh, S. (2006, June 14). Students double-dosing on reading and math: Schools aim to improve state test scores—and satisfy federal education laws. *Education Week.* Retrieved September 3, 2006, from http://www.all4ed.org/press/ EdWeek_061406_ StudentsDoubleDosingReadingMath.pdf

Centers for Disease Control and Prevention. (2000). *Youth risk behavior surveillance—United States, 1999.* In CDC surveillance summaries, June 9, 2000, MMRW. Atlanta, GA: Author.

Crick, N. R., Bigbee, M. A., & Howe, C. (1996). How do I hurt thee? Let me count the ways. *Child Development, 67,* 1003–1014.

Demorest, A., Meyer, C., Phelps, E., Gardner, H., & Winner, E. (1984). Words speak louder than actions: Understanding deliberately false remarks. *Child Development, 55,* 1527–1534.

Dews, S., & Winner, E. (1995). Muting the meaning: A social function of irony. *Metaphor and Symbolic Activity, 10,* 3–18.

Elias, M. J., & Zins, J. E. (2003). Bullying, other forms of peer harassment, and victimization in the schools: Issues for school psychology research and practice. In M. J. Elias & J. E. Zins (Eds.), *Bullying, peer harassment, and victimization in the schools: The next generation of prevention* (pp. 1–5). Binghamton, NY: Haworth.

Fisher, D. (2005). The literacy educator's role in suicide prevention. *Journal of Adolescent and Adult Literacy, 48,* 364–373.

Friedman, T. L. (2005). *The world is flat: A brief history of the twenty-first century.* New York: Farrar, Straus and Giroux.

Goldschmidt, P., & Wang, J. (1999). When can schools affect dropout behavior? A longitudinal multilevel analysis. *American Education Research Journal, 36,* 715–738.

Klein, J. D. (2005). Adolescent pregnancy: Current trends and issues. *Pediatrics, 116,* 281–286.

Martin, W. B. W. (1987). Students' perceptions of causes and consequences of embarrassment in the school. *Canadian Journal of Education, 12,* 277–293.

Midgely, C., & Urdan, T. (1995). Predictors of middle school students' use of self-handicapping strategies. *The Journal of Early Adolescence, 15,* 389–411.

Mooney, J., & Cole, D. (2000). *Learning outside the lines: Two Ivy League students with learning disabilities and ADHD give you the tools for academic success and educational revolution.* New York: Simon & Schuster.

National Association of Secondary School Principals. (2006). *Breaking ranks in the middle: Strategies for leading middle level reform.* Reston, VA: Author.

Nishina, A., & Juvonen, J. (2005). Daily reports of witnessing and experiencing peer harassment in middle school. *Child Development, 76,* 435–450.

Olweus, D. (1993). *Bullying at school: What we know and what we can do.* Oxford, UK: Blackwell.

Pellgrini, A. D., & Bartini, M. (2000). A longitudinal study of bullying, victimization, and peer affiliation during the transition from primary school to middle school. *American Educational Research Journal, 37,* 699–725.

Perry, D. G., Williard, J. C., & Perry, L. C. (1990). Peers' perceptions of the consequences that victimized children provide aggressors. *Child Development, 61,* 1310–1325.

Rumberger, R. W. (1995). Dropping out of middle school: A multilevel analysis of students and schools. *American Educational Research Journal, 32,* 583–625.

Shakeshaft, C., Mandel, L., Johnson, Y. M., Sawyer, J., Hergenrother, M. A., & Barber, E. (1997). Boys call me cow. *Educational Leadership, 55*(2), 22–25.

Simmons, R. (2002). Odd girl out: *The hidden culture of aggression in girls.* New York: Harcourt.

Slavin, R. E. (1993). Ability grouping in the middle grades: Achievement effects and alternatives. *The Elementary School Journal, 93,* 535–552.

Tapper, K., & Boulton, M. J. (2005). Victim and peer group responses to different forms of aggression among primary school children. *Aggressive Behavior, 31,* 238–253.

Tomlinson, C. A., & Eidson, C. C. (2003). *Differentiation in practice: A resource guide for differentiating curriculum grades 5–9.* Alexandria, VA: Association for Supervision and Curriculum Development.

Turner, J. C., Midgley, C., Meyer, D. K., Gheen, M., Anderman, E. M., Kang, Y., & Patrick, H. (2002). The classroom environment and students' reports of avoidance strategies in Mathematics: A multimethod study. *Journal of Educational Psychology, 94,* 88–106.

Vail, K., (1999). Words that wound. *American School Board Journal,* 186(9), 37–40.

Wehlage, G. (1991). School reform for at-risk students. *Equity and Excellence, 25,* 15–24.

Wessler, S. L. (2003). It's hard to learn when you're scared. *Educational Leadership, 61*(1), 40–43.

Vail, K., (1999). Words that wound. *American School Board Journal,* 186(9), 37–40.

Wehlage, G. (1991). School reform for at-risk students. *Equity and Excellence, 25,* 15–24.

Wessler, S. L. (2003). It's hard to learn when you're scared. *Educational Leadership, 61*(1), 40–43.

NANCY FREY is an associate professor of teacher education at San Diego State University, California.

DOUGLAS FISHER is a professor of teacher education at San Diego State University, California. Email: dfisher@mail.sdsu.edu

Risk Taking in Adolescence
New Perspectives from Brain and Behavioral Science

Trying to understand why adolescents and young adults take more risks than younger or older individuals do has challenged psychologists for decades. Adolescents' inclination to engage in risky behavior does not appear to be due to irrationality, delusions of invulnerability, or ignorance. This paper presents a perspective on adolescent risk taking grounded in developmental neuroscience. According to this view, the temporal gap between puberty, which impels adolescents toward thrill seeking, and the slow maturation of the cognitive-control system, which regulates these impulses, makes adolescence a time of heightened vulnerability for risky behavior. This view of adolescent risk taking helps to explain why educational interventions designed to change adolescents' knowledge, beliefs, or attitudes have been largely ineffective, and suggests that changing the contexts in which risky behavior occurs may be more successful than changing the way adolescents think about risk.

LAURENCE STEINBERG

A dolescents and college-age individuals take more risks than children or adults do, as indicated by statistics on automobile crashes, binge drinking, contraceptive use, and crime; but trying to understand why risk taking is more common during adolescence than during other periods of development has challenged psychologists for decades (Steinberg, 2004). Numerous theories to account for adolescents' greater involvement in risky behavior have been advanced, but few have withstood empirical scrutiny (but see Reyna & Farley, 2006, for a discussion of some promising approaches).

False Leads in Risk-Taking Research

Systematic research does not support the stereotype of adolescents as irrational individuals who believe they are invulnerable and who are unaware, inattentive to, or unconcerned about the potential harms of risky behavior. In fact, the logical-reasoning abilities of 15-year-olds are comparable to those of adults, adolescents are no worse than adults at perceiving risk or estimating their vulnerability to it (Reyna & Farley, 2006), and increasing the salience of the risks associated with making a potentially dangerous decision has comparable effects on adolescents and adults (Millstein & Halpern-Felsher, 2002). Most studies find few age differences in individuals' evaluations of the risks inherent in a wide range of dangerous behaviors, in judgments about the seriousness of the consequences that might result from risky behavior, or in the ways

that the relative costs and benefits of risky activities are evaluated (Beyth-Marom, Austin, Fischoff, Palmgren, & Jacobs-Quadrel, 1993).

Because adolescents and adults reason about risk in similar ways, many researchers have posited that age differences in actual risk taking are due to differences in the information that adolescents and adults use when making decisions. Attempts to reduce adolescent risk taking through interventions designed to alter knowledge, attitudes, or beliefs have proven remarkably disappointing, however (Steinberg, 2004). Efforts to provide adolescents with information about the risks of substance use, reckless driving, and unprotected sex typically result in improvements in young people's thinking about these phenomena but seldom change their actual behavior. Generally speaking, reductions in adolescents' health-compromising behavior are more strongly linked to changes in the contexts in which those risks are taken (e.g., increases in the price of cigarettes, enforcement of graduated licensing programs, more vigorously implemented policies to interdict drugs, or condom distribution programs) than to changes in what adolescents know or believe.

The failure to account for age differences in risk taking through studies of reasoning and knowledge stymied researchers for some time. Health educators, however, have been undaunted, and they have continued to design and offer interventions of unproven effectiveness, such as Drug Abuse Resistance Education (DARE), driver's education, or abstinence-only sex education.

A New Perspective on Risk Taking

In recent years, owing to advances in the developmental neuroscience of adolescence and the recognition that the conventional decision-making framework may not be the best way to think about adolescent risk taking, a new perspective on the subject has emerged (Steinberg, 2004). This new view begins from the premise that risk taking in the real world is the product of both logical reasoning and psychosocial factors. However, unlike logical-reasoning abilities, which appear to be more or less fully developed by age 15, psychosocial capacities that improve decision making and moderate risk taking—such as impulse control, emotion regulation, delay of gratification, and resistance to peer influence—continue to mature well into young adulthood (Steinberg, 2004; see Figure 1). Accordingly, psychosocial immaturity in these respects during adolescence may undermine what otherwise might be competent decision making. The conclusion drawn by many researchers, that adolescents are as competent decision makers as adults are, may hold true only under conditions where the influence of psychosocial factors is minimized.

Evidence from Developmental Neuroscience

Advances in developmental neuroscience provide support for this new way of thinking about adolescent decision making. It appears that heightened risk taking in adolescence is the product of the interaction between two brain networks. The first is a socioemotional network that is especially sensitive to social and emotional stimuli, that is particularly important for reward processing, and that is remodeled in early adolescence by the hormonal changes of puberty. It is localized in limbic and

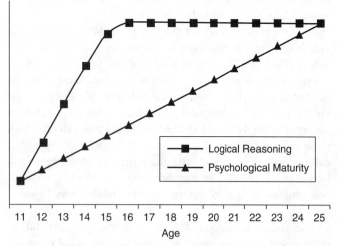

Figure 1   Hypothetical graph of development of logical reasoning abilities versus psychosocial maturation. Although logical reasoning abilities reach adult levels by age 16, psychosocial capacities, such as impulse control, future orientation, or resistance to peer influence, continue to develop into young adulthood.

paralimbic areas of the brain, an interior region that includes the amygdala, ventral striatum, orbitofrontal cortex, medial prefrontal cortex, and superior temporal sulcus. The second network is a cognitive-control network that subserves executive functions such as planning, thinking ahead, and self-regulation, and that matures gradually over the course of adolescence and young adulthood largely independently of puberty (Steinberg, 2004). The cognitive-control network mainly consists of outer regions of the brain, including the lateral prefrontal and parietal cortices and those parts of the anterior cingulate cortex to which they are connected.

In many respects, risk taking is the product of a competition between the socioemotional and cognitive-control networks (Drevets & Raichle, 1998), and adolescence is a period in which the former abruptly becomes more assertive (i.e., at puberty) while the latter gains strength only gradually, over a longer period of time. The socioemotional network is not in a state of constantly high activation during adolescence, though. Indeed, when the socioemotional network is not highly activated (for example, when individuals are not emotionally excited or are alone), the cognitive-control network is strong enough to impose regulatory control over impulsive and risky behavior, even in early adolescence. In the presence of peers or under conditions of emotional arousal, however, the socioemotional network becomes sufficiently activated to diminish the regulatory effectiveness of the cognitive-control network. Over the course of adolescence, the cognitive-control network matures, so that by adulthood, even under conditions of heightened arousal in the socioemotional network, inclinations toward risk taking can be modulated.

It is important to note that mechanisms underlying the processing of emotional information, social information, and reward are closely interconnected. Among adolescents, the regions that are activated during exposure to social and emotional stimuli overlap considerably with regions also shown to be sensitive to variations in reward magnitude (cf. Galvan, et al., 2005; Nelson, Leibenluft, McClure, & Pine, 2005). This finding may be relevant to understanding why so much adolescent risk taking—like drinking, reckless driving, or delinquency—occurs in groups (Steinberg, 2004). Risk taking may be heightened in adolescence because teenagers spend so much time with their peers, and the mere presence of peers makes the rewarding aspects of risky situations more salient by activating the same circuitry that is activated by exposure to nonsocial rewards when individuals are alone.

The competitive interaction between the socioemotional and cognitive-control networks has been implicated in a wide range of decision-making contexts, including drug use, social-decision processing, moral judgments, and the valuation of alternative rewards/costs (e.g., Chambers, Taylor, & Potenza, 2003). In all of these contexts, risk taking is associated with relatively greater activation of the socioemotional network. For example, individuals' preference for smaller immediate rewards over larger delayed rewards is associated with relatively increased activation of the ventral striatum, orbitofrontal cortex, and medial prefrontal cortex—all regions linked to the socioemotional network—presumably because immediate rewards are especially emotionally arousing (consider the difference between how you might feel if a crisp $100 bill were held in front of you versus being told that you will receive $150 in 2 months). In contrast, regions implicated in cognitive control are engaged equivalently across decision conditions (McClure, Laibson, Loewenstein, & Cohen, 2004). Similarly, studies show that increased activity in regions of the socioemotional network is associated with the selection of comparatively risky (but potentially highly rewarding) choices over more conservative ones (Ernst et al., 2005).

Evidence from Behavioral Science

Three lines of behavioral evidence are consistent with this account. First, studies of susceptibility to antisocial peer influence show that vulnerability to peer pressure increases between preadolescence and mid-adolescence, peaks in mid-adolescence—presumably when the imbalance between the sensitivity to socioemotional arousal (which has increased at puberty) and capacity for cognitive control (which is still immature) is greatest—and gradually declines thereafter (Steinberg, 2004). Second, as noted earlier, studies of decision making generally show no age differences in risk processing between older adolescents and adults when decision making is assessed under conditions likely associated with relatively lower activation of brain systems responsible for emotion, reward, and social processing (e.g., the presentation of hypothetical decision-making dilemmas to individuals tested alone under conditions of low emotional arousal; Millstein, & Halpern-Felsher, 2002). Third, the presence of peers increases risk taking substantially among teenagers, moderately among college-age individuals, and not at all among adults, consistent with the notion that the development of the cognitive-control network is gradual and extends beyond the teen years. In one of our lab's studies, for instance, the presence of peers more than doubled the number of risks teenagers took in a video driving game and increased risk taking by 50% among college undergraduates but had no effect at all among adults (Gardner & Steinberg, 2005; see Figure 2). In adolescence, then, not only is more merrier—it is also riskier.

What Changes during Adolescence?

Studies of rodents indicate an especially significant increase in reward salience (i.e., how much attention individuals pay to the magnitude of potential rewards) around the time of puberty (Spear, 2000), consistent with human studies showing that increases in sensation seeking occur relatively early in adolescence and are correlated with pubertal maturation but not chronological age (Steinberg, 2004). Given behavioral findings indicating relatively greater reward salience among adolescents than adults in decision-making tasks, there is reason to

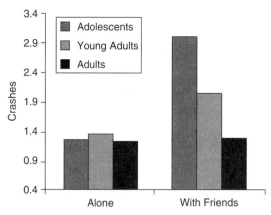

Figure 2 Risk taking of adolescents, young adults, and adults during a video driving game, when playing alone and when playing with friends. Adapted from Gardner & Steinberg (2004).

speculate that, when presented with risky situations that have both potential rewards and potential costs, adolescents may be more sensitive than adults to variation in rewards but comparably sensitive (or perhaps even less sensitive) to variation in costs (Ernst et al., 2005).

It thus appears that the brain system that regulates the processing of rewards, social information, and emotions is becoming more sensitive and more easily aroused around the time of puberty. What about its sibling, the cognitive-control system? Regions making up the cognitive-control network, especially prefrontal regions, continue to exhibit gradual changes in structure and function during adolescence and early adulthood (Casey, Tottenham, Liston, & Durston, 2005). Much publicity has been given to the finding that synaptic pruning (the selective elimination of seldom-used synapses) and myelination (the development of the fatty sheaths that "insulate" neuronal circuitry)—both of which increase the efficiency of information processing—continue to occur in the prefrontal cortex well into the early 20s. But frontal regions also become more integrated with other brain regions during adolescence and early adulthood, leading to gradual improvements in many aspects of cognitive control such as response inhibition; this integration may be an even more important change than changes within the frontal region itself. Imaging studies using tasks in which individuals are asked to inhibit a "prepotent" response—like trying to look away from, rather than toward, a point of light—have shown that adolescents tend to recruit the cognitive-control network less broadly than do adults, perhaps overtaxing the capacity of the more limited number of regions they activate (Luna et al., 2001).

In essence, one of the reasons the cognitive-control system of adults is more effective than that of adolescents is that adults' brains distribute its regulatory responsibilities across a wider network of linked components. This lack of cross-talk across brain regions in adolescence results not only in individuals acting on gut feelings without fully thinking (the stereotypic portrayal of teenagers) but also in thinking too much when gut feelings ought to be attended to (which teenagers also do from time to time). In one recent study, when asked whether some obviously dangerous activities (e.g., setting one's hair on fire) were "good ideas," adolescents took significantly longer than adults to respond to the questions and activated a less narrowly distributed set of cognitive-control regions (Baird, Fugelsang, & Bennett, 2005). This was not the case when the queried activities were not dangerous ones, however (e.g., eating salad).

The fact that maturation of the socioemotional network appears to be driven by puberty, whereas the maturation of the cognitive-control network does not, raises interesting questions about the impact—at the individual and at the societal levels—of early pubertal maturation on risk-taking. We know that there is wide variability among individuals in the timing of puberty, due to both genetic and environmental factors. We also know that there has been a significant drop in the age of pubertal maturation over the past 200 years. To the extent that the temporal disjunction between the maturation of the socioemotional system and that of the cognitive-control system contributes to adolescent risk taking, we would expect to see higher rates of risk taking among early maturers and a drop over time in the age of initial experimentation with risky behaviors such as sexual intercourse or drug use. There is evidence for both of these patterns (Collins & Steinberg, 2006; Johnson & Gerstein, 1998).

Implications for Prevention

What does this mean for the prevention of unhealthy risk taking in adolescence? Given extant research suggesting that it is not the way adolescents think or what they don't know or understand that is the problem, a more profitable strategy than attempting to change how adolescents view risky activities might be to focus on limiting opportunities for immature judgment to have harmful consequences. More than 90% of all American high-school students have had sex, drug, and driver education in their schools, yet large proportions of them still have unsafe sex, binge drink, smoke cigarettes, and drive recklessly (often more than one of these at the same time; Steinberg, 2004). Strategies such as raising the price of cigarettes, more vigilantly enforcing laws governing the sale of alcohol, expanding adolescents' access to mental-health and contraceptive services, and raising the driving age would likely be more effective in limiting adolescent smoking, substance abuse, pregnancy, and automobile fatalities than strategies aimed at making adolescents wiser, less impulsive, or less shortsighted. Some things just take time to develop, and, like it or not, mature judgment is probably one of them.

The research reviewed here suggests that heightened risk taking during adolescence is likely to be normative, biologically driven, and, to some extent, inevitable. There is probably very little that can or ought to be done to either attenuate or delay the shift in reward sensitivity that takes place at puberty. It may be possible to accelerate the maturation of self-regulatory competence, but no research has examined whether this is possible. In light of studies showing familial influences on psychosocial maturity in adolescence, understanding how contextual factors influence the development of self-regulation and knowing the neural underpinnings of these processes should be a high priority for those interested in the well-being of young people.

References

Baird, A., Fugelsang, J., & Bennett, C. (2005, April). *"What were you thinking?": An fMRI study of adolescent decision making.* Poster presented at the annual meeting of the Cognitive Neuroscience Society, New York.

Beyth-Marom, R., Austin, L., Fischoff, B., Palmgren, C., & Jacobs-Quadrel, M. (1993). Perceived consequences of risky behaviors: Adults and adolescents. *Developmental Psychology, 29,* 549–563.

Casey, B.J., Tottenham, N., Liston, C., & Durston, S. (2005). Imaging the developing brain: What have we learned about cognitive development? *Trends in Cognitive Science, 9,* 104–110.

Chambers, R.A., Taylor, J.R., & Potenza, M.N. (2003). Developmental neurocircuitry of motivation in adolescence: A critical period of addiction vulnerability. *American Journal of Psychiatry, 160,* 1041–1052.

Collins, W.A., & Steinberg, L. (2006). Adolescent development in interpersonal context. In W. Damon & R. Lerner (Series Eds.) & N. Eisenberg (Vol. Ed.), *Handbook of Child Psychology: Social, emotional, and personality development* (Vol. 3, pp. 1003–1067). New York: Wiley.

Drevets, W.C., & Raichle, M.E. (1998). Reciprocal suppression of regional cerebral blood flow during emotional versus higher cognitive processes: Implications for interactions between emotion and cognition. *Cognition and Emotion, 12,* 353–385.

Ernst, M., Jazbec, S., McClure, E.B., Monk, C.S., Blair, R.J.R., Leibenluft, E., & Pine, D.S. (2005). Amygdala and nucleus accumbens activation in response to receipt and omission of gains in adults and adolescents. *Neuroimage, 25,* 1279–1291.

Galvan, A., Hare, T., Davidson, M., Spicer, J., Glover, G., & Casey, B.J. (2005). The role of ventral frontostriatal circuitry in reward-based learning in humans. *Journal of Neuroscience, 25,* 8650–8656.

Gardner, M., & Steinberg, L. (2005). Peer influence on risk-taking, risk preference, and risky decision-making in adolescence and adulthood: An experimental study. *Developmental Psychology, 41,* 625–635.

Johnson, R., & Gerstein, D. (1998). Initiation of use of alcohol, cigarettes, marijuana, cocaine, and other substances in US birth cohorts since 1919. *American Journal of Public Health, 88,* 27–33.

Luna, B., Thulborn, K.R., Munoz, D.P., Merriam, E.P., Garver, K.E., Minshew, N.J., et al. (2001). Maturation of widely distributed brain function subserves cognitive development. *Neuroimage, 13,* 786–793.

McClure, S.M., Laibson, D.I., Loewenstein, G., & Cohen, J.D. (2004). Separate neural systems value immediate and delayed monetary rewards. *Science, 306,* 503–507.

Millstein, S.G., & Halpern-Felsher, B.L. (2002). Perceptions of risk and vulnerability. *Journal of Adolescent Health, 31S,* 10–27.

Nelson, E., Leibenluft, E., McClure, E., & Pine, D. (2005). The social re-orientation of adolescence: A neuroscience perspective on the process and its relation to psychopathology. *Psychological Medicine, 35,* 163–174.

Reyna, V., & Farley, F. (2006). Risk and rationality in adolescent decision-making: Implications for theory, practice, and public policy. *Psychological Science in the Public Interest, 7,* 1–44.

Spear, P. (2000). The adolescent brain and age-related behavioral manifestations. *Neuroscience and Biobehavioral Reviews, 24,* 417–463.

Steinberg, L. (2004). Risk-taking in adolescence: What changes, and why? *Annals of the New York Academy of Sciences, 1021,* 51–58.

Acknowledgments—Thanks to Nora Newcombe for comments on an earlier draft and to Jason Chein for his expertise in developmental neuroscience.

Address correspondence to Laurence Steinberg, Department of Psychology, Temple University, Philadelphia, PA 19122; lds@temple.edu.

UNIT 3

Individual Differences among Learners

Unit Selections

Key Points to Consider

- What are some of the issues and concerns of including children with special needs in regular classrooms?

- Who are the gifted and talented students? How can knowledge of their characteristics and learning needs help to provide them with an appropriate education?

- How will understanding the needs of culturally diverse and language minority students help them achieve success in school?

- What instructional strategies are more successful with boys as opposed to girls, and why?

Student Web Site

www.mhcls.com

Internet References

The Council for Exceptional Children
http://www.cec.sped.org/index.html

Global SchoolNet Foundation
http://www.gsn.org

International Project: Multicultural Pavilion
http://curry.edschool.virginia.edu/curry/centers/multicultural/papers.html

Let 100 Flowers Bloom/Kristen Nicholson-Nelson
http://teacher.scholastic.com/professional/assessment/100flowers.htm

National Association for Multicultural Education
http://www.nameorg.org

National Attention Deficit Disorder Association
http://www.add.org

National MultiCultural Institute (NMCI)
http://www.nmci.org

Tolerance.org
http://www.tolerance.org

The Equal Educational Opportunity Act for All Handicapped Children (Public Law 94–142) gives children with disabilities the right to an education in the least-restrictive environment, due process, and an individualized educational program that is specifically designed to meet their needs. Professionals and parents of children with special needs are responsible for developing and implementing an appropriate educational program for each child. The application of these ideas to classrooms across the nation at first caused great concern among educators and parents. Classroom teachers whose training did not prepare them for working with children who have special needs expressed negative attitudes about mainstreaming. Special resource teachers also expressed concern that mainstreaming would mitigate the effectiveness of special programs for the disabled and would force cuts in services. Parents feared that their children would not receive the special services they required because of governmental red tape and delays in proper diagnosis and placement.

In 1991, P.L. 94–142 was amended as the Individuals with Disabilities Education Act (IDEA) and the term "inclusion" was introduced. Inclusion tries to assure that children with disabilities will be fully integrated within the classroom. Many of the above concerns have been studied by psychologists and educators, and their findings have often influenced policy. For example, research has indicated that inclusion is more effective when regular classroom teachers and special resource teachers collaborate and work cooperatively.

The articles concerning students with exceptional learning needs confront some of these issues. The first article by Michael Giangreco discusses curricular modifications that can be used to meet the needs of students with special needs in an inclusive classroom. Jody Sherman, Carmen Rasmussen, and Lola Baydala help us understand the positive qualities of students with ADHD, and the instructional strategies that support those strengths. The article by Margaret Flores addresses issues of universal design, and how curriculum and instruction can be designed to benefit all struggling learners.

Other exceptional children are the gifted and talented. These children are rapid learners who can absorb, organize, and apply concepts more effectively than the average child. They often have IQs of 140 or more and are convergent thinkers (i.e., they give the correct answer to teacher or test questions). Convergent thinkers are usually models of good behavior and academic performance, and they respond to instruction easily; teachers generally value such children and often nominate them for gifted programs. There are other children, however, who

© Nicola Sutton/Life File/Getty Images

do not score well on standardized tests of intelligence because their thinking is more divergent (i.e., they can imagine more than one answer to teacher or test questions). These gifted divergent thinkers may not respond to traditional instruction. They may become bored, respond to questions in unique and disturbing ways, and appear uncooperative and disruptive. Many teachers do not understand these unconventional thinkers and fail to identify them as gifted. In fact, such children are sometimes labeled as emotionally disturbed or mentally retarded because of the negative impressions they make on their teachers. Because of the differences between these types of students, a great deal of controversy surrounds programs for the gifted. Such programs should enhance the self-esteem of all gifted and talented children, motivate and challenge them, and help them realize their creative potential. The first article in the subsection on gifted children considers the characteristics of giftedness, and explains how to identify gifted students and provide them with an appropriate education. The second article discusses how to address perfectionism typically seen with gifted students.

The third subsection of this unit concerns student diversity. Just as labeling may adversely affect the disabled child, it may also affect the child who comes from a minority ethnic background where the language and values are quite different from those of the mainstream culture. The term "disadvantaged" is often used to describe these children, but it is negative, stereotypical, and apt to result in a self-fulfilling prophecy whereby teachers perceive such children as incapable of learning. Teachers should provide academically and culturally diverse children with experiences that they might have missed in the restricted environment of their homes and neighborhoods. This section starts off with an article describing the benefits of a culturally diverse city. The remainder of the articles in this section suggest ways to create culturally compatible classrooms. The first article describes interventions to help low-income students be successful. The second article specifies ways to meet the needs of dialectically diverse students. The third article identifies general qualities of culturally responsive teaching. The last two articles concern gender differences in the classroom and creating classrooms that meet the needs of both boys and girls. These articles consider instructional techniques that accommodate the needs of boys and girls in the classroom.

Thinking Positively

How Some Characteristics of ADHD Can Be Adaptive and Accepted in the Classroom

Jody Sherman, Carmen Rasmussen, and Lola Baydala

Attention deficit/hyperactivity disorder (ADHD) has received much attention over the past several years in both the scientific literature and the popular press, yet confusion still exists with respect to the origin of the disorder, factors that trigger or aggravate it, the trajectory of symptoms, and treatment options, particularly for young children (Gimpel & Kuhn, 2000; Mash & Wolfe, 1999). Entering the term "ADHD" into a popular search engine revealed 624,000 hits on the Web, highlighting the diversity and overwhelming range of information available to those seeking to learn about this condition. Most, if not all, sources describe ADHD as a "disorder," and list the various deficits and difficulties that children with ADHD experience. Parents, teachers, health care professionals, and the children themselves can become discouraged as they learn about the negative aspects associated with a diagnosis of ADHD. This article reviews the challenges associated with ADHD, as well as more recent discussions that center around a positive view of this "disorder."

ADHD occurs in 3 to 5 percent of school-age children, making it the most common psychiatric disorder among children.

ADHD occurs in 3 to 5 percent of school-age children (MTA Cooperative Group, 1999), making it the most common psychiatric disorder among children (Sciutto, Terjesen, & Bender Frank, 2000). ADHD's characteristics can be broken down into specific subtypes that capture differences in children who display predominantly hyperactive and impulsive behaviors, inattentive behaviors, or a combination of both (American Psychiatric Association, 2000). Because some children will exhibit mainly inattentive behaviors and some children will exhibit mainly hyperactive behaviors, not all treatments work equally well with all children diagnosed with ADHD. Most children with ADHD will continue to experience symptoms into adulthood (Mercugliano, Power, & Blum, 1999), although the behaviors tend to change over the course of development. The disorder often manifests in difficulties in school, trouble creating and maintaining social relations, low self-esteem, and deficits in the area of executive functioning (Barkley, 1998). Executive functioning refers to goal-directed, future-oriented behaviors, including planning, organized searches, inhibition, working memory, set-shifting, strategy employment, and fluency (Welsh & Pennington, 1988; Welsh, Pennington, & Grossier, 1991). Barkley (1998) proposed a model of executive functions in children with ADHD that includes deficits in inhibition, working memory, and self-regulation, which relates to the deficits children with ADHD typically demonstrate on tasks requiring split attention and organization (Zentall, 1993).

After reviewing the literature related to academic deficits in children with ADHD, Zentall (1993) noted that children with ADHD selectively attend to stimuli that are salient and/or novel in some way, such as color or movement. This characteristic may compromise performance on tasks in which selective attention is required for stimuli that are subtle or neutral. Selective attention is required to learn most new tasks, whereas tasks that are practiced and have a fairly constant level of performance, such as reading, require sustained attention. Thus, attention problems can interfere with both the learning of new tasks and the rehearsal of tasks requiring sustained attention, such as reading and writing. Teaching children with ADHD to read and write may be optimized when modifications address the unique needs of children with the disorder. Rief (2000) suggested numerous strategies for helping these children read, including paraphrasing, limiting distractions, and scanning for chapter headings and outlines. Writing can be enhanced by using such graphic organizers as flow charts, providing models of written work, and aiding in self-editing. The author also noted that most children with ADHD will need additional help with studying and organizational skills. Rief further noted that most teaching strategies found to be useful for children with ADHD are actually ideal for the entire classroom.

Changing the Way We Think of ADHD

Despite the negative attitudes toward behavior consistent with a diagnosis of ADHD, not all of those characteristics should be thought of negatively. In fact, many researchers now view some ADHD behaviors as potentially adaptive in some situations and contexts (Hartmann, 1996, 2003; Jensen et al., 1997), and they believe that parents, teachers, and health care professionals may need to reconsider the way they view the disorder. The very name, which includes the word "disorder," does not reflect the variability among children diagnosed with ADHD, and may bias individuals against realizing the potential, strengths, and gifts that many children with ADHD have. Similarly, Hallowell and Ratey (1994), both psychiatrists who happen to have ADHD, state that the diagnosis can become a way of life, and they place a more optimistic spin on the topic than is found in typical medical discussions on ADHD.

Having ADHD can be viewed either as a disorder defined by deficits, or as an advantage defined by unique characteristics and strengths that, in the appropriate contexts, are adaptive and advantageous (Hartmann, 2003). Had he lived today, the famous composer Wolfgang Amadeus Mozart might have been diagnosed as having ADHD, as his behaviors contribute to his description as being: "impatient, impulsive, distractible, energetic, emotionally needy, creative, innovative, irreverent, and a maverick" (Hallowell & Ratey, 1994, p. 43). These behaviors worked together in a beneficial manner for the musical genius, and may be part of what makes ADHD "powerfully positive" (Hallowell & Ratey, 1994, p. 43). Although Hallowell and Ratey believe that ADHD is a serious condition that should be treated sensitively and appropriately when diagnosed, they also point out that many historical figures, including Albert Einstein, Edgar Allan Poe, Salvador Dali, and Henry Ford, displayed characteristics consistent with ADHD, and that every individual with or without ADHD carries within him or herself extraordinary potential. It is this process of identifying potential, capitalizing on unique strengths, and encouraging physical, academic, and social/emotional development that is especially important to apply with every child who is diagnosed with ADHD.

Some researchers and authors do not believe that ADHD is a negative diagnosis at all, but rather it is society's perception of the diagnosis that is negative. Hartmann referred to ADHD as a *trait* rather than a *disorder*, and outlined an argument in which ADHD characteristics are associated with a specific gene, which he called the "Edison gene" after the inventor who is believed to have had ADHD. The trait, Hartmann claimed, is associated with behaviors and skills that worked to the advantage of hunter-gatherer societies and has been passed down over the course of evolution. He described how many of the symptoms of ADHD, including short attention spans, poor planning skills, daydreaming, and impatience, can be viewed as adaptive characteristics. That is, these characteristics were perhaps vital to the survival of hunter-gatherer societies. For example, what might be considered "short attention span" and "poor planning" also could be described as continually monitoring the environment and being flexible, ready to change strategies and react

instantly to new sights or sounds. These characteristics stand in contrast to what so-called "farmer" societies possess. Farmers exhibit such characteristics as patience, being purposefully organized, and focusing on tasks until completion. Although being alert to changes in surroundings and reacting quickly may be advantageous to hunters, farmers fare better when they plan ahead, are patient, and maintain focus until goal completion.

Unfortunately for children with hunter-like traits, modern North American cultures typically favor farmer characteristics over hunter traits, particularly in the classroom. Children are expected to sit at their desks quietly and keep their hands still as they listen to the teacher; they must work on projects or topics for prolonged periods of time; homework must be completed after school hours; and information is typically absorbed through reading, listening, or seeing as opposed to doing. Children with farmer characteristics often perform well under these "normal" conditions. Children with ADHD characteristics, on the other hand, often find it difficult to achieve academic goals and obey classroom rules. Learning about how ADHD can be a positive trait in the classroom, however, can affect how educators deal with students diagnosed with ADHD, and, in turn, can benefit such students' academic, social, and behavioral outcomes.

The manner in which ADHD is viewed can affect the strategies that teachers employ in the classroom. Alcock and Ryan (2000) state that ADHD could be thought of as a gift, despite its negative reputation. They suggest that teachers should attempt to identify the unique ADHD characteristics of each child, and tailor their instruction and teaching behaviors to emphasize the child's strengths and abilities. ADHD can give children an advantage in that they are "polyactive"—that is, they are able to work on numerous tasks—and that they are often excellent brainstormers (Alcock & Ryan, 2000, p. 9). The notion of being polyactive, however, may refer more to the tendency to pursue multiple activities, rather than the ability to coordinate and process numerous tasks simultaneously. That is, although children with ADHD may be able to carry out various tasks sequentially and with great energy and enthusiasm, their ability to pursue multiple tasks simultaneously typically is compromised. Often, children's attention to one task is diverted to new tasks or stimuli, resulting in fragmented attention rather than processing numerous task demands at one time. Alcock and Ryan recommend techniques for making use of students' excess energy, such as allowing these children to do classroom errands. Such errands can include walking notes from the teacher down to the school's administrative office, putting chairs up on desks at the end of the day, and helping the teacher put supplies away or hanging up visuals. They also suggest that teachers establish quiet zones, create times for one-on-one interactions, and listen to students' needs and solve problems together. Based on the research, teachers may consider valuing and exploiting students' natural energy by engaging them in numerous activities, both academic and otherwise. Yet, they also must realize that being polyactive may not equate to success and appropriate focus on all the tasks simultaneously.

Just as Hartmann (1996, 2003) and others (Jensen et al., 1997) believe that ADHD is actually an adaptive trait with a negative image, Hughes (1990) also cautions about the danger of labeling children with diagnoses that may carry prejudicial stereotypes. Hughes (1990) suggests that teachers go beyond the label of ADHD and identify the specific needs of their students. Too often, the label marks the child as somehow inadequate, rather than identifying a specific pattern of learning and behaving. Even pointing out that children with ADHD have attention difficulties may be simplistic, because attention has many facets, including the ability to be directed, switched, divided, sustained, or withheld. Hughes recommends that teachers determine the specific characteristics and difficulties of each child and states that, with appropriate programming, children with ADHD can succeed academically, and even achieve average levels of attentional performance when tasks are self-paced. With respect to classroom instruction, the author suggests that teachers call on the students frequently, use various cues and immediate feedback, be specific about lesson goals, and emphasize the importance of setting goals.

Schirduan (2001) found that children with ADHD are successful in situations in which their unique learning patterns and strengths were identified. Specifically, Schirduan examined 87 students (Grades 2–7) from Schools Using a Multiple Intelligences Theory (SUMIT). In these schools, the curricula were designed to reflect the various cognitive profiles of the students. The author pointed out that traditional schools use curricula that reflect the dominant culture, rather than addressing individual children's learning styles, intelligences, and interests. In considering Gardner's (1993) eight intelligences (musical, bodily kinesthetic, logical mathematical, spatial, linguistic, interpersonal, intrapersonal, and naturalist), Schirduan found that most schools focus on logical mathematical and linguistic domains at the expense of the other areas (see Table 1). This focus places students whose primary areas of intelligence lie in one or some of the other six domains at a disadvantage. Schirduan found that most of the children in the program had average self-concepts, as well as average achievement levels. Because academic underachievement is a valid concern for most children with ADHD (Barkley, 1998), the results from this study were encouraging. When taught in settings that implement a multiple intelligences approach, children with ADHD perform and feel better than children with ADHD in traditional school settings (Schirduan, 2001).

Working With ADHD in the Classroom

Children with ADHD often are polyactive, excellent brainstormers, eager to please, energetic, and creative. Teachers can use these gifts in the classroom by asking students to carry out special tasks (such as those mentioned above), and creating hands-on lessons and stimuli to keep students with ADHD engaged. Teachers can capitalize on children's creativity and natural desire for exploration by setting up mini-experiments and lessons presented in various media (such as through music, art, crafts, and dance). Teachers also can enhance and capitalize on students' gifts by recognizing each child's individual learning styles, and by using a multiple intelligences approach to teaching. To help children achieve their best academically, Alcock and Ryan (2000) suggest that educators teach demanding course work in the morning hours, keep the classroom setting structured, and use a variety of media in their instruction (such as chalkboards, overhead projectors, objects, charts, videos, etc.).

Altering perceptions and classroom practices to benefit the whole classroom is a larger goal related to reshaping our views of ADHD. Realizing that children with ADHD may have strengths that are hidden behind misleading terminology and restrictive requirements can help teachers and support staff to re-examine many of their approaches to education and behavior management. Cooper and O'Regan (2001) proposed that teachers arrange their classrooms to limit distraction and increase teacher availability to address attention and behavioral issues. Furthermore, the authors suggested that complex tasks and instructions be broken down into smaller, more manageable components. Students with ADHD may need additional support completing multiple tasks. The authors recommended that teachers should provide students with a written copy of the instructions that they can refer back to,

Table 1 Children's Strengths in Relation to Gardner's Intelligences

Intelligences:	Potential Strengths:
Linguistic	Child expresses him- or herself clearly through written or spoken language; can use language to achieve goals
Musical	Child has strong musical talents or inclinations; can appreciate musical patterns, rhythms, etc.
Logical-Mathematical	Child is good at reasoning logically, solving mathematical problems, and/or exploring issues scientifically
Spatial	Child is aware of the space, locations, and/or dimensions around him or her
Bodily-Kinesthetic	Child performs well at sports, is aware of his or her body in motion, and can use mental ability to coordinate physical movements
Interpersonal	Child has success at interacting with other people, having empathy for others' feelings, and interpreting others' motivations and desires
Intrapersonal	Child is good at interpreting his or her own feelings
Naturalist	Child knows a lot about nature; can retain facts about the environment, animals, etc.

or have students repeat instructions back to the teacher. Lerner, Lowenthal, and Lerner (1995) discussed how educators might help children with ADHD improve their organizational and listening skills, and how to sustain their attention (De La Paz, 2001; DuPaul & Stoner, 1994; Hughes, 1990). Lerner et al. (1995) state that students with ADHD often need an external structure to help them organize and prioritize assignments, including rewards for being prepared, as well as such tools as day-planners to list homework assignments and deadlines. To increase sustained attention, the authors suggest that teachers shorten task and instructions, and include interesting and novel stimuli.

Taking some measures, such as shortening instructions and re-arranging desk in the classroom, can help children diagnosed with ADHD reach their creative, academic, and behavioral goals. Perhaps more fundamentally, altering perceptions about the disorder, if it is in fact a disorder, is vital to unlocking the unique strengths and skills of children diagnosed with ADHD. For example, although children with ADHD often are accused of daydreaming, Hartmann (2003) suggests that teachers view such behavior as an indication that children are bored with mundane tasks and that all the students would benefit from a change. Another example is the common complaint by teachers that students with ADHD have difficulty converting ideas into words. If ADHD is in fact an adaptive trait, rather than a disorder, then teachers would do well to realize that many students are visual or concrete thinkers who can clearly visualize a goal or product, even when they do not have the words to describe it. Allowing children to represent their ideas, inventions, or emotions through other means can open up alternative means of communication and education. Many students in the classroom, whether or not they are diagnosed with ADHD, could have more success solving problems or summarizing stories by using paints, molding clay, dramatic skits, or music. In fact, Zentall (1993) proposed that teachers incorporate new activities and experiences into their lesson plans. The author found that children with ADHD behaved better while watching films and during games than when they were partaking in more mundane tasks. In addition, art provides many therapeutic benefits for children with ADHD by giving the children an opportunity to express themselves; in addition, art is associated with increased attention and decreased impulsive behavior (Safran, 2002; Smitheman-Brown & Church, 1996). When implementing curricula, teachers should select hands-on material whenever possible, use multiple modalities when presenting information, modify testing strategies in accordance to students' special needs, and introduce any new vocabulary prior to delivering lessons (Lerner et al., 1995).

To deny that students diagnosed with ADHD experience various degrees of difficulty in academic, social, and behavioral domains would be, at the very least, irresponsible. At worst, denying the challenges associated with ADHD might hinder students from receiving the attention and help they may need to achieve their potential. Although some ADHD characteristics may be adaptive and despite the fact that North American societies' overwhelming allegiance to a farmer-type behavioral system may be limiting, some genuine concerns must be addressed. In fact, some researchers vehemently oppose viewing ADHD as an adaptive trait at all cautioning that doing so might underestimate the specific needs and limitations associated with the disorder (Barkley, 2000; Goldstein & Barkley, 1998). For example, children with ADHD frequently disrupt classroom tasks and other classmates, are often defiant, and have problems with peers and difficulty making friends (DuPaul & Stoner, 1994). Furthermore, students diagnosed with ADHD may have difficulty with selective and sustained attention (Zentall, 1993). Many teachers and educators face challenges associated with teaching children with ADHD. These students often have behavioral problems, difficulties maintaining focus in the classroom, and challenges meeting academic and social goals. Unfortunately for students diagnosed with ADHD, many teachers and health care professionals view the disorder as just that, a disorder. Yet, maintaining a positive attitude about ADHD can allow parents and educators to move beyond the diagnosis and focus on children's strengths and unique learning styles to encourage optimal development.

Conclusion

The authors are not denying that children diagnosed with ADHD do in fact face many real challenges, nor are we necessarily supporting the notion that ADHD is an evolved, adaptive trait. Rather, we argue that thinking positively about ADHD and recognizing all children's unique strengths is important for helping children reach their social emotional, and academic potential.

References

Alcock, M. W., & Ryan, P. M. (2000). ADD, type, and learning. *Journal of Psychological Type, 52,* 5–10.

American Psychiatric Association. (2000). *Diagnostic and statistical manual of mental disorders* (4th ed., text revision). Washington, DC: Author.

Barkley, R. A. (1998). *Attention-deficit disorder: A handbook for diagnosis and treatment* (2nd ed.). New York: Guilford Press.

Barkley, R. A. (2000). More on evolution, hunting, and ADHD. *The ADHD Report, 8,* 1–7.

Cooper, P., & O'Regan, F. J. (2001). *Educating children with AD/HD: A teacher's manual.* London: RoutledgeFalmer.

De La Paz, S. (2001). Teaching writing to students with attention deficits disorders and specific language impairment. *Journal of Educational Research, 95,* 37–47.

DuPaul, G. J., & Stoner, G. (1994). *ADHD in the schools: Assessment and intervention strategies.* New York: Guilford Press.

Gardner, H. (1993). *Frames of mind: The theory of multiple intelligences.* New York: Basic Books.

Gimpel, G. A., & Kuhn, B. R. (2000). "Maternal report of attention deficit hyperactivity disorder symptoms in preschool children": Authors' response. *Child: Care, Health and Development, 26,* 178–179.

Goldstein, S., & Barkley, R. A. (1998). Commentary: ADHD, hunting and evolution: "Just so" stories. *The ADHD Report, 6,* 1–4.

Hallowell, E. M., & Ratey, J. J. (1994). *Driven to distraction: Recognizing and coping with attention deficit disorder from childhood through adulthood.* New York: Touchstone.

Hartmann, T. (1996). *Beyond ADD: Hunting for reasons in the past and present.* Grass Valley, CA: Publishers Group West.

Hartmann, T. (2003). *The Edison gene: ADHD and the gift of the hunter child.* Rochester, VT: Park Street Press.

Hughes, S. (1990). Appropriate programming for children with attention deficits. *Arizona Reading Journal, 19,* 21–22.

Jensen, P. S., Mrazek, D., Knapp, P., Steinberg, L., Pfeffer, C., Schowalter, J., & Shapiro, T. (1997). Evolution and revolution in child psychiatry: ADHD as a disorder of adaptation. *Journal of the American Academy of Child & Adolescent Psychiatry, 36,* 1672–1681.

Lerner, J. W., Lowenthal, B., & Lerner, S. R. (1995). *Attention deficit disorders: Assessment and teaching.* Pacific Grove, CA: Brooks/Cole Publishing.

Mash, E. J., & Wolfe, D. A. (1999). Attention-deficit/hyperactivity disorder. In E. J. Mash & D. A. Wolfe (Eds.), *Abnormal child psychology* (pp. 143–184). Belmont, CA: Books/Cole-Wadsworth Publishing.

Mercugliano, M., Power, T. J., & Blum, N. J. (1999). *The clinician's practical guide to attention-deficit/hyperactivity disorder.* Baltimore: Paul H. Brookes.

MTA Cooperative Group. (1999). A 14-month randomized clinical trial of treatment strategies for attention-deficit/hyperactivity disorder. *Archives of General Psychiatry, 56,* 1073–1086.

Rief, S. (2000). ADHD: Common academic difficulties and strategies that help. Attention!, *September/October,* 47–51.

Safran, D. S. (2002). *Art therapy and AD/HD: Diagnostic and therapeutic approaches.* London: Jessica Kingsley.

Schirduan, V. (2001, April). *Mindful curriculum leadership for students with attention deficit hyperactivity disorder (ADHD): Leading in elementary schools by using multiple intelligences theory (SUMIT).* Paper presented at the annual meeting of the American Educational Research Association, Seattle, WA.

Sciutto, M. J., Terjesen, M. D., & Bender Frank, A. S. (2000). Teachers' knowledge and misperceptions of attention-deficit/hyperactivity disorder. *Psychology in the Schools, 37,* 115–122.

Smitheman-Brown, V., & Church, R. P. (1996). Mandala drawing: Facilitating creative growth in children with ADD or ADHD. *Art Therapy, 13,* 252–260.

Welsh, M. C., & Pennington, B. F. (1988). Assessing frontal lobe function in children: Views from developmental psychology. *Developmental Neuropsydtology, 4,* 199–230.

Welsh, M. C., Pennington, B. F., & Grossier, D. B. (1991). A normative-developmental study of executive function: A window of prefrontal function in children. Developmental *Neuropsychology, 7,* 131–149.

Zentall, S. S. (1993). Research on the educational implications of attention deficit hyperactivity disorder. *Exceptional Children, 60,* 143–153.

JODY SHERMAN is graduate student, Department of Psychology, **CARMEN RASMUSSEN** is Research Associate, PhD, Department of Pediatrics, and **LOLA BAYDALA** is MD, MSc, FRCP, FAAP, Department of Pediatrics, University of Alberta, Edmonton, Alberta, Canada.

Authors' Note—This project was funded by the Charles Fried Memorial Fund through the Misericordia Hospital, Edmonton, Alberta, Canada.

Universal Design in Elementary and Middle School

Designing Classrooms and Instructional Practices to Ensure Access to Learning for All Students

Margaret M. Flores

The Association for Childhood Education International's (ACEI) mission includes helping educators meet the needs of students in a climate of societal change. One such change is the increasing diversity of learning needs within elementary and middle school classrooms. Increased numbers of students with disabilities served within the general education classroom have contributed to this diversity (U.S. Department of Education, 2005). Students with diverse needs present a challenge for elementary and middle school teachers because it may be difficult to ensure that all students meet expectations. Under current legislation, such as the No Child Left Behind Act (2002), all students, including those with disabilities, are expected to be proficient at grade level by 2013. Similarly, the Individuals With Disabilities Education Improvement Act (2004) states that students with disabilities should have increased access to the general education curriculum and that accommodations should be designed according to the students' needs.

In carrying out the mission of ACEI and complying with federal legislation, it is important that students with disabilities have accommodations written into their individualized educational programs (IEPs) and that these students receive accessible instruction. General education teachers play a critical role in both IEP development and implementation of accessible instruction. As members of the multidisciplinary IEP team, general education teachers have a unique understanding of curricular materials, texts, equipment, and technology within the general education setting that is critical in designing appropriate accommodations. These accommodations should support teachers' other role, that of implementing instruction that is assessible to all students. While this role may seem daunting, tools are available for designing classroom environments and instruction that are conducive to the learning of all students.

Universal Design for Instruction (UDI) is a set of principles helpful in guiding this process. UDI, designed by the Center for Applied Special Technology, is a framework that has been successful for all students, including those with disabilities in general education settings (Cawley, Foley, & Miller, 2003; McGuire, Scott, & Shaw, 2006; Pisha & Coyne, 2001; Pisha & Stahl, 2005). UDI ensures that all students have access to instruction through the following principles: 1) equitable use, 2) flexibility in use, 3) simple and intuitive, 4) perceptible information, 5) tolerance for error, 6) low physical effort, and 7) size and space for approach and use. The purpose of this article is to provide an overview of UDI, as well as practical classroom applications for elementary and middle school teachers.

Equitable Use

Equitable use means that all students can use materials, equipment, and technology in the classroom. The most common materials that can be inaccessible to students with disabilities are textbooks. As students advance in school, the emphasis on reading to learn increases and accessibility of textbooks becomes increasingly important in the content areas as students move through to middle school. Textbooks are inaccessible if students' reading levels are several levels below their grade placement, students cannot read the print due to its small size, and/or students have difficulty holding a book due to its size and weight. However, textbooks can be made accessible to students through the use of books on tape and through digital texts (Boyle et al., 2003; Twyman & Tindal, 2006). Books on tape are available through such nonprofit organizations as Readings for the Blind and Dyslexic, a free service for school districts and individuals with reading and visual disabilities. Digital texts allow for physical access, magnification of print, changes in contrast (i.e., increased color contrast between the print and page background), as well as audio output.

Technology, classroom equipment, and materials may not be accessible to all students, due to various student characteristics. Equipment and materials maybe difficult to grasp or manipulate and/or visually perceive. Fortunately, equipment and materials used for instruction can be made accessible to all students through the use of grips, changes in size and dimension, and high-contrast materials. For lower and intermediate elementary students, these materials might include: special grips for pencils or other writing utensils; adaptive scissors; use of high contrast and/or large print, pictorial directions, and/or audio directions within learning centers; use of paper with raised lines; and manipulatives that are made easier to grip through size and texture (D'Angiulli, 2007; Judge, 2006; Russell et al., 2007). Although these materials will continue to be helpful for students at the late elementary and middle school level, additional items might include high-contrast print materials and graphic organizers or diagrams, and the use of graphic organizers and diagrams with raised lines (D'Angiulli, 2007; Russell et al., 2007).

Technology difficulties include becoming "lost" when searching the Internet for research, the computer font being too small or lacking color contrast, motor difficulties interfering with mouse manipulation, keyboard keys being too small, or the keyboard's lack of color contrast. As students progress through elementary and middle school, they will use technology more independently for research. Technology solutions for these students include the creation of web quests, in which the necessary websites are linked and/or the sites are contained within a single main site (Skylar, Higgins, & Boone, 2007). For all students, regardless of their grade level, computer equipment can be modified through the use of mouse balls that accommodate for fine motor difficulty, high contrast, and/or large-print stickers placed on top of keyboard keys. Keyboards are also available with large keys. Computer software is available to provide audio output so that print can be read to the student. The contrast of the screen and print can be adjusted to provide appropriate color contrast.

Flexibility in Use

Flexible use means that instruction and accompanying activities accommodate a wide range of individual preferences and abilities. Instruction can be designed in a variety of ways to accommodate a variety of learning strengths. It is helpful to design instruction using several different modes in order to make learning accessible for students with diverse learning needs.

Visual representation. Adding visual representations in the form of graphic organizers or schematic maps helps students organize concepts and information (Boulineau,

Fore, & Hagan-Burke, 2004; Ives, 2007; Lovitt, & Horton, 1994; McCoy & Ketterlin-Geller, 2004; Williams et al., 2007). These tools also help students recognize relationships between ideas and concepts. Students who have difficulties processing information, and students who lack background knowledge, may have difficulty connecting ideas and understanding how ideas come together to form overall concepts. Emphasis on pictures and symbols may be more appropriate when designing graphic organizers for elementary students. For middle school students, the use of graphic organizers or schematic maps may be helpful as instructional advance organizers and as instructional guides throughout units. The use of color, size, and shape also can be helpful in emphasizing relationships and hierarchies within graphic organizers. Other ways to appeal to visual learners at all grade levels is through pictures and videos. Visual depictions of information and relationships also may be helpful for memory or retention by providing students with an avenue for "picturing information in their mind."

Hands-on activities. Hands-on activities can be helpful for students, at all grade levels, who have difficulty acquiring information by more traditional means (Butler, Miller, Crehan, & Babbitt, 2003; Cass, Cares, Smith, & Jackson, 2003; Kerry–Moran, 2006; Kinniburgh & Shaw, 2007; Mastropieri et al., 2006; Witzel, Mercer, & Miller, 2003). Although these types of activities may be associated with science in the form of experiments and demonstrations, they provide opportunities throughout content areas. In mathematics, the use of manipulatives is a way to increase understanding of concepts and procedures, regardless of grade level. Although using and managing the use of manipulatives may be challenging, research has shown that students with learning disabilities need an average of three experiences with manipulatives in order to understand mathematical concepts (Mercer & Miller, 1992). In addition to building understanding, hands-on and participatory activities provide students who have difficulty expressing themselves through oral and written language with an opportunity to demonstrate their understanding.

Assignment completion. It is important to assess students' understanding of concepts and ideas; however, providing one avenue for expression of one's understanding may lead to inaccurate results. For example, students with learning disabilities in writing may not be able to fully express their ideas in writing, but they could discuss them in detail. Offering assignment or project menus could provide a variety of ways in which students can demonstrate their understanding. A menu allows all students to choose their preferred format without singling out particular students. For example, students might be given the option of writing a paragraph (for younger students) or an essay (for older students), an oral report to a group or through audio recording, or a multimedia presentation. The choices offered should each allow for appropriate assessment of students' understanding of the target objective or concept.

Another way to be flexible about assignment completion throughout elementary and middle levels is through cooperative grouping. Cooperative groups should be structured so that all members of the group have roles and responsibilities. These roles should be tailored to students' strengths and weaknesses and lead to active participation for all students. Each student should be accountable for his or her contribution to the group, as well as for the overall group's performance. The provision of individual roles ensures that all students actively learn and contribute, rather than only a few members of the group completing the work.

Simple and Intuitive

Simple and intuitive means that instruction is easily understood, regardless of students' experience, knowledge, or language skills. This includes priming students' background knowledge prior to beginning instruction. Priming background knowledge involves explaining how new information is connected to prior knowledge and experience. For example, an instructional unit about the American Civil War might include discussions about instances when students might have felt that another person or group did not attend to their point of view or needs. The experiences of students and how this discussion is moderated will differ depending on the grade level. Another way to make instruction simple and intuitive for elementary and middle school students is through analogies between new concepts and well-known concepts. It is important to be aware of students' diverse experiences while creating or designing these analogies, so that all students easily connect the two concepts.

Using consistent language is another way of making instruction simple and intuitive for elementary and middle school students. Students with language processing deficits and/or students who are second language learners have difficulty understanding instruction when each explanation involves different vocabulary and terminology. Therefore, using similar language each time an explanation is provided will lead to more efficient learning and understanding. In addition, language should be not only appropriate for a given skill, task, or concept, but also easily understood by students. Keep explanations as simple as possible, adding vocabulary instruction, if needed.

Perceptible Information

Perceptible information refers to that information that can be perceived regardless of skill and ability. This includes the use of instructional materials with appropriate color contrast for students with visual impairments. Black and yellow provide the highest color contrast, and computer screens, PowerPoint presentations, keys on computer keyboards, and handouts

can be adjusted to allow for increased visual perception. Seating within the classroom also can provide for increased perception. Placing students near the instructor and away from windows and hallways will increase students' ability to hear, see, and attend to instructional activities. Assignments and instructional materials also can be made more perceptible by changing their format. This begins with directions that are written clearly and at a level that students with various reading abilities can understand. Format also includes the amount of space between activities or problems, the use of lines for written responses, the layout, and the order of questions. Activities and assignments that involve written problems or scenarios can be adjusted for readability. Tests and quizzes that accompany textbooks may not be written at a level that all students understand. The wording of questions can be changed so that students are assessed based on their level of subject matter knowledge, rather than on their reading ability.

Tolerance for Error

Tolerance for error means that students have the opportunity to engage in ongoing assignments and projects. This allows for revision and editing over time, and students receive credit for correcting their errors. Students have the opportunity for feedback and ongoing learning. Over time, students learn from their mistakes and practice the appropriate skill, an opportunity that is lost with one-time assignments. These ongoing assignments and projects would be appropriate, regardless of students' grade placement.

Low Physical Effort

Low physical effort means that all students have access to materials and activities without great physical effort. The use of technology can decrease the amount of physical effort (Bahr & Nelson, 1996; Strassman & D'Amore, 2002; Tumlin & Heller, 2004). For example, if writing is physically taxing for students with fine motor difficulties, then the use of a keyboard can be of assistance. Hardware, software, and accessories are available to make computers accessible to students with more significant motor difficulties. Classroom materials, such as scissors, writing utensils, lab equipment, and desks, are all available in versions that are easily accessible for students with physical disabilities (Judge, 2006). These accommodations allow students to focus their attention and energy on learning rather than on manipulating materials.

Size and Space for Approach and Use

Size and space for approach and use means enough space is available so that all students can participate. The classroom is set up so that all students can maneuver throughout the room and participate in a variety of activities without

Mr. Jackson teaches 3rd grade at North Hills Elementary School and utilizes UDI in order to make his classroom accessible to a diverse group of learners. Mr. Jackson's room includes three types of learning centers (mathematics, writing, and reading), a classroom library (which includes audio books), an area for small-group instruction, and an area for whole-group instruction. Therefore, he has flexibility in his grouping, allowing him to individualize instruction for a small group while others are engaged in alternate learning activities. He places the learning centers along one side of the room, far enough apart so that students in one center will not be distracted by students in another, but still allowing easy movement from one to another. The large group area consists of grouped desks (conducive for cooperating group work) placed in a semicircle formation in front of the classroom's whiteboard. The classroom library (close to the reading center) and the small-group area are situated on each end of the room. Mr. Jackson has instituted a class book club in which students chose books based on the groups' interests. Mr. Jackson has acquired audio-books from the Association for the Blind and Dyslexic so that all students can participate fully in the experience. Each learning center includes written (large print, high contrast) directions, pictorial directions, and audio directions through headsets. Menus of activities also are included for each center in order to differentiate them based on students' strengths. The materials for the centers are modified according to students' needs. For example, the math center's manipulatives are large, with high-contrast coloring. The keyboards are portable and can be moved throughout learning areas. The students' written work can be saved on the classroom computer so it can be downloaded for editing and printing later.

Figure 1   Mr. Jackson's 3rd-grade Classroom: UDI Example for Elementary Level Classroom.

Ms. Vargas is a member of a four-person team and teaches 7th-grade science at Green Oaks Middle School. She utilizes the principles of UDI to make her science class accessible to diverse groups of learners. Ms. Vargas' science textbook package includes audio versions of the text that she makes available to students with visual and learning disabilities. Ms. Vargas has acquired software and hardware that allows students to scan print materials into the classroom computer, which then converts the print into an audio format. Prior to beginning an instructional unit, Ms. Vargas provides all students with a schematic map for the unit. She refers to the map often and highlights important connections between concepts learned previously and those in the current lesson. When instruction involves lecture and note taking, Ms. Vargas provides all students with an outline that includes key words and a hierarchical structure to ensure that students have useful study notes. Students also may audio-record classroom instruction. During these lectures, Ms. Vargas uses PowerPoint presentations with a large, high-contrast font. During laboratory activities, students work in pairs, with each person responsible for specific duties. Plastic (rather than glass) containers and equipment are used and materials are kept on a series of lazy Susans so that they may be accessed easily. When needed, Ms. Vargas modifies the procedures so that larger weights and volumes can be used, allowing students with fine motor problems to grip and move containers and objects more easily. Laboratory reports can be produced either in writing (handwritten or word processed) or as an audio recording. More complicated lab reports and projects are ongoing assignments in which students complete the product in stages and receive feedback.

Figure 2   Ms. Vargas' 7th-grade Classroom: UDI Example for a Middle Level Classroom.

excess physical effort. Students with physical disabilities have enough space to engage in the same types of activities as students without disabilities. Movement throughout the room and transition to activities is facilitated by its layout and design. Enough space is available between learning centers within elementary classrooms and middle school classrooms. Students should be able to move easily from small-group instruction to other areas within the room. As students begin to change classrooms, backpacks and other student materials can create clutter and hazards for students with visual impairments, physical disabilities, and/or students who use wheelchairs. Providing a special area within the room for these materials or using individual storage crates under chairs or tables can alleviate this problem.

Conclusion

The scenarios in Figures 1 and 2 are from elementary and middle level classrooms that exemplify different UDI principles in action. Figure 1 describes a 3rd-grade classroom

in which the following principles are emphasized: equitable use, flexibility in use, perceptible information, low physical effort, and size and space for approach. Figure 2 describes a 7th-grade classroom in which the following principles are emphasized: equitable use, flexibility in use, simple and intuitive, perceptible information, tolerance for error, and size and space for approach.

Students with disabilities have IEPs that are written each year by a multidisciplinary team, including, but not limited to, general education teachers, special education teachers, parents, and administrators. The general education teacher has the most experience and information about the curriculum, activities, and materials used within the general education setting. In order to ensure that instruction is accessible to all students, appropriate modifications and accommodations need to be planned and implemented. The general education teacher is a critical participant in this process because of his or her knowledge of the general education setting. Parents, special education teachers, and administrators might not be as knowledgeable about what might be needed within this setting. The general education teacher could add valuable

Table 1 Books That Provide Resources and Additional Information About Implementation of Universal Design for Instruction

Rose, D. H., Meyer, A., & Hichcock, C. (2005). *The universally designed classroom.* Cambridge, MA: Harvard University Press.

This book provides an introduction to Universal Design and is useful for teachers, administrators, and parents. It includes strategies and resources for creating a classroom that provides access to the general education curriculum for all students.

Rose, D. H., & Meyer, A. (2002). *Teaching every student in the digital age: Universal design for learning.* Alexandria, VA: Association for Supervision and Curriculum Development.

This book provides an overview of Universal Design for Learning, as well as real-world strategies for implementing Universal Design in the classroom. The authors explicitly connect ideas and concepts, using graphic organizers and examples throughout the book.

Council for Exceptional Children. (2005). *Universal design for learning.* Upper Saddle River, NJ: Prentice Hall.

This book serves as a practical guide to implementing Universal Design in the classroom. It includes a case-based scenario about teachers' experiences with Universal Design. Discussion questions throughout the book offer opportunities for application and reflection upon the content.

Table 2 Interactive Websites That Provide Tools for the Implementation of Universal Design for Instruction Principles

Websites

Lesson Builder: http://lessonbuilder.cast.org

This site provides models and tools to create and adapt lessons in order to increase accessibility for all students. Model lesson plans across content areas and grade levels are included.

Book Builder: http://bookbuilder.cast.org

This site provides information and the tools to create engaging digital books for students. Universally designed books will engage, and provide access for, diverse groups of students.

Creating Accessible WebQuests and Web-based Student Activities: www.4teachers.org

This site offers tools and resources to integrate technology into the classroom. These include Web lessons, quizzes, rubrics, classroom calendars, and other tools for student use.

suggestions about modifications and accommodations that might be otherwise overlooked. The principles of universal design should guide this planning process. The general education classroom should be thought of with regard to the students' accessibility, specifically in terms of equitable use, flexibility in use, simple and intuitive, perceptive in formation, perceptible in formation, tolerance for error, low physical effort, and size and space for approach and use.

The No Child Left Behind Act (2002) requires that students with disabilities perform proficiently on grade level in all areas by 2013. These are high expectations to meet. Therefore, it is critical that all students have access to instruction within the general education classroom. Students' IEPs provide for the necessary accommodations and modifications for access to instruction. The multidisciplinary team who creates a student's IEP is responsible for assessing the student's needs and designing the necessary modifications. The general education teacher has unique knowledge of the curricular standards, instructional activities, materials, and physical design of the classroom. The awareness of these factors, as well as the knowledge of the principles of universal design, provides teachers with the tools necessary to fully participate in this process of meeting students' needs and ensuring that all students have access to instruction.

References

Bahr, C. M., & Nelson, N. W. (1996). The effects of text-based and graphics-based software tools on planning and organizing of stories. *Journal of Learning Disabilities, 22,* 355–270.

Boulineau, T., Fore, C., & Hagan-Burke, S. (2004). Using story mapping to increase the story grammar of elementary students with learning disabilities. *Learning Disability Quarterly, 27*(2), 105–114.

Boyle, E. A., Rosenberg, M. S., Connelly, V. J., Gallin-Washburg, S., Brinckerhoff, L. C., & Banerjee, M. (2003). Effects of audio-texts on the acquisition of secondary level content by students with mild disabilities. *Learning, Disability Quarterly, 26,* 204–214.

Butler, F. M., Miller, S. P., Crehan, K., & Babbitt, B. P. (2003). Fraction instruction for students with mathematics disabilities: Comparing two teaching sequences. *Learning Disabilities Research and Practice, 18*(2), 99–111.

Cass, M., Cates, D., Smith, M., & Jackson, C. (2003). Effects of manipulative instruction on solving area and perimeter problems by students with learning disabilities. *Learning Disabilities Research and Practice, 18*(2), 112–120.

Cawley, J. F., Foley, T. E., & Miller, J. (2003). Science and students with mild disabilities. *Intervention in School and Clinic 38,* 160–171.

D'Angiulli, A. (2007). Raised-line pictures, blindness, and tactile beliefs: An observational case study. *Journal of Visual Impairment and Blindness, 101,* 172–178.

Individuals with Disabilities Education Improvement Acts of 2004, Pub. L. No. 108–446, 118 Stat. 2647 (2004) (amending 20 U.S.C.§§ 1440 et seq.).

Ives, B. (2007). Graphic organizers applied to secondary algebra instruction for students with learning disorders. *Learning Disabilities Research and Practice, 22*(2), 110–118.

Judge, S. (2006). Constructing an assistive technology toolkit for young children: Views from the field. *Journal of Special Education Technology, 21*(4), 17–24.

Kerry-Moran, K.J. (2006). Nurturing emergent readers through readers' theater. *Early Childhood Education Journal, 33,* 317–323.

Kinniburgh, L., & Shaw, E. (2007). Building reading fluency in elementary science through readers' theater. *Science Activities, 44*(1), 16–20.

Lovitt, T. C, & Horton, S. V. (1994). Strategies for adapting textbooks for youth with learning disabilities. *Remedial and Special Education, 15,* 105–116.

Mastropieri, M. A., Scruggs, T. E., Norland, J. J., Berkley, S., McDuffie, K., Tornquist, E. H., & Connors, N. (2006). Differentiated curriculum enhancement in inclusive middle school science: Effects on classroom and high stakes tests. *Journal of Special Education, 40*(3), 130–137.

McCoy, J. D., & Ketterlin-Geller, R. (2004). Rethinking instructional delivery for diverse student populations: Serving all learners with concept-based instruction. *Intervention in School and Clinic, 40*(2), 88–95.

McGuire, J. M., Scott, S. S., Shaw, S. F. (2006). Universal design and its application in educational environments. *Remedial and Special Education, 27,* 166–175.

Mercer, C. D., & Miller, S. P. (1992). Teaching students with learning problems in math to acquire, understand, and apply basic math facts. *Remedial and Special Education, 13*(3), 19–35.

Pisha, B., & Coyne, P. (2001). Smart from the start. *Remedial and Special Education, 22,* 197–203.

Pisha, B., & Stahl, S. (2005). The promise of new learning environments for students with disabilities. *Intervention in School and Clinic, 41,* 67–75.

Russell M. E., Jutai, J. W., Strong, J. G., Campbell, K. A., Gold, D., Pretty, L., & Wilmot, L. (2007). The legibility of typefaces for readers with low vision: A research review. *Journal of Visual Impairments and Blindness, 101,* 402–415.

Skylar, A. A., Higgins, K., & Boone, R. (2007). Strategies for adapting webquests for students with learning disabilities. *Intervention in School and Clinic, 43*(1), 20–28.

Strassman, B. K., & D'Amore, M. (2002). The write technology. *Teaching Exceptional Children, 34*(6), 28–31.

Tumlin, J., & Heller, K. W. (2004). Using word prediction software to increase fluency with students with physical disabilities. *Journal of Special Education Technology, 19*(3), 5–14.

Twyman, T., & Tindal, G. (2006). Using computer-adapted, conceptually based history text to increase comprehension and problem-solving skills of students with disabilities. *Journal of Special Education Technology, 21*(2), 5–16.

U.S. Department of Education. (2002). *No Child Left Behind: A desktop reference.* Washington, DC: Author.

U.S. Department of Education, National Center for Education Statistics. (2005). *The condition of education 2005* (NCES 2005–094).

Williams, J. P., Nubla-Kung, A. M., Pollini, S., Stafford, K. B., Garcia, A., & Snyder, A. E. (2007). Teaching cause and effect text structure through social studies content to at-risk second graders. *Journal of Learning Disabilities, 40*(2), 111–120.

Witzel, B. S., Mercer, C. D., & Miller, S. P. (2003). Teaching algebra to students with learning difficulties: An investigation of an explicit instruction approach. *Learning Disabilities Research and Practice, 18*(2), 121–131.

MARGARET M. FLORES is Assistant Professor, Special Education, Department of Interdisciplinary Learning and Teaching, University of Texas at San Antonio.

Recognizing Gifted Students
A Practical Guide for Teachers

By watching for certain behaviors and characteristics, teachers in the general education classroom can identify and better understand exceptional students.

SANDRA MANNING

Today, more than ever, student diversity typifies the general education classroom (Tomlinson 2004). In most classrooms, the range of cognitive abilities is vast. Inclusion and legislative mandates challenge general educators to design and implement teaching and behavior management strategies that will ensure success for all student groups—including the gifted and highly able. Research indicates, however, that a majority of teachers have little specific knowledge about this group of children (Archambualt et al. 1993; Robinson 1998; Westberg and Daoust 2003; Whitton 1997).

Lacking awareness of the characteristics and instructional requirements of high ability students, teachers are at a disadvantage. This article explores the characteristics of gifted children and offers the general classroom teacher tips and ideas for understanding the gifted children they teach.

Gifted students routinely exhibit academic and emotional traits that may be described as intense and, at times, even extreme.

Defining 'Gifted'

High ability students have been labeled in many ways. Currently, the label "gifted" is used to indicate high intellectual or academic ability, and "gifted education" is recognized as the educational field devoted to the study of this student population. However, defining "gifted" is no easy task. The earliest use of this word to identify high ability students was by Lewis Terman in 1925 (Stephens and Karnes 2000; Morelock 1996). This usage came on the heels of the first IQ test developed in the early 1900s by Alfred Binet (Morelock 1996; Morgan 1996; Sarouphim 1999). Terman identified students scoring in the top 2 percent in general intelligence on the Binet test or a similar measure as gifted (Clark 2002).

Over the years, many definitions of this term have been proposed by scholars and researchers. From natural talent awaiting development (Gagne 1995; Tannenbaum 2003) to the ability to use life situations successfully (Sternberg 2003), the common factors in defining giftedness appear to be potential and opportunity.

Clark (2002) defined "gifted" as a label for the biological concepts of superior development of various brain functions. These functions, according to Clark, may be manifested in the areas of cognition, creativity, academics, leadership, or the arts. Clark subtly emphasized the natural aspects of the child's ability, as opposed to learned aspects, and most nearly matched the popular definition of the word gifted—"endowed with a special aptitude or ability" (Webber 1984, 295). Clark (2002, 25), however, went on to say that "Growth of intelligence depends on the interaction between biological inheritance and environmental opportunities." With this phrase, Clark inferred a union of the nature/nurture debate, designating giftedness as partially due to inherited traits of information processing with an integral portion attributed to the environmental experiences the child encounters to develop those traits.

Less formal definitions of the word gifted include those offered by parent groups and gifted students themselves. Russell, Hayes, and Dockery (1988, 2) reported a definition created by a parent group: "Giftedness is that precious endowment of potentially outstanding abilities which allows a person to interact with the environment with remarkably high levels of achievement and creativity." Gifted student Amanda Ashman (2000, 50) defined being gifted as "not something that you can develop. You are born with a capacity for knowledge. Learning and understanding come naturally for the gifted."

These definitions further the meaning of giftedness as an endowment of natural ability apart from learning that takes place in the home or at school. Unfortunately, these types of definitions have given the field of gifted education the reputation of elitism (Morelock 1996) and perhaps have been the impetus of the popular myth that "gifted students will get it on their own." To refute that myth and highlight the need for talent development in all students, growing interest in the idea of multiple intelligences has challenged the singular idea of "general intelligence org" (Gardner 1983; Von Károlyi, Ramos-Ford, and Gardner 2003) and suggested that strengths in many areas more aptly define giftedness in individuals. Further, Sternberg (2003) advocated in his theory of successful intelligence that giftedness is manifested in individuals who are able to take the raw materials of their life situations and transform them into successful experiences. Renzulli (1978; 2003) added that task commitment and creativity must be considered when defining giftedness.

Whether giftedness is inherited, developed, manifested in the ability to manipulate life situations, or a result of some combination of these ideas, it is imperative for the regular classroom teacher to be cognizant of the fact that high ability students are in the classroom. Because these students are present, teachers have a responsibility to create a learning environment conducive to gifted student success.

Characteristics of Gifted Students

One key way classroom teachers can broaden understanding of gifted students is through knowledge of the general characteristics intellectually gifted children exhibit. Characteristics in the cognitive and affective domains most commonly appear in general classroom behavior and, therefore, may be observed by the classroom teacher.

Table 1 highlights general cognitive characteristics of intellectually gifted students. Notice that gifted students often possess an intense desire to learn about their own interests. Their ability to think at abstract levels earlier than same-aged peers and form their own ways of thinking about problems and ideas indicates that intellectually gifted students need advanced content and choice in learning activities. Gifted students' high energy levels and ability to extend the range of projects signify that independent studies may be an option for differentiating instruction for these students.

Varied behaviors and preferences arise from giftedness. An awareness of the social and emotional characteristics of gifted students can further help teachers understand many of the classroom behaviors they observe in these children. For example, the gifted child's desire to share knowledge may be seen by others as an attempt to show off and may lead to peer rejection. Gifted students' high expectations of themselves and others can lead to perfectionism, personal dissatisfaction, or feelings of hopelessness (Clark 2002). Table 2 gives an overview of the characteristics of intellectually gifted students in the affective domain.

Table 1 Cognitive Characteristics of Intellectually Gifted Students

- Process and retain large amounts of information
- Comprehend materials at advanced levels
- Curious and have varied and sometimes intense interests
- High levels of language development and verbal ability
- Possess accelerated and flexible thought processes
- Early ability to delay closure of projects
- See unusual relationships among disciplines or objects
- Adept at generating original ideas and solutions to problems
- Persistent, goal-oriented, and intense on topics of interest
- Form their own ways of thinking about problems and ideas
- Learn things at an earlier age than peers
- Need for freedom and individuality in learning situations
- High desire to learn and seek out their own interests
- Abstract thinkers at an earlier age than peers
- Prefer complex and challenging work
- Transfer knowledge and apply it to new situations
- May prefer to work alone
- May be early readers
- May possess high energy levels and longer attention spans

(Chuska 1989; Clark 2002; Silverman 2000; Winebrenner 2001)

Table 2 Affective Characteristics of Intellectually Gifted Students

- Possess large amounts of information about emotions
- May possess an unusual sensitivity to the feelings of others
- Possess a keen or subtle sense of humor
- Possess a heightened sense of self-awareness
- Idealism and sense of justice appear at an early age
- Develop inner controls early
- Possess unusual emotional depth and intensity
- Exhibit high expectations of self and others
- Display a strong need for consistency in themselves and others
- Possess advanced levels of moral judgment

(Chuska 1989; Clark 2002; Silverman 2000; Winebrenner 2001)

Gifted students routinely exhibit academic and emotional traits that may be described as intense and, at times, even extreme. They are more curious, demanding, and sensitive than their typical developing peers. Gifted children are unique and require parents and educators to modify both home and school environments to meet their strong need to know. Modification is imperative if gifted students are to reach full potential.

Teachers should keep in mind that the traits listed are not exhaustive and that every gifted child will not display each characteristic stated. In fact, intellectually gifted students referred to in the literature as atypical may display their giftedness in other ways. There are many groups to consider when identifying an atypical gifted student, including, but not limited to, non-English speaking students and students from low socioeconomic circumstances. Unfortunately, research has shown that teachers often overlook atypical gifted students and refer a disproportionately high number of European-American children with "teacher-friendly" characteristics such as good behavior and high academic achievement to gifted education programs (Plata and Masten 1998; Bonner 2000). This reality points to the need for additional information on the characteristics of atypical gifted students such as listed in Table 3.

Many traits of atypical gifted students are evident in all intellectually gifted students. However, a strong sense of family, responsibility for adult roles—such as assuming additional tasks in the classroom setting, inner-strength, and self-worth—are key factors for the classroom teacher to look for in recognizing atypical gifted students. These children have the same general abilities as many gifted students. Yet, because of cultural differences or lack of early experiences, they may not display the typical characteristics of intellectually gifted students that often are considered by teachers when making referrals to gifted education programs.

Table 3 Characteristics of Atypical Gifted Students

- Ability to manipulate a symbol system
- Think logically
- Ability to use stored knowledge to solve problems
- Reason by analogy
- Transfer knowledge to new circumstances
- May possess creative and artistic abilities
- Resilient; able to cope with trying family situations
- Take on adult roles in the home
- Strong sense of pride and self-worth
- Exhibit leadership ability and independent thinking
- Possess a strong desire to learn about and understand their culture
- Display a strong inner will
- May display a heightened sensitivity to others and the world around them

(Bonner 2000; Hebert and Reis 1999; Schwartz 1997)

Classroom Behaviors

Because of the unique characteristics gifted students possess, teachers need to be aware of the ways in which these attributes manifest themselves in observable classroom behaviors. Some behaviors can be troubling to the classroom teacher; however, being aware of their root causes will help teachers more fully meet gifted students' needs and build positive relationships vital to meaningful classroom experiences.

The following classroom problem situations (Clark 2002; Winebrenner 2001; Smutny, Walker, and Meckstroth 1997) are offered for consideration.

- Unfinished work may be the result of varied interests and inability to narrow down a topic. Poor work habits might also reveal student feelings that he or she already knows about a particular topic and does not feel the need for practice.
- Poor class work by gifted students is often a sign of disinterest in subject matter. Gifted children may question the appropriateness of classroom activities to their needs, but will work diligently and well on topics of high interest.
- Sensitivity to the attitudes and perceptions of others may cause gifted students to fall into the perfectionism trap or to fear failure. These feelings can lead to unfinished work, procrastination, or underachievement.
- Poor group work often is the result of gifted students' feelings that they will have the burden of the group's work. Gifted students also may prefer to work alone because of feelings that their ideas will be misunderstood or unappreciated by the group.
- Bossiness in group work could be an indicator of younger students practicing their leadership abilities to find the most effective leadership style. Overbearing behavior also may stem from gifted students' desire for control in their lives and their characteristics of independence and nonconformity.
- Slow workers who are gifted may be ensuring that their work is perfect.
- Behavior problems in gifted students could be a result of boredom or the feeling that class work is too easy or beneath them.
- Being the "class clown" may be the result of the gifted student's keen sense of humor being exhibited in unacceptable ways. The behavior also might be an attempt to gain acceptance among peers who may perceive the student negatively because of his or her "gifted" label.
- Emotional outbursts or periods of withdrawal in gifted students may be due to their highly sensitive natures.

Close Observation

Given that gifted students clearly do not always exhibit classroom work, behavior, and dispositions that are "teacher friendly," how can classroom teachers make informed decisions about the children they refer for gifted education programs?

A list of pertinent questions follows. An affirmative and detailed answer to some of these questions regarding a particular student might serve as a signal to begin observing the child more closely and keeping anecdotal records to document patterns of behavior. Such activities not only aid teachers in identifying the student for assessment, but also provide valuable information on the frequency of gifted behaviors to professionals who eventually may assess the student formally for gifted education services.

- Is this student highly verbal in spoken language, written language, or both?
- Does this student use art materials either creatively or uniquely?
- Does this student offer insightful contributions to class discussions that are of interest to him or her?
- Is this student able to comprehend, synthesize, or evaluate story material in unique ways from personal readings or from teacher read-alouds?
- Does this student have unique or varied interests?
- Is this student highly passionate or excited about his or her own interests?
- Does this student have a strong sense of family or interest in family-related topics?
- Does this child get good test grades but often turns in poor class work?

Final Thoughts

This sampling of characteristics and concomitant problems points to the need for classroom teachers to heighten their awareness of issues related to gifted students in their classrooms. Keeping abreast of research and information by reading journals devoted to gifted children and gifted education is a good starting place. Becoming more reflective by asking internal "why" questions to understand the root causes of student behaviors will help teachers as they strive to provide the most meaningful education for all the students they teach.

References

Archambault, F. X., Jr., K. L. Westberg, S. W. Brown, B. W. Hallmark, C. L. Emmons, and W. Zhang. 1993. *Regular classroom practices with gifted students: Results of a national survey of classroom teachers* (Research Monograph 93102). Storrs, CT: University of Connecticut, National Research Center on the Gifted and Talented.

Ashman, A. 2000. Through another's eyes: Amanda's perspective on being gifted. *Gifted Child Today* 23(1): 50–53.

Bonner, F. A., II. 2000. African American giftedness. *Journal of Black Studies* 30(5): 643–63.

Chuska, K. R. 1989. *Gifted learners K–12: A practical guide to effective curriculum and teaching.* Bloomington, IN: National Educational Service.

Clark, B. 2002. *Growing up gifted: Developing the potential of children at home and at school,* 6th ed. Upper Saddle River, NJ: Prentice Hall.

Gagne, F. 1995. From giftedness to talent: A developmental model and its impact on the language of the field. *Roeper Review* 18(2): 103–11.

Gardner, H. 1983. *Frames of mind: The theory of multiple intelligences.* New York: Basic Books.

Hebert, T. P., and S. M. Reis. 1999. Culturally diverse high-achieving students in an urban high school. *Urban Education* 34(4): 428–57.

Morelock, M. J. 1996. On the nature of giftedness and talent: Imposing order on chaos. *Roeper Review* 19(1): 4–12.

Morgan, H. 1996. An analysis of Gardner's theory of multiple intelligence. *Roeper Review* 18(4): 263–69.

Plata, M., and W. G. Masten. 1998. Teacher ratings of Hispanic and Anglo students on a behavior rating scale. *Roeper Review* 21(2): 139–44.

Renzulli, J. S. 1978. What makes giftedness? Re-examining a definition. *Phi Delta Kappan* 60(3): 180–84, 261.

Renzulli, J. S. 2003. A conception of giftedness and its relationship to the development of social capital. In *Handbook of gifted education,* 3rd ed., ed. N. Colangelo and G. A. Davis, 75–87. Boston: Allyn & Bacon.

Robinson, G. J. 1998. Classroom practices with high achieving students: A national survey of middle school teachers. Ph.D. diss., University of Connecticut, Storrs.

Russell, D. W., D. G. Hayes, and L. B. Dockery. 1988. *My child is gifted! Now what do I do?* 2nd ed. Winston-Salem: North Carolina Association for the Gifted and Talented.

Sarouphim, K. M. 1999. Discover: A new promising alternative assessment for the identification of gifted minorities. *Gifted Child Quarterly* 43(4): 244–51.

Schwartz, W. 1997. *Strategies for identifying the talents of diverse students.* New York: ERIC Clearinghouse on Urban Education. ERIC ED 410 323.

Silverman, L. 2000. Characteristics of giftedness scale. Denver, CO: Gifted Development Center. Available at: www.gifteddevelopment.com/Articles/Characteristics_Scale.htm.

Smutny, J. F., S. Y. Walker, and E. A. Meckstroth. 1997. *Teaching young gifted children in the regular classroom: Identifying, nurturing, and challenging ages 4–9.* Minneapolis, MN: Free Spirit Publishing.

Stephens, K. R., and F. A. Karnes. 2000. State definitions for the gifted and talented revisited. *Exceptional Children* 66(2): 219–38.

Sternberg, R. J. 2003. Giftedness according to the theory of successful intelligence. In *Handbook of gifted education*, 3rd ed., ed. N. Colangelo and G. A. Davis, 55–60. Boston: Allyn & Bacon.

Tannenbaum, A. J. 2003. Nature and nurture of giftedness. In *Handbook of gifted education*, 3rd ed., ed. N. Colangelo and G. A. Davis, 45–59. Boston: Allyn & Bacon.

Tomlinson, C. A. 2004. Differentiation in diverse settings. *School Administrator* 61(7): 28–33.

Von Károlyi, C., V. Ramos-Ford, and H. Gardner. 2003. Multiple intelligences: A perspective on giftedness. In *Handbook of gifted education*, 3rd ed., ed. N. Colangelo and G. A. Davis, 100–12. Boston: Allyn & Bacon.

Webber, H., ed. 1984. *Webster's II new Riverside dictionary*. Boston: Houghton Mifflin.

Westberg, K. L., and M. E. Daoust. 2003. The results of the replication of the classroom practices survey replication in two states. *The National Research Center on the Gifted and Talented Newsletter* Fall: 3–8. Available at: www.gifted.uconn.edu/nrcgt/newsletter/fall03/fall032.html.

Whitton, D. 1997. Regular classroom practices with gifted students in grades 3 and 4 in New South Wales, Australia. *Gifted Education International* 12(1): 34–38.

Winebrenner, S. 2001. *Teaching gifted kids in the regular classroom: Strategies and techniques every teacher can use to meet the academic needs of the gifted and talented,* revised, expanded, and updated edition, ed. P. Espeland. Minneapolis, MN: Free Spirit Publishing.

SANDRA MANNING is Associate Director for The Frances A. Karnes Center for Gifted Studies at The University of Southern Mississippi. Her research interests include young gifted children and differentiating instruction for high ability students. She also holds National Board Teacher Certification.

Mélange Cities

The disruption that immigrants bring is often a benefit.

BLAIR A. RUBLE

Tensions and conflict get the headlines when peoples make contact, but historically migration is not a singular event tied always to a "crisis." Migrants of all sorts—immigrants, emigrants, refugees, displaced persons, guest workers—have become a significant presence in cities around the world. According to the UN Human Settlements Program, there are approximately 175 million official international migrants worldwide, not including those without complete documentation. Even this massive movement of people is not unprecedented. During the past 500 years, Europeans began to inhabit the rest of the world and nearly 10 million African slaves were forced to migrate to the Americas; another 48 million people left Europe for the Americas and Australia between 1800 and 1925. That is not to mention the tens of millions of people who have migrated across other national boundaries, continental divides, and oceans during the past half-century. Migration is simply part and parcel of human existence. And it has always brought fruitful encounters as well as conflict.

The transformative power of today's migration is easiest to see not in established "mélange cities" such as New York but in traditionally more insular communities such as Washington, D.C., and Montreal, which were long divided by race, language, culture, religion, ethnicity, or class. Once split along single fault lines between two core groups—whites and blacks in Washington, French-speakers and English-speakers in Montreal—these urban centers have become new mélange cities, and the evidence suggests that we should view such transformations with more hope than fear.

Montreal offers the clearest example in North America of the creative disruption wrought by new immigrants. In that city divided—and defined—for decades by conflicts between Francophones and Anglophones, a curious story appeared in the press a couple of years ago. During the depths of a typically harsh Quebec February, it was reported that Filipino and Hispanic parents were trekking with their sick children through snow-filled streets to a small apartment complex in the fringe neighborhood of St.-Laurent, where they desperately beseeched an iconlike portrait of the Virgin Mary to cure them. Abderezak Mehdi, the Muslim manager of the low-rise building, claimed to have discovered the Virgin's image in the garbage. According to Mehdi and Greek Melkite Catholic priest Michel Saydé, the Virgin shed tears of oil that could cure the ill and tormented. Michel Parent, the chancellor of the Roman Catholic archdiocese of Montreal, cautioned skepticism, noting that "while it is true that nothing is impossible for God, historically, that is not how God acts."

This small and almost comically inclusive multicultural scene of healing, which unfolded in a dreary neighborhood built at a time when Montreal was starkly divided between speakers of French and of English, captures some of the positive aspects, as well as some of the tensions, of a change that has occurred over the past three decades or so, as immigrants and their Canadian-born children have grown to number more than a quarter of the city's population.

Immigrants are not the only force for change. Montreal's growth into a sprawling metropolitan region laced by freeways that provide a new organizing structure of daily life has rendered many old cultural and geographical boundaries meaningless. The Internet is likewise no friend to the old order. But it is the newcomers, who have no stake in the city's past divisions, who have had a singular impact on its political life. The once-powerful Francophone *sovereigntiste* movement, which long pressed for the secession of the entire province of Quebec from Canada, has lost momentum in considerable measure because of opposition from immigrant groups. Those groups were an essential component of the very narrow majority that defeated the last referendum on Quebec sovereignty in 1995, 50.6 percent to 49.4 percent. Pro-sovereignty politicians have since been looking for ways to court the immigrant vote. The communally based populism that once dominated Montreal politics is giving way, slowly but surely, to a new pragmatism more suited to a world in which communities compete for investment and bond ratings.

Montreal may be further along the road to true cultural diversity than most North American cities, but its experience is hardly unique. Metropolitan Washington, D.C., another historically divided city, was the United States' fifth largest recipient of legal migrants during the 1990s, and it is beginning to experience some of the same sort of change affecting Montreal.

Twenty-first-century Washington is already dramatically different from the "Chocolate City, Vanilla Suburbs" days of the 1970s. New arrivals from El Salvador and Ukraine, Ethiopia and Vietnam, Brazil and India, and dozens of other countries, as well as other areas of the United States, have fanned out across an expanding metropolitan region that extends from Frederick, Maryland, 50 miles to the west, to the shores of the Chesapeake Bay and beyond to the east; from north of Baltimore more than 100 miles south to Fredericksburg, Virginia. The region as a whole is an incredible polyglot blend. The neighborhoods in the inner-ring Virginia suburb of South Arlington defined by zip code 22204, as well as zip code 20009 in the city's trendy Adams Morgan–Mt. Pleasant area, are each home to residents from more than 130 different countries, according to a group of Brookings Institution analysts led by Audrey Singer. Yet not very many Americans or even Washingtonians appear aware that their capital has become a mélange city.

New arrivals from El Salvador, Ukraine, Ethiopia, Vietnam, Brazil, India, and many other countries have made America's capital a mélange city.

After Congress gave up its direct oversight of the capital city and reinstated partial home rule in the 1970s, local affairs quickly came to be dominated by the polities of race. As children of the civil rights battles of the 1960s, many of Washington's first elected officials appeared to view local politics as a new version of the nation's great racial struggle, and symbolic polities took precedence over pragmatic city management. This civil rights regime began to flay as the city's financial and management problems grew, and by the time Mayor Marion Barry was arrested in 1990 on charges of smoking crack cocaine, the dream of the city's activist leadership to transform D.C. into a showcase for their values and policies had been shattered. Congress essentially placed the city in receivership by appointing a financial control board in 1995.

The collapse of local government prompted a new generation of neighborhood leaders to enter local politics, shifting attention to pragmatic concerns about city services and neighborhood quality of life—a focus that began to allow immigrants into the city's political mix even as their presence became a subject of debate. During his 2002 reelection campaign, for example, Mayor Anthony Williams stirred controversy by proposing that noncitizens should be allowed to vote in local elections. Arriving in large numbers just at the moment of municipal regime shift, immigrants helped mold a new, broader political environment in which race yielded its preeminence to more pragmatic concerns. When the first major issue of the new era emerged in 2004 in the form of a controversy over the financing of a new baseball stadium, most local observers were not prepared for the spectacle of a raging city council debate waged virtually without any reference to race.

In other new mélange cities, the story plays out in different ways. The Latinization of Denver's population and voter base has encouraged both political parties to reach out to minority voters. Once-sleepy Charlotte, North Carolina, has been transformed by, among other things, a 932 percent increase in its Hispanic population between 1980 and 2000. The country's second-largest city, Los Angeles, elected Antonio Villaraigosa in 2005 as its first Hispanic mayor since it was a village of 6,000 people, back in 1872.

Similar shifts are occurring throughout the world. In the Ukrainian capital of Kyiv, immigrants from Vietnam, China, Pakistan, and the Middle East are blunting the force of a nationwide population decline, and officials are beginning to speak of migration as a long-term answer to the country's economic and demographic decline.

Even as seemingly homogenous a society as Japan has felt the impact of immigration. Japan's shrinking population and economic uncertainty are helping to drive companies to relocate factories abroad. Japan's reputation for homogeneity is not unearned, and national policies do not encourage immigration, but local leaders in some cities have decided that the best way to keep their local economies healthy is to actively seek out migrants from abroad.

Few cities anywhere in the world have been as aggressive in pursing international migrants as Hamamatsu. A city of more than half a million located half way between Tokyo and Osaka, Hamamatsu boasts major Honda, Yamaha, and Suzuki factories. Realizing that the city would lose its economic base without new residents, municipal officials began to recruit workers from Japanese migrant communities in Brazil and Peru. The officials assumed—rather naively, it would seem to American eyes—that given their Japanese heritage, the immigrants would easily fit into local neighborhoods and workplaces. In fact, the migrants were descendants of Japanese who had left the home islands as much as a century before. They were Brazilian and Peruvian more than they were Japanese.

As a result, Hamamatsu—like Montreal, Washington, and many other mélange cities—is no longer the community it was. There are four Portuguese newspapers, four Brazilian schools and a Peruvian school, Portuguese and Spanish community centers, and numerous samba nightclubs. City hall now publishes local laws and regulations in several languages, and municipal leaders have learned to embrace Brazilian holidays as their own, often using them as launching pads for local political campaigns.

Other cities in Japan have been changing as well. Osaka, long the home of Japan's largest Korean community, publishes city documents in nearly a half-dozen languages. Sapporo and other communities on the island of Hokkaido post street signs in Russian. Tens of thousands of city residents of all ages and races turn out for Kobe's annual samba festival.

Migrants, though still few in number, have brought significant change to Japan. Some of that change is measurable and lamentable, such as increasing income inequality, rising crime rates, and enervated traditional institutions. Other changes that cannot be measured neatly may be creating opportunities for communities to escape dysfunctional institutions and patterns of life. One unexpected effect of the search by Hamamatsu and other Japanese cities for labor from abroad has been pressure from below on the traditionally hyper-centralized Japanese state to cede some central control over immigration policy.

How should we weigh the negative and positive impacts of immigration? Is all change for the worse? Heightened anxiety over international terrorism has cast suspicion on cities themselves as a social form and on migration as a social phenomenon. The impulse to withdraw into a cocoon of homogeneity increasingly undermines the acceptance of difference. The experiences of mélange cities such as Montreal, Washington, and Hamamatsu show us another course. Voluntarily or not, such cities have come to represent lively alternatives to a 21st-century metropolitan future in which everyone seeks protection from others unlike themselves. Despite the new mélange cities' obvious imperfections, their enormous intercultural vitality provides the basis for successful strategies for a 21st century in which people's movement around the world remains a fact of human existence.

BLAIR A. RUBLE is the director of the Wilson Center's Kennan Institute and its Comparative Urban Studies Program. His most recent book, *Creating Diversity Capital* (2005), examines the impact of transnational migrants on Montreal, Washington, and Kyiv.

Reprinted with permission from *The Wilson Quarterly*, Summer 2006, pp. 56–59. Copyright © 2006 by Blair A. Ruble. Reprinted by permission of the author.

Nine Powerful Practices

Nine Strategies Help Raise the Achievement of Students Living in Poverty

RUBY PAYNE

Students from families with little formal education often learn rules about how to speak, behave, and acquire knowledge that conflict with how learning happens in school. They also often come to school with less background knowledge and fewer family supports. Formal schooling, therefore, may present challenges to students living in poverty. Teachers need to recognize these challenges and help students overcome them. In my work consulting with schools that serve a large population of students living in poverty, I have found nine interventions particularly helpful in raising achievement for low-income students.

1. Build Relationships of Respect

James Comer (1995) puts it well: "No significant learning occurs without a significant relationship." Building a respectful relationship doesn't mean becoming the student's buddy. It means that teachers both insist on high-quality work and offer support. When my colleagues and I interviewed high school students in 1998 about what actions show that a teacher has respect for them, students identified the following:

- The teacher calls me by my name.
- The teacher answers my questions.
- The teacher talks to me respectfully.
- The teacher notices me and says "Hi."
- The teacher helps me when I need help.

The nonverbal signals a teacher sends are a key part of showing respect. I have found that when students feel they have been "dissed" by a teacher, they almost always point to nonverbals, rather than words, as the sign of disrespect. Nonverbal signals communicate judgment, and students can sense when a teacher's intent is to judge them rather than to offer support. Although it's hard to be conscious of nonverbal signals at times, one way to sense how you're coming across is to deeply question your intent. Your gestures and tone will likely reflect that intent.

2. Make Beginning Learning Relational

When an individual is learning something new, learning should happen in a supportive context. Teachers should help all students feel part of a collaborative culture. Intervene if you see an elementary student always playing alone at recess or a middle or high school student eating lunch alone. Assign any new student a buddy immediately and ensure that each student is involved with at least one extracurricular group at lunch or after school. Whenever possible, introduce new learning through paired assignments or cooperative groups.

3. Teach Students to Speak in Formal Register

Dutch linguist Martin Joos (1972) found that every language in the world includes five registers, or levels of formality: frozen, formal, consultative, casual, and intimate. Both school and work operate at the consultative level (which mixes formal and casual speech) and the formal level (which uses precise word choice and syntax). All people use the casual and intimate registers with friends, but students from families with little formal education may default to these registers. Researchers have found that the more generations a person lives in poverty, the less formal the register that person uses, with the exception of people from a strong religious background, who frequently encounter formal religious texts (Montana-Harmon, 1991). Hart and Risley's (1995) study of 42 families indicated that children living in families receiving welfare heard approximately 10 million words by age three, whereas children in families in which parents were classified as professional heard approximately 30 million words in the same period. Teachers conduct most tests through formal register, which puts poor students at a disadvantage. Teachers should address this issue openly and help students learn to communicate through consultative and formal registers. Some students may object that formal register is "white talk"; we tell them it's "money talk."

Have students practice translating phrases from casual into formal register. For example, a student I worked with was sent to the office because he had told his teacher that something "sucked." When I asked him to translate that phrase into formal register, he said, "There is no longer joy in this activity." Teachers should use consultative language (a mix of formal and casual) to build relationships and use formal register to teach content, providing additional explanation in consultative register.

4. Assess Each Student's Resources

One way to define poverty and wealth is in terms of the degree to which we have access to the following eight resources.

- Financial: Money to purchase goods and services.
- Emotional: The ability to control emotional responses, particularly to negative situations, without engaging in self-destructive behavior. This internal resource shows itself through stamina, perseverance, and good decision making.
- Mental: The mental abilities and acquired skills (such as reading, writing, and computing) needed for daily life.
- Spiritual: Some belief in a divine purpose and guidance.
- Physical: Good physical health and mobility.
- Support systems: Friends, family, and resource people who are available in times of need.
- Relationships and role models: Frequent contact with adults who are appropriate role models, who nurture the child, and who do not engage in self-destructive behavior.
- Knowledge of unspoken rules: Knowing the unspoken norms and habits of a group.

School success, as it's currently defined, requires a huge amount of resources that schools don't necessarily provide. Teachers need to be aware that many students identified as "at risk" lack these outside resources. Interventions that require students to draw on resources they do not possess will not work. For example, many students in households characterized by generational poverty have a very limited support system. If such a student isn't completing homework, telling that student's parent, who is working two jobs, to make sure the student does his or her homework isn't going to be effective. But if the school provides a time and place before school, after school, or during lunch for the student to complete homework, that intervention will be more successful.

5. Teach the Hidden Rules of School

People need to know different rules and behaviors to survive in different environments. The actions and attitudes that help a student learn and thrive in a low-income community often clash with those that help one get ahead in school. For example, when adult family members have little formal schooling, the student's environment may be unpredictable. Having reactive skills might be particularly important. These skills may be counterproductive in school, where a learner must plan ahead, rather than react, to succeed. If laughter is often used to lessen conflict in a student's community, that student may laugh when being disciplined. Such behavior is considered disrespectful in school and may anger teachers and administrators.

Educators often tell students that the rules they come to school with aren't valuable anywhere. That isn't true, and students know it. For example, to survive in many high-poverty neighborhoods, young people have to be able to fight physically if challenged—or have someone fight for them. But if you fight in school, you're usually told to leave.

The simple way to deal with this clash of norms is to teach students two sets of rules. I frequently say to students,

> You don't use the same set of rules in basketball that you use in football. It's the same with school and other parts of your life. The rules in school are different from the rules out of school. So let's make a list of the rules in school so we're sure we know them.

6. Monitor Progress and Plan Interventions

One teacher alone cannot address all students' achievement issues. Monitoring and intervening with at-risk kids must be a schoolwide process. Take the following steps:

- Chart student performance and disaggregate this data by subgroups and individuals.
- Keeping in mind your district's learning standards, determine which content you need to spend the most time on. Bloom (1976) found that the amount of time devoted to a content area makes a substantial difference in how well students learn that content. Set up a collaborative process for teachers to discuss learning standards and make these determinations.
- Plan to use the instructional strategies that have the highest payoff for the amount of time needed to do the activity. For example, teaching students to develop questions has a much higher payoff for achievement than completing worksheets.
- Use rubrics and benchmark tests to identify how well students are mastering standards; discuss the results.
- Identify learning gaps and choose appropriate interventions. Interventions can include scheduling extra instruction time, providing a supportive relationship, and helping students use mental models.
- Schedule these activities on the school calendar regularly.

7. Translate the Concrete into the Abstract

To succeed in school, students need to move easily from the concrete to the abstract. For example, a kindergarten teacher may hold up a real apple and tell students to find a drawing of an apple on a given page. Even though the two-dimensional apple on the page doesn't look like the real apple, students come to understand that the drawing represents the apple. In math, students need to understand that a numeral represents a specific number of items.

Teachers can help students become comfortable with the abstract representations characteristic of school by giving them *mental models*—stories, analogies, or visual representations. Mental models enable the student to make a connection between something concrete he or she understands and a representational idea. For example, in math, one can physically form a square with the number of items represented by any square number. We can teach students this concept quickly by drawing a box with nine *X*s in it. The student can visually see that 3 is the square root of 9, because no matter how the student looks at the model, there are 3 *X*s on each side.

Excellent teachers use mental models all the time, although they may not call them that. I have found that using mental models decreases the amount of time needed to teach and learn a concept.

8. Teach Students How to Ask Questions

When you have asked a student what part of a lesson he or she didn't understand, have you heard the reply, "All of it"? This response may indicate that the student has trouble formulating a specific question. Questions are a principal tool to gain access to information, and knowing how to ask questions yields a huge payoff in achievement (Marzano, 2007). In their research on reading, Palincsar and Brown (1984) found that students who couldn't ask good questions had many academic struggles.

To teach students how to ask questions, I assign pairs of students to read a text and compose multiple-choice questions about it. I give them sentence stems, such as "When _____ happened, why did _____ do _____?" Students develop questions using the stems, then come up with four answers to each question, only one of which they consider correct and one of which has to be funny.

9. Forge Relationships with Parents

Many low-income parents are so overwhelmed with surviving daily life that they can't devote time to their children's schooling. Even when time is available, the parent may not know how to support the child's learning.

It is essential to create a welcoming atmosphere at school for parents. Ask yourself these questions about the kind of experience parents have when they enter your building:

- How are parents usually greeted? With a smile, a command, a look, or the parents' names?
- What is the ratio of educators to parents in meetings? Six educators to one parent? Many parents experience such a situation as being "ganged up on." To avoid this perception, designate a person to greet the parent five minutes before the meeting starts and tell him or her who will be present and what is likely to happen. This is much better than having the parent walk into the room cold. When the meeting is over, have all the educators leave the room (and don't have another obvious consultation in the parking lot). The person who met the parent ahead of time should walk the parent out of the building, ask how he or she is feeling, and find out whether the parent has more questions.
- Is the language used in parent meetings understandable, or is it "educationese"?
- Are parents often asked to make interventions they do not have the resources to make?
- Do parents realize that people at the school care about their children? Parents want to know first whether the school cares about and respects their child. Communicate this message early in the conference. It also helps to say, "We know that you care about your child, or you wouldn't be here."

I recommend doing home visits. Arrange to have a substitute for a particular day and send a letter home to a few parents saying that because teachers always ask parents to come to school, a pair of teachers would like to come by their house, say hello, and bring a gift. The gift should be something small, such as a magnet listing the school's name, phone number, and hours. If a parent wants to have an in-depth talk about the child, schedule a time that's good for both parties to talk further. Schools that have taken this approach, such as East Alien County Schools in Fort Wayne, Indiana, have strengthened the rapport between parents and teachers and lessened discipline referrals.

The Gift of Education

Educators can be a huge gift to students living in poverty. In many instances, education is *the* tool that gives a child life choices. A teacher or administrator who establishes mutual respect, cares enough to make sure a student knows how to survive school, and gives that student the necessary skills is providing a gift that will keep affecting lives from one generation to the next. Never has it been more important to give students living in poverty this gift.

References

Bloom, B. (1976). *Human characteristics and school learning.* New York: McGraw-Hill.

Comer, J. (1995). Lecture given at Education Service Center, Region IV. Houston, TX.

Hart, B., & Risley, T. R. (1995). *Meaningful differences in the everyday experience of young American children.* Baltimore: Paul H. Brookes.

Joos, M. (1972). The styles of the five clocks. In R. D. Abrahams & R. C. Troike (Eds.), *Language and cultural diversity in American education* (pp. 145–149). Englewood Cliffs, NJ: Prentice-Hall.

Marzano, R. J. (2007). *The art and science of teaching. A comprehensive framework for effective instruction.* Alexandria, VA: ASCD.

Montana-Harmon, M. R. (1991). Discourse features of written Mexican Spanish: Current research in contrastive rhetoric and its implications. *Hispania, 74*(2), 417–425.

Palincsar, A. S., & Brown, A. L. (1984). The reciprocal teaching of comprehension-fostering and comprehension-monitoring activities. *Cognition and Instruction, 1*(2), 117–175.

RUBY PAYNE is President of aha! Process. Her most recent book is *Under-resourced Learners: Eight Strategies to Boost Student Achievement* (aha! Process, 2008); RubyPayne@msn.com.

Becoming Adept at Code-Switching

By putting away the red pen and providing structured instruction in code-switching, teachers can help urban African American students use language more effectively.

REBECCA S. WHEELER

It was September, and Joni was concerned. Her 2nd grade student Tamisha could neither read nor write; she was already a grade behind. What had happened? Joni sought out Melinda, Tamisha's 1st grade teacher. Melinda's answer stopped her in her tracks. "Tamisha? Why, you can't do *anything* with that child. Haven't you heard how she talks?" Joni pursued, "What *did* you do with her last year?" "Oh, I put her in the corner with a coloring book." Incredulous, Joni asked, "All year?" "Yes," the teacher replied.

Although extreme, Melinda's appraisal of Tamisha's performance and potential as a learner is not isolated. In standardized assessments of language acquisition, teachers routinely underrate the language knowledge and the reading and writing performance of African American students (Cazden, 2001; Ferguson, 1998; Godley, Sweetland, Wheeler, Minnici, & Carpenter, 2006; Scott & Smitherman, 1985). A typical reading readiness task asks the student to read five sentences (*The mouse runs. The cat runs. The dog runs. The man runs. Run, mouse, run!*). As Jamal reads, *Da mouse run. Da cat run. Da dog run. Da man run. Run, mouse, run,* his teacher notes 8/15 errors, placing him far below the frustration level of 3/15. She assesses Jamal as a struggling reader and puts him in a low reading group or refers him to special education.

Through a traditional language arts lens, Tamisha's 1st grade teacher saw "broken English" and a broken child. Through the same lens, Jamal's teacher heard mistakes in Standard English and diagnosed a reading deficit. These teachers' lack of linguistic background in the dialects their students speak helps explain why African American students perform below their white peers on every measure of academic achievement, from persistent over-representation in special education and remedial basic skills classes, to under-representation in honors classes, to lagging SAT scores, to low high school graduation rates (Ogbu, 2003).

Across the United States, teacher education and professional development programs fail to equip teachers to respond adequately to the needs of many African American learners. We know that today's world "demands a new way of looking at teaching that is grounded in an understanding of the role of culture and language in learning" (Villegas & Lucas, 2007, p. 29). Unfortunately, many teachers lack the linguistic training required to build on the language skills that African American students from dialectally diverse backgrounds bring to school. To fill this need, elementary educator Rachel Swords and I have developed a program for teaching Standard English to African American students in urban classrooms (Wheeler & Swords, 2006). One linguistic insight and three strategies provide a framework for responding to these students' grammar needs.

One Linguistic Insight

When African American students write *I have two sister and two brother, My Dad jeep is out of gas,* or *My mom deserve a good job,* teachers traditionally diagnose "poor English" and conclude that the students are making errors with plurality, possession, or verb agreement. In response, teachers correct the students' writing and show them the "right" grammar.

Research has amply demonstrated that such traditional correction methods fail to teach students the Standard English writing skills they need (Adger, Wolfram, & Christian, 2007). Further, research has found strong connections among teachers' negative attitudes about stigmatized dialects, lower teacher expectations for students who speak these dialects, and lower academic achievement (Godley et al., 2006; Nieto, 2000).

An insight from linguistics offers a way out of this labyrinth: Students using vernacular language are not making errors, but instead are speaking or writing correctly following the language patterns of their community (Adger el al., 2007; Green, 2002; Sweetland, 2006; Wheeler & Swords, 2006). With this insight, teachers can transform classroom practice and student learning in dialectally diverse schools.

Three Strategies

Equipped with the insight that students are following the grammar patterns of their communities, here is how a teacher can lead students through a critical-thinking process to help them understand and apply the rules of Standard English grammar.

Scientific Inquiry

As the teacher grades a set of papers, she may notice the same "error" cropping up repeatedly in her students' writing. My work in schools during the past decade has revealed more than 30 Informal English grammar patterns that appear in students' writing. Among these, the following patterns consistently emerge (see also Adger et al., 2007; Fogel & Ehri, 2000):

- Subject-verb agreement (*Mama walk the dog every day.*)
- Showing past time (*Mama walk the dog yesterday* or *I seen the movie.*)
- Possessive (*My sister friend came over.*)
- Showing plurality (*It take 24 hour to rotate.*)
- "A" versus "an" (*a elephant, an rabbit*)

A linguistically informed teacher understands that these usages are not errors, but rather grammar patterns from the community dialect transferred into student writing (Wheeler, 2005). Seeing these usages as data, the teacher assembles a set of sentences drawn from student writing, all showing the same grammar pattern, and builds a code-switching chart (see Fig. 1). She provides the Formal English equivalent of each sentence in the right-hand column. She then leads students through the following steps:

- *Examine sentences.* The teacher reads the Informal English sentences aloud.
- *Seek patterns.* Then she leads the students to discover the grammar pattern these sentences follow. She might say, "*Taylor cat is black.* Let's see how this sentence shows ownership. Who does the cat belong to?" When students answer that the cat belongs to Taylor, the teacher asks, "How do you know?" Students answer that it says *Taylor cat,* or that the word *Taylor* sits next to the word cat.
- *Define the pattern.* Now the teacher helps students define the pattern by repeating their response, putting it in context: "Oh, *Taylor* is next to *cat.* So you're saying that the owner, *Taylor,* is right next to what is owned, cat. Maybe this is the pattern for possessives in Informal English: *owner + what is owned?*" The class has thus formulated a hypothesis for how Informal English shows possession.
- *Test the hypothesis.* After the teacher reads the next sentence aloud, she asks the students to determine whether the pattern holds true. After reading *The boy coat is torn,* the teacher might ask, "Who is the owner?" The students respond that *the boy* is the owner. "What does he own?" The students say that he owns *the coat.* The teacher then summarizes what the students have discovered: "So *the boy* is the owner and *the coat* is what he owns. That follows our pattern of *owner + what is owned.*" It is important to test each sentence in this manner.
- *Write Informal English pattern.* Finally, the teacher writes the pattern, *owner + what is owned,* under the last informal sentence (Wheeler & Swords, 2006).

Possessive Patterns

Informal English	Formal English
Taylor cat is black.	Taylor's cat is black.
The boy coat is torn.	The boy's coat is torn.
A giraffe neck is long.	A giraffe's neck is long.
Did you see the teacher pen?	Did you see the teacher's pen?
The Patterns	**The Patterns**
owner + what is owned	owner + 's + what is owned
noun + noun	noun + 's + noun

Figure 1   Code-Switching Chart for Possessive Patterns.

Comparison and Contrast

Next, the teacher applies a teaching strategy that has been established as highly effective—comparison and contrast (Marzano, Pickering, & Pollock, 2001). Using *contrastive analysis,* the teacher builds on students' existing grammar knowledge. She leads students in contrasting the grammatical patterns of Informal English with the grammatical patterns of Formal English written on the right-hand side of the code-switching chart. This process builds an explicit, conscious understanding of the differences between the two language forms. The teacher leads students to explore what changed between the Informal English sentence *Taylor cat is black* and the Formal English sentence *Taylor's cat is black.* Through detailed comparison and contrast, students discover that the pattern for Formal English possessive is owner + 's + what is owned.

Code-Switching as Metacognition

After using scientific inquiry and contrastive analysis to identify the grammar patterns of Informal and Formal English, the teacher leads students in putting their knowledge to work. The class uses *metacognition,* which is knowledge about one's own thinking processes. Students learn to actively code-switch—to assess the needs of the setting (the time, place, audience, and communicative purpose) and intentionally choose the appropriate language style for that setting. When the teacher asks, "In your school writing, which one of these patterns do you think you need to use: *Owner + what is owned?* or *owner + 's + what is owned?*" students readily choose the Standard English pattern.

Because code-switching requires that students think about their own language in both formal and informal forms, it builds cognitive flexibility, a skill that plays a significant role in successful literacy learning (Cartwright, in press). Teaching students to consciously reflect on the different dialects they use and to choose the appropriate language form for a particular situation provides them with metacognitive strategies and the cognitive flexibility to apply those strategies in daily practice. With friends and family in the community, the child will choose the language of the community, which is often Informal English. In school discussions, on standardized tests, in analytic essays, and in the

ANNUAL EDITIONS

world of work, the student learns to choose the expected formal language. In this way, we add another linguistic code, Standard English, to the students language toolbox.

A Successful Literacy Tool

Research and test results have demonstrated that these techniques are highly successful in fostering the use of Standard English and boosting overall student writing performance among urban African American students at many different grade levels (Fogel & Ehri, 2000; Sweetland, 2006; Taylor, 1991). Using traditional techniques as a teacher at an urban elementary school on the Virginia peninsula, Rachel Swords saw the usual 30-point gap in test scores between her African American and white 3rd grade students. In 2002, her first year of implementing code-switching strategies, she closed the achievement gap in her classroom; on standardized state assessments, African American students did as well as white students in English and history and outperformed white students in math and science. These results have held constant in each subsequent year. In 2006, in a class that began below grade level, 100 percent of Sword's African American students passed Virginia's year-end state tests (Wheeler & Swords, 2006).

Transforming Student Learning

Fortunately, Joni knew that Tamisha was not making grammatical mistakes. Tamisha *did* know grammar—the grammar of her community. Now the task was to build on her existing knowledge to leverage new knowledge of Standard English. When Joni tutored her after school, Tamisha leapfrogged ahead in reading and writing. Despite having started a year behind, she was reading and writing on grade level by June. How did she achieve such progress? Her teacher possessed the insights and strategies to foster Standard English mastery among dialectally diverse students. Even more important, Joni knew that her student did not suffer a language deficit. She was able to see Tamisha for the bright, capable child she was.

Using *contrastive analysis*, the teacher builds on students' existing grammar knowledge.

Joni has laid down the red pen and adopted a far more effective approach, teaching students to reflect on their language using the skills of scientific inquiry, contrastive analysis, and code-switching. We have the tools to positively transform the teaching and learning of language arts in dialectally diverse classrooms. Isn't it time we did?

References

Adger, C. T., Wolfram, W., & Christian, D. (Eds.). (2007). *Dialects in schools and communities.* Mahwah, NJ: Erlbaum.

Cartwright, K. B. (in press). *Literacy processes: Cognitive flexibility in learning and teaching.* New York: Guilford Press.

Cazden, C. B. (2001). *Classroom discourse: The language of teaching and learning* (2nd ed.). Portsmouth, NH: Heinemann.

Ferguson, R. F. (1998). Teachers' perceptions and expectations and the black-white test score gap. In C. Jencks & M. Phillips (Eds.), *The black-white test score gap* (pp. 273–317). Washington, DC: Brookings Institution.

Fogel, H., & Ehri, L. (2000). Teaching elementary students who speak Black English vernacular to write in Standard English: Effects of dialect transformation practice. *Contemporary Educational Psychology, 25,* 212–35.

Godley, A., Sweetland, J., Wheeler, S., Minnici, A., & Carpenter, B. (2006). Preparing teachers for dialectally diverse classrooms. *Educational Researcher, 35*(8), 30–37.

Green, L. (2002). *African American English: A linguistic introduction.* Cambridge, UK: Cambridge University Press.

Marzano, R., Pickering, D., & Pollock, J. (2001). *Classroom instruction that works: Research-based strategies for increasing student achievement.* Alexandria, VA: ASCD.

Nieto, S. (2000). *Affirming diversity: The sociopolitical context of multicultural education* (3rd ed.). White Plains, NY: Longman.

Ogbu, J. (2003). *Black American students in an affluent suburb: A study of academic disengagement.* Mahwah, NJ: Erlbaum.

Scott, J. C., & Smitherman, G. (1985). Language attitudes and self-fulfilling prophecies in the elementary school. In S. Greenbaum (Ed.), *The English language today* (pp. 302–314). Oxford, UK: Pergamon.

Sweetland, J. (2006). *Teaching writing in the African American classroom: A sociolinguistic approach.* Unpublished doctoral dissertation, Stanford University.

Taylor, H. U. (1991). *Standard English, Black English, and bidialectalism: A controversy.* New York: Lang.

Villegas, A. M., & Lucas, T. (2007). The culturally responsive teacher. *Educational Leadership, 64*(6), 28–33.

Wheeler, R. (2005). Code-switch to teach Standard English. *English Journal, 94*(5), 108–112.

Wheeler, R., & Swords, R. (2006). *Code-switching. Teaching Standard English in urban classrooms.* Urbana, IL: National Council of Teachers of English.

REBECCA S. WHEELER is Associate Professor of English Language and Literacy, Department of English, Christopher Newport University, Newport News, Virginia; rwheeler@cnu.edu.

Author's note—Kelly B. Cartwright, Associate Professor of Psychology, Christopher Newport University, crafted the section "Code-Switching as Metacognition."

Boys and Girls Together
A Case for Creating Gender-Friendly Middle School Classrooms

DAVID KOMMER

Are Boys and Girls Really Different?

Close your eyes and picture an average grade school class. Watch the boys and girls as they learn, interact, and deal with problems. Do they look alike in your mind's eye? Do they learn the same way? Do they interact with you and with one another similarly? Do they solve problems—both relationship and academic—in the same ways? Not likely. No, there appears to be a very real difference between boys and girls.

What is the nature of that difference, and from where does it come? Moreover, if there is such a striking difference, are there things we should be doing in the classroom to accommodate for these differences? These are all significant questions that might affect the academic growth of our students.

As young people move into adolescence, they begin to explore gender roles. Finding their way through this potential minefield is complicated and challenging for middle school students. The process of determining the variations in masculinity and femininity is largely a social function, not a biological one (Rice and Dolgin 2002). What it means to be a man, and what it means to be a woman, are communicated to children by all the adults in a child's life, including teachers.

"Peers may play a particularly important role in the development of children's gender identities" (Rice and Dolgin 2002, 195). Boys and girls create very distinct cultures; when they are in same-gender groups they act and play very differently. Girls are talkative and cooperative, boys are competitive and physical (Rice and Dolgin). Teachers need to understand these differences and be purposeful in the treatment of each so as to send the healthiest messages to adolescents.

Looking closely at middle schools, two questions surface: Are boys and girls treated differently from one another? *should* boys and girls be treated differently?

In 1992, the American Association of University Women (AAUW) published a groundbreaking study about how schools were not meeting the needs of young girls. Their schools short-changed girls in many ways: when questioned in class, girls were less likely to receive a prompt to clarify thinking if they answered incorrectly; boys were more regularly called on, and if not, they were just as likely to shout out an answer, leaving girls to sit quietly; and girls were not encouraged to take advanced math and science classes (AAUW 1992). Perhaps not surprisingly, then, in their middle school years, girls stopped being successful in math and science.

A large concern that must be addressed by middle level educators is the decrease in confidence that girls experience throughout middle school. One recent study shows that just prior to their entry into pre-adolescence, 60 percent of girls had positive feelings about themselves and their ability. Only 29 percent of high school girls felt the same confidence. (This compares with 67 percent of young boys feeling confident, and 46 percent of high school-aged boys having the same confidence.) Confidence fell during middle school (Santrock 2001). I am not suggesting that there is something toxic about middle school, but I am suggesting that while students are on our watch, we can and must do better.

The AAUW (1992) study focused our attention on the issue of educational equity. It was difficult to argue with the findings, and teachers all over the country began to reevaluate their teaching in light of the study. Several years later, the AAUW found that significant progress was made, as evidenced by gains in girls' success in math and science (AAUW 1998). Nevertheless, the story is not yet finished, for it appears now the boys were also often the victims of our educational system. Consider the following gender questions:

1. Who is more likely to drop out of high school?
2. Who is more likely to be sent to the principal's office for a disciplinary referral?
3. Who is more likely to be suspended or expelled?
4. Who is more likely to be identified as a student needing special education?
5. Who is more likely to need reading intervention?

The answer to all of the above questions is "boys" (Taylor and Lorimer 2003). Clearly, the educational system is discouraging some of them. However, even that conclusion is too simple;

ot a problem that can be solved with a quick fix. Looking again at the questions above, you might also add, "Not all oys are being discouraged/exhibiting behavior problems." And you would be correct: some girls also show these behaviors and problems. The evidence seems to show that, although there are differences in general, it is not possible to put all the boys on one side and all the girls on the other. In fact, there seems to be some type of spectrum with "maleness" on one end and "femaleness" on the other. Everyone exists somewhere in the spectrum, and generally boys cluster toward one end, and girls toward the other. This also has ramifications for classrooms. But perhaps there is an effective way to address gender differences.

So what do we do? The first thing is to become aware of the differences between genders. Once these differences are explained and accepted, educators must be proactive in the way boys and girls are treated in schools. This is not a call for separate schools, for we do not live in a gender-segregated world. Indeed, there are distinct advantages to educating boys and girls together appropriately, for in doing so, each gender will begin to see how the other thinks, feels, responds, and reacts. Such understanding is in itself a major goal for gender-friendly classrooms.

We should also consider the nature of the differences between boys and girls. The question of nature versus nurture is always an intriguing one, but is similarly enigmatic as the one about the chicken and the egg. Most psychologists agree that gender differences may be a function of biological forces, but that they are also shaped by the environments in which our children grow up (Rice and Dolgin 2002). When studying this it is helpful to observe some of the factors and looking more closely at each.

Brain Theory

As you scan the room in which students are supposed to be reading silently, you see that most of the girls are engaged with their books. Because the reading is student selected, the girls have chosen the books that focus on relationships. The boys seem to be more easily distractible and are not, as a rule, focusing their full attention on the text. Some read for a while, then gaze about the room. If they are reading, they are more likely to have selected action books or sports magazines.

Boys and girls have slightly different brain chemistry that may cause each to think differently. While not yet conclusive, research has uncovered many intriguing possibilities that might provide some explanations.

In addition to having slightly different chemistry, the structure of the male and female brain is actually different (Gurian 2001; Sax 2005; Sousa 2001). As most of us have learned, girls mature more quickly than boys, but what does this mean exactly? Gurian suggests that as the individual grows there is an increase in myelin, a coating that transmits electrical impulses through the nervous system. This accumulating coat of myelin occurs earlier in females.

The most striking difference, Gurian and others suggest, is the system of nerves, the corpus callosum, which connect the right and left hemispheres of the brain. In females this structure is, on average, 20 percent larger than it is in males (Gurian, 2001; Sousa 2001; Walsh 2004). Is this why females seem to be able to use both sides of the brain in processing information and are able to multitask more efficiently than males?

Studies on boys and girls also point out some interesting differences in both hearing and seeing (Sax 2005). Studies reported by Sax indicate that girls hear at different levels—in effect, better—than boys. Other studies show that girls are able to read facial expressions more astutely than boys, and this difference is related to a different chemistry in the eye and corresponding receptor in the brain (Sax).

Girls "tend to take in more sensory data than boys" (Gurian 2001, 27). Boys are more likely to engage in physically risky behaviors as a result. Although the effects of testosterone on the adolescent brain spark some controversy, there seems to be wide acceptance of the fact that testosterone leads males into more aggressive and risky actions than estrogen does with girls (Walsh 2004). "Girls and boys assess risk differently, and they differ in their likelihood of engaging in risky behaviors" (Sax 2005, 41). Might there be ramifications for this in the classroom? You bet. Walsh suggests that the initial burst of hormones that come earlier for girls gives their brains a head start in developing the prefrontal cortex, or rational part or the brain. This allows girls to engage in more complex rational thought than boys. By the end of adolescence, boys have caught up with girls.

Girls tend to be less hemisphere dominant than boys, who seem to be largely right hemisphere dominant. As a result, boys are better at spatial tasks, which gives them an advantage in areas such as mathematics, graphs, and maps. Girls seem to use both sides of the brain and tend to be better at literacy-related activities (Gurian and Stevens 2004; Sax 2005).

In addition to the structural differences, there may be differences caused by the hormones that each gender receives. While this is somewhat more controversial, there is some evidence that the progesterone that girls receive is a bonding hormone, and the testosterone of boys is much more aggressive (Gurian 2001; Sax 2005). It appears that boys receive about a half-dozen spikes of testosterone each day: these spikes may result in boys becoming more anxious, moody, and even aggressive. Estrogen and progesterone, the female hormones, rise and fall throughout the female cycle. Girls experience an increase in mood swings, as well, but they tend to be spread over time rather than the intense change that boys experience. Interestingly, there is evidence that during these hormone infusions in girls, they actually have an increased academic upsurge (Gurian 2001). In short, they are smarter during this peak.

There are many more aspects to this emerging information on brain development and function. However, it should also be noted that although much of what we are learning about the brain is intriguing and may offer keys to helping both genders become more academically successful, perhaps there are other reasons that boys and girls are different.

Social Differences

As the school day begins, students are all congregated in class. They are not really moving to their workplaces as you would like, but are engaged with each other, seemingly oblivious to the fact that you have an educational agenda ready. So what is their agenda, you wonder? The girls all seem to be huddled in groups whispering and looking about to see who might be paying attention to them. The boys are much more physically active as four boys play a game of trying to slap the other's hand before the other moves it away. Others are playing "basketball" with clean sheets of paper rolled up and tossed at the wastebasket.

Perhaps the issue does not lie in nature, but in nurture—that is, in the way we socialize our young people. "Society prescribes how a male ought to look and behave, what type of personality he ought to have, and what roles he should perform" (Rice and Dolgin, 2002, 193). Girls receive these messages equally as strongly. All adolescents receive messages from adults as they grow; from teachers who encourage and discourage in word and deed; from signals sent by peers; and from the media that also contribute to their developing gender identification.

Boys seem to present the most problems in the academic setting. They often are detached from the learning objective and would prefer to goof off—or so it seems. Why do boys seem ready to respond to any problem by either silence or lashing out? In *Raising Cain: Protecting the Emotional Lives of Boys*, Kindlon and Thompson (2000) argue that boys have been miseducated. Boys get very conflicting messages from everyone: parents, peers, teachers, coaches, and the media. Boys do, in fact, feel they are told not to show emotions; they are told, "Big boys don't cry." And when they hurt, they are told to walk it off. Boys receive strong messages that they must be in control and that any show of emotion is unacceptable, with the result that boys are trying to put their feelings someplace where they will not be betrayed by their own emotions.

What we are beginning to see is that boys, like girls, have many of the same feelings of inadequacy. Boys, however, seem ill-prepared to deal with these feelings, and often, the response from those who might guide them is that boys should "suck it up." Pollack refers to this as "boy code" which society teaches all young males as they grow up (1998). Indeed, the feeling that boys can handle the slings and arrows of adolescence with resilience and fortitude is a myth that has come to hurt boys. Given both lack of an emotional vocabulary and permission to deal with their feelings, boys have difficulty understanding and controlling their emotions. The result is that we see both stoic and self-destructive behaviors (Kindlon and Thompson 2001; Pollack).

Girls also encounter a constant stream of messages, ones that have a strong influence on the way they succeed in school, deal with others, and feel about themselves as people of worth. As educators we must be mindful of these messages and head off the negative ones as much as we can.

In *Reviving Ophelia: Saving the Selves of Adolescent Girls*, Pipher (1994) relates how young girls have an almost effervescent quality and a feeling that they can do anything. Somewhere in early adolescence this buoyancy begins to erode. Is it the demands that girls begin to fit into the roles our society has carved for them that extinguishes that exuberance? Those demands are powerful influences.

Girls begin to judge themselves relative to how they are perceived by the opposite gender. In the attempt to become what they feel others expect them to be, girls quickly lose their own. They hide their true selves to their friends and family (Pipher 1994; Powell 2004). Girls are "sugar and spice and everything nice." But during adolescence, this message is lost in a bewildering array of swirling images. They must "[b]e beautiful, but beauty is only skin deep. Be sexy, but not sexual. Be honest, but don't hurt anyone's feelings. Be independent, but be nice. Be smart, but not so smart that you threaten boys" (Pipher, 35–36).

Most girls like being at school, but there is strong evidence that, as a social institution, schools can damage girls at the same time that they educate them (Sax 2005). One reason might be that girls recognize that schools can be male oriented and male dominated; the books they read are most frequently written by men; they know the hierarchy of the school district is dominated by men; science classes frequently focus on male achievements; and math is presented as a male domain. Although our schools are becoming more aware of the sexist nature of education, there is still a great deal to do (AAUW 1998; Pipher 1994).

As a social institution, schools can do a great deal to educate both boys and girls about the messages they receive every day. For example, media literacy should be taught in all schools, so the culture of appearance is laid bare for all to see. Also, sexual harassment must be eliminated from school hallways and classrooms. Teachers need to be trained in gender issues so they can recognize the features that are detrimental to boys, girls, or both genders.

Making Classrooms Appropriate for Both Genders

The students are all in groups and they have projects each group has selected. You have carefully arranged the groups to allow for as much diversity as you can, and you told the students that is why they are placed that way. Within each project are a number of tasks which use several multiple intelligence strategies and learning preferences. It is your hope that each student can contribute to this project using his or her strength.

The goal is not to treat boys and girls equally, but to create equity by purposefully addressing the particular needs of each gender. If you believe that education causes the brain to develop and change, then there are things we can do to offset the gender influences whether they are biological or sociological

(Sousa 2001). In the process, we can encourage students to develop more sensitivity and greater academic character than we are currently seeing. Our goal is not to try to make boys and girls the same; we tried that several decades ago. We might have more success if we teach boys and girls to respond to each other as people (Santock 2001).

Creating a gender-friendly classroom does not mean that you create gender-specific activities, divide your classroom, or even insist on single-sex classes. Remembering that everyone lives in a bigendered world makes it necessary to teach your students ways to be successful in that world. Students should at some times have an opportunity to work in a gender-matched activity, while at other times they should learn to function in a more typical gender-mismatched one. This allows students to experience instructional times that are more comfortable for students when the activities are matched to their nature. But they also learn to function outside that comfort area when they are in a mismatched situation, and thus strengthen weaker areas.

For teachers the imperative is to learn about the differences in gender. Teachers need to accept that learning occurs differently for each gender, and to measure out activities and experiences that favor one some of the time, and the other some of the time. Keep in mind that although some girls may be more linguistically advanced than boys, some boys are just as advanced, although some boys manipulate objects well and see patterns better than girls, some girls are headed toward engineering school. So, to teach only one way for each gender would do a disservice to the boys and girls who do not fit the stereotype.

When teachers plan learning experiences that favor one gender, they are also doing a great thing for the other. For as boys see girls appropriately modeling relationship behaviors, the boys learn how to be more sensitive and open. Likewise, when girls see the appropriate use of assertiveness that boys learn early, the girls see that this can be used to their advantage as well.

Students appreciate knowing the reasons for classroom activities. Teach them the differences between genders and explain why you teach things a certain way (Casky and Ruben 2003). It has amazed me over the last several decades as we learn more about the brain how much we keep from our students. Teachers understand Bloom's Taxonomy, Gardner's Multiple Intelligences, and other theories, but do not let the students in on the secret. Teaching young adolescents about the brain and brain chemistry helps them through these confusing times.

Keep the parents of your students in the information loop as well. By educating them about these differences, they can support your activities at home. This entire concept would make a great parent education evening sponsored by a team.

Begin exploring various gender-friendly strategies in your classrooms. Maintain a balance between competitive and cooperative activities, use gender as a consideration when you regroup, provide movement and energy release activities, build in character education lessons, call on students equally, be aware that some content may be intimidating to one gender or the other, use graphic organizers, provide effective notetaking strategies, provide gender role models, teach students how to be media literate, and provide a positive environment that is gender neutral—these are all ways to make your classroom gender friendly.

Conclusion

In the past decade or so, much progress has been made in understanding the human brain, both physiologically and environmentally. We are now beginning to see that there may even be gender implications in the way the brain receives and uses information. These differences have implications for teachers striving to make learning more effective and efficient for students.

Whether the differences are genetic, or social, or both is not as important to us as the fact that boys and girls do learn in different ways. The quest is not to create classrooms that focus on one or the other gender. Instead, it is to purposefully structure our classroom so that some activities favor one gender's learning style and some favor the other's. Specifically, it is critical that teachers know the differences and structure the learning environment so that the students work sometimes reinforces individuals' stronger area, and sometimes strengthens a weaker one.

We can use this new and exciting information to make students more academically successful and to make classrooms more gender-friendly.

References

AAUW. 1992. *How schools shortchange girls*. New York: American Association of University Women.

_____. 1998. *Gender gaps: Where schools still fail our children*. New York: American Association of University Women.

Caskey, M. M., and B. Ruben. (2003). Awakening adolescent brains. *Middle Matters* 12 (1): 4–5.

Gurian, M. 2001. *Boys and girls learn differently! A guide for teachers and parents*. San Francisco: Jossey-Bass.

Gurian, M., and A. C. Ballew. 2003. *The boys and girls learn differently action guide for teachers*. San Francisco: Jossey-Bass.

Gurian, M., and K. Stevens. 2004. With boys and girls in mind. *Educational Leadership* (62)3:21–26.

Kindlon, D., and M. Thompson. 2000. *Raising Cain: Protecting the emotional life of boys*. New York: Ballantine.

Pipher, M. 1994. *Reviving Ophelia: Saving the selves of adolescent girls*. New York: Ballantine.

Pollack, W. 1998. *Real boys: Rescuing our sons from the myths of boyhood*. New York: Random House.

Powell, K. C. 2004. Developmental psychology of adolescent girls: Conflicts and identity issues. *Education* 125 (1):77–87.

Rice, F. P., and K. G. Dolgin. 2002. *The adolescent: Development, relationships and culture*. 10th ed. Boston: Allyn and Bacon.

Santrock, J. W. 2001. *Adolescence*. 8th ed. Boston. McGraw-Hill.

Sax, L. 2005. *Why gender matters: What parents and teachers need to know about the emerging science of sex differences*. New York: Doubleday.

Sousa, D. A. 2001. *How the brain learns*. 2nd ed. Thousand Oaks, CA: Corwin Press.

Taylor, D., and M. Lorimer. 2003. Helping boys succeed: Which research-based strategies curb negative trends now facing boys? *Educational Leadership* 60 (4):68–70.

Walsh, D. 2004. *Why do they act that way?* New York: Free Press.

DAVID KOMMER is an associate professor at Ashland University.

From *The Clearing House,* July/August 2006, pp. 247–251. Reprinted by permission of the Helen Dwight Reid Educational Foundation. Published by Heldref Publications, 1319 Eighteenth St., NW, Washington, DC 20036-1802. Copyright © 2006. www.heldref.org

UNIT 4
Learning and Instruction

Unit Selections

Key Points to Consider

- What are some of the principles for effective teaching that derive from constructivist and social psychological theories of learning?

- How would you go about adapting your instructional methods to teach students who are culturally and linguistically diverse?

- What is "critical thinking?" How does it differ from other types of thinking? Why is it important to encourage students to think critically?

- What teaching strategies can you use to promote student engagement in the classroom?

- If you wanted to create a constructivist classroom in the subject area and/or grade in which you want to teach, what would the classroom look like? What would you emphasize and how would your actions reflect constructivist principles and research on intelligence?

- How would technology be used in an effective manner with constructivist approaches?

- What are some specific ways you could differentiate content and learning experiences in your classroom to meet the needs of all students?

- How would you utilize students' errors or mistakes as positive learning experiences that offer them an opportunity to develop a deeper understanding of the content?

Student Web Site
www.mhcls.com

Internet References

The Critical Thinking Community
http://criticalthinking.org
Education Week on the Web
http://www.edweek.org
Online Internet Institute
http://www.oii.org
Teachers Helping Teachers
http://www.pacificnet.net/~mandel/
The Teachers' Network
http://www.teachers.net/

Although there are many theories of how people learn, learning can be broadly defined as a relatively permanent change in behavior or thinking due to experience. Learning is not a result of change due to maturation or temporary influences. Changes in behavior and thinking of students result from complex interactions between their individual characteristics and environmental factors. A continuing challenge in education is understanding these interactions so that learning can be enhanced. This unit focuses on ways of viewing a variety of processes related to learning and instructional strategies that can be supportive to a broad range of learner needs. Each article emphasizes a different set of personal and environmental factors that influence students, with a common theme that learning is an active process requiring students to construct meaning from their interactions with their environment. The articles in this section reflect a recent emphasis on research-based strategies that have been applied in schools to improve learning.

Until recently, behaviorism was the best-known theory of learning. Most practicing and prospective teachers are familiar

with concepts such as classical conditioning, reinforcement and punishment, and there is no question that behaviorism has made significant contributions to our understanding of human learning. More recently, educational psychologists have focused on constructivist and social psychological theories to explain how students learn.

According to constructivists, it is important for students to actively create their own understanding and reorganize existing knowledge to incorporate this new knowledge. This emphasizes the importance of providing students with meaningful, authentic contexts so students develop understandings that allow them to connect their learning to real-world applications and existing knowledge. Social psychology is the study of the nature of interpersonal relationships in social situations. Social psychological theories emphasize the affective, social, moral, and personal learning of students. Both constructivist and social psychological theories highlight the importance of social context of learning environments and the need for students to interact with others in order for learning to occur.

The section begins with an article that focus on improving learning for groups of diverse learners. The first article discusses the importance of differentiating instruction for middle school students in ways that support student autonomy and choice while working within the developmental needs of this age group.

Cognitive psychologists and researchers are continually expanding our knowledge of how the brain works, as well as our understanding of complex cognitive processes. Both areas focus on important procedures related to how we receive, process, and store information, as well as access information for later use that are essential for all learning. Psychologists and educators alike acknowledge that critical thinking and metacognition are cognitive skills essential to student learning. Article 17 argues that critical thinking needs to be viewed as a type of thought that is domain specific rather than a set of skills, which explains why it can be so difficult to teach students. In article 18, the authors suggest integrating technology in the classroom using principles of constructivist theory and as a metacognitive tool to enhance learning.

Finally, both social-psychological and constructivist approaches emphasize the important roles of self-efficacy and self-regulation to student learning. The last article in this section provides a framework based on research in these two areas to assist and promote growth with struggling learners that would be beneficial for all students.

Instructional strategies are teacher behaviors and methods of conveying information that affect learning. Teaching methods or techniques can vary greatly, depending on objectives, group size, types of students, and personality of the teacher. For example, discussion classes are generally more effective for enhancing thinking skills than are individualized sessions or lectures. In addition, constructivist approaches to instruction such as problem- or project-based learning have gained popularity, particularly in math and science. For the final subsection,

six articles have been selected that help illustrate how teachers can apply principles of educational psychology to their classrooms. In the first article, a framework is presented for teachers to evaluate instruction and assess student learning as a means of fostering deep, as opposed to surface, learning. The second article highlights how teachers can improve their verbal questioning of students during instruction to support effective higher level thinking. The fourth article in this section summarizes the collaborative efforts of a high school teacher and university researcher to implement a design-based learning unit in science.

Student engagement is perhaps one of the more important concepts that is essential for student learning. Successful teachers implement instructional strategies that actively engage students in a variety of ways. In the fourth article in this unit, the authors identify a number of strategies that can be utilized to foster student engagement; and although they target elementary students, much of what they present can be used by teachers at any grade level. With the ever increasing diversity of our student population, teachers are presented with the challenge of meeting the unique learning needs of all students. The fifth article in this section provides an overview of strategies that can be implemented to assist teachers in differentiating instruction for all students. In contrast to the article in the previous section, this article focuses on grouping and assessment practices that can allow teachers to be flexible with regard to both content and learning styles of their students.

The final article in this section, "What's Right about Looking at What's Wrong" focuses on how teachers can use student mistakes to improve learning and reasoning skills in mathematics. The focus of the article, having students examine their mistakes in depth in order to develop a greater understanding, is well-documented in both learning and motivational research and can be applied universally across all content areas.

Differentiating for Tweens

Teaching tweens requires special skills—and the willingness to do whatever it takes to ensure student success.

RICK WORMELI

Effective instruction for 12-year-olds looks different from effective instruction for 8-year-olds or 17-year-olds. Combine the developmental needs of typical tweens and the wildly varying needs of individuals within this age group, and you can see that flourishing as a middle-grades teacher requires special skills.

It's not as overwhelming as it sounds, however. There are some commonsense basics that serve students well. The five strategies described here revolve around the principles of differentiated instruction, which does not always involve individualized instruction. Teachers who differentiate instruction simply do what's fair and developmentally appropriate for students when the "regular" instruction doesn't meet their needs.

Strategy 1: Teach to Developmental Needs

Reports from the Carnegie Corporation (Jackson & Davis, 2000) and the National Middle School Association (2003), as well as the expertise of veteran middle school teachers, point to seven conditions that young adolescents crave: competence and achievement; opportunities for self-definition; creative expression; physical activity; positive social interactions with adults and peers; structure and clear limits; and meaningful participation in family, school, and community. No matter how creatively we teach—and no matter how earnestly we engage in differentiated instruction, authentic assessment, and character education—the effects will be significantly muted if we don't create an environment that responds to students' developmental needs. Different students will require different degrees of attention regarding each of these factors.

Integrating developmental needs into tweens' learning is nonnegotiable.

Take tweens' need for physical movement. It's not enough for tweens to move between classes every 50 minutes (or every 80 minutes on a block schedule). Effective tween instruction incorporates movement every 10 to 15 minutes. So we ask all students to get up and walk across the room to turn in their papers, not just have one student collect the papers while the rest of them sit passively. We let students process information physically from time to time: for example, by using the ceiling as a massive organizer matrix and asking students to hold cards with information for each matrix cell and stand under the proper location as indicated on the ceiling. We use flexible grouping, which allows students to move about the room to work with different partners.

Every topic in the curriculum can be turned into a physical experience, even if it's very abstract. We can do this for some or all of our students as needed. We can use simulations, manipulatives, body statues (frozen tableau), and finger plays to portray irony, metabolism, chromatic scale, republics, qualitative analysis, grammar, and multiplying binomials (Glynn, 2001; Wormeli, 2005). These aren't "fluff" activities; they result in real learning for this age group.

To address students' need for self-definition, we give them choices in school projects. We help students identify consequences for the academic and personal decisions they make. We also teach students about their own learning styles. We put students in positions of responsibility in our schools and communities that allow them to make positive contributions and earn recognition for doing so. We provide clear rules and enforce them calmly—even if it's the umpteenth time that day that we've needed to enforce the same rule—to help students learn to function as members of a civilized society.

Integrating developmental needs into tweens' learning is nonnegotiable. It's not something teachers do only if we have time in the schedule; it's vital to tween success. As teachers of this age group, we need to apply our adolescent development expertise in every interaction. If we don't, the lesson will fall flat and even worse, students will wither.

Strategy 2: Treat Academic Struggle as Strength

Young adolescents readily identify differences and similarities among themselves, and in their efforts to belong to particular groups, they can be judgmental about classmates' learning styles or progress (Jackson & Davis, 2000). At this junction, then, it's important to show students that not everyone starts at the same point along the learning continuum or learns in the same way. Some classmates learn content by drawing it, others by writing about it, and still others by discussing it—and even the best students are beginners in some things.

Unfortunately, students in nondifferentiated classes often view cultural and academic differences as signs of weakness and inferiority. Good students in these classes often try to protect their reputations as being the kids who always get the problems right or finish first. They rarely take chances and stretch themselves for fear of faltering in front of others. This approach to learning rarely leads to success in high school and beyond.

Educators of tweens need to make academic struggle virtuous. So we model asking difficult questions to which we don't know the answers, and we publicly demonstrate our journey to answer those questions. We affirm positive risk taking in homework as well as the knowledge gained through science experiments that fail. We push students to explore their undeveloped skills without fear of grade repercussions, and we frequently help students see the growth they've made over time.

In one of my classes, Jared was presenting an oral report on Aristotle's rhetorical triangle (*ethos, pathos, logos*), and he was floundering. Embarrassed because he kept forgetting his memorized speech, he begged me to let him take an *F* and sit down. Instead, I asked Jared to take a few deep breaths and try again. He did, but again, he bombed. I explained that an oral report is not just about delivering information; it's also about taking risks and developing confidence. "We're all beginners at one point, Jared," I explained:

> This is your time to be a beginner. The worst that can happen is that you learn from the experience and have to do it again. That's not too bad.

After his classmates offered encouraging comments, Jared tried a third time and got a little farther before stopping his speech. I suggested that he repeat the presentation in short segments, resting between each one. He tried it, and it worked. After Jared finished, he moved to take his seat, but I stopped him and asked him to repeat the entire presentation, this time without rests.

As his classmates grinned and nodded, Jared returned to the front of the room. This time, he made it through his presentation without a mistake. His classmates applauded. Jared bowed, smiled, and took his seat. His eyes watered a bit when he looked at me. Adrenalin can do that to a guy, but I hoped it was more. Everyone learned a lot about tenacity that day, and Jared took his first steps toward greater confidence (Wormeli, 1999).

Strategy 3: Provide Multiple Pathways to Standards

Differentiation requires us to invite individual students to acquire, process, and demonstrate knowledge in ways different from the majority of the class if that's what they need to become proficient. When we embrace this approach, we give more than one example and suggest more than one strategy. We teach students eight different ways to take notes, not just one, and then help them decide when to use each technique. We let students use wide- or college-ruled paper, and we guide them in choosing multiple single-subject folders or one large binder for all subjects—whichever works best for them.

We don't limit students' exposure to sophisticated thinking because they have not yet mastered the basics. Tweens are capable of understanding how to solve for a variable or graph an inequality even if they struggle with the negative/positive signs when multiplying integers. We can teach a global lesson on a sophisticated concept for 15 minutes, and then allow students to process the information in groups tiered for different levels of readiness—or we can present an anchor activity for the whole class to do while we pull out subgroups for minilessons on the basics or on advanced material. Our goal is to respond to the unique students in front of us as we make learning coherent for all.

In the area of assessment, we should never let the test format get in the way of a student's ability to reveal what he or she knows and is able to do. For example, if an assessment on Ben Mikaelsen's novel *Touching Spirit Bear* (Harper Trophy, 2002) required students to create a poster showing the development of characters in the story, it would necessarily assess artistic skill in addition to assessing the students' understanding of the novel. Students with poor artistic skills would be unable to reveal the full extent of what they know. Consequently, we allow students to select alternative assessments through which they can more accurately portray their mastery.

In differentiated classes, grading focuses on clear and consistent evidence of mastery, not on the medium through which the student demonstrates that mastery. For example, we may give students five different choices for showing what they know about the rise of democracy: writing a report, designing a Web site, building a library display, transcribing a "live" interview with a historical figure, or creating a series of podcasts simulating a discussion between John Locke and Thomas Jefferson about where governments get their authority. We can grade all the projects using a common scoring rubric that contains the universal standards for which we're holding students accountable.

Every topic in the curriculum can be turned into a physical experience.

Of course, if the test format *is* the assessment, we don't allow students to opt for something else. For example, when we ask students to write a well-crafted persuasive essay, they can't

The Day I was Caught Plagiarizing

Young adolescents are still learning what is moral and how to act responsibly. I decided to help them along.

One day, I shared a part of an education magazine column with my 7th grade students. I told them that I wrote it and was seeking their critique before submitting it for publishing. In reality, the material I shared was an excerpt from a book written by someone else. I was hiding the book behind a notebook from which I read.

A parent coconspirator was in the classroom for the period, pretending to observe the lesson. While I read the piece that I claimed as my own, the parent acted increasingly uncomfortable. Finally, she interrupted me and said that she just couldn't let me go on. She had read the exact ideas that I claimed as my own in another book. I assured her that she was confused, and I continued.

She interrupted me again, this time angrily. She said she was not confused and named the book from which I was reading, having earlier received the information from me in our pre-class set-up. At this point, I let myself appear more anxious about her words. Her concern grew, and she persisted in her comments until I finally admitted that I hadn't written the material. Acting ashamed, I revealed the book to the class. The kids' mouths opened, some in confused grins, some greatly concerned, not knowing what to believe.

The parent let me have it then. She reminded me that I was in a position of trust as a teacher—how dare I break that trust! She said that I was being a terrible role model and that my students would never again trust my writings or teaching. She declared that this was a breach of professional conduct and that my principal would be informed. Throughout all of this, I countered her points with the excuses that students often make when caught plagiarizing: It's only a small part. The rest of the writing is original; what does it matter that this one part was written by someone else? I've never done it before, and I'm not ever going to do it again, so it's not that bad.

The students' faces dissolved into disbelief, some into anger. Students vicariously experienced the uncomfortable feeling of being trapped in a lie and having one's reputation impugned. At the height of the emotional tension between the parent and me, I paused and asked the students, "Have you had enough?" With a smile and a thank-you to the parent assistant, I asked how many folks would like to learn five ways not to plagiarize material; then I went to the chalkboard.

Students breathed a sigh of relief. Notebooks flew onto desktops, and pens raced across paper to get down everything I taught for the rest of class; they hung on every word. Students wanted to do anything to avoid the "yucky" feelings associated with plagiarism that they had experienced moments ago. I taught them ways to cite sources, how to paraphrase another's words, and how many words from an original source we could use before we were lifting too much. We discussed the legal ramifications of plagiarism. Later, we applauded the acting talent of our parent assistant.

One student in the room that day reflected on this lesson at the end of the year:

> I know I'll never forget when my teacher got "caught" plagiarizing. The sensations were simply too real. . . . Although my teacher is extremely moral, it was frightening how close to home it struck. The moment when my teacher admitted it, the room fell silent. It was awful. All my life, teachers have preached about plagiarism, and it never really sank in. But when you actually experience it, it's a whole different story.

To this day, students visit me from high school and college and say, "I was tempted to plagiarize this one little bit on one of my papers, but I didn't because I remembered how mad I was at you." That's a teacher touchdown.

—Rick Wormeli

---

instead choose to write a persuasive dialogue or create a poster. Even then, however, we can differentiate the pace of instruction and be flexible about the time required for student mastery. Just as we would never demand that all humans be able to recite the alphabet fluently on the first Monday after their 3rd birthday, it goes against all we know about teaching tweens to mandate that all students master slope and y-intercept during the first week of October in grade 7.

In 2001, 40.7 percent of students in grades 3–5 and 41.7 percent of students in grades 6–8 participated in after-school activities (such as school sports, religious activities, scouts, and clubs) on a weekly basis.
—NCES, *The Condition of Education 2004*

Thus, we allow tweens to redo work and assessments until they master the content, and we give them full credit for doing so. Our job is to teach students the material, not to document how they've failed. We never want to succumb to what middle-grades expert Nancy Doda calls the "learn or I will hurt you" mentality by demanding that all students learn at the same pace and in the same manner as their classmates and giving them only one chance to succeed.

Strategy 4: Give Formative Feedback

Tweens don't always know when they don't know, and they don't always know when they do. One of the most helpful strategies we can employ is to provide frequent formative feedback. Tween learning tends to be more multilayered and episodic than linear; continual assessment and feedback correct misconceptions before they take root. Tweens learn more when teachers take off the evaluation hat and hold up a mirror to students, helping them compare what they did with what they were supposed to have done.

Because learning and motivation can be fragile at this age, we have to find ways to provide that feedback promptly. We do this by giving students short assignments—such as one-page writings instead of multipage reports—that we can evaluate and return in a timely manner. When we formally assess student writing, we focus on just one or two areas so that students can assimilate our feedback.

To get a quick read on students' understanding of a particular lesson, we can use exit card activities, which are quick products created by students in response to prompts. For example, at the end of a U.S. history lesson, we might ask, "Using what we've learned today, make a Venn diagram that compares and contrasts World Wars I and II." The 3-2-1 exit card format can yield rich information (Wormeli, 2005). Here are two examples:

3—Identify *three* characteristic ways Renaissance art differs from medieval art.

2—List *two* important scientific debates that occurred during the Renaissance.

1—Provide *one* good reason why *rebirth* is an appropriate term to describe the Renaissance.

3—Identify at least *three* differences between acids and bases.

2—List *one* use of an acid and *one* use of a base.

1—State *one* reason why knowledge of acids and bases is important to citizens in our community.

Strategy 5: Dare to Be Unconventional

Curriculum theorists have often referred to early adolescence as the age of romanticism: Tweens are interested in that which is novel, compels them, and appeals to their curiosity about the world (Pinar, Reynolds, Slattery, & Taubman, 2000). To successfully teach tweens, we have to be willing to transcend convention once in a while. It's not a lark; it's essential.

Being unconventional means we occasionally teach math algorithms by giving students the answers to problems and asking them how those answers were derived. We improve student word savvy by asking students to conduct an intelligent conversation without using verbs. (They can't; they sound like Tarzan.) We ask students to teach some lessons, with the principal or a parent as coteacher. Students can make a video for 4th graders on the three branches of government, convey Aristotle's rhetorical triangle by juggling tennis balls, or correspond with adult astronomers about their study of the planets. They can create literary magazines of science, math, or health writing that will end up in local dentist offices and Jiffy Lube shops. They can learn about the Renaissance through a "Meeting of Minds" debate in which they portray Machiavelli, da Vinci, Erasmus, Luther, Calvin, and Henry VIII.

The power of such lessons lies in their substance and novelty, and young adolescents are acutely attuned to these qualities.

Ninety percent of what we do with young adolescents is quiet, behind-the-scenes facilitation. Ten percent, however, is an inspired dog and pony show without apologies. At this "I dare you to show me something I don't know" and "Shake me out of my self-absorption" age, being unconventional is key.

Thus, when my students were confusing the concepts of adjective and adverb, I did the most professional thing I could think of: I donned tights, shorts, a cape, and a mask, and became Adverb Man. I moved through the hallways handing out index cards with adverbs written on them. "You need to move quickly," I said, handing a student late to class a card on which the word *quickly* was written. "You need to move now," I said to another, handing him a card with the adverb on it. Once in a while, I'd raise my voice, Superman-style, and declare, "Remember, good citizens of Earth, what Adverb Man always says: 'Up, up, and modify adverbs, verbs, and adjectives!'" The next day, one of the girls on our middle school team came walking down the hallway to my classroom dressed as Pronoun Girl. One of her classmates preceded her—he was dressed as Antecedent Boy. Both wore yellow masks and had long beach towels tucked into the backs of their shirt collars as capes. Pronoun Girl had taped pronouns across her shirt that corresponded with the nouns taped across Antecedent Boy's shirt.

It was better than *Schoolhouse Rock*. And the best part? There wasn't any grade lower than a *B*+ on the adverbs test that Friday (Wormeli, 2001).

Navigating the Tween River

Of all the states of matter in the known universe, tweens most closely resemble liquid. Students at this age have a defined volume, but not a defined shape. They are ever ready to flow, and they are rarely compressible. Although they can spill, freeze, and boil, they can also lift others, do impressive work, take the shape of their environment, and carry multiple ideas within themselves. Some teachers argue that dark matter is a better analogy—but those are teachers trying to keep order during the last period on a Friday.

To successfully teach tweens, we have to be willing to transcend convention once in a while.

Imagine directing the course of a river that flows through a narrow, ever-changing channel toward a greater purpose yet to be discovered, and you have the basics of teaching tweens. To chart this river's course, we must be experts in the craft of guiding young, fluid adolescents in their pressure-filled lives, and we must adjust our methods according to the flow, volume, and substrate within each student. It's a challenging river to navigate, but worth the journey.

References

Glynn, C. (2001). *Learning on their feet*. Shoreham, VT: Discover Writing Press.

Jackson, A., & Davis, G. (2000). *Turning points 2000: Educating adolescents in the 21st century*. New York: Carnegie Corporation.

National Middle School Association. (2003). *This we believe: Successful schools for young adolescents*. Westerville, OH: Author.

Pinar, W. F., Reynolds, W. M., Slattery, P., & Taubman, P. M. (2000). *Understanding curriculum*. New York: Peter Lang Publishing.

Wormeli, R. (1999). The test of accountability in middle school. *Middle Ground, 3*(7), 17–18, 53.

Wormeli, R. (2001). *Meet me in the middle*. Portland, ME: Stenhouse Publishers.

Wormeli, R. (2005). *Summarization in any subject: 50 techniques to improve student learning*. Alexandria, VA: ASCD.

RICK WORMELI (703-620-2447; rwormeli@cox.net) taught young adolescents for 25 years. He is now a consultant who works with administrators and teachers across the United States. He resides in Herndon, Virginia.

From *Educational Leadership,* April 2006, pp. 14–19. Copyright © 2006 by ASCD. Reprinted by permission. The Association for Supervision and Curriculum Development is a worldwide community of educators advocating sound policies and sharing best practices to achieve the success of each learner. To learn more, visit ASCD at www.ascd.org

Critical Thinking
Why Is It So Hard to Teach?

Daniel T. Willingham

Virtually everyone would agree that a primary, yet insufficiently met, goal of schooling is to enable students to think critically. In layperson's terms, critical thinking consists of seeing both sides of an issue, being open to new evidence that disconfirms your ideas, reasoning dispassionately, demanding that claims be backed by evidence, deducing and inferring conclusions from available facts, solving problems, and so forth. Then too, there are specific types of critical thinking that are characteristic of different subject matter: That's what we mean when we refer to "thinking like a scientist" or "thinking like a historian."

This proper and commonsensical goal has very often been translated into calls to teach "critical thinking skills" and "higher-order thinking skills"—and into generic calls for teaching students to make better judgments, reason more logically, and so forth. In a recent survey of human resource officials[1] and in testimony delivered just a few months ago before the Senate Finance Committee,[2] business leaders have repeatedly exhorted schools to do a better job of teaching students to think critically. And they are not alone. Organizations and initiatives involved in education reform, such as the National Center on Education and the Economy, the American Diploma Project, and the Aspen Institute, have pointed out the need for students to think and/or reason critically. The College Board recently revamped the SAT to better assess students' critical thinking. And ACT, Inc. offers a test of critical thinking for college students.

These calls are not new. In 1983, *A Nation At Risk,* a report by the National Commission on Excellence in Education, found that many 17-year-olds did not possess the "'higher-order' intellectual skills" this country needed. It claimed that nearly 40 percent could not draw inferences from written material and only one-fifth could write a persuasive essay.

Following the release of *A Nation At Risk,* programs designed to teach students to think critically across the curriculum became extremely popular. By 1990, most states had initiatives designed to encourage educators to teach critical thinking, and one of the most widely used programs, Tactics for Thinking, sold 70,000 teacher guides.[3] But, for reasons I'll explain, the programs were not very effective—and today we still lament students' lack of critical thinking.

After more than 20 years of lamentation, exhortation, and little improvement, maybe it's time to ask a fundamental question: Can critical thinking actually be taught? Decades of cognitive research point to a disappointing answer: not really. People who have sought to teach critical thinking have assumed that it is a skill, like riding a bicycle, and that, like other skills, once you learn it, you can apply it in any situation. Research from cognitive science shows that thinking is not that sort of skill. The processes of thinking are intertwined with the content of thought (that is, domain knowledge). Thus, if you remind a student to "look at an issue from multiple perspectives" often enough, he will learn that he ought to do so, but if he doesn't know much about an issue, he *can't* think about it from multiple perspectives. You can teach students maxims about how they ought to think, but without background knowledge and practice, they probably will not be able to implement the advice they memorize. Just as it makes no sense to try to teach factual content without giving students opportunities to practice using it, it also makes no sense to try to teach critical thinking devoid of factual content.

Critical thinking is not a set of skills that can be deployed at any time, in any context. It is a type of thought that even 3-year-olds can engage in—and even trained scientists can fail in.

In this article, I will describe the nature of critical thinking, explain why it is so hard to do and to teach, and explore how students acquire a specific type of critical thinking: thinking scientifically. Along the way, we'll see that critical thinking is not a set of skills that can be deployed at any time, in any context. It is a type of thought that even 3-year-olds can engage in—and even trained scientists can fail in. And it is very much dependent on domain knowledge and practice.

Why Is Thinking Critically So Hard?

Educators have long noted that school attendance and even academic success are no guarantee that a student will graduate an effective thinker in all situations. There is an odd tendency for rigorous thinking to cling to particular examples or types of problems. Thus, a student may have learned to estimate the answer to a math problem before beginning calculations as a way of checking the accuracy of his answer, but in the chemistry lab, the same student calculates the components of a compound without noticing that his estimates sum to more than 100 percent. And a student who has learned to thoughtfully discuss the causes of the American Revolution from both the British and American perspectives doesn't even think to question how the Germans viewed World War II. Why are students able to think critically in one situation, but not in another? The brief answer is: Thought processes are intertwined with what is being thought about. Let's explore this in depth by looking at a particular kind of critical thinking that has been studied extensively: problem solving.

Imagine a seventh-grade math class immersed in word problems. How is it that students will be able to answer one problem, but not the next, even though mathematically both word problems are the same, that is, they rely on the same mathematical knowledge? Typically, the students are focusing on the scenario that the word problem describes (its surface structure) instead of on the mathematics required to solve it (its deep structure). So even though students have been taught how to solve a particular type of word problem, when the teacher or textbook changes the scenario, students still struggle to apply the solution because they don't recognize that the problems are mathematically the same.

Thinking Tends to Focus on a Problem's "Surface Structure"

To understand why the surface structure of a problem is so distracting and, as a result, why it's so hard to apply familiar solutions to problems that appear new, let's first consider how you understand what's being asked when you are given a problem. Anything you hear or read is automatically interpreted in light of what you already know about similar subjects. For example, suppose you read these two sentences: "After years of pressure from the film and television industry, the President has filed a formal complaint with China over what U.S. firms say is copyright infringement. These firms assert that the Chinese government sets stringent trade restrictions for U.S. entertainment products, even as it turns a blind eye to Chinese companies that copy American movies and television shows and sell them on the black market." Background knowledge not only allows you to comprehend the sentences, it also has a powerful effect as you continue to read because it narrows the interpretations of new text that you will entertain. For example, if you later read the word "Bush," it would not make you think of a small shrub, nor would you wonder whether it referred to the former President Bush, the rock band, or a term for rural hinterlands. If you read "piracy," you would not think of eye-patched swabbies shouting "shiver me timbers!" The cognitive system gambles that incoming information will be related to what you've just been thinking about. Thus, it significantly narrows the scope of possible interpretations of words, sentences, and ideas. The benefit is that comprehension proceeds faster and more smoothly; the cost is that the deep structure of a problem is harder to recognize.

The narrowing of ideas that occurs while you read (or listen) means that you tend to focus on the surface structure, rather than on the underlying structure of the problem. For example, in one experiment,[4] subjects saw a problem like this one:

> Members of the West High School Band were hard at work practicing for the annual Homecoming Parade. First they tried marching in rows of 12, but Andrew was left by himself to bring up the rear. Then the director told the band members to march in columns of eight, but Andrew was still left to march alone. Even when the band marched in rows of three, Andrew was left out. Finally, in exasperation, Andrew told the band director that they should march

How Do Cognitive Scientists Define Critical Thinking?

From the cognitive scientist's point of view, the mental activities that are typically called critical thinking are actually a subset of three types of thinking: reasoning, making judgments and decisions, and problem solving. I say that critical thinking is a subset of these because we think in these ways all the time, but only sometimes in a critical way. Deciding to read this article, for example, is not critical thinking. But carefully weighing the evidence it presents in order to decide whether or not to believe what it says is. *Critical* reasoning, decision making, and problem solving—which, for brevity's sake, I will refer to as critical thinking—have three key features: effectiveness, novelty, and self-direction. Critical thinking is effective in that it avoids common pitfalls, such as seeing only one side of an issue, discounting new evidence that disconfirms your ideas, reasoning from passion rather than logic, failing to support statements with evidence, and so on. Critical thinking is novel in that you don't simply remember a solution or a situation that is similar enough to guide you. For example, solving a complex but familiar physics problem by applying a multi-step algorithm isn't critical thinking because you are really drawing on memory to solve the problem. But devising a new algorithm is critical thinking. Critical thinking is self-directed in that the thinker must be calling the shots: We wouldn't give a student much credit for critical thinking if the teacher were prompting each step he took.

—D.W.

in rows of five in order to have all the rows filled. He was right. Given that there were at least 45 musicians on the field but fewer than 200 musicians, how many students were there in the West High School Band?

Earlier in the experiment, subjects had read four problems along with detailed explanations of how to solve each one, ostensibly to rate them for the clarity of the writing. One of the four problems concerned the number of vegetables to buy for a garden, and it relied on the same type of solution necessary for the band problem—calculation of the least common multiple. Yet, few subjects—just 19 percent—saw that the band problem was similar and that they could use the garden problem solution. Why?

When a student reads a word problem, her mind interprets the problem in light of her prior knowledge, as happened when you read the two sentences about copyrights and China. The difficulty is that the knowledge that seems relevant relates to the surface structure—in this problem, the reader dredges up knowledge about bands, high school, musicians, and so forth. The student is unlikely to read the problem and think of it in terms of its deep structure—using the least common multiple. The surface structure of the problem is overt, but the deep structure of the problem is not. Thus, people fail to use the first problem to help them solve the second: In their minds, the first was about vegetables in a garden and the second was about rows of band marchers.

With Deep Knowledge, Thinking Can Penetrate Beyond Surface Structure

If knowledge of how to solve a problem never transferred to problems with new surface structures, schooling would be inefficient or even futile—but of course, such transfer does occur. When and why is complex,[5] but two factors are especially relevant for educators: familiarity with a problem's deep structure and the knowledge that one should look for a deep structure. I'll address each in turn.

When one is very familiar with a problem's deep-structure, knowledge about how to solve it transfers well. That familiarity can come from long-term, repeated experience with one problem, or with various manifestations of one type of problem (i.e., many problems that have different surface structures, but the same deep structure). After repeated exposure to either or both, the subject simply perceives the deep structure as part of the problem description. Here's an example:

A treasure hunter is going to explore a cave up on a hill near a beach. He suspected there might be many paths inside the cave so he was afraid he might get lost. Obviously, he did not have a map of the cave; all he had with him were some common items such as a flashlight and a bag. What could he do to make sure he did not get lost trying to get back out of the cave later?

The solution is to carry some sand with you in the bag, and leave a trail as you go, so you can trace your path back when you're ready to leave the cave. About 75 percent of American college students thought of this solution— but only 25 percent of Chinese students solved it.[6] The experimenters suggested that Americans solved it because most grew up hearing the story of Hansel and Gretel, which includes the idea of leaving a trail as you travel to an unknown place in order to find your way back. The experimenters also gave subjects another puzzle based on a common Chinese folk tale, and the percentage of solvers from each culture reversed. (To read the puzzle based on the Chinese folk tale, and the tale itself, go to www.aft.org/ pubs-reports/ american_educator/index.htm.)

It takes a good deal of practice with a problem type before students know it well enough to immediately recognize its deep structure, irrespective of the surface structure, as Americans did for the Hansel and Gretel problem. American subjects didn't think of the problem in terms of sand, caves, and treasure; they thought of it in terms of finding something with which to leave a trail. The deep structure of the problem is so well represented in their memory, that they immediately saw that structure when they read the problem.

Looking for a Deep Structure Helps, but It Only Takes You So Far

Now let's turn to the second factor that aids in transfer despite distracting differences in surface structure—knowing to look for a deep structure. Consider what would happen if I said to a student working on the band problem, "this one is similar to the garden problem." The student would understand that the problems must share a deep structure and would try to figure out what it is. Students can do something similar without the hint. A student might think "I'm seeing this problem in a math class, so there must be a math formula that will solve this problem." Then he could scan his memory (or textbook) for candidates, and see if one of them helps. This is an example of what psychologists call metacognition, or regulating one's thoughts. In the introduction, I mentioned that you can teach students maxims about how they ought to think. Cognitive scientists refer to these maxims as metacognitive strategies. They are little chunks of knowledge—like "look for a problem's deep structure" or "consider both sides of an issue"—that students can learn and then use to steer their thoughts in more productive directions.

Helping students become better at regulating their thoughts was one of the goals of the critical thinking programs that were popular 20 years ago. As the box on the following page explains, these programs are not very effective. Their modest benefit is likely due to teaching students to effectively use metacognitive strategies. Students learn to avoid biases that most of us are prey to when we think, such as settling on the first conclusion that seems reasonable, only seeking evidence that confirms one's beliefs, ignoring countervailing evidence, overconfidence, and others.[7] Thus, a student who has been encouraged many times to see both sides of an issue, for example, is probably more likely to spontaneously think "I should look at both sides of this issue" when working on a problem.

Unfortunately, metacognitive strategies can only take you so far. Although they suggest what you ought to do, they don't provide the knowledge necessary to implement the strategy. For

Critical Thinking Programs: Lots of Time, Modest Benefit

Since the ability to think critically is a primary goal of education, it's no surprise that people have tried to develop programs that could directly teach students to think critically without immersing them in any particular academic content. But the evidence shows that such programs primarily improve students' thinking with the sort of problems they practiced in the program—not with other types of problems. More generally, it's doubtful that a program that effectively teaches students to think critically in a variety of situations will ever be developed.

As the main article explains, the ability to think critically depends on having adequate content knowledge; you can't think critically about topics you know little about or solve problems that you don't know well enough to recognize and execute the type of solutions they call for.

Nonetheless, these programs do help us better understand what can be taught, so they are worth reviewing briefly.

A large number of programs[1] designed to make students better thinkers are available, and they have some features in common. They are premised on the idea that there is a set of critical thinking skills that can be applied and practiced across content domains. They are designed to supplement regular curricula, not to replace them, and so they are not tied to particular content areas such as language arts, science, or social studies. Many programs are intended to last about three years, with several hours of instruction (delivered in one or two lessons) per week. The programs vary in how they deliver this instruction and practice. Some use abstract problems such as finding patterns in meaningless figures (Reuven Feuerstein's Instrumental Enrichment), some use mystery stories (Martin Covington's Productive Thinking), some use group discussion of interesting problems that one might encounter in daily life (Edward de Bono's Cognitive Research Trust, or CoRT), and so on. However it is implemented, each program introduces students to examples of critical thinking and then requires that the students practice such thinking themselves.

How well do these programs work? Many researchers have tried to answer that question, but their studies tend to have methodological problems.[2] Four limitations of these studies are especially typical, and they make any effects suspect: 1) students are evaluated just once after the program, so it's not known whether any observed effects are enduring; 2) there is not a control group, leaving it unclear whether gains are due to the thinking program, to other aspects of schooling, or to experiences outside the classroom; 3) the control group does not have a comparison intervention, so any positive effects found may be due, for example, to the teacher's enthusiasm for something new, not the program itself; and 4) there is no measure of whether or not students can transfer their new thinking ability to materials that differ from those used in the program. In addition, only a small fraction of the studies have undergone peer review (meaning that they have been impartially evaluated by independent experts). Peer review is crucial because it is known that researchers unconsciously bias the design and analysis of their research to favor the conclusions they hope to see.[3]

Studies of the Philosophy for Children program may be taken as typical. Two researchers[4] identified eight studies that evaluated academic outcomes and met minimal research-design criteria. (Of these eight, only one had been subjected to peer review.) Still, they concluded that three of the eight had identifiable problems that clouded the researchers' conclusions. Among the remaining five studies, three measured reading ability, and one of these reported a significant gain. Three studies measured reasoning ability, and two reported significant gains. And, two studies took more impressionistic measures of student's participation in class (e.g., generating ideas, providing reasons), and both reported a positive effect.

Despite the difficulties and general lack of rigor in evaluation, most researchers reviewing the literature conclude that some critical thinking programs do have some positive effect.[5] But these reviewers offer two important caveats. First, as with almost any educational endeavor, the success of the program depends on the skill of the teacher. Second, thinking programs look good when the outcome measure is quite similar to the material in the program. As one tests for transfer to more and more dissimilar material, the apparent effectiveness of the program rapidly drops.

Knowing that one should think critically is not the same as being able to do so. That requires domain knowledge and practice.

Both the conclusion and the caveats make sense from the cognitive scientist's point of view. It is not surprising that the success of the program depends on the skill of the teacher. The developers of the programs cannot anticipate all of the ideas—right or wrong—that students will generate as they practice thinking critically, so it is up to the teacher to provide the all-important feedback to the students.

It is also reasonable that the programs should lead to gains in abilities that are measured with materials similar to those used in the program. The programs that include puzzles like those found on IQ tests, for instance, report gains in IQ scores. In an earlier column,* I described a bedrock principle of memory: You remember what you think about. The same goes for critical thinking: You learn to think critically in the ways in which you practice thinking critically. If you practice logic puzzles with an effective teacher, you are likely to get better at solving logic puzzles. But substantial improvement requires a great deal of practice. Unfortunately, because critical thinking curricula include many different types of problems, students typically don't get enough practice with any one type of problem. As explained in the main article, the modest benefits that these programs seem to produce are likely due to teaching students metacognitive strategies—like "look at both sides of an issue"—that cue them to try to think critically. But knowing that one should think critically is not the same as being able to do so. That requires domain knowledge and practice.

—D.W.

*See "Students Remember . . . What They Think About" in the Summer 2003 issue of *American Educator;* online at www.aft. org/ pubs-reports/american_educator/ summer2003/cogsci.html.

example, when experimenters told subjects working on the band problem that it was similar to the garden problem, more subjects solved the problem (35 percent compared to 19 percent without the hint), but most subjects, even when told what to do, weren't able to do it. Likewise, you may know that you ought not accept the first reasonable-sounding solution to a problem, but that doesn't mean you know how to come up with alterative solutions or weigh how reasonable each one is. That requires domain knowledge and practice in putting that knowledge to work.

Since critical thinking relies so heavily on domain knowledge, educators may wonder if thinking critically in a particular domain is easier to learn. The quick answer is yes, it's a *little* easier. To understand why, let's focus on one domain, science, and examine the development of scientific thinking.

Teaching students to think critically probably lies in large part in enabling them to deploy the right type of thinking at the right time.

Is Thinking Like a Scientist Easier?

Teaching science has been the focus of intensive study for decades, and the research can be usefully categorized into two strands. The first examines how children acquire scientific concepts; for example, how they come to forgo naive conceptions of motion and replace them with an understanding of physics. The second strand is what we would call thinking scientifically, that is, the mental procedures by which science is conducted: developing a model, deriving a hypothesis from the model, designing an experiment to test the hypothesis, gathering data from the experiment, interpreting the data in light of the model, and so forth.[†] Most researchers believe that scientific thinking is really a subset of reasoning that is not different in kind from other types of reasoning that children and adults do.[8] What makes it *scientific* thinking is knowing when to engage in such reasoning, and having accumulated enough relevant knowledge and spent enough time practicing to do so.

Recognizing *when* to engage in scientific reasoning is so important because the evidence shows that being able to reason is not enough; children and adults use *and* fail to use the proper reasoning processes on problems that seem similar. For example, consider a type of reasoning about cause and effect that is very important in science: conditional probabilities. If two things go together, it's possible that one causes the other. Suppose you start a new medicine and notice that you seem to be getting headaches more often than usual. You would infer that the medication influenced your chances of getting a headache. But it could also be that the medication increases your chances of getting a headache only in certain circumstances or

conditions. In conditional probability, the relationship between two things (e.g., medication and headaches) is dependent on a third factor. For example, the medication might increase the probability of a headache *only* when you've had a cup of coffee. The relationship of the medication and headaches is conditional on the presence of coffee.

Understanding and using conditional probabilities is essential to scientific thinking because it is so important in reasoning about what causes what. But people's success in thinking this way depends on the particulars of how the question is presented. Studies show that adults sometimes use conditional probabilities successfully,[9] but fail to do so with many problems that call for it.[10] Even trained scientists are open to pitfalls in reasoning about conditional probabilities (as well as other types of reasoning). Physicians are known to discount or misinterpret new patient data that conflict with a diagnosis they have in mind,[11] and Ph.D.-level scientists are prey to faulty reasoning when faced with a problem embedded in an unfamiliar context.[12]

And yet, young children are sometimes able to reason about conditional probabilities. In one experiment,[13] the researchers showed 3-year-olds a box and told them it was a "blicket detector" that would play music if a blicket were placed on top. The child then saw one of the two sequences shown below in which blocks are placed on the blicket detector. At the end of the sequence, the child was asked whether each block was a blicket. In other words, the child was to use conditional reasoning to infer which block caused the music to play.

Note that the relationship between each individual block (yellow cube and blue cylinder) and the music is the same in sequences 1 and 2. In either sequence, the child sees the yellow cube associated with music three times, and the blue cylinder associated with the absence of music once and the presence of music twice. What differs between the first and second sequence is the relationship between the blue and yellow blocks, and therefore, the conditional probability of each block being a blicket. Three-year-olds understood the importance of conditional probabilities. For sequence 1, they said the yellow cube was a blicket, but the blue cylinder was not; for sequence 2, they chose equally between the two blocks.

"Teaching content alone is not likely to lead to proficiency in science, nor is engaging in inquiry experiences devoid of meaningful science content."

—National Research Council

This body of studies has been summarized simply: Children are not as dumb as you might think, and adults (even trained scientists) are not as smart as you might think. What's going on? One issue is that the common conception of critical thinking or scientific thinking (or historical thinking) as a set of skills is not accurate. Critical thinking does not have certain characteristics normally associated with skills—in particular, being able to use that skill at any time. If I told you that I learned to read music, for

---

[†]These two strands are the most often studied, but these two approaches—content and process of science—are incomplete. Underemphasized in U.S. classrooms are the many methods of scientific study, and the role of theories and models in advancing scientific thought.

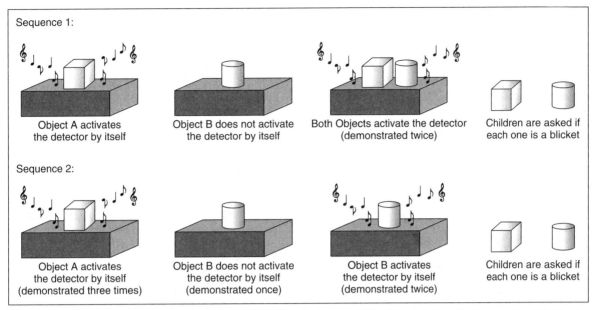

Sequence 1:

Object A activates
the detector by itself

Object B does not activate
the detector by itself

Both Objects activate the detector
(demonstrated twice)

Children are asked if
each one is a blicket

Sequence 2:

Object A activates
the detector by itself
(demonstrated three times)

Object B does not activate
the detector by itself
(demonstrated once)

Object B activates
the detector by itself
(demonstrated twice)

Children are asked if
each one is a blicket

Source: Gopnik, A. and Schulz, L.E. (2004). "Mechanisms of theory formation in young children," *Trends in Cognitive Sciences,* 8, p. 373, Elsevier.

example, you would expect, correctly, that I could use my new skill (i.e., read music) whenever I wanted. But critical thinking is very different. As we saw in the discussion of conditional probabilities, people can engage in some types of critical thinking without training, but even with extensive training, they will sometimes fail to think critically. This understanding that critical thinking is not a skill is vital.[‡] It tells us that teaching students to think critically probably lies in small part in showing them new ways of thinking, and in large part in enabling them to deploy the right type of thinking at the right time.

Returning to our focus on science, we're ready to address a key question: Can students be taught when to engage in scientific thinking? Sort of. It is easier than trying to teach general critical thinking, but not as easy as we would like. Recall that when we were discussing problem solving, we found that students can learn metacognitive strategies that help them look past the surface structure of a problem and identify its deep structure, thereby getting them a step closer to figuring out a solution. Essentially the same thing can happen with scientific thinking. Students can learn certain metacognitive strategies that will cue them to think scientifically. But, as with problem solving, the metacognitive strategies only tell the students what they should do—they do not provide the knowledge that students need to actually do it. The good news is that within a content area like science, students have more context cues to help them figure out which metacognitive strategy to use, and teachers have a clearer idea of what domain knowledge they must teach to enable students to do what the strategy calls for.

For example, two researchers[14] taught second-, third-, and fourth-graders the scientific concept behind controlling vari-

ables; that is, of keeping everything in two comparison conditions the same, except for the one variable that is the focus of investigation. The experimenters gave explicit instruction about this strategy for conducting experiments and then had students practice with a set of materials (e.g., springs) to answer a specific question (e.g., which of these factors determine how far a spring will stretch: length, coil diameter, wire diameter, or weight?). The experimenters found that students not only understood the concept of controlling variables, they were able to apply it seven months later with different materials and a different experimenter, although the older children showed more robust transfer than the younger children. In this case, the students recognized that they were designing an experiment and that cued them to recall the metacognitive strategy, "When I design experiments, I should try to control variables." Of course, succeeding in controlling all of the relevant variables is another matter—that depends on knowing which variables may matter and how they could vary.

Why Scientific Thinking Depends on Scientific Knowledge

Experts in teaching science recommend that scientific reasoning be taught in the context of rich subject matter knowledge. A committee of prominent science educators brought together by the National Research Council[15] put it plainly: "Teaching content alone is not likely to lead to proficiency in science, nor is engaging in inquiry experiences devoid of meaningful science content."

The committee drew this conclusion based on evidence that background knowledge is necessary to engage in scientific thinking. For example, knowing that one needs a control group in an experiment is important. Like having two comparison conditions, having a control group in addition to an experimental group helps you focus on the variable you want to study. But knowing that you need a control group is not the same as being able to create one. Since it's not always possible to have two

---

[‡]Although this is not highly relevant for K–12 teachers, it is important to note that for people with extensive training, such as Ph.D.-level scientists, critical thinking does have some skill-like characteristics. In particular, they are better able to deploy critical reasoning with a wide variety of content, even that with which they are not very familiar. But, of course, this does not mean that they will never make mistakes.

Did Sherlock Holmes Take a Course in Critical Thinking?

No one better exemplifies the power of broad, deep knowledge in driving critical thinking than Sherlock Holmes. In his famous first encounter with Dr. Watson, Holmes greets him with this observation: "You have been in Afghanistan, I perceive." Watson is astonished—how could Holmes have known? Eventually Holmes explains his insight, which turns not on incredible intelligence or creativity or wild guessing, but on having relevant knowledge. Holmes is told that Watson is a doctor; everything else he deduces by drawing on his knowledge of, among other things, the military, geography, how injuries heal, and current events. Here's how Holmes explains his thought process:

> I knew you came from Afghanistan. From long habit the train of thoughts ran so swiftly through my mind, that I arrived at the conclusion without being conscious of intermediate steps. There were such steps, however. The train of reasoning ran, "Here is a gentleman of a medical type, but with the air of a military man. Clearly an army doctor, then. He has just come from the tropics, for his face is dark, and that is not the natural tint of his skin, for his wrists are fair. He has undergone hardship and sickness, as his haggard face says clearly. His left arm has been injured. He holds it in a stiff and unnatural manner. Where in the tropics could an English army doctor have seen much hardship and got his arm wounded? Clearly in Afghanistan." The whole train of thought did not occupy a second. I then remarked that you came from Afghanistan, and you were astonished.

—Editors

Source: *A Study in Scarlet* by Sir Arthur Conan Doyle.

groups that are *exactly* alike, knowing which factors can vary between groups and which must not vary is one example of necessary background knowledge. In experiments measuring how quickly subjects can respond, for example, control groups must be matched for age, because age affects response speed, but they need not be perfectly matched for gender.

More formal experimental work verifies that background knowledge is necessary to reason scientifically. For example, consider devising a research hypothesis. One could generate multiple hypotheses for any given situation. Suppose you know that car A gets better gas mileage than car B and you'd like to know why. There are many differences between the cars, so which will you investigate first? Engine size? Tire pressure? A key determinant of the hypothesis you select is plausibility. You won't choose to investigate a difference between cars A and B that you think is unlikely to contribute to gas mileage (e.g., paint color), but if someone provides a reason to make this factor more plausible (e.g., the way your teenage son's driving habits changed after he painted his car red), you are more likely to say that this now-plausible factor should be investigated.[16] One's judgment about the plausibility of a factor being important is based on one's knowledge of the domain.

Other data indicate that familiarity with the domain makes it easier to juggle different factors simultaneously, which in turn allows you to construct experiments that simultaneously control for more factors. For example, in one experiment,[17] eighth-graders completed two tasks. In one, they were to manipulate conditions in a computer simulation to keep imaginary creatures alive. In the other, they were told that they had been hired by a swimming pool company to evaluate how the surface area of swimming pools was related to the cooling rate of its water. Students were more adept at designing experiments for the first task than the second, which the researchers interpreted as being due to students' familiarity with the relevant variables. Students are used to thinking about factors that might influence creatures' health (e.g., food, predators), but have less experience working with factors that might influence water temperature (e.g., volume, surface area). Hence, it is not the case that "controlling variables in an experiment" is a pure process that is not affected by subjects' knowledge of those variables.

Subjects who started with more and better integrated knowledge planned more informative experiments and made better use of experimental outcomes.

Prior knowledge and beliefs not only influence which hypotheses one chooses to test, they influence how one interprets data from an experiment. In one experiment,[18] undergraduates were evaluated for their knowledge of electrical circuits. Then they participated in three weekly, 1.5-hour sessions during which they designed and conducted experiments using a computer simulation of circuitry, with the goal of learning how circuitry works. The results showed a strong relationship between subjects' initial knowledge and how much subjects learned in future sessions, in part due to how the subjects interpreted the data from the experiments they had conducted. Subjects who started with more and better integrated knowledge planned more informative experiments and made better use of experimental outcomes.

Other studies have found similar results, and have found that anomalous, or unexpected, outcomes may be particularly important in creating new knowledge—and particularly dependent upon prior knowledge.[19] Data that seem odd because they don't fit one's mental model of the phenomenon under investigation are highly informative. They tell you that your understanding is incomplete, and they guide the development of new hypotheses. But you could only recognize the outcome of an experiment as anomalous if you had some expectation of how it would turn out. And that expectation would be based on domain knowledge, as would your ability to create a new hypothesis that takes the anomalous outcome into account.

The idea that scientific thinking must be taught hand in hand with scientific content is further supported by research on scientific problem solving; that is, when students calculate an answer to a textbook-like problem, rather than design their own experiment. A meta-analysis[20] of 40 experiments investigating methods for teaching scientific problem solving showed that effective approaches were those that focused on building complex, integrated knowledge bases as part of problem solving, for

example by including exercises like concept mapping. Ineffective approaches focused exclusively on the strategies to be used in problem solving while ignoring the knowledge necessary for the solution.

What do all these studies boil down to? First, critical thinking (as well as scientific thinking and other domain-based thinking) is not a skill. There is not a set of critical thinking skills that can be acquired and deployed

Teaching Critical Thinking

Teaching students to think critically is high on any teacher's to-do list. So what strategies are consistent with the research?

• *Special programs aren't worth it.* In the box, "Critical Thinking Programs: Lots of Time, Modest Benefit," I've mentioned a few of the better known programs. Despite their widespread availability, the evidence that these programs succeed in teaching students to think critically, especially in novel situations, is very limited. The modest boost that such programs may provide should be viewed, as should all claims of educational effectiveness, in light of their opportunity costs. Every hour students spend on the program is an hour they won't be learning something else.

• *Thinking critically should be taught in the context of subject matter.* The foregoing does not mean that teachers shouldn't teach students to think critically—it means that critical thinking shouldn't be taught on its own. People do not spontaneously examine assumptions that underlie their thinking, try to consider all sides of an issue, question what they know, etc. These things must be modeled for students, and students must be given opportunities to practice—preferably in the context of normal classroom activity. This is true not only for science (as discussed in the main article), but for other subject matter. For example, an important part of thinking like a historian is considering the source of a document—who wrote it, when, and why. But teaching students to ask that question, independent of subject matter knowledge, won't do much good. Knowing that a letter was written by a Confederate private to his wife in New Orleans just after the Battle of Vicksburg won't help the student interpret the letter unless he knows something of Civil War history.

• *Critical thinking is not just for advanced students.* I have sometimes heard teachers and administrators suggest that critical thinking exercises make a good enrichment activity for the best students, but struggling students should just be expected to understand and master more basic material. This argument sells short the less advanced students and conflicts with what cognitive scientists know about thinking. Virtually everyone is capable of critical thinking and uses it all the time—and, as the conditional probabilities research demonstrated, has been capable of doing so since they were very young. The difficulty lies not in thinking critically, but in recognizing when to do so, and in knowing enough to do so successfully.

• *Student experiences offer entrée to complex concepts.* Although critical thinking needs to be nested in subject matter, when students don't have much subject matter knowledge, introducing a concept by drawing on student experiences can help. For example, the importance of a source in evaluating a historical document is familiar to even young children; deepening their understanding is a matter of asking questions that they have the knowledge to grapple with. Elementary school teachers could ask: Would a letter to a newspaper editor that criticized the abolishment of recess be viewed differently if written by a school principal versus a third-grader? Various concepts that are central to scientific thinking can also be taught with examples that draw on students' everyday knowledge and experience. For example, "correlation does not imply causation" is often illustrated by the robust association between the consumption of ice cream and the number of crimes committed on a given day. With a little prodding, students soon realize that ice cream consumption doesn't cause crime, but high temperatures might cause increases in both.

Knowing that a letter was written by a Confederate private to his wife in New Orleans just after the Battle of Vicksburg won't help the student interpret the letter—unless he knows something of Civil War history.

• *To teach critical thinking strategies, make them explicit and practice them.* Critical thinking strategies are abstractions. A plausible approach to teaching them is to make them explicit, and to proceed in stages. The first time (or several times) the concept is introduced, explain it with at least two different examples (possibly examples based on students' experiences, as discussed above), label it so as to identify it as a strategy that can be applied in various contexts, and show how it applies to the course content at hand. In future instances, try naming the appropriate critical thinking strategy to see if students remember it and can figure out how it applies to the material under discussion. With still more practice, students may see which strategy applies without a cue from you.

—D.W.

regardless of context. Second, there are metacognitive strategies that, once learned, make critical thinking more likely. Third, the ability to think critically (to actually do what the metacognitive strategies call for) depends on domain knowledge and practice. For teachers, the situation is not hopeless, but no one should underestimate the difficulty of teaching students to think critically.

Notes

1. Borja, R. R. (2006). "Work Skills of Graduates Seen Lacking," *Education Week, 26,* 9, 10.

2. Green, W. D. (2007). "Accenture Chairman and CEO William D. Green Addresses Senate Finance Committee," Accenture, www.accenture.com.

3. Viadero, D. (1991). "Parents in S.C. Attack Alleged 'New Age' Program." *Education Week,* www.edweek.org.

4. Novick, L. R. and Holyoak, K. J. (1991). "Mathematical problem-solving by analogy," *Journal of Experimental Psychology: Learning, Memory and Cognition, 17,* 398–415.

5. For reviews see: Reeves, L. M. and Weisberg, R. W. (1994), "The role of content and abstract information in analogical transfer," *Psychological Bulletin, 115,* 381–400; Barnett, S. M. and Ceci, S. J. (2002), "When and where do we apply what we learn? A taxonomy for far transfer," *Psychological Bulletin, 128* (4), 612–637.

6. Chen, Z., Mo, L., and Honomichl, R. (2004). "Having the memory of an elephant: Long-term retrieval and the use of analogues in problem solving," *Journal of Experimental Psychology: General, 133,* 415–433.

7. For a readable review see: Baron, J. (2000). *Thinking and Deciding,* Cambridge, UK: Cambridge University Press.

8. For example see: Klahr, D. (2000). *Exploring science: The cognition and development of discovery processes,* Cambridge, Mass.: MIT press.

9. Spellman, B. A. (1996). "Acting as intuitive scientists: Contingency judgments are made while controlling for alternative potential causes," Psychological Science, 7, 337–342

10. For example see: Kuhn, D., Garcia-Mila, M., and Zohar, A. (1995). "Strategies of knowledge acquisition," *Monographs of the Society for Research in Child Development, 60,* 1–128.

11. Groopman, J. (2007). *How Doctors Think,* New York: Houghton Mifflin.

12. Tweney, R. D. and Yachanin, S. A. (1985), "Can scientists rationally assess conditional inferences?" *Social Studies of Science, 15,* 155–173; Mahoney, M. J. and DeMonbreun, B. G. (1981), "Problem-solving bias in scientists," in R. D. Tweney, M. E. Doherty, and C. R. Mynatt (eds.) *On Scientific Thinking,* 139–144, New York:Columbia University Press.

13. Gopnik, A., Sobel, D. M., Schulz, L. E., and Glymour, C. (2001). "Causal learning mechanisms in very young children: Two-, three-, and four-year- olds infer causal relations from patterns of variation and covariation," *Developmental Psychology, 37*(5), 620–629.

14. Chen, Z. and Klahr, D. (1999). "All Other Things Being Equal: Acquisition and Transfer of the Control of Variables Strategy," *Child Development, 70* (5), 1098–1120.

15. National Research Council (2007). *Taking Science to School,* Washington, D.C.: National Academies Press.

16. Koslowski, B. (1996). *Theory and Evidence: The Development of Scientific Reasoning,* Cambridge, Mass.: MIT Press.

17. Friedler, Y., Nachmias, R., and Linn, M. C. (1990). "Learning scientific reasoning skills in microcomputer-based laboratories," *Journal of Research in Science Teaching, 27,* 173–191.

18. Schauble, L., Glaser, R., Raghavan, K., and Reiner, M. (1991). "Causal models and experimentation strategies in scientific reasoning," *The Journal of Learning Sciences, 1,* 201–238.

19. For example see: Dunbar, K. N. and Fugelsang, J. A. (2005), "Causal thinking in science: How scientists and students interpret the unexpected," in M. E. Gorman, R. D. Tweney, D. C. Gooding, and A. P. Kincannon (eds.) *Scientific and Technological Thinking,* 57–79, Mahwah, N.J.: Erlbaum; Echevarria, M. (2003), "Anomalies as a catalyst for middle school students' knowledge construction and scientific reasoning during science inquiry," *Journal of Educational Psychology, 95,* 357–374.

20. Taconis, R., Ferguson-Hessler, M.G.M., and Broekkamp, H., (2001). "Teaching science problem solving: An overview of experimental work," *Journal of Research in Science Teaching, 38*(4), 442–468.

Box Notes

1. Adams, M. J. (1989), "Thinking skills curricula: Their promise and progress," *Educational Psychologist, 24,* 25–77; Nickerson, R. S., Perkins, D. N., and Smith, E. E. (1985), *The Teaching of Thinking,* Hillsdale, N.J.: Erlbaum; Ritchart, R. and Perkins, D. N. (2005), "Learning to think: The challenges of teaching thinking," in K. J. Holyoak and R. G. Morrison (eds.) *The Cambridge Handbook of Thinking and Reasoning,* Cambridge, UK: Cambridge University Press.

2. Sternberg, R. J. and Bhana, K. (1986). "Synthesis of research on the effectiveness of intellectual skills programs: Snake-oil remedies or miracle cures?" *Educational Leadership, 44,* 60–67.

3. Mahoney, M. J. and DeMonbreun, B. G. (1981). "Problem-solving bias in scientists," in R. D. Tweney, M. E. Doherty, and C. R. Mynatt (eds.) *On Scientific Thinking,* 139–144, New York: Columbia University Press.

4. Trickey, S. and Topping, K. J. (2004). "Philosophy for Children: A Systematic Review," *Research Papers in Education 19,* 365–380.

5. Adams, M. J. (1989). "Thinking skills curricula: Their promise and progress." *Educational Psychologist, 24,* 25–77; Nickerson, R. S., Perkins, D. N., and Smith, E. E. (1985), *The Teaching of Thinking,* Hillsdale, N.J.: Erlbaum; Ritchart, R. and Perkins, D. N. (2005), "Learning to think: The challenges of teaching thinking," in K. J. Holyoak and R. G. Morrison (eds.) *The Cambridge Handbook of Thinking and Reasoning,* Cambridge, UK: Cambridge University Press.

DANIEL T. WILLINGHAM is professor of cognitive psychology at the University of Virginia and author of *Cognition: The Thinking Animal* as well as over 50 articles. With Barbara Spellman, he edited *Current Directions in Cognitive Science.* He regularly contributes to *American Educator* by writing the *"Ask the Cognitive Scientist"* column. His research focuses on the role of consciousness in learning.

Constructing Learning

Using Technology to Support Teaching for Understanding

THOMAS M. SHERMAN AND BARBARA L. KURSHAN

A frequent criticism of technology applications in classrooms is that they are little more than extraneous bells and whistles pointlessly tacked onto routine instruction. The flash and splash of a PowerPoint presentation may look good, but many question the value added to student learning. This leads to the question, how can technologies genuinely contribute to enhanced learning? We need to show explicitly how a constructivist perspective can be helpful in planning and delivering instruction and how technologies can significantly support effective and theoretically sound teaching.

We discussed contructivism in depth in our article last month (December–January). Briefly, constructivism is based on the conception that we learn by relating new experiences to our prior knowledge; we construct new understandings based on what we already know. This theory has emerged from research across a broad range of disciplines, but the challenge has been to understand how to promote deeper, more substantive learning. Three principles capture the essence of the challenge. Understanding is:

- the product of actively relating new and prior experiences
- a function of learning facts and core principles of a discipline
- a consequence of using and managing intellectual abilities well

As educators, our challenge is to identify, invent, adopt, and use classroom practices that are consistent with these principles. However, this is no easy quest. For example, one common concern relates to the central role of individual prior knowledge. How can we measure and tailor instruction to each individual's unique experiences? Our response is to identify key characteristics of effective teaching consistent with constructivist theory. Then, for each characteristic we identify ways you can use technology to make these characteristics regular features of your classroom.

Consistency between theoretical conceptions of learning and teaching practice has been shown to support effective applications of technologies to increase achievement. We explore eight teaching characteristics that are consistent with constructivist principles:

- Learner centered
- Interesting
- Real life
- Social
- Active
- Time
- Feedback
- Supportive

Learner Centered

Learner-centered classrooms focus instruction on the intellectual strategies, experiences, culture, and knowledge that students bring into classrooms. The instruction you create uses these experiences as learning paths for students to follow as they examine and transform the new ideas into their own understanding. You can use technology to support this transformation in two important ways.

First, you can use access to extensive libraries of teaching examples and suggestions to tune your instruction to student needs, experiences, and unique situations. For example, Edgate and ProQuestK-12 provide large repertoires of Web-based teaching resources. (*Editor's note:* Find these URLs and other information in the Resources section on p. 102.) Using online resources such as these, you can search for activities that are consistent with students' learning needs. For example, consider teaching a geography lesson in a classroom where students have limited and extensive experiences with local conditions such as a central business district. You could also use the Edgate site to design language lessons that are related to student cultural experiences from home, such as recipes from Mexico. You can personalize study by using local information resources (e.g., GIS databases, museum records and images online, property records, census data), as a focus for study in science (investigating pollution issues), literature (reading local stories), and social studies (examining the politics of local decisions).

Students can use geographic principles to study data about their own neighborhoods as well as examine other features of interest specifically to them.

Interested students challenge their existing knowledge and are more likely to develop conceptual frameworks that integrate prior knowledge and new information into understanding.

Second, you can teach students to organize their knowledge using computer-based tools and software simulations that model forming and expressing alternate conceptions of concepts and strategies. For example, CSILE (Computer-Supported Intentional Learning Environments) offers several projects and many application examples in which the technology is integrated into curricula so that students' thinking is revealed. With sites such as these, you can help students focus on their thinking as well as look for information. As students develop understandings, you guide them to examine their conclusions based on interactions between their peers, their writing, the information they collect, and their prior knowledge. By trying to explain their ideas to other students and interacting with their peers around academic content, students improve their thinking skills and gain new knowledge. In addition, by reviewing students' CSILE entries, you can find evidence of the kinds of help students provide for each others' thinking and communication skills.

Interesting

Interested students challenge their existing knowledge and are more likely to develop conceptual frameworks that integrate prior knowledge and new information into understanding. Lack of interest is generally the number one reason that students give for not learning to mastery. By focusing on students' current beliefs, you increase the probabilities that students will be intrigued and explore their understandings. Technologies can be an effective tool to promote this interested and active exploration.

Technology-based demonstrations and illustrations such as the math and science animations at ExploreLearning, the Day in the Life Series, and MathMagic stimulate discussions in which students' current beliefs are expressed and tested. By creating classroom environments that encourage manipulating and discussing new ideas, you build opportunities for students to engage their interests and examine the perceptions of others. Although these opportunities can be very rich, it is also important to ensure that students have the skills to interact with each other. Sites such as these usually are open to teacher-led and whole class discussion as well as small and independent group work. Technology enables students to propose an effect and then to test that proposal with a virtual manipulative.

Manipulatives are concrete or symbolic artifacts that students interact with while learning new topics. They are powerful instructional aids because they provide active, hands-on

exploration of abstract concepts. Research supports the premise that computer-based manipulatives are often more effective than ones involving physical objects, in part because they can dynamically link multiple representations together.

In addition, because there is a wide range of technology-based materials available on many topics, you can provide opportunities for students to self-select learning activities that are developmentally and topic appropriate as well as capture their personal interests. Thus, rather than a single demonstration of a reaction of chemicals or one perspective on a war battlefield, you can open a broad range of options for students to select those that are most interesting to them.

Real Life

Constructivist teaching incorporates students' communities as the context for learning. Consider the Schools For Thought (SFT) project of the Learning Sciences Institute at Vanderbilt University. In the SFT Jasper Woodbury series, students are presented with computer-based scenarios that involve complex information and sophisticated decisions. You contribute to successful learning by guiding students' inquiry through focused questions and directing students to consider how these principles affect their community-generated questions. As students work through the SFT dilemmas, you can help them recognize the many ways they have used information they learned in math, science, social studies, and literature to address the issues raised.

You can also facilitate depth of understanding by integrating technologies into the fabric of teaching as intellectual tools that students use to study, learn, and communicate with others in their classes as well as others in different locations. Students can respond by using organizing tools, making complex calculations, and employing search engines to mirror the strategies they will use outside of school to seek answers. In this way, real life in school becomes as much a second nature response as real life outside of school. The result should be a much higher potential for transfer in addition to deeper and more meaningful learning.

Social

Constructing meaning comes from interacting with others to explain, defend, discuss, and assess our ideas and challenge, question, and comprehend the ideas of others. Social activities allow students to express and develop their understandings with peers as they pursue projects through conversations that stimulate examining and expanding their understandings.

One increasingly common technology-based strategy is to create online communities of students and adults who collaborate on specific problems. For example, Global Lab and CoVis link students from as many other sites as you choose to monitor, collect, and share scientific data. The Global Lab project was tested in more than 300 schools in 30 countries. These technologies provide opportunities for students to join a large community and analyze data in a very diverse social environment.

Understanding grows from studying difficult concepts several times and in different ways.

As students analyze and share conclusions across different cultures and perspectives, you have the opportunity to help them evaluate the quality and quantity of the evidence on which they build their conceptions. One outcome is that you can demonstrate the effects of cultural and geographical perspectives by discussing the reasons for differences. These technology-based collaborative social classrooms create learning environments in which students can openly express their conclusions, challenge the conclusions of others, and build extensive information resources. Your role is to help students develop standards to judge evidence, lead students as they reflect on and discuss issues, and encourage students to form conceptual frameworks based on social considerations of the ideas they are studying.

Active

The visible learning actions students use to gather and consider information include writing, discussing, and searching. The covert actions that result in monitoring and choosing how to learn are reading, listening, monitoring, reflecting, considering, evaluating, and checking.

Technology-based interactivity can be a tool to facilitate active learning with dialogue between students as well as to evaluate and revise their propositions. WebPals is a collaborative interaction between teacher education students and middle school students in which they jointly read and discuss their interpretations of novels and review implications for their communities and lives. You would moderate these discussions by posing stimulating questions to your students about the novels they read and also about the observations that their Web pals make. By emphasizing thoughtful interpretation of their questions and observations, you show students that how they think is as important as mastering details.

Time

Time and carefully planned experiences are necessary for broad and deep understanding. Two overarching outcomes from in-depth study are essential. First, understanding is the result of well-organized and widely linked concepts. This allows learners to recall and use their knowledge quickly and appropriately in unfamiliar situations. Second, understanding consists of knowing the important questions and cognitive strategies that characterize the disciplines they are studying.

You can employ technology to increase the efficiency and personalization of the time to learn new ideas as well as to rethink and revise existing ideas. Technologies can facilitate these recursive processes in several ways. Word processors and databases can be used to record thoughts and observations so that students can review them regularly and revise as needed. You can embed this individual review in student self-directed routines guided by metacognitive questions such as: Why are

you learning this? What do you already know that relates to this information? How interested are you in learning this? How difficult will it be for you to learn? Are you checking your understanding as you study? How should you correct errors? Are there other ways you can study that may be better? These questions focus students to use their time well and to maximize success by selecting and applying the most effective learning strategies.

Supportive scaffolding shows students that you understand their needs and "walk" with them as they work to meet learning goals.

Understanding grows from studying difficult concepts several times and in different ways. You can use technologies to foster these recursive learning processes by providing the same information in different formats and for different situations. For example, presenting math from sites such as Global Grocery List and MathMagic provides variety and maintains students' interest.

Technology can help teachers and students use time more efficiently. Students are empowered to control and organize their learning in programs that respond to their specific needs. Some examples of tutoring programs that use time efficiently are Get A Clue, which provides vocabulary development through stories, and HomeworkSpot, which provides homework help through access to subject-specific links. With sites such as these, you can link students to many help and reference sites. For structured practice, students can be directed to use many available drill and practice programs tailored to independent use. These resources offer students multiple presentations of classroom lessons that use time efficiently and promote greater understanding.

Feedback

Feedback is essential to the process of acquiring and reflecting on the relation between existing knowledge and new information. The feedback you provide is most effective as a continual stream of performance-based observations from which students can revise their thinking as they work on projects. When teachers successfully integrate feedback authentically into projects to support and guide students, learning becomes a journey that is constantly being adjusted as students individually and collectively pursue solving problems or explaining observed phenomena.

Software such as Logal Simulations in Science and Math and Decisions, Decisions in Social Studies and others in nearly all disciplines offer students the opportunity to plug in data or observations and model the results of their efforts. Technology-based feedback is immediate and focused on the learning at hand. Feedback can be presented in graphs that illustrate the effects of the students' propositions and by indicating if a test question has been answered correctly. Test questions can also be put into databases from which practice questions can be generated for students to test their own knowledge. Computer simulations can give students realistic problems to solve for evaluating their use of their knowledge and understanding.

This kind of feedback lets students know what they have and have not learned; students then have the ability to manage their own learning, use their metacognitive skills, and establish personal goals. You can promote this sense of efficacy when students make data-based judgments about what they know and how well they know it. Your models of how to think about using feedback are an important ingredient in students learning to make the most of the feedback they receive.

Supportive

Instructional support provides the right assistance at the right time for learners. You can support or scaffold learning by doing things such as reducing the complexity of a task, limiting the steps needed to solve a problem, providing cues, identifying critical errors, and demonstrating how tasks can be completed.

This kind of supportive scaffolding shows students that you understand their needs and enables you to "walk" with them as they work to meet learning goals. A key part of this support is to determine when students are ready for a nudge and then to provide the scaffold that will support them as they make progress. As learners develop new concepts, the scaffolds are removed.

You can provide opportunities for students to self-select learning activities that are developmentally and topic appropriate as well as capture their personal interests.

When you use technologies such as calculators, spreadsheets, and graphing and modeling programs, you help students as they develop their understandings. In addition, you can use computer programs that serve as mentors to students as they develop their skills and knowledge. Programs with access to experts and tutoring also offer scaffolding for students to question their knowledge and find support for exploring questions with multiple correct answers. For example, the site Smarthinking is designed to increase academic retention and achievement for individual students with interactive mentors and tutors. The Electronic Emissary Project is another site that connects online mentors with K–12 students in collaborative and team projects that are curriculum based.

Conclusion

We have described eight characteristics of effective learning environments consistent with modern constructivist theory. As we see research becoming more interdisciplinary—including not only education but also the physiology of the brain, neurology, psychology, and medicine—the constructivist explanation of how to influence learning and learners appears more and more consistent with the emerging evidence. This research has direct and important implications for what we do in classrooms. Classrooms that are active, interesting, learner centered, focused on real life, and social and provide time to learn, frequent and

facilitative feedback, and support both learning to be good learners as well as learning content have consistently been shown to be more effective with all learners.

Creating these environments is a daunting challenge and requires considerable restructuring of classroom routines and teaching practices. Nobody denies the challenge is great, and we do not claim that technologies will make the task easy. But, as we have illustrated, technologies can provide teaching tools that you can genuinely integrate into the instructional fabric of classrooms. In addition, we can teach our students to use technologies to meet their own responsibility to become good learners and also use these technologies as effective tools to teach content. The goal of constructivism—teaching students so they know how and what to learn—is the path to fuller and more relevant understanding of life's important lessons.

Resources

CoVis: http://www.covis.nwu.edu

CSILE: http://www.ed.gov/pubs/EdReform-Studies/EdTech/csile.html

Day in the Life Series: http://www.colonial-williamsburg.com/History/teaching/Day-series/ditl_index.cfm

Decisions, Decisions in Social Studies: http://www.scholastic.com/products/tomsnyder.htm

Edgate: http://www.edgate.com

Electronic Emissary Project: http://emissary.wm.edu

ExploreLearning: http://www.explorelearning.com

Get A Clue: http://www.getaclue.com

Global Grocery List: http://landmark-project.com/ggl/

Global Lab: http://globallab.terc.edu

HomeworkSpot: http://homeworkspot.com

Logal Simulations in Science and Math: http://www.riverdeep.com/products/logal

MathMagic: http://mathforum.org/mathmagic/

ProQuestK-12: http://www.proquestk12.com

Schools For Thought: http://peabody.vanderbilt.edu/projects/funded/sft/general/sfthome.html

Smarthinking: http://www.smarthinking.com

WebPals: http://teacherbridge.cs.vt.edu/public/projects/Web+Pals/Home

THOMAS M. SHERMAN is a professor of education in the College of Liberal Arts and Human Sciences at Virginia Tech. He teaches courses in educational psychology, evaluation, and instructional design and has written more than 100 articles for professional publications. Tom works regularly with practicing teachers and students in the areas of learning improvement and teaching strategies. He is also active in civic affairs, serving on local and state committees. **DR. BARBARA KURSHAN** is the president of Educorp Consulting Corporation. She has a doctorate in education with an emphasis on computer-based applications. She has written numerous articles and texts and has designed software and networks to meet the needs of learners. She works with investment banking firms and venture groups on companies related to educational technology. She serves on the boards of Fablevision, Headsprout, and Medalis, and on the advisory boards of Pixel, WorldSage, and Tegrity.

Successful Teachers Develop Academic Momentum with Reluctant Students

Last year, I couldn't keep track of my work. I lost homework on the way to school or forgot it at home. I got in a lot of trouble. This year I'm staying out of trouble. I have more friends, some of them are better, some still get in trouble, but not as much as they used to. I'm on the ABC honor roll, so I get to go on the honor roll trips. That's something I've never done before. (Randy, 01/05)

DAVID STRAHAN

As an eighth grader, Randy's academic engagement increased dramatically. He rarely got in trouble. He became a leader on community service projects. He qualified for the honor roll. His scores on statewide achievement tests rose significantly. He and his teachers reversed the negative dynamics that had plagued him in years past. Their story demonstrated a pattern of performance that has grown clearer in recent research reports.

In a series of investigations, my colleagues and I have examined ways that students who once did poorly in school made progress and how their teachers nurtured their accomplishments (Strahan, Smith, McElrath, & Toole, 2001; Strahan, 2003; Strahan, Faircloth, Cope, & Hundley, 2007; Strahan & Layell, 2006). We have chronicled ways that successful teachers learned to understand why students are reluctant to do their work, how to help them think through their choices, and how to create classroom learning communities. These practices create "academic momentum."

In the physical sciences, momentum is "a strength or force that keeps growing" (Neufeldt, 1996, p. 874). Athletes and coaches talk of momentum in sports. Advertisers try to create momentum for new products. Politicians try to strengthen momentum for candidates and ideas. In a school setting, momentum is the strength of a student's engagement with learning activities. Students with strong academic momentum approach new assignments with confidence. Based on previous experiences with similar tasks, they know they are likely to do well. If a task proves to be difficult, they know they have a repertoire of skills and strategies they can employ. Students with little academic momentum show little confidence and doubt their ability to do well. In some cases, they have internalized a sense of inadequacy that makes it very difficult to invest effort on assignments. To observers, they may appear "unmotivated," "turned off," or "disconnected."

In our studies, successful teachers have encouraged momentum with reluctant students in similar ways. This article describes these central dynamics and presents a case study to illustrate how one middle school team put research into practice. These insights suggest ways for other teachers and administrators to enhance their efforts to engage reluctant students more productively.

In developmental language, academic momentum is the integration of "skill" and "will." For some time, researchers have used these constructs to describe how students achieve success in school.

> Since at least the 1980s there has been a sustained research focus on how motivational and cognitive factors interact and jointly influence student learning and achievement. In more colloquial terms, there is recognition that students need both the cognitive skills and the motivational will to do well in school. (Linneback & Pintrich, 2002, p. 313)

To learn new concepts in meaningful ways, students need the *will* to want to understand the information and the *skill* to know how best to invest their energies in the learning process (Zimmerman, 1989; McCombs & Marzano, 1990; Linnenbrink & Pintrich, 2002). For example, a student who has previously done well in school will approach a difficult homework assignment with an expectation to understand what she reads. She believes she can figure out the meaning of the text by focusing on what she reads and taking notes. If she gets confused, she may employ strategies she has learned to make sense of the material. She might ask herself questions, re-read passages, or jot down key words. She might take a brief break and return to the task with greater determination. These strategies give her the will to persist to meet her goal of understanding the material and getting a good grade.

How Young Adolescents Experience Academic Momentum

In recent years, researchers have identified two connected ways of thinking that create skill and will in academic settings. Students who do well in school have developed *self-efficacy,* that is, they believe they can perform the academic task. They have also internalized a high level of *self-regulation,* believing they can control the factors necessary to perform the task. A growing number of studies have documented how the development of self-efficacy and self-regulation strengthen achievement. Figure 1 presents a brief summary of some of these studies.

These studies describe ways that young adolescents gain academic momentum. Students need self-efficacy to choose to engage with academic tasks and to persist when learning becomes more difficult. Self-efficacy is not a general belief. It is task specific and based on actual accomplishments. For example, a student might believe he can solve computational problems in his math class. When he sees that the problems require addition, subtraction, multiplication, or division, he invests a great deal of energy in solving them, even as they grow more complex. If he has less self-efficacy about solving equations, however, he may give up at an early stage of deliberation.

Academic momentum also requires the internalization of the skills of self-regulation. As noted in Figure 1, these skills connect self-observation, self-evaluation, goal setting and strategic planning, and monitoring. By examining their work, successful students identify ways they want to improve. They then use specific study strategies to try to reach these goals. Based on their progress, they adjust their work plans to improve their performance. When students set meaningful, realistic goals and accomplish them, they become more confident in their abilities as students and assume more responsibility for their learning. This integration of skill and will accelerates academic progress.

How Successful Teachers Nurture Academic Momentum

Teachers play an essential role in nurturing students' integration of skill and will. Joyce, Wolf, and Calhoun (1993) concluded that successful teaching begins by establishing supporting relationships: "The literature is full of examples of teachers enabling students, even the most unlikely ones, to learn to outstanding degrees and reach beyond prediction to a self-confident, socially committed state of growth" (p. ix).

Teachers play an essential role in nurturing students' integration of skill and will.

Such relationships are especially important when students have rarely experienced academic success. Years ago, we had an opportunity to examine the perceptions of a group of students who entered seventh grade with very little academic

Research Reports	Conclusions
Zimmerman (1989)	Successful students more consistently set goals for themselves, used their prior knowledge, considered alternative strategies, developed plans of attack, and considered contingency plans when they ran into trouble. Less successful students were less aware of these learning behaviors and less likely to assume responsibility for their own learning.
Csikszentmihalyi (1989, 1990)	As adolescents performed tasks that were clearly directed toward immediate goals, they reported that they strengthened the skills needed to perform these tasks well. Participants often noted that they felt best about themselves when they were doing well with a task that mattered to them.
McCombs and Marzano (1990)	Learning to think about their thoughts (metacognition) was important to students' development of self-efficacy and self-regulation. Students who succeeded academically understood that they made choices about how to approach tasks and how much to engage.
Zimmerman, Bonner, and Kovach (1996)	Researchers identified a cycle of four connected thinking processes that characterized self-regulation in school settings: self-observation and evaluation, goal setting and strategic planning, strategy implementation and monitoring, and strategic outcome monitoring.
Paris and Paris (2001)	Researchers documented six types of instructional support that encouraged self-regulation: providing a variety of strategies for completing academic tasks; showing students how, when, and why to apply these strategies; helping students see how their use of strategies promotes academic successes; helping students see how their peers use strategies; helping students use strategies in other academic subjects; helping students integrate the use of strategies across the curriculum (p. 93).
Linnenbrink and Pintrich (2002)	Motivation was situated, contextual, and domain-specific. Not only were students motivated in multiple ways, but their motivation varied depending on the situation or context in the classroom or school.
Schunk (2003)	In studies that documented growth in literacy, teachers explained and demonstrated specific strategies for reading and writing, showed how these strategies related to students' goals, and helped students evaluate their own progress using these strategies.

Figure 1 Representative studies of self-efficacy and self-regulation.

momentum and "bounced back" to do well that year (Strahan, 1988). We gathered work samples and interviews from a team of seventh graders across an entire school year. At the end of the year, we compared the responses of students who made progress with a matched group of students on the same team who did not make progress. Students who made little progress made few connections with the academic life of their school. When reflecting on their responses to lessons, they expressed a "survival orientation," describing ways they tried to look busy or ask for help. Some took pride in creating disruptions, "getting into it" with classmates and teachers as a way to avoid work. In contrast, students who made progress reported functional strategies for completing assignments and ways they avoided getting in trouble. They attributed their success to supportive relationships with their teachers and to academic tasks they could accomplish.

Since that early study, we have analyzed these dynamics in greater detail. A series of case studies with teachers who were successful in challenging settings showed how they developed a strong working rapport with students (Strahan, Smith, McElrath & Toole, 2001). Teachers in these case studies demonstrated warm, supportive relationships by showing a deep knowledge of individual students. Not only could they describe in detail the emotional, physical, cognitive, intellectual, and family needs and circumstances of students in their classes, they addressed these needs by responding to students as individuals. A longitudinal study (Strahan & Layell, 2006) chronicled ways that one middle school team accomplished success across a school year. Students on this team made significant growth, higher than that of the school as a whole. Results documented three principal ways that this team promoted academic achievement. Teachers (a) created a climate of shared responsibility through team building and positive discipline, (b) taught explicit strategies for performing academic tasks, and (c) developed instructional activities that linked inquiry, collaboration, and real-world experiences.

These accomplishments are only possible when teachers have created a climate of trust. Goddard, Tschannen-Moran, and Hoy (2001) examined ways that learning depends on trust, especially in regard to language. Data from 47 elementary schools showed that measures of trust consistently predicted achievement differences in mathematics and reading, even when they controlled for race, gender, socioeconomic status, and past achievement. They concluded that "when teachers believe their students are competent and reliable, they create learning environments that facilitate students' academic success. When students trust their teachers, they are more likely to take the risks that new learning entails" (p. 14). Unfortunately, when the opposite dynamics occur, a "self-reinforcing spiral of blame and suspicion" hampers student achievement (p. 15).

To explore ways that teachers might rekindle trust with students who have struggled in school, Smith-McIlwain (2005) conducted an intensive case study with a ninth grade teacher and seven of her students. Based on observations, interviews, and analysis of writing samples, Smith-McIlwain identified three types of care that contributed to trusting relationships with students who gained academic momentum.

- *Discovery talk*—conversation aimed at discovering the details of students' personal lives to extend understanding in the classroom and "just to find out if everything is okay"
- *Help* (two types)—help for personal problems and the instructional help that actually enables the student to improve academically
- *Friendly listening*—listening to discover personal issues that affect classroom behaviors and academic performance

Because she spent a great deal of time in conversations with participating students discussing the papers they were writing, Smith-McIlwain was able to document what she called "watershed events," which she defined as "specific events that provided the opportunity for the extension of care that resulted in the establishment of a positive personal relationship between teacher and student" (p. 10). For example, one of the participants in her study rarely completed an essay or revealed much of his thinking in writing conferences. One day, in a meeting with this student, the teacher shifted discussion away from his paper to ask about a reference he made to a family event in conversation. After sharing some of his family story, he asked the teacher to suggest ways he could write about these events in his paper. He began to talk specifically about his essay and completed it within a few days. This was his first complete paper. After that, he participated in writing conferences and submitted papers regularly. His writing began to improve. Smith-McIlwain identified the conference about this student's family as a watershed event.

As this study progressed, trust promoted positive actions toward improving performance and diminished the fear of risk. Students became increasingly aware of the types of care they expected from their teacher and described them explicitly. Once this trust was in place, students expected the teacher to provide an honest assessment of their writing and to follow it with specific suggestions. Smith-McIlwain concluded that caring relationships were the key to reengaging disengaged learners, more so than any specific instructional practice or classroom procedure.

When considered together, these studies help us better understand the dynamics of academic momentum. Students who have struggled with reading, writing, or mathematics have often experienced a vicious cycle of poor performance and limited effort. With few successes, they have limited "skills" to invest in new tasks and little "will" to take the risks necessary to improve their skills. Learning to trust a teacher seems to be the only way to break this cycle. When a student learns to trust a caring teacher, he or she can begin to take chances, find the will to invest effort in a task, and receive the guidance needed to improve skills. Trusting relationships thus constitute a "threshold" of action, a point beyond which meaningful learning can occur. Figure 2 presents a graphic representation of these dynamics.

From the bottom up, this figure suggests that successful teachers create classroom communities that invite students to trust them and trust each other. They engage students in conversations that allow them to learn more about them as individuals,

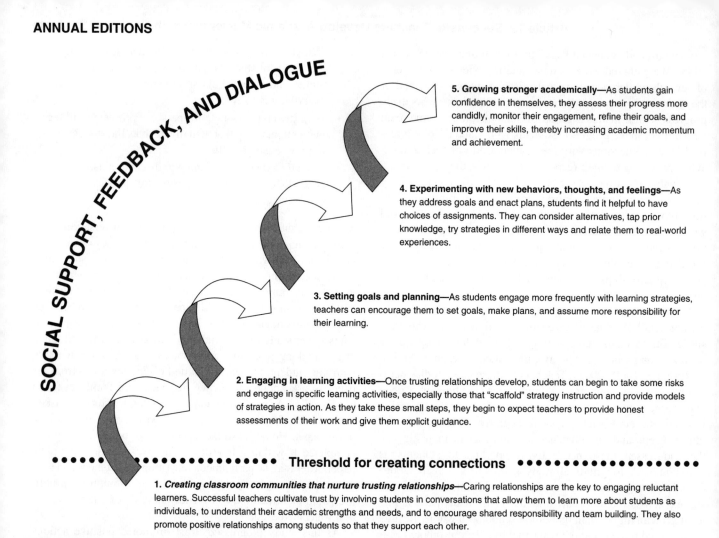

SOCIAL SUPPORT, FEEDBACK, AND DIALOGUE

5. Growing stronger academically—As students gain confidence in themselves, they assess their progress more candidly, monitor their engagement, refine their goals, and improve their skills, thereby increasing academic momentum and achievement.

4. Experimenting with new behaviors, thoughts, and feelings—As they address goals and enact plans, students find it helpful to have choices of assignments. They can consider alternatives, tap prior knowledge, try strategies in different ways and relate them to real-world experiences.

3. Setting goals and planning—As students engage more frequently with learning strategies, teachers can encourage them to set goals, make plans, and assume more responsibility for their learning.

2. Engaging in learning activities—Once trusting relationships develop, students can begin to take some risks and engage in specific learning activities, especially those that "scaffold" strategy instruction and provide models of strategies in action. As they take these small steps, they begin to expect teachers to provide honest assessments of their work and give them explicit guidance.

● **Threshold for creating connections** ●

1. *Creating classroom communities that nurture trusting relationships*—Caring relationships are the key to engaging reluctant learners. Successful teachers cultivate trust by involving students in conversations that allow them to learn more about students as individuals, to understand their academic strengths and needs, and to encourage shared responsibility and team building. They also promote positive relationships among students so that they support each other.

Figure 2   The dynamics of developing academic momentum with reluctant students.

understand their academic strengths, and listen actively to clarify these dynamics. As students learn to trust their teachers and their classmates, they cross a threshold. They begin to engage more frequently in lesson activities, especially those that scaffold instruction and teach strategies explicitly. Because they trust their teachers and their classmates, students begin to assess their own work more candidly and seek explicit guidance from their teachers. Using the academic successes they experience, they begin to set goals for themselves, make plans, and assess their progress more specifically. As they gain confidence, they begin to experiment with new learning behaviors, thoughts, and feelings until they reach a point where they gain enough self-efficacy and self-regulation to learn more independently.

Each step of the way, three sources of energy fuel these dynamics. Ongoing *personal support* reminds students that their teachers and classmates care about them as individuals— who they are and how they feel, in and out of school. *Candid feedback* helps them increase their academic understanding and their skills of self-regulation. *Dialogue regarding academic and personal choices* helps them internalize a sense of responsibility. As this growth spiral strengthens, teachers can increase the levels of challenge, foster an even greater sense of "connectedness" among students, and strengthen academic momentum.

Academic Momentum in Action— Illustrations from a Case Study

Examples from one of our most intensive case studies provide illustrations of these dynamics in action (Strahan, Faircloth, Cope, & Hundley, 2006). For three semesters, we chronicled the responses of middle school students to their teachers' efforts to reengage them in school. Working with two teachers and their team of 42 eighth graders selected as "academically at-risk," we interviewed participants, observed interactions, and gathered follow-up data from students' first semester of high school. Results documented ways that teachers established a sense of community and co-constructed experiential learning experiences with students. During their eighth grade year, 35 students on the team (83%) developed a stronger sense of academic momentum, consistently demonstrating three patterns of behavior: cooperating with classmates and teachers, engaging with academic tasks, and expressing a sense of progress. They attributed their accomplishments to changes in attitude, task-specific successes, supportive relationships with teachers, better self-control, and opportunities for community service. To explore the dynamics of academic momentum in greater detail, we conducted more intensive case studies with seven of the students. Of these seven, Randy demonstrated some of the most dramatic growth in academic momentum.

As Randy noted in the quotation at the beginning of this article, he "got in a lot of trouble" and did not do well academically as a seventh grader. He "hated reading" and did not complete many of his assignments. In one of his interviews as an eighth grader, he reported an incident that gave us a glimpse of his previous experiences in school. He told us another student spilled water on the table during a science experiment, and the teacher blamed him. He refused to take the punishment and received two days of in-school suspension. When we asked him if it was worth it, he replied, "It really wasn't worth it, because they threatened to get an officer in there, and they moved all my friends into lunch detention with me, and they got mad at me" (4/19/05). These types of incidents, in combination with poor grades and inconsistent attendance, made Randy a good candidate for the Sage Program.

Nancy and Terri (pseudonyms) began the Sage program in 2002 as a way to engage students who had grown school weary. Based on their experiences on a regular eighth grade team, they developed a plan for a two-teacher, self-contained team that would work with students struggling in school. To acknowledge the wisdom of each person, they called themselves the Sage Team.

> Anything that we felt was hindering kids, we got rid of. And anything that we felt would help, we would try. We knew that these kids were a lot smarter than they tested. We knew that in order to convince them that we were going to do something different; we had to get rid of the textbooks and see that active learning doesn't come through a textbook. (T, 01/05)

Building on their successes with hands-on, minds-on activities, they developed more "responsive" approaches to teaching.

> I like the term "responsive teaching" a lot, because it brings in the idea we are "responsive" to what they need. It also reminds us that things are coming from realistic situations. Every moment has to become a teaching moment. (T, 01/05)

Two major goals shaped the program: promote students' respect for themselves and others and encourage them to take responsibility for their personal and academic decisions.

> We wanted these kids to be involved, to be positive, to be an asset to the community. We wanted them to be able to see themselves as, "I mean something. I can do something." And so we just thought that, in building their self-esteem, their self-confidence, that aspect of it, we needed to get them involved. (N, 01/05)

Their work with Randy demonstrated how they nurtured academic momentum in ways that illustrate the model for developing academic momentum with reluctant students (Figure 2).

1. Creating Classroom Communities That Nurture Trusting Relationships

To encourage self-confidence and involvement, Nancy and Terri began the school year with activities designed to create a sense of community. On the first day of school, they established a daily routine that featured classroom meetings. In these meetings, they defined their expectations for team behavior, taught procedures explicitly, and clarified rules. They planned outdoor learning experiences that built camaraderie such as Hacky Sack® competitions and team football games. They created lessons that required teamwork and peer tutoring, held conversations about teams and working together, and guided reflections about team events. During classroom meetings, they planned team field trips and asked students to make basic decisions about these trips. To make teamwork more concrete and specific, they asked students to plan community service activities. Students decided to volunteer at a nearby elementary school, an elder care facility, and a local soup kitchen. Other students chose to work on the school grounds. Randy quickly became the leader of the team that worked on the school garden with students from one of the special education classes. "We show them how we can garden and improve the community. It's a benefit for them to get out and do stuff that they normally can't do. I enjoy doing that, helping people and doing something outside" (01/05).

When students misbehaved, Nancy and Terri conducted extensive individual conversations with them. Early in the year, Randy became distracted during a math lesson and had to miss his service learning time. He reported to us later that this was a turning point for him. He decided he did not want to miss his service learning time again. He told us, "If I do my part in the garden, I get a reward and can come back next time. You show teachers you're responsible, they let you come back and do it again. You have to be trusted by them so you can leave class. Rewards work better than ISS and OSS" (01/05). For Randy, this realization became a threshold event. He did not miss service learning again for the rest of the year. In January he reported, "I've really paid attention in class, and I've had all my work. I'm on the ABC honor roll, so I get to go on the honor roll trips. That's something I've never done before" (01/05).

2. Engaging in Learning Activities

Nancy and Terri developed project assignments that addressed inquiry-oriented, student-selected issues. When reading *The Outsiders,* for example, they asked students to identify ways that the social dynamics of high school in the 1960s were similar to those they experienced in school now. They raised questions related to the process of conflict resolution, analyzed choices characters made, and examined the consequences of those decisions. Randy reported that he thought the book was "pretty weird and cool at the same time."

> There were some parts that were sad, because this one boy died. The weird part was the two different sides, the rich and poor people, and they were always fighting; there was never any peace. The part that really stung me was that there were some Greasers who tried to go out with the Socs, and when they did that, they stirred up trouble. Some of that stuff still takes place, because people think they're better than someone else. It still causes fights. Everybody tries to be better than one another. (04/05)

In several other interviews, Randy described how he was engaging in learning activities in ways that were new for him. For example, he described a writing assignment in February as follows:

> We are working on a children's book as one of the projects in class. We're learning different parts of language, how to write, and we're going to try to get our book published when it's finished. We've had to learn about different types of writing, like setting, simile, metaphor, personification, protagonist, antagonist, different views of people speaking, onomatopoeia (he read off a handout). We have to have a pretty good story, and paying attention—that's hard to do, because I'm not into writing. I think it's going to be pretty hard. We have to talk about the Civil War, but in a way that makes sense to first or second graders. We know a lot about the Civil War that shouldn't be discussed with little kids, like how they killed people, and all that, because some people would run away, and they'd get killed by a firing squad—just some things that might upset them to read. It's interesting, because I've learned more on the Civil War; I know some background about how a person in the South could use the land to navigate back to his camp. It's pretty interesting. I've not liked writing in the past. Now I'm writing about something interesting, so it could be okay. I'm trying to get back to where I enjoy writing. (02/05)

Assignments like these encouraged Randy to take risks, learn new ways of thinking, and make personal connections. His successes with these activities strengthened his self-efficacy. Even when he perceived that tasks were difficult, he wanted to do well and could be candid about his performance.

3. Setting Goals and Planning

Nancy and Terri developed a daily routine that featured goal setting and reflective writing assignments. Each morning, they gave students an agenda of daily events and gave them opportunities for input to change the agenda. Morning meetings often centered on the attitudes and behaviors that would lead to success with the day's events. Each grading period, teachers asked students to identify, in writing, their own goals for the progress report period and then to reflect on how well they believed they had accomplished those goals. At the end of the day, they often asked students to reflect on a decision scenario that might put these values into action. One of these scenarios asked students to describe what they might do if a teacher had to leave the room during silent reading time and a few students started to talk. Randy wrote the following:

> I could just sit and read, or I could join them, or I could try to stop them. Most importantly, I would just sit and read, because if you were to try and got mad at them and trying to get them to stop and the teacher comes back in the door, you'd get in trouble for talking also. Sometimes, if someone was to speak to me, I'd turn around and answer them, but most of the time, I'd just keep reading. I know if I'm good, something good will happen to me, and I don't want to get caught not working. (04/06)

Opportunities to set goals and reflect on decision scenarios helped Randy think through the choices he was making and assume more responsibility for his learning.

4. Experimenting with New Behaviors, Thoughts and Feelings

In his interviews, Randy often described how he was trying to think more productively about his assignments. When asked to reflect on how well he was reading *The Outsiders,* he reported

> Some of it was hard to read, they'd skip from talking about one person to another, and you'd get lost. They'd talk about at the movies and skip to a gas station, and then back to the movies. That was the hard part for me. When I got lost, I talked to friends, some of them—you could work together and get a better understanding, because you get information from them. Sometimes I'll go back and reread it and see if I can understand. Other times, I'll have to go through and just read ahead, and that will help give a clue to what happened earlier. I'm trying to get to a higher level of reading, but I'm really low, because in lower grades they'd push me. I don't really like reading because of that. I'm starting to read more. (04/05)

As Randy reflected on his work, he became more aware of ways he was using specific learning strategies. This heightened sense of self-regulation reinforced his growing confidence, encouraged him to think at deeper levels, and led him to set higher goals for himself.

5. Growing Stronger Academically

Randy's new habits of mind seemed to serve him well. He completed his eighth grade with all As and Bs and qualified for the honor roll for the first time. He made dramatic gains on his end-of-year achievement tests, gaining 16 points in mathematics and 8 points in reading, far surpassing the expectation of 4 developmental scale points per year. When we interviewed him after his first semester of ninth grade, he told us

> There is a real big difference at the high school because of changing classes; finding all the buildings and all the classrooms was real hard at first. Now that I'm up here, it is easier to get around. Everything keeps getting harder and harder. I'm doing pretty good. I'm passing all my classes now (two weeks into the second semester). I am in a drama class for an art credit. We have to interact with people, and that helps me improve my speaking skills and not be scared. I used not to interact with many people. (Randy, 02/06)

Conclusions

Our study with Nancy, Terri, Randy, and his classmates documented many of the ways that teachers and students can work together to strengthen academic momentum. As a seventh grader, Randy and his friends displayed a survival orientation toward school, looking busy, forgetting homework, and disrupting class as ways to avoid work. When he joined the Sage

Team, he and his classmates found that Nancy and Terri worked hard to understand them as individuals and identify their academic strengths and needs. They planned lessons that drew on these strengths and scaffolded strategy instruction to build higher levels of understanding. At the same time, they encouraged shared responsibility and held students accountable for their actions. They promoted higher levels of trust by providing ongoing personal support, giving candid feedback, and promoting dialogue regarding academic and personal choices. As the year progressed and the classroom learning community grew stronger, they provided increasingly challenging tasks, fostering even stronger academic momentum.

In this environment, Randy and many of his class mates developed higher levels of both skill and will. They assumed more responsibility for their own learning and understood how to invest energy in lesson activities. As they began to understand concepts in deeper ways, new insights kindled higher levels of self-efficacy and self-regulation. Stronger skills and tangible moments of success convinced them they could make progress. This sense of momentum fueled stronger levels of engagement. As a result, Randy and many of his classmates entered high school with greater confidence and persistence, a work ethic that he described vividly in his final interview:

> Algebra class is advancing, and now there are things I don't understand. My grade was going down, but I am bringing it back up. Graphing is tough. We have to solve for equations that are about six inches long, and you have to narrow it down. It's hard to figure it all out. It's hard when you first get into it. I understand things a bit better now. The teacher gives us notes with examples. The notes help, because they show me how to break it down in steps. The teacher helps too. When someone says he's lost, she goes back and reworks it to show us how she got the answer. That really helps me. (02/06)

References

Csikszentmihalyi, M. (1990). Literacy and intrinsic motivation. *Daedalus, 119*(2), 115–140.

Csikszentmihalyi, M. (1989). The dynamics of intrinsic motivation: A study of adolescents. *Research on Motivation in Education, 3,* 45–71.

Goddard, R. D., Tschannen-Moran, M., & Hoy, W. K. (2001). A multilevel examination of the distribution and effects of teacher trust in students and parents in urban elementary schools. *The Elementary School Journal, 102*(1), 3–17.

Joyce, B., Wolf, J., & Calhoun, E. (1993). *The self-renewing school.* Alexandria, VA: Association for Supervision and Curriculum Development.

Linneback, E. A., & Pintrich, P. R. (2002). Motivation as an enabler for academic success. *School Psychology Review, 31*(3), 313–327.

McCombs, B., L., & Marzano, R. J. (1990). Putting the self in self-regulated learning: The self as agent in integrating will and skill. *Educational Psychologist, 25*(1), 51–69.

Neufeldt, V. (Ed.). (1996). *Webster's new world college dictionary.* New York: Macmillan.

Paris, S. G., & Paris, A. H. (2001). Classroom applications of research on self-regulated learning. *Educational Psychologist, 36*(2), 89–101.

Schunk, D. (2003). Self efficacy for reading and writing: Influence of modeling, goalsetting and self evaluation. *Reading and Writing Quarterly, 19,* 159–172.

Smith-McIlwain, K. (2005). *A study of trust in the motivation and academic performance of disengaged writers.* Greensboro, NC: University of North Carolina Greensboro.

Strahan, D. (1988). Life on the margins: How academically at-risk early adolescents view themselves and school. *Journal of Early Adolescence, 8*(4), 373–390.

Strahan, D. (2003). Promoting a collaborative professional culture in three elementary schools that have beaten the odds. *Elementary School Journal, 104*(2), 127–146.

Strahan, D., Faircloth, C., Cope, M., & Hundley, S. (2006, April). Students' responses to an experiential learning program: Exploring academic momentum with eighth graders who have not done well in school. Paper presented at American Educational Research Association, San Francisco.

Strahan, D., Faircloth, C., Cope, M., & Hundley, S. (2007). Exploring the dynamics of academic reconnections: A case study of middle teachers' efforts and students' responses. *Middle Grades Research Journal, 2*(2), 19–41.

Strahan, D., & Layell, K. (2006). Connecting caring and action through responsive teaching: How one team accomplished success in a struggling middle school. *The Clearing House, 9*(3), 147–154.

Strahan, D., Smith, T., McElrath, M., & Toole, C. (2001). Profiles in caring: Teachers who create learning communities in their classrooms. In T. Dickinson (Ed.), *Reinventing the middle school* (pp. 96–116). New York: Routledge Press.

Zimmerman, B. J. (1989). Models of self regulated learning and academic achievement. In B. J. Zimmerman & D. H. Schunk (Eds.), *Self regulated learning and academic achievement: Theory, research, and practice* (pp. 1–25). New York: Springer and Verlag.

Zimmerman, B. J., Bonner, S., & Kovach, R. (1996). *Developing self-regulated learners: Beyond achievement to self-efficacy.* Washington, DC: American Psychological Association.

DAVID STRAHAN is Taft B. Botner Distinguished Professor of Elementary and Middle Grades Education at Western Carolina University, Cullowhee. E-mail: strahan@email.wcu.edu.

Teaching for Deep Learning

The authors have been engaged in research focused on students' depth of learning as well as teachers' efforts to foster deep learning. Findings from a study examining the teaching practices and student learning outcomes of sixty-four teachers in seventeen different states (Smith et al. 2005) indicated that most of the learning in these classrooms was characterized by reproduction, categorizing of information, or replication of a simple procedure. In addition to these and other findings, in this article, the authors provide a definition of surface and deep learning and describe the structure of the observed learning outcome taxonomy, which was used to evaluate depth of learning. The authors also provide implications for practitioners interested in fostering deep student learning.

TRACY WILSON SMITH AND SUSAN A. COLBY

In public education and in a democratic society, few could question the spirit and intention of the moral imperative to provide all children the opportunity to learn and meet high standards. However, in recent years, our approaches to help all students meet higher standards have resulted in the establishment of a system in which we equate high standards with high test scores. At times, it seems such a system limits students' prospects for moving beyond superficial thinking (Kohn 2000). As educators, we must advocate for a focus on learning that fosters students' opportunities to reach for deeper levels of understanding. Evidence has shown that teachers can adopt a surface or deep approach to teaching, which has consequential effects on what and how students learn (Boulton-Lewis et al. 2001).

Recently, we completed a study examining the teaching practices and student learning outcomes of sixty-four teachers in seventeen states (Smith, Gordon, Colby, and Wang 2005). The sample included elementary, middle, and high school teachers. Thirty-five (55 percent) of the participants had achieved National Board Certification, and twenty-nine (45 percent) had attempted but had not achieved National Board Certification. Specifically, we designed the study to answer two research questions: (*a*) Do students taught by National Board Certified teachers produce deeper responses (to class assignments and standardized writing assessments) than students of teachers who attempted National Board Certification but were not certified? (*b*) Do National Board Certified teachers develop instruction and structure class assignments designed to produce deeper responses than teachers who attempted National Board Certification but were not certified?

The findings of our study yielded statistically significant differences between the comparison groups; however, some of the most interesting results of the study were related to teachers' efforts to elicit and obtain deep learning outcomes with their students, regardless of their National Board Certification status. We assessed teachers' instructional aims through qualitative and quantitative analyses of work samples submitted based on a unit of instruction. The findings indicated that a majority of the teachers (64 percent), regardless of certification status, aimed instruction and assignments toward surface learning outcomes. Additionally, analysis of student work samples collected in the study suggested that the student outcomes in most of the teachers' classrooms were at the surface level (78 percent). These findings suggest that most of the learning in these classrooms was characterized by reproduction or categorizing of information or replication of a simple procedure.

In our study, we learned that our teacher participants tended to teach at surface levels; therefore, their students generated surface responses. Furthermore, we suspect that this finding is not uncommon among the general population of teachers and students. To reverse this trend, we propose that teachers need to understand, value, and foster deep approaches to learning in their students.

Defining Surface and Deep Learning

Although the distinction between surface and deep learning seems intuitive to most educators, it has also been well documented. Marton and Säljö (1976) completed the original work related to deep and surface approaches to learning. Their study examined students' approaches to a particular task. They instructed students participating in the study to read a text and told them that they would later be asked questions about it. Students adopted two differing approaches to this task. The first approach was to try to understand the big ideas in the passage; their focus was on comprehending and understanding the text. The researchers characterized students using this approach as adopting a deep approach to learning. The second approach involved an attempt to remember the facts and details from the text and a focus on what they thought they would be asked later. This group demonstrated rote learning, or a superficial, surface approach to the task.

According to Marton's framework, a surface approach involves minimum engagement with the task, typically a focus on memorization or applying procedures that do not involve reflection, and usually an intention to gain a passing grade. In contrast, a deep approach to learning involves an intention to understand and impose meaning. Here, the student focuses on relationships between various aspects of the content, formulates hypotheses or beliefs about the structure of the problem or concept, and relates more to obtaining an intrinsic interest in learning and understanding. High-quality learning outcomes are associated with deep approaches whereas low-quality outcomes are associated with surface approaches (Biggs 1987; Entwistle 2001; Marton and Säljö 1984). Teachers who are more likely to lead students to deep learning structure lessons, set tasks, and provide feedback

and challenge that encourage the development of deep processing (Hattie 1998, 2002).

The SOLO Taxonomy

In our study, we used a research-based framework to assess teachers' instructional approaches and students' learning outcomes. This framework, the structure of the observed learning outcome (SOLO) taxonomy, is a promising tool that educators can use to understand and examine the depth of teaching and learning. Informed by the work of Marton (1976, 1984) and his colleagues, Biggs and Collis (1982) created the SOLO taxonomy that illustrates a continuum from surface to deep learning. The SOLO taxonomy is structured into five major hierarchical levels that reflect the quality of learning of a particular episode or task. In his most recent book, Biggs (1999) represented the SOLO taxonomy graphically, as shown in Figure 1.

The first level, prestructural, represents a response that is irrelevant or misses the point. The next two levels, unistructural and multistructural, correspond to surface learning, and the final two (relational and extended abstract) correspond to deep learning. An advantage and unique distinction of the SOLO model is that it can be used to reliably analyze and interpret classroom lessons and assignments, and the student work produced in response to those assignments (Bond et al. 2000; Boulton-Lewis et al. 2001; Boulton-Lewis, Wilss, and Mutch 1996; Burnett 1999; Chan et al. 2002; Hattie 1998, 2002; Hattie et al. 1996).

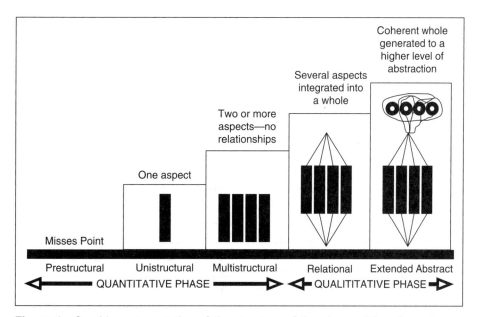

Figure 1 Graphic representation of the structure of the observed learning outcome (SOLO) taxonomy (Biggs 1999).

A Call to Action: Implications for Practitioners

What prevented the teachers in our study from fostering deep learning outcomes among their students? One possibility is that these teachers had not been given the training, tools, and time to engage in practices that contribute to these outcomes. Educators must engage in intentional efforts to foster deep learning in their students. This section gives recommendations for promoting deep learning among students. We have also used a high school world history class scenario to illustrate how the SOLO taxonomy can be translated into practice.

Engage in Dialogue about Deep Learning

A critical first step in the effort to foster deep student learning is to raise and cultivate awareness regarding the characteristics of deep and surface learning. One way to accomplish this is to engage all members of the learning community in intentional, substantive, and inclusive dialogue about student learning. Some of these conversations should take place as part of formal professional development sessions focused on understanding what deep learning looks like. Other conversations, although more informal, should occur more frequently among teams of colleagues. For example, in a typical ninth grade world history course, students might be asked to analyze the causes and results of twentieth-century conflicts among nations (North Carolina standard course of study). Prior to developing this set of lessons, world history teachers might engage in collegial dialogue focused on the following questions: (a) What does a deep understanding of twentieth-century conflicts look like? (b) How will we know that students have a deep understanding of these conflicts? A deep level of learning related to this outcome might be characterized by a response that uses multiple independent details about the causes and effects of specific conflicts to support a general understanding of how conflicts have affected our nation and our world. If a student is able to construct such a sophisticated response, that student will be more able to develop and support generalizations in a different context (e.g., current global conflicts). Collegial dialogue related to deep learning outcomes is essential as teachers progress from identifying what deep learning looks like in their content area to developing activities and assessments correlated with deep learning outcomes.

In the early stages of our study, the research team found our dialogue about learning to be particularly helpful as we worked collaboratively to design a writing assessment that would elicit deep student learning. Prior to designing the writing assessment, we engaged in multiple discussions focused on the question: What is depth of knowledge of writing? As we began to formulate our thoughts, we real-ized how important our dialogue was to our understanding of what deep learning looks like in the area of writing. We then envisioned how helpful similar conversations would be to students engaged in the learning process. From our experiences, we discovered that students who move beyond a surface approach to learning consider any given task as a series of internal rhetorical questions: What do I know about this subject? How does this information relate to what I already know? What is the broader implication or significance of what I've learned? If students do not naturally ask these questions, their teachers must model aloud thought processes that lead to deep outcomes and support students as they are engaged in reflecting about the quality of their own learning. Our goal as teachers should be to help students ask questions of themselves as they are learning and to help them establish habits for continually using a deep approach to learning.

Examine Teaching and Learning

In addition to raising awareness and understanding about the quality of student learning through dialogue, educators must engage in purposeful, systematic examinations of their teaching and the resultant student learning. Teachers must critically examine the teaching resources they are using, the types of questions they are asking students, the assignments they are developing and requiring of students, and their methods of assessing the quality of student learning. One repeating pattern in the teachers' artifacts was that the teachers' expectations or the design of the instructional materials seemed to limit students. It was often difficult to determine students' actual depth of learning because the tasks and questions assigned to them aimed only at surface outcomes. Students rarely demonstrated a deep understanding when the tasks were not aimed at fostering deep learning outcomes.

The SOLO taxonomy is particularly helpful as a tool for examining the quality of teaching and learning. Teachers can use the SOLO taxonomy to construct and categorize questions and assignments (Hattie and Purdie 1998) and to determine whether their instructional goals and tasks will promote deep student learning. Returning to our world history class scenario, a high school world history teacher adopting a surface approach to learning may teach about the causes and results of World War II by lecturing, assigning readings, and conducting multiple-choice tests that evaluate a student's ability to memorize, recall, and even categorize the specific causes and results previously reviewed. In contrast, a high school world history teacher adopting a deep approach to learning may require students to develop a more conceptual understanding about war. The teacher may require students to use this understanding when proposing solutions to current conflicts around the world. Using the SOLO taxonomy in content-specific instruction and assessment allows teachers to determine whether they are facilitating a surface or deep approach to learning.

The usefulness of the taxonomy was evident in our study. When we evaluated the teachers' materials, we realized that many of the resources were commercially made. We worked with our scorers to defuse the bias that often accompanies the observation of worksheet-driven instruction. We trained scorers to assess the value and intent of materials for eliciting deep student learning based on the SOLO taxonomy rubrics created for this study. Even when teachers had not created the materials, we assumed that they purposely selected them for the particular lessons. If the teaching resources were designed to elicit surface responses, usually students responded in like manner. If, however, the instructional materials were designed to foster the understanding of concepts, relationships, and other deep outcomes, students made connections among the facts and details presented to arrive at more sophisticated understandings. By examining the learning goals, resources, content, and sequence of instruction with the SOLO taxonomy in mind, teachers can ascertain if their instructional materials and approaches have potential to move students beyond surface into deep learning.

Likewise, teachers can use the SOLO taxonomy to evaluate the work and responses of students. Examining student learning is essential if we are to understand the results of our efforts to support students in achieving deep learning. Our analyses of student work should be collaborative and independent. Collaborative examinations of student work help teachers determine the concepts, principles, and generalizations they value in their respective content areas. By examining student work samples collaboratively, with others who teach the same course or content, teachers can identify student work at different levels of the continuum and analyze how and why particular work samples represent various levels. More important, what practitioners learn from this process can inform discussions about how they might help students in achieving deep learning outcomes.

Equally as important are independent examinations of student work that, conducted regularly, allow teachers to determine their own effectiveness in helping students achieve deep learning outcomes. Using the SOLO taxonomy as a framework when examining work produced by their students, teachers can begin to understand what type of learning their instructional methods are yielding and how well their students are performing. They can then use this information to support students in achieving deep learning outcomes related to specific content. Because the SOLO taxonomy represents a learning cycle, we must continually support students as we introduce new ideas. We cannot assume that because a student has reached a deep level of understanding with one idea, the student will understand other ideas at the

same level. One simple method for supporting students in the attainment of deep learning outcomes is to assist them in reaching for the next level on the SOLO taxonomy. Our experiences as researchers and classroom teachers indicate that the taxonomy is so straightforward that students in upper elementary, high school, and college can understand its value for evaluating their own learning.

Rethink Classroom Assessment

One of the greatest values of the SOLO taxonomy is that it provides a framework for accomplishing a critical aim of classroom assessment: improving student understanding and performance. Wiggins (1998) suggested, "the aim of assessment is primarily to *educate and improve* student performance, not merely to *audit* it" (original emphasis, 7). Wiggins contended that when we test what is easy to test, we sacrifice our aims, our children's intellectual needs, and information regarding what we truly want to assess. Instead, we settle for score accuracy and efficiency. If we do not study how students learn and demonstrate their learning, we can never understand how to help them learn better. Similarly, Hattie and Jaeger (1998) argued for an approach to assessment that acknowledges its importance in the learning process. They contend "assessment needs to be an integral part of a model of teaching and learning if it is to change from its present status as an adjunct to 'see' if learning has occurred, to a new status of being part of the teaching and learning process" (111). The SOLO taxonomy has potential for helping practitioners assess student learning in process. It not only acknowledges the importance of facts and information, but also provides a way to think about the progression of student learning to higher levels.

For example, the SOLO taxonomy has practical benefits when used as the framework for communicating expectations and creating rubrics to evaluate student work. If the teacher of the world history course asked students to describe the relationships between the causes and effects of twentieth-century conflicts among nations, the responses he or she might receive are likely to represent a range of complexity. If the teacher wants to evaluate students' depth of learning relative to the curriculum goal, the task must be open enough that students have flexibility in their responses. She can provide feedback to students who provided surface responses and guide them to deeper levels of learning. In this way, SOLO is used as an instructional and an evaluative tool. Table 1 provides characteristics of possible responses for each level of the SOLO taxonomy.

Our study provides evidence that although deep learning can happen, most often it does not. Promising steps along the way to helping students achieve deep learning include (*a*) supporting teachers as they engage in dialogue about surface and deep learning, (*b*) examining teaching practices and the resultant student learning, and (*c*) rethinking classroom

Table 1 Characteristics of Possible Student Responses Corresponding to Structure of the Observed Learning Outcome (SOLO) Levels

	SOLO Level	Characteristics of Possible Student Response	Rationale for SOLO Rating
Surface	Prestructural	The student response indicates that there were many causes and effects of conflicts in the twentieth century.	The student misses the point and generates a response that merely repeats the question.
	Unistructural	The student response provides one cause and effect pair related to World War II.	The response focuses on only one aspect of the task. The student has defined the task in a limited way, focusing only on one specific twentieth-century conflict.
	Mulistructural	The student response provides multiple cause and effect pairs related to World War II.	The student has provided multiple relevant details but has not discussed the relationship among those details. The teacher knows that the student used a recall strategy to generate the response because all cause and effect pairs had been discussed in class.
Deep	Relational	The student response provides multiple cause and effect pairs related to multiple twentieth-century conflicts. Additionally, the student discusses the relationships between the causes and effects and uses examples from various conflicts as support.	The student has identified multiple relevant details and has discussed the relationship between these details.
	Extended abstract	The student response provides multiple cause and effect pairs related to multiple twentieth-century conflicts. Additionally, the student discusses the relationships between the causes and effects and uses examples from various conflicts as support. Finally, the student hypothesizes how similar cause and effect pairs might play out in specific current conflicts (or in conflicts in regions of the world not previously discussed).	The student has identified multiple relevant details, discussed the relationships among these details, and has constructed principles about conflict that he or she has used to develop hypotheses about global conflicts that might not have been explicitly studied in the twentieth-century conflicts unit.

assessment with deep learning approaches in mind. Abigail Adams stated, "learning is not attained by chance; it must be sought for with ardor and attended to with diligence" (Howe 2003). Our research has shown that teachers' efforts to foster deep learning outcomes do make a difference. As educators, we must devote ourselves to intentional rather than happenstance efforts to teach for deep student learning.

References

Biggs, J. 1987. *Student approaches to learning and studying.* Melbourne: Australian Council for Educational Research.

———. 1999. *Teaching for quality learning at university.* England: Society for Research into Higher Education and Open University Press.

Biggs, J., and K. F. Collis. 1982. *Evaluating the quality of learning: The SOLO taxonomy.* New York: Academic.

Bond, L., T. W. Smith, W. K. Baker, and J. A. C. Hattie. 2000. *The certification system of the national board for professional teaching standards: A construct and consequential validity study.* http://www.nbpts.org/research/research_archive.cfm (accessed October 1, 2000).

Boulton-Lewis, G. M., D. Smith, A. R. McCrindle, P. C. Burnett, and K. J. Campbell. 2001. Secondary teachers' conceptions of teaching and learning. *Learning and Instruction* 11 (1): 35–51.

Boulton-Lewis, G. M., L. Wilss, and S. Mutch. 1996. Teachers as adult learners: Their knowledge of their own learning and implications for teaching. *Higher Education* 32 (1): 89–106.

Burnett, P. C. 1999. *Assessing the outcomes of counseling within a learning framework.* Paper presented at the annual conference of the American Educational Research Association, Montreal, Canada.

Chan, C. C., M. Tsui, M. Y. C. Chan, and J. H. Hong. 2002. Applying the structure of the observed learning outcomes (SOLO) taxonomy on student's learning outcomes: An empirical study. *Assessment and Evaluation in Higher Education* 27 (6): 511–17.

Entwistle, N. 2001. Conceptions, styles and approaches within higher education: Analytic abstractions and everyday experience. In *Perspectives on cognitive, learning, and thinking styles,* ed. R. Sternberg and L. F. Zhang, 103–36. Mahwah, NJ: Erlbaum.

Hattie, J. A. C. 1998. *Evaluating the Paideia program in Guilford County schools: First year report: 1997–1998.* Greensboro: Center for Educational Research and Evaluation, University of North Carolina, Greensboro.

———. 2002. What are the attributes of excellent teachers? In *Teachers make a difference: What is the research evidence?*, ed. Bev Webber, 1–17. Wellington: New Zealand Council for Educational Research.

Hattie, J. A. C., J. C. Clinton, M. Thompson, and H. Schmitt-Davis. 1996. *Identifying expert teachers.* Technical report presented to the National Board for Professional Standards, Detroit, MI.

Hattie, J. A. C., and R. Jaeger. 1998. Assessment and classroom learning: A deductive approach. *Assessment in Education* 5 (1): 111–21.

Hattie, J. A. C., and N. Purdie. 1998. The SOLO model: Addressing fundamental measurement issues. In *Teaching and learning in higher education,* ed. B. Dart and G. Boulton-Lewis, 72–101. Melbourne: ACER Press.

Howe, R., ed. 2003. *The quotable teacher.* Guilford, CT: Lyons.

Kohn, A. 2000. Standardized testing and its victims. *Education Week.* http://www.alfiekohn.org/teaching/edweek/staiv.htm (accessed September 27, 2000).

Marton, F., and R. Säljö. 1976. On qualitative differences in learning: Outcome as a function of learners' conception of task. *British Journal of Educational Psychology* 46: 115–27.

———. 1984. Approaches to learning. In *The experience of learning,* ed. F. Marton, D. Hounsell, and D. N. Entwistle, 39–58. Edinburgh: Scottish Academic Press.

Smith, T. W., B. Gordon, S. A. Colby, and J. Wang. 2005. *An examination of the relationship between depth of student learning and national board certification status.* http://www.nbpts.org/UserFiles/File/Applachian_State_study_D_-_Smith.pdf (accessed January 8, 2007).

Wiggins, G. 1998. *Educative assessment: Designing assessments to inform and improve student performance.* San Francisco: Josey-Bass.

TRACY WILSON SMITH, PhD, is an associate professor in the Department of Curriculum and Instruction at Appalachian State University in Boone, North Carolina, where she also serves as assistant middle grades education program coordinator. **SUSAN A. COLBY,** EdD, is assistant professor in the Department of Curriculum and Instruction at Appalachian State University in Boone, North Carolina.

From *The Clearing House,* May/June 2007, pp. 205–210. Reprinted by permission of the Helen Dwight Reid Educational Foundation. Published by Heldref Publications, 1319 Eighteenth St., NW, Washington, DC 20036-1802. Copyright © 2007. www.heldref.org

Improve Your Verbal Questioning

Kenneth E. Vogler

Most teachers are well aware that verbal questioning can aid student learning. Asking questions can stimulate students to think about the content being studied (Carlson 1997; Good and Brophy 2000; Graesser and Person 1994; Wilen 2004; Wilen 2001), connect it to prior knowledge (Good and Brophy 2000; Graesser and Person 1994; Wilen 2001), consider its meanings and implications (Carlson 1997; Good and Brophy 2000; Graesser and Person 1994; Seymour and Osana 2003; Wilen 2004), and explore its applications (Carlson 1997; Good and Brophy 2000; Graesser and Person 1994; Wilen 2001). Researchers have found that teachers ask about 300–400 questions per day (Levin and Long 1981), and depending on the type of lesson, as many as 120 questions per hour (Carlson 1991; Carlson 1997; Graesser and Person 1994). With teachers asking this many questions, it is essential that they be skilled in using verbal questioning. Unfortunately, research on teachers' use of verbal questioning has shown that this skill is typically less effective than it could be (Anderson and Burns 1989; Dantonio 1990; Graesser and Person 1994; Seymour and Osana 2003).

A common problem with many teachers' use of verbal questioning is a lack of knowledge about questioning taxonomies and sequencing, knowledge essential for productive verbal questioning (Barnes 1979; Good and Brophy 2000; Lucking 1978; Pollack 1988; Rice 1977; Wilen 2001). Without an understanding of the different cognitive levels of questions, teachers could quite possibly be asking questions at only one or two cognitive levels, probably asking low cognitive level questions that require students to merely recall knowledge or information, rather than asking high cognitive level questions that require students to perform higher order thinking (see Martin 1979; Redfield and Rousseau 1981; Wilen and Clegg 1986; Wilen 2001; Wimer et al. 2001). Without an understanding of the sequence to ask questions, delivery techniques such as the use of wait time, prompting, probing, and refocusing become less effective. And if the questions are poorly worded or the sequence is haphazard, even skillfully used delivery techniques will not prevent student confusion and frustration (Good and Brophy 2000). This article will begin by comparing different question taxonomies, recognizing the importance of knowing the right question to ask and when to ask it, as well as understanding that verbal questioning is a skill that must be practiced before it can be effectively used. Next, it will review relevant research on question sequencing and patterns. Finally, it will present an activity using colleague classroom observations to improve teachers' verbal question sequencing.

Question Taxonomies

Taxonomies are human constructs used to classify questions based on the intellectual behavior or mental activity needed to formulate an answer (Morgan and Schreiber 1969). They are very similar to a continuum. Questions that may have only one "correct" answer and require only minimal mental activity are at one end of the continuum. More complex questions requiring greater mental activity are at the other end of the continuum.

Arguably, the most well-known question taxonomy was created by Benjamin Bloom and his associates—known formally as Bloom's Taxonomy of the Cognitive Domain, or more commonly, Bloom's Taxonomy. Bloom's Taxonomy is comprised of six levels of intellectual behavior (Bloom 1956).

1. *Knowledge.* The knowledge level is the lowest level. At this level, students are only asked to recall information.
2. *Comprehension.* At the comprehension level, students are asked only to put information in another form.
3. *Application.* At this level, students are asked to apply known facts, principles, and/or generalizations to solve a problem.
4. *Analysis.* A question at the analysis level asks students to identify and comprehend elements of a process, communication, or series of events.
5. *Synthesis.* At this level, students are asked to engage in original creative thinking.
6. *Evaluation.* This is the highest questioning level. Students are asked to determine how closely a concept or idea is consistent with standards or values.

Bloom's Taxonomy is just one of a number of questioning taxonomies. Table 1 compares Bloom's Taxonomy with the questioning taxonomies of Krathwohl (2002) and Gallagher and Ascher (1963).

As shown in Table 1, Krathwohl's Taxonomy, sometimes referred to as "the revised Bloom's Taxonomy" or simply "the revised Taxonomy"

Table 1 Comparison of Different Questioning Taxonomies

Bloom	Krathwohl	Gallagher and Ascher
Knowledge	Remember	Cognitive-memory
Comprehension	Understand	Convergent thinking
Application	Apply	
Analysis	Analyze	Divergent thinking
Synthesis	Evaluate	
Evaluation	Create	Evaluative thinking

Sources. Airasian, P. W., K. A. Cruikshank, R. E. Mayer, P. R. Pintrich, J. Raths, and M. C. Wittrock. 2001. *A taxonomy for learning, teaching, and assessing: A revision of Bloom's taxonomy of educational objectives.* Ed. L. W. Anderson and D. R. Krathwohl. New York: Longman, Bloom, B. S. 1956. *Taxonomy of educational objectives, handbook I: Cognitive domain.* New York: David McKay. Gallagher, J. J., and M. J. Ascher, 1963. A preliminary report on analyses of classroom interaction. *Merrill-Palmer Quarterly 9* (1): 183–94.

(see Airasian and Miranda 2002; Byrd 2002; Krathwohl 2002), uses the same number of categories as Bloom's Taxonomy, but there are some differences. Knowledge, the first category in Bloom's Taxonomy, was renamed Remember, and Comprehension was renamed Understand. These category changes do not reflect a difference in the cognitive level of the questions between the two taxonomies, but in their description. The terms "Remember" and "Understand" were chosen because they are commonly used by teachers to describe their work (Krathwohl 2002). For example, a question from the Remember category would be, "What is a noun?" An example of a question from the Understand category is, "What is another way of stating the results of your experiment?" Of the remaining categories, Application, Analysis, and Evaluation were changed to Apply, Analyze, and Evaluate. And finally, Synthesis switched places with Evaluation and was renamed Create.

Gallagher and Ascher (1963) use memory, and three different types of thinking, to describe the question levels in their taxonomy. The lowest question level is Cognitive-Memory. A Cognitive-Memory question only requires simple processes such as recognition, rote memory, and selective recall. For example, "What do you call the angle of elevation of a roof?" Convergent Thinking is the next level, and is a combination of Bloom's Application and Analysis levels. It is convergent because there is only one expected answer, but it requires an analysis and integration of given or remembered data. An example from this category would be, "How would you sum up in one sentence why the main character decided to leave home?" Divergent Thinking, the next level in this taxonomy, requires using independently generated data or a new direction or perspective on a given topic. For example, "Suppose the United States had won the Vietnam War. What impact would that have on foreign policy in Southeast Asia?" Evaluative Thinking is the highest level in this taxonomy. This level requires dealing with matters of judgment, value, and choice. An example from this category would be, "Should an applicant's race be a factor in college admissions decisions? Explain."

Question Sequencing and Patterns

Being a skillful questioner requires not only an understanding of the cognitive levels of individual questions, but also an understanding of question sequencing and patterns (Barnes 1979; Good and Brophy 2000). Question sequencing is a series of questions designed so that each question builds on the answer to the previous one (Wragg and Brown 2001). Wragg and Brown analyzed more than a thousand questions asked by teachers during classroom discussions. They found that 53 percent of questions stood alone and 47 percent were part of a sequence of two or more questions. But of the questions that were part of a sequence, only 10 percent were part of a sequence of more than four questions (Wragg and Brown 2001).

Researchers have noted six patterns of questions (Brown and Edmondson 1989; Good and Brophy 2000; Taba 1971; Wilen and White 1991; Wilen 2001; Wragg and Brown 2001). The first pattern is called extending and lifting (Taba 1971). This questioning pattern involves asking a number of questions at the same cognitive level, or extending, before lifting the level of questions to the next higher level. For example, a science teacher reviewing a chapter on cell division could ask the following series of questions: "What four events must occur in order for any cell to divide?" "What is mitosis?" "What are the five phase of mitosis division?" "What is meiosis?" "What are the five phases of meiotic division?" "How is cell division different in prokaryotic cells and eukaryotic cells?" In this pattern, the first five questions are all at the same cognitive level—extending. Finally, the sixth question requires students to think at a higher level to answer.

The circular path is the second questioning pattern (Brown and Edmondson 1989). This pattern involves asking a series of questions that eventually lead back to the initial position or question. A humorous example of this pattern begins with the question, "Which came first, the chicken or the egg?" After a number of subsequent questions based on responses, the discussion will inevitably lead back to the initial question—a circular path.

The third pattern is called same path, or extending (Brown and Edmondson 1989). This involves asking questions all at the same cognitive level. For example, a teacher questioning students about the sun and the energy it produces could ask the following: "How far away is the sun from the earth?" "What is the temperature of the sun in degrees Fahrenheit?" "What is the diameter of the sun in miles?" "What is the process that causes the sun to release energy as light and heat?" "How does the energy of the sun reach the earth?" This pattern uses all lower level, specific questions.

Narrow to broad is the fourth questioning pattern (Brown and Edmondson 1989; Good and Brophy 2000; Taba 1971; Wilen and White 1991; Wilen 2001). This pattern involves asking lower level, specific questions followed by higher level, general questions. For example, a history teacher discussing the American Revolution could ask the following series of questions: "Why is there a statue of Benedict Arnold's boot in Saratoga, New York?" "Why was the Battle of Saratoga considered a major turning point in the American Revolutionary War?" "Why did 'Americans' feel a revolution was necessary?" "Should rights be given or earned? Explain." In this pattern, the questions start with a lower level, specific question, and progress to higher level, general questions.

The fifth questioning pattern is called broad to narrow, or funneling (Brown and Edmondson 1989; Good and Brophy 2000; Wilen and White 1991, Wilen 2001). This question sequence begins with low level, general questions followed by higher level, specific questions. For example, a teacher could ask the following questions about ecology and the environment: "What is ecology?" "What are ecosystems?" "What are some ways ecosystems can change due to nature?" "Explain how 'succession' affects an ecosystem." "How did Rachel Carson's *Silent Spring* impact perceptions about the relationship between environment and ecosystem?" This pattern, the exact opposite of the narrow to broad questioning pattern, begins with low level, general questions followed by increasingly higher level, specific questions.

The last questioning pattern is called a backbone of questions with relevant digressions (Brown and Edmondson 1989). In this sequence, the focus is not on the cognitive level of the questions but on how closely they relate to the central theme, issue, or subject of the discussion. For example, in a lesson on creative writing and imagery, an English teacher could ask the following sequence of questions about a television commercial: "Who is being targeted?" "What kind of lifestyle is presented?" "How old are the characters?" "What is the literal meaning of the message?" "What is the underlying message?" "How does the way the characters are dressed add to the message?" "If you could create another commercial about this subject, what would you say and how would you say it?" The focus of this pattern has nothing to do with the cognitive level of the questions but how they relate to the theme of script writing and imagery in a television commercial.

Colleague Classroom Observations

Obviously, merely understanding the cognitive level of individual questions and question sequencing and patterns will not, by themselves, make teachers skilled in using verbal questioning. The key to developing and mastering any skill is practicing. Teachers must use their knowledge of cognitive levels of individual questions to practice question sequencing and patterns.

Teacher's Name _____ Date _____

Observer's Name _____ Date _____

Front of Room

Symbols for this observation:

Question Cognitive Level		Question Sequence
CM = Cognitive-memory question	N = Non-volunteering student	EL = Extending and lifting
CT = Convergent thinking question	V = Volunteering student	CP = Curcular path
DT = Divergent thinking question		SP = Same path
ET = Evaluative thinking question		NB = Narrow to broad
		F = Funneling
		B = Backbone

Figure 1   Classroom observation instrument.

An effective activity to help teachers develop verbal questioning skills is colleague classroom observations. Working in pairs, teachers observe their partner, as well as are observed, leading classroom discussions. A classroom observation instrument (see Figure 1) adapted from Sadker and Sadker (1997) can be used to record these observations. Note that the instrument shown in Figure 1 employs a traditional classroom seating configuration. For actual use, the instrument must accurately represent the seating arrangement of the classroom to be observed. The classroom observation instrument utilizes Gallagher and Ascher's (1963) questioning taxonomy because there are just enough categories in this taxonomy for even a novice observer to recognize different levels of questions without having difficulty identifying which category questions belong (see Riley 1980). For each classroom observation, the observer must identify the number of each question, the level (category) of each question asked, the student (whether volunteering or non-volunteering) who answered the question, and the question sequence used. For instance, if the first question asked was a cognitive-memory question answered by a volunteering student, the observer would write "1CMV" in the space on the instrument that corresponds to where the student who answered the question sat. If the next question was a convergent thinking question answered by a non-volunteering student, it would be labeled "2CTN." Once question sequences are recognized, they are also labeled. For example, if the first question sequence was funneling, it would be labeled "1F." At a pre-observation conference, a review can be made of questions that will be asked during the lesson, otherwise known as a question script. After the lesson, during a post-observation conference, a completed classroom observation instrument can provide valuable feedback on the cognitive level of individual questions asked and question sequences used.

I have used this activity for the past six years with a number of colleagues. At first glance, it seems like a very demanding and intimidating activity. The teacher being observed must write out, or at least accurately describe, the individual questions and question sequences they will be using during the observation. The teacher doing the observing is responsible for keeping track of the number of questions asked, making a quick judgment on the cognitive level of each question, locating who answered the question and if they volunteered the answer, and recognizing the question pattern used—things that only someone confident in their ability to recognize cognitive levels and patterns would feel comfortable doing. But a lot can and should be done during the pre-observation conference to alleviate any apprehension about participating in the activity. For instance, colleagues can agree on a "formal" observation for a limited number of question patterns. This allows the teacher being observed not to have to write or describe all the questions they plan to ask during the observation. This also allows the observer, after the agreed-on number of question patterns have been completed, to listen and ideally recognize cognitive levels of questions and question patterns without feeling compelled to write it all out. Sometimes, observations made during this time lead to wonderful post-observation discussions.

Speaking of post-observation discussions, there are a number of topics a new team can focus on to begin their post-observation conference. The first topic has to do with the use of a question script. A discussion about this topic usually can be started by asking questions such as: Did the question script work as planned? Was there a need to ask more questions than originally scripted? Were students able to follow your line of questioning? Why or why not? Often, answers include an acknowledgment that a few more questions were needed than anticipated. Sometimes, this can lead to a discussion about the cognitive level of questions students seem to respond to the best and possible reasons why. Another interesting topic is question transition—whether it is question level to another question level, or question sequence to another question sequence. This discussion could begin with a question such as: Was the transition from _____ to _____ as smooth as you anticipated? Why or why not? Finally, a discussion about question sequences is another good way to begin a post-observation conference. In many instances a teacher may have only used one or two types of question sequences during the observation—question sequences the teacher often used in the past. In this situation, the discussion should focus on getting the teacher out of his or her "comfort zone" and trying other question sequences. Remember, practice builds confidence and competence.

Conclusion

Asking questions and leading classroom discussions can have a positive impact on student learning. They can monitor student comprehension, help make connections to prior knowledge, and stimulate cognitive growth. But good questions and classroom discussions don't just happen. Verbal questioning is a skill, and like any skill, it must be practiced before it is mastered. It is hoped that this knowledge about sequencing and patterns, as well as the classroom observation activity, will help teachers become skilled in using verbal questioning effectively and productively.

References

Airasian, P. W., and H. Miranda. 2002. The role of assessment in the revised taxonomy. *Theory into Practice* 41 (4): 249–54.

Anderson, L., and R. Burns. 1989. *Research in classrooms: The study of teachers, teaching and instruction.* New York: Pergamon.

Barnes, C. P. 1979. Questioning strategies to develop critical thinking skills. Paper presented at the 46th annual meeting of the Claremont Reading Conference, California. ERIC, ED 169486.

Bloom, B. S. 1956. *Taxonomy of educational objectives, handbook I: Cognitive domain.* New York: David McKay.

Brown, G. A., and R. Edmondson. 1989. Asking questions. In *Classroom teaching skills,* ed. E. C. Wragg, 97–120. New York: Nichols.

Byrd, P. A. 2002. The revised taxonomy and prospective teachers. *Theory into Practice* 41 (4): 244–48.

Carlson, W. S. 1991. Questioning in classrooms: A sociolinguistic perspective. *Review of Educational Research* 61 (2): 157–78.

———. 1997. Never ask a question if you don't know the answer. *Journal of Classroom Interaction* 32 (2): 14–23.

Dantonio, M. 1990. *How can we create thinkers? Questioning strategies that work for teachers.* Bloomington, IN: National Education Service.

Gallagher, J. J., and M. J. Ascher. 1963. A preliminary report on analyses of classroom interaction. *Merrill-Palmer Quarterly* 9 (1): 183–94.

Good, T. J., and J. Brophy. 2000. *Looking in classrooms.* 8th ed. New York: Longman.

Graesser, A. C., and N. K. Person. 1994. Question asking during tutoring. *American Educational Research Journal* 31 (2): 104–37.

Krathwohl, D. R. 2002. A revision of Bloom's taxonomy: An overview. *Theory into Practice* 41 (4): 212–18.

Levin, T., and R. Long. 1981. *Effectiveness instruction.* Alexandria, VA: Association for Supervision and Curriculum Development.

Lucking, R. A. 1978. Developing question-conscious language arts teachers. *Language Arts* 55 (5): 578–82.

Martin, J. 1979. Effects of teacher higher-order questions on student process and product variables in a single-classroom study. *Journal of Educational Research* 72 (2): 183–87.

Morgan, J. C., and J. E. Schreiber. 1969. *How to ask questions.* Washington, DC: National Council for the Social Studies. ERIC, ED 033887.

Pollack, H. 1988. *Questioning strategies to encourage critical thinking.* ERIC, ED 297210.

Redfield, D. L., and E. W. Rousseau. 1981. A meta-analysis of experimental research on teacher questioning behavior. *Review of Educational Research* 51 (3): 237–45.

Rice, D. R. 1977. The effect of question-asking instruction on preservice elementary science teachers. *Journal of Research in Science Teaching* 14 (4): 353–59.

Riley, J. P. 1980. A comparison of three methods of improving preservice science teachers' questioning knowledge and attitudes toward questioning. *Journal of Research in Science Teaching* 17 (5): 419–24.

Sadker, M., and D. Sadker. 1997. *Teachers, schools and society.* Boston: McGraw-Hill.

Seymour, J. R., and H. P. Osana. 2003. Reciprocal teaching procedures and principles: Two teachers' developing understanding. *Teaching and Teacher Education* 19 (3): 325–44.

Taba, H. 1971. *Teaching strategies and cognitive function in elementary school children.* San Francisco: San Francisco State College.

Wilen, W. W. 2001. Exploring myths about teacher questioning in the social studies classroom. *Social Studies* 92 (1): 26–32.

———. 2004. Refuting misconceptions about classroom discussion. *Social Studies* 95 (1): 33–39.

Wilen, W. W., and A. Clegg. 1986. Effective questions and questioning: A research review. *Theory and Research in Social Education* 14 (2): 53–62.

Wilen, W. W., and J. White. 1991. Interaction and discourse in social studies classrooms. In *Handbook of research in social studies teaching and learning,* ed. J. P. Shaver, 483–95. New York: Macmillan.

Wimer, J. W., C. S. Ridenour, K. Thomas, and A. W. Place. 2001. Higher order teacher questioning of boys and girls in elementary mathematics classrooms. *Journal of Educational Research* 95 (2): 84–92.

Wragg, E. C., and G. Brown. 2001. *Questioning in the primary school.* London: Routledge Falmer.

KENNETH E. VOGLER is an assistant professor in the Department of Instruction and Teacher Education at the University of South Carolina.

From *The Clearing House,* November/December 2005, pp. 98–103. Reprinted by permission of the Helen Dwight Reid Educational Foundation. Published by Heldref Publications, 1319 Eighteenth St., NW, Washington, DC 20036-1802. Copyright © 2005. www.heldref.org

Designing Learning through Learning to Design

This paper represents a conversation between a high school science teacher and a university researcher as they found common ground in the theory and experiences of designing powerful learning experiences. The teacher describes an instructional unit in which students designed a complex, interactive display showing what life may have been like during the Mesozoic Era. The researcher offers analysis of that activity through the lens of design and design-based learning. Their voices intentionally co-mingle as they illuminate aspects of one another's work—the pedagogical work of the teacher, and the theoretical analysis of the researcher. The conversation provides useful insight for teachers wishing to employ design-based learning in their classrooms and an important analytic lens for researchers to view teaching and learning.

PUNYA MISHRA AND MARK GIROD

Introduction

Much is written today about design-based learning (Author, Zhao, & Tan, 1999; Author & Koehler, in press; Kafai & Resnick, 1996;). Design, as a pedagogical activity, has come to be perceived as forward-looking, reform-oriented, and progressive (Roth, 1998). Reformers and writers commonly support design-based learning for its authentic outcomes and activities, and collaborative and cross-curricular nature (Brown, 1992). These, however, are only surface-level characteristics of design-based learning that fail to capture three, much deeper, psychologically-based characteristics, that illuminate the efficacy and potential of design-based learning.

This paper provides one teacher's account of a unique design-based learning situation in which 40 high school students worked to represent life during the Mesozoic age. Students' design projects had to: a) communicate (teach) a particular element related to life during the Mesozoic period such as plant and animal life, climate, or physiographic features of the earth's surface; b) provide something for both children and adults to do to help them learn or understand the point being made by the representation, and; c) be scientifically accurate and artistically crafted to provide a unique experience to those viewing the representations. Projects were displayed in a community open-house referred to as the Mesozoic Resource Center (MRC). Woven throughout an extended pedagogical description of the MRC, as told by the teacher (in italics), is a parallel, theoretical analysis through the lens of design, as told by the university researcher (in plain text). The intent is to illuminate salient features of both the pedagogical description and the theoretical analysis in ways educative to both teachers and researchers.

The Case of the Mesozoic Resource Center[1]

As I looked around my classroom I saw Reuben, a known gang member, reading a story he had written and illustrated about a young Pachycephalosaurus to five first graders. Chris, an eighteen-year-old sophomore labeled severely emotionally disturbed, was smiling and enthusiastically debating the feasibility of the asteroid impact theory with our school superintendent. Linda and Becky, both of whom had failed other science classes, were surrounded by several parents as they described the nesting behavior of hadrosaurs.

This was the scene at the opening of my classes' Mesozoic Resource Center. Forty high school science students and I had been working diligently for ten weeks in preparation for this evening. We had set up displays on both floors of our unusual two-story classroom. Downstairs visitors browsed through student constructed displays ranging from the diversity of pterosaurs to a debate over whether dinosaurs were warm or cold-blooded. Students manned their displays clarifying ideas and offering additional information to visitors as they passed.

In one corner, elementary children were invited to excavate dinosaur toys from a simulated paleontological dig, pour resin over insects to simulate the famous mosquito stuck in amber from Jurassic Park, or use a rubber stamp kit to construct their own dinosaurs. Each group was closely supervised by my students.

Upstairs, another group was conducting tours of a lost age. Guides assigned to each period, Triassic, Jurassic, and Cretaceous, led visitors through their respective age describing the plants, animals, and climate of that time. Visitors stood stunned at the bleakness of the dry, sandy, desert-like surroundings in the Triassic, marveled at the 8 meter long Apatosaurus model being eyed by the head of a Parasaurolophus peering through ferns and lush greenery, and were amazed by the 3 meter tall Tyrannosaurus Rex model glaring down at them as the first flowering plants appeared in the Cretaceous Period. The sights and conversation were academic, enthusiastic, and engaging for everyone involved.

What started as a trial in self-directed learning exploded in both size and scope. Before I knew it, these students, most previously characterized as disinterested, unmotivated, and apathetic, were tearing down the walls of traditional learning. In its place they built a community of scholars each working toward understanding and communicating what life was like millions of years ago in the Mesozoic Era. As their teacher, I could barely keep up.

New to teaching about dinosaurs and the era in which they lived, I had few resources and even less personal knowledge about these topics. I chose to involve my students, as well as myself, with a book called Dinosaur! (Norman, 1991). It is filled with information about current thinking regarding dinosaurs and is richly illustrated. We supplemented our reading with the four-part A&E television series by the same name. In areas where these two sources were insufficient in providing enough information, students consulted our school library, the Internet, local experts, university libraries, and even college professors. Just learning how to gather information was a worthwhile experience for many of my students.

We soon realized that to get a complete picture of life in the Mesozoic Era we needed to split up and become experts in many different areas. With a little guidance, my students were able to focus their inquiry into very specific topics. With their topic in mind, they had one goal. Each student was to become an expert in a particular area. I challenged each student to develop their knowledge of the subject far beyond mine or anyone else's in our school. These were empowering words for largely disenfranchised students. They eagerly accepted the challenge! As students' knowledge grew it became clear that I had to find a way to showcase their work. Our simple dinosaur projects became the Mesozoic Resource Center described above.

Ready to show off their products, my students suggested that I call the local newspaper and television station. To our surprise, both agencies were eager to come and do short stories. Everyone was thrilled to be on television but the pressure to look and sound impressive was mounting. The television crew arrived a couple hours before the grand opening as my high school students were hosting groups of second and third graders from our local elementary school. One of the requirements for each student display was that it must have something for both child and adult visitors to do. In this case, the elementary teachers examined the computer-generated overlays describing dinosaur anatomy while children distinguished Ornithischians from Saurischians using very realistic plastic models.

By far, the biggest hit of the Mesozoic Resource Center was the walk-through-diorama showing how life might have been during the each of the three periods of the Mesozoic. Together with my students and our school janitors, we had built fake

walls of black plastic to separate the ages. Across several days we hauled in 500 gallons of sand and rocks to spread across the floor. Students working on the diorama spent two Saturdays hauling brush, driftwood, and small shrubbery to "plant" in our 200-million-year-old setting. Our local florist donated several large boxes of ferns to add to the realism. With back lighting and sound effects piped in through a hidden stereo system, our diorama became very impressive.

The highlights of the diorama were two very large dinosaur models built and assembled by my students. We ordered balsa wood snap-together models from a supply house and traced each of the pieces. Using an opaque projector and very steady hands, six students made patterns of dinosaur bones approximately 1/4 normal scale. The students traced the patterns onto sheets of plywood, and using jigsaws, cut them out. After sanding and painting all the pieces and using a few bolts and clamps, we assembled these massive dinosaur models in their appropriate time periods.

Second only to the huge dinosaur models in impressiveness were two dinosaur heads painted in exquisite detail. A student who was an avid hunter found a taxidermy magazine that sold closed-cell styrofoam forms of dinosaur heads. Taxidermists buy and display them on their wall in jest like any other trophy animal. But this student imagined the heads mounted on the wall peering out of bushes that would be planted in front. After airbrushing the forms to amazing realism, the effect was quite startling. Imagine walking through a darkened classroom, marveling at the magnitude of the dinosaur models in front of you, listening intently as students explained the hunting habits of small, carnivorous dinosaurs, and then suddenly eyeing one, head sticking out of some bushes lit by a soft green glow. The effect was fantastic. In fact, one first grader wet his pants!

A Researcher's Conceptualization of "Design"

Design activities are one class of activities that fall under the broader rubric of project-based activities. In such activities, students design complex interactive artifacts to be used by other students for learning about a particular subject (Harel, 1991). Design-based projects have involved the development of presentations, instructional software, simulations, publications, journals, and games (Carver, 1991; Guzdial, 1993; Kafai, 1995, 1996; Lehrer, 1991; Vyas & Author, 2002). With such projects, students learn both about design—through the process of developing complex artifacts—and a variety of academic disciplines, such as programming, social studies, language arts, etc.

Research and theory suggest that design-based activities provide a rich context for learning (Willet 1992). Within the context of social constructivism (Cole, 1997; Vygotsky, 1978) or constructionism (Papert, 1991), design projects lend themselves to sustained inquiry and revision of ideas. Other scholars have emphasized the value of complex, self-directed, personally motivated and meaningful design projects for students (Blumenfeld, Soloway, Marx, Krajcik, Guzdial, & Palinscar, 1991; Collins, Brown & Newman, 1990, Harel & Papert, 1990, Kafai, 1996).

Such design-based, informal learning environments offer a sharp contrast to regular classroom instruction, the effectiveness of which has been questioned by many scholars (Papert, 1991, 1993; Pea, 1993; Lave & Wenger, 1991). As one might imagine, adapting such open-ended problem solving situations into the structure and organization of the conventional classroom is often difficult to manage logistically.

Design, broadly speaking, can be seen as "structure adapted to a purpose" (Perkins, 1986, p. 2). Perkins' definition captures elegantly an essential quality of design: it is a process of constructing artifacts that exhibit "goodness of fit." Design can be seen both in material artifacts, such as a hammer or a piece of software, as well as in non-material artifacts, such as a poem, a theory or a scientific experiment. This conceptualization of design can play itself out within multiple contexts. In the MRC project, for instance, students designed complex educational artifacts based on their understanding of important ideas in science and art. Further, they acted as social scientists designing usability studies and evaluation tools to test how their exhibits were used by exhibit visitors.

At another level, design applies to educational researchers attempting to better understand the pragmatic and theoretical aspects of developing design-based activities. In essence, our perspective sees design as being both "an object of study as well as context for a study of learning" (Author, Zhao, & Tan, 1999; Kafai 1996, pg. 72; Koehler, Author, Hershey & Peruski, under review). This view of design as adaptation generates several significant implications that can help us understand the pedagogical value of design-based learning activities. These implications are discussed in terms of the MRC.

Design in Analysis of the Mesozoic Resource Center

One of the most interesting aspects of the MRC project is the multiple levels of understanding that were required for completing the design task. Students surely gained a deep understanding of the core ideas of deep-time and evolutionary biology, and the manner in which they play out in different domains. Students also developed strategies and techniques to help others learn these concepts through their exhibit. This required them to think beyond the science concepts to consider ways in which others would generate their own understandings of these ideas. Further, students needed to develop technological skills in order to construct the artifacts that embodied their ideas. To understand this, we can apply the design experiment approach (Brown, 1992), focusing on the following social and cognitive aspects of the design activities to help interpret what was observed:

- The role of knowledge in design, technology, and subject matter content in learning to design, the patterns of interaction among knowledge in different domains
- The role of audience, mentors, leaders, collaborators, and peers in learning and design; patterns of interaction, both face-to-face and online and their effects on learning and design

- The role of artifacts and ideas as tools for construction, expression, communication and inquiry
- The nature of representation and manipulation of symbols in the process of design

As these aspects of the design experiment approach suggest, design works at multiple levels; thus, understanding what happened in this classroom requires analysis at multiple levels as well. The unit of analysis is not merely the individual, but rather the interaction of the learner, the practices, the resources being used, the community within which these practices are nested and the constraints of the situation—i.e. the intersection of individual, activity, and context (Lave & Wenger, 1991; Roth, 1998).

Three themes emerge from this juxtaposition of the pedagogical instantiation of the Mesozoic Resource Center and the psychological analysis via design. Each theme is illustrated by a brief vignette drawn from the teacher's account of experiences during production of the Mesozoic Resource Center. The vignettes are designed to be broadly representative of the experiences of students' learning in this design-based setting. They should not be considered atypical or unusual. Three different stories could have been easily selected to illustrate these same three design themes. As with the intertwining of voices used previously, these themes as offered by the researcher appear in plain text, and their corresponding illustrative stories, supplied by the teacher, appear in italics.

Theme I: Design as a Transformative Experience

Vygotsky (1978) and Dewey (1933) emphasize the role of dialogue or interplay in learning. As the individual acts on the environment, the environment also acts upon the individual. Inquiry and learning, like design, are not simply about understanding and assembling materials. They are fundamentally about ideas and transforming oneself and the world through the process of working with those ideas.

At the heart of design is an interplay between theory and practice, between constraints and trade-offs, between designer and materials, and between designer and user/learner. Through this dialogue, meanings and artifacts are defined and understood (Dewey, 1934). The interaction is bi-directional and open-ended.

Design also requires that learners discern the essential qualities of an idea and represent it in a compelling manner. To have new ideas is more than simply labeling or thinking about the world differently; rather, it is to have a new way of *being* in the world. To have an idea is to be more fully alive with thought, feeling, and action (Dewey, 1934; Jackson, 1998). It is to have an "energy-for-action" that is directed by thought and fueled by emotion. The having of a new idea is more than the acquisition or application of information. It is, therefore, critical to have students work with ideas that are inherently empowering and generative.

Story I: Seeing the World Differently

Oscar was particularly captivated by the debate over the warm or cold-bloodedness of dinosaurs. After much research on predator to prey ratios, body mass to energy expenditure ratios, and heat dissipation and conservation anatomy and strategies, Oscar literally began to see the world through the eyes of this debate. Oscar told a story about seeing a mouse in his mother's kitchen to illustrate his new-found worldview, "See how it moves in quick, darting motions. I bet it needs to eat all the time because it expends so much energy moving in that jerking way." At our open-house, I overheard him explain to his mother, "Scientists believe these fin-backed dinosaurs actually pumped blood up in this sail-like thing to help cool off or warm up." This uniquely energizing idea had transformed Oscar's world from static observations of nature to more alive and dynamic ways of seeing and experiencing the world. In fact, Oscar enrolled in zoology class the next semester because he said he found animals interesting for the first time in his life. Design put Oscar in contact with powerful, transformative ideas in ways that led him into further inquiry and further educative experiences.

Theme II: Design as Inquiry

Design activities create opportunities to learn about the nature of inquiry itself. First, design forces students to pay attention to the process and consequences of their actions. Second, students learn to appreciate the nonlinear, often messy nature of inquiry. Design tasks are often ill-structured and afford many viable solutions. This perspective on knowledge and inquiry is quite different from the epistemological illusion typically found in classrooms, where problems are well-defined with clear-cut solutions. Additionally, to design is to engage in a fundamentally social activity. Students learn the value of communicating effectively and of attending to the experience of others. The design process requires building and negotiating ideas in a community of practice, just as ideas are generated and validated among practicing scientists. Students become experts in specific domains and share their knowledge with one another. Data gathering, validation, and accurate representation of those data force students to move beyond the constraints of their classroom, and school.

Story II: Imagining the Past

The guiding task was to present life in the Mesozoic in as much reality and detail as possible. Rachel, Heather, and Desiree thought deeply about the climate and plant life of the Mesozoic as they were assigned the task of making scenery for the walk-through diorama. They assumed their task would be to examine, and try to reproduce, artwork that portrayed dinosaurs, plant and animal life, and climate in the Mesozoic. However, after some research, they discovered that flowering plants did not appear until the Cretaceous period—no where near the Triassic period in which so many flowers appeared in our textbook! After a few more discoveries of inconsistencies, the three girls embarked on an all-out study of flora, fauna, and climate in the

Mesozoic. They wanted their contribution to the MRC to be as scientifically accurate as possible to provide the most authentic experience to visitors. Gradually, their understanding of the period developed and the scenery they produced was stunning in its accuracy and attention to detail. The opportunity to design had forced them to investigate best and most accurate ways to represent their ideas.

Theme III: Design Is Expression

Design is the process of exploring new ways of being in the world, and hence a deeply personal and expressive act. Design is an inner idea expressed outwardly—it is a private possibility acted upon publicly. Design-based activities, therefore, give students opportunities to bring their own unique interpretations to subject matter ideas. We contend that this idea stands in significant contrast with conventional schooling, where ideas are impressed rather then expressed and where, too often, artistic activity is seen as separate from scientific activity. Too often learning in science is viewed as solely cognitive. We believe the power and beauty of ideas to move and inspire is often disregarded. By allowing students to construct artifacts that are personally meaningful and communicative we allow students to tap into the aesthetic aspects of learning ideas. It allows students to develop their artistic potential as well, all within the overarching goal of developing expressive and engaging artifacts that communicate to an audience.

Story III: The Art of Science

Ruben had an incredible talent for art. Typically pensive and brooding, he wasn't interested in the difficult and academic tasks with which the rest of the class was engaged. After a few days considering options, halfhearted attempts, and dead-ends, Ruben remembered one of our goals was to share our findings with the community—in particular K–3 students from our local elementary school. Ruben posed to me his plan to author and illustrate a scientifically accurate story about a dinosaur as it moved through a day in the Cretaceous period. Ruben was able to couch his academic learning in the personal expression of his developing story. The end result was a well-written, conceptually faithful, wildly personalized and expressive story about Packy—a young Pachycephalosaur living and learning 80 million years ago. He joyfully read his story several times to different groups of young, enthusiastic MRC visitors. Ruben, who had been in trouble with the law, drugs, and violence, was newly perceived as a teacher, explorer, and artist by these young children and their parents. Ruben was clearly proud of his accomplishment and through this design process changed both his perceptions of himself and the world in ways that possibly no other school related experience had before.

Discussion

It is clear that not all design (or project based) activities have equal educational value. Merely giving students "something to construct" may keep them busy but it is unclear as to what pedagogical value exists in doing so. Elucidation of the pedagogical and psychological elements of design offer educators a framework useful in developing project-based experiences for students that can motivate, challenge and teach as well as researchers a framework for thinking more clearly about powerful classroom teaching and learning.

In this vein, valuable design based projects will be centered on important subject matter ideas that are powerful, generative, and expansive; ideas that move students to see the world in different ways. Powerful ideas lie at heart of all disciplines, though too often obscured by terminology and shallow understandings. Design based activities allow students to engage with these powerful ideas in a serious manner, and, most importantly, to act on them in ways that move students into the world engaged, curious, and poised to learn more.

Design-based learning centers learning on this goal of "acting on" an idea, both intellectually and physically. Intellectually, the designer engages with the ideas and concepts and attempts to learn more. Physically the designer works with the artifact, modifying, manipulating objects to fit the desired ends. This is essentially a dialogue between ideas and world, between theory and its application, a concept and its realization, tools and goals. This dialogue is at the heart of inquiry, involving as it does the construction of meaning and the evolution of understanding through a dialogic, transactional process. Thus, sound design-based projects carefully incorporate opportunities for inquiry within them.

Finally, design based activities hold the artistic/aesthetic aspects of learning as of equal value to the cognitive. Notions of the aesthetic are fundamental to both the intellectual and physical aspects of the design process. Intellectually, students learn to appreciate the beauty of ideas; physically, they learn the beauty of constructing an aesthetically pleasing artifact. In this view, design based projects offer students opportunities to explore affective aspects of learning and should be rewarded for doing so successfully.

Pedagogy centered on design raises important issues that effectively "raise the bar" on what a powerful, constructivist education entails. As a psychological lens, design expands definitions of teaching and learning in ways that bring other outcomes to bear on educational problems. In this way, we hope design and design-based learning enrich the work of both teachers and researchers.

Note

1. Some of the text describing the Mesozoic Resource Center has appeared previously as Author (1998). Educational Leadership.

References

Author (1998). *Educational Leadership.*

Author, & Koehler, M. J. (in press). In Y. Zhao (Ed.). *What teachers should know about technology: Perspectives and practices.*

Author, Yong, Z., & Tan, S. (1999). *Journal of Research on Computing in Education.*

Blumenfeld, P. C., Soloway, E., Marx, R. W., Krajcik, J. S., Guzdial, M., & Palincsar, A. (1991). Motivating project-based learning: Sustaining the doing, supporting the learning. *Educational Psychologist, 26* (2 & 4), 369–398.

Brown, A. L. (1992). Design experiments: theoretical and methodological challenges in creating complex interventions in classroom settings. *The Journal of the Learning Sciences 2:* 141–178.

Carver, S. (1991). *Interdisciplinary problem solving.* Paper presented at the American Educational Research Association, Chicago, IL.

Cole, M. (1997). *Cultural psychology: A once and future discipline.* Cambridge: Harvard University Press.

Collins, A. S., Brown, J. S., & Newman, S. (1990). Cognitive apprenticeship: Teaching the craft of reading, writing, and mathematics. In L. B. Resnick (Ed.), *Cognition and instruction: Issues and agendas* (p. 453–434). Hillsdale, NJ: Lawrence Erlbaum Associates.

Dewey, J. (1933). *How we think: A restatement of the relation of reflective thinking to the educative process.* Boston, MA: Heath.

Dewey, J. (1934). *Art as experience.* New York: Perigree.

Guzdial, M. (1993). *Emile: Software-realized scaffolding for science learners programming in mixed media.* Unpublished doctoral dissertation, Ann Arbor, MI: University of Michigan.

Harel, I. (1991). *Children designers.* Norwood, NJ: Ablex.

Harel, I., & Papert, S. (1990). Software design as a learning environment. *Interactive Learning Environment, 1* (1), 1–32.

Jackson, P. W. (1998). *John Dewey and the lessons of art.* New Haven: Yale University Press.

Kafai, Y., & Resnick, M. (Eds.)(1996). *Constructionism in practice: Designing, thinking and learning in a digital world.* Mahwah, NJ: Lawrence Erlbaum Associates.

Kafai, Y. (1995). *Minds in play: Computer game design as a context for children's learning.* Hillsdale, NJ: Lawrence Erlbaum Associates.

Kafai, Y. (1996). Learning design by making games: Children's development of design strategies in the creation of a complex computational artifact. In Y. Kafai & M. Resnick, (Eds.), (pp. 71–96). *Constructionism in practice: Designing, thinking and learning in a digital world.* Mahwah, NJ: Lawrence Erlbaum Associates.

Koehler, M. J., Author, Hershey, K., & Peruski, L. (under review). With a little help from your students: A new model for faculty development and online course design. *Journal of Technology and Teacher Education.*

Lave, J. & Wenger, E. (1991). *Situated learning: Legitimate peripheral participation.* New York: Cambridge University Press.

Lehrer, R. (1991). *Knowledge as design.* Paper presented at the American Educational Research Association, Chicago, IL.

Norman, D. (1991). *Dinosaur!* Upper Saddle River, NJ: Prentice Hall.

Papert, S. (1991). Situating constructionism. In I. Harel & S. Papert. (Ed.) *Constructionism.* Norwood, NJ: Ablex.

Papert, S. (1993). *The children's machine: Rethinking school in the age of the computer.* New York: Basic Books.

Pea, R. (1993). Practices of distributed intelligence and designs for education. In G. Salomon (Ed.), *Distributed cognitions: Psychological and educational considerations.* (pp. 47–87). Cambridge, UK: Cambridge University Press.

Perkins, D. N. (1986). *Knowledge as design.* Hillsdale, NJ: Lawrence Erlbaum Associates.

Roth, W.-M. (1998). *Designing communities.* Dordrecht: Kluwer Academic Publishers.

Vyas, S., & Author (2002). Experiments with design in an after-school Asian literature club. In R. Garner, M. Gillingham, Y. Zhao (Eds.). *Hanging out: After-school community based programs for children.* Greenwood Publishing Group: CT. 75–92.

Vygotsky, L. S. (1978). *Mind in society: The development of higher psychological processes.* Cambridge: Harvard University Press.

Willett, L. V. (1992). *The efficacy of using the visual arts to teach math and reading concepts.* Paper presented at the annual meeting of the American Educational Research Association, San Francisco, CA.

Using Engagement Strategies to Facilitate Children's Learning and Success

JUDY R. JABLON AND MICHAEL WILKINSON

The third-graders in Ms. Neil's classroom begin a lesson on dictionaries with a whole-group discussion about what the children already know about the purpose and organization of these resources. Ms. Neil then explains to the children that they will work in small groups to examine the dictionary carefully; make observations about the book's organization, structure, and format; and record their group's findings on a chart. After ensuring that everyone is clear about the task, she posts a chart showing six teams of four children and sends them off with a task sheet to begin work.

The teams disperse to get the necessary materials: chart paper, dictionaries, and a basket with markers, pencils, and sticky notes. A few minutes later, a buzz of activity and conversation fills the room as all six teams pore over dictionary pages, discuss their observations, collaborate, and debate how to keep track of the information on their charts. Ms. Neil circulates around the room talking with each group, posing questions to promote thinking, responding to children's questions, and noting to individual children what she observes about their work. Within the groups, laughter is interspersed with argument as children comment on humorous or unfamiliar words, multiple meanings, and unusual punctuation. Twenty minutes into the work period, the six charts are filling up with lots of information.

Picture your classroom. Are there moments like this one when children are fully involved, curious about finding answers to real questions, taking initiative, enthusiastic? The room hums with positive energy and children are deeply engaged in their learning. You step back with a deep sense of satisfaction and think, "Wow! They are working well together. I wish it were always like this." You recognize that the children are a community of learners.

In this article we define what engagement is and why it is important to children's success as learners. We offer strategies for facilitating children's engagement in learning and provide some tips for implementing them.

Defining Engagement

Children begin life eager to explore the world around them. Watching a baby fascinated by the hands she has just discovered as hers or a toddler as he carefully lifts a shovel full of sand, spills it into the colander, then watches, eyes wide open, as the sand flows through the tiny holes—for the fifth time—is seeing engagement at its best!

Research about engagement in the classroom describes both psychological and behavioral characteristics (Finn & Rock 1997; Brewster & Fager 2000; Marks 2000). Psychologically, engaged learners are intrinsically motivated by curiosity, interest, and enjoyment, and are likely to want to achieve their own intellectual or personal goals. In addition, the engaged child demonstrates the behaviors of concentration, investment, enthusiasm, and effort.

In the opening example the children demonstrate engagement through their curiosity, effort, and persistence. They can be described as busy and on task. But they are also using their minds, hearts, and even their bodies to learn. In his book *Shaking Up the School House,* Schlechty captures the difference between being engaged and being on task:

> Engagement is active. It requires that students be attentive as well as in attendance; it requires the student to be committed to the task and find some inherent value in what he or she is being asked to do. The engaged student not only does the task assigned but also does it with enthusiasm and diligence. Moreover, the student performs the task because he or she perceives the task to be associated with a near-term end that he or she values. (2001, 64)

What Does Research Tell Us about Engagement in the Classroom?

Not surprisingly, research shows a significant correlation between high levels of engagement and improved attendance and achievement as measured through direct observations and interviews with and questionnaires to children and teachers (Finn & Rock 1997; Marks 2000; Roderick & Engle 2001; Willingham, Pollack, & Lewis 2002). After children enter school, their natural motivation and interest in learning do not always persist. Research also tells us that disengagement increases as children progress from elementary to middle to high school (Graham & Weiner 1996; Felner et al. 1997; Brewster & Fager 2000). Children may lose interest in classroom activities, respond poorly to teacher direction and classroom interaction, and perform significantly lower on tests. Studies have shown that patterns of educational disengagement begin as early as third grade (Rossi & Montgomery 1994).

Research shows a significant correlation between high levels of engagement and improved attendance and achievement as measured through direct observations and interviews with and questionnaires to children and teachers.

As important as engagement is for children's success as learners, strategies for promoting engagement are not emphasized or even present in the vast majority of school settings (Marks 2000; McDermott, Mordell, & Stolzfus 2001). Instruction that promotes passivity, rote learning, and routine tends to be the rule rather than the exception (Yair 2000; Goodlad 2004). Because children with low levels of engagement are at risk for disruptive behavior, absenteeism, and eventually dropping out of school (Roderick & Engle 2001), the need to increase engagement is critical to children's success in school.

Engaging Children in the Classroom

Educators of young children tend to share the goal of fostering children's successful learning and achievement. As the pressure to emphasize academic standards increases, it is all the more essential to reflect on the most effective practices for ensuring that children are actually learning what is being taught. Some factors related to children's achievement are not in teachers' control, but creating a climate of engagement in the classroom

is. The use of engagement strategies is a powerful teaching tool critical in promoting children's achievement because it

- focuses children on learning;
- supports learning specific skills and concepts; and
- provides children positive associations with learning.

The authors' experiences observing in classrooms and talking with teachers show that many teachers use strategies throughout the day to engage children in learning. In a recent conversation with a group of K–3 teachers, one teacher remarked, "I care a lot about engaging my kids. But it just comes naturally to me. I'm not sure I actually use strategies." Another teacher added, "It's just part of the culture of my classroom." These teachers work hard to foster positive relationships with children and create a learning community. But the more we talked, they gradually began to analyze the little things they do and concluded collectively that they do use strategies to facilitate engagement.

Some teachers use engagement strategies to introduce children to new ideas or bring a topic of study to conclusion. Others use them to keep children focused, energize the group, manage behavior, and avoid chaos during transitions. Engagement strategies can be used for different purposes and in different settings.

Below are some engagement strategies for use with whole groups, small groups, and individual learners:

KWL—To begin a new study or theme, teachers ask children, "What do you already *know*, what do you *wonder* about, and what do you want to *learn?*" Use of this strategy tells children that their prior knowledge and interests are valued.

How many ways can you do this?—Teachers pose this question or organize an activity with this as the opener in various situations. For example, how many ways can you create shapes on a geoboard? or how many ways can you sort bottle caps? As soon as you ask children to come up with many different ways to use a material, answer a question, or end a story, their desire to make choices and be inventive comes into play and leads to engagement.

Think, pair, share—This strategy works well at group time to ensure that each child has an opportunity to respond to questions. After posing a question, the teacher tells children to take a moment to think of an answer and then turn to a partner to talk. After everyone has had a chance to talk with their partners, volunteers share a few ideas with the whole group.

Dramatic touch—Teachers can use drama and humor to enhance child interest. For example, to encourage children to use other words for *said* in their writing, a teacher darkened the room, lit a flashlight, and attached a card with the word *said* written on it to a make-believe tombstone. Then the class brainstormed other words they could use.

See what you can find out—The primary purpose of this approach is to introduce children to a new topic, material, book, or tool. Ms. Neil used it to encourage children to further explore a valuable resource tool.

Characteristics of Engaging Experiences

- activate prior knowledge
- foster active investigation
- promote group interaction
- encourage collaboration
- allow for choice
- include games and humor
- support mastery
- nurture independent thinking
- do not make children wait

Quick games—Twenty Questions, I'm Thinking of a Number, and other games that capture children's interest can be applied to different subject areas and often work especially well to keep children engaged during transition times.

Understanding Why Engagement Strategies Work

Think back to the story of Ms. Neil's classroom at the beginning of the article. Amidst an atmosphere of energy, enthusiasm, and productivity, the children are actively acquiring and applying skills related to using a dictionary. They are purposeful while investigating how to understand and use an important reference tool. They are researchers working in teams to discover, share, and organize information. Ms. Neil carefully selected the engagement strategy See What You Can Find Out because it addresses the purposes of her lesson:

- **to expose children to new information**—Ms. Neil is teaching how to learn about and use reference materials. She also addresses a third grade state literacy standard: determine the meanings and other features of words (for example, pronunciation, syllabication, synonyms, parts of speech) using the dictionary and thesaurus (and CD-ROM and Internet when available).
- **to promote excitement through discovery**—In this lesson Ms. Neil exposes children to all that the dictionary offers as a research tool.

See What You Can Find Out engages children because it includes instructional methods that fit well with how children learn. This approach

- **activates prior knowledge**—Children answer "What do you already know about [in our example, the dictionary]?"
- **requires active investigation**—Children answer "What can you find out about_____?"
- **encourages collaboration**—Children work in teams of four, divide responsibilities, and share information and knowledge with peers.

- **allows choice**—Children determine how to go about the task, what information they will gather, and how to record it on their chart.

Teachers tell us that they themselves are energized by the children's increased enthusiasm and success.

Using this strategy gives children greater responsibility for their learning, a prerequisite for high achievement.

As stated earlier, research tells us that teacher awareness and the use of engagement strategies benefit children tremendously. Their interest in learning and their confidence as learners will increase, and hopefully those children who are engaged learners in the early grades will bring this characteristic with them as they continue in school. What's more, teachers tell us that they themselves are energized by the children's increased enthusiasm and success.

Facilitating Engagement Strategies

The engagement strategies you choose depend on your purpose, teaching style, and the children in your classroom. Regardless of the strategies selected, effective facilitation is a key to making them work. By facilitation we mean the techniques used to execute a strategy.

When Ms. Neil uses the See What You Can Find Out strategy to encourage children to explore the dictionary, she facilitates the lesson by providing

- **a clearly stated purpose**—She lets children know the overall purpose of the task and why they are being asked to do it: they are researchers finding out about how to use a powerful tool.
- **explicit directions**—Ms. Neil provides directions about the what and how of the task at each step, both verbally and in writing.
- **needed materials**—Children have dictionaries, chart paper, and baskets with pencils, markers, and sticky notes.
- **guidance**—Ms. Neil circulates among groups, asking and answering questions as well as giving feedback.

Conclusion

Ideally, teachers should use a wide range of engagement strategies and then masterfully facilitate their implementation. Not only do engagement strategies enable teachers to capture the interest of children as they learn the skills and concepts necessary for success in school, but children also experience what it feels like to be engaged in learning—a lifelong gift.

References

Brewster, C., & J. Fager. 2000. *Increasing student engagement and motivation: From time on task to homework.* Portland, OR: Northwest Regional Educational Laboratory. Online: www .nwrel.org/request/oct00/textonly.html.

Felner, R. D., A.W. Jackson, D. Kasak, P. Mulhall, S. Brand, & N. Flowers. 1997. The impact of school reform for the middle years: Longitudinal study of a network engaged in *Turning Points*-based comprehensive school transformation. *Phi Delta Kappan* 78 (March): 528–32; 541–50.

Finn, J. D., & D. A. Rock. 1997. Academic success among students at risk for school failure. *Journal of Applied Psychology* 82 (2): 221–34.

Goodlad, J. I. 2004. *A place called school: Prospects for the future.* 20th anniversary ed. New York: McGraw-Hill.

Graham, S., & B. Weiner. 1996. Theories and principles of motivation. In *Handbook of educational psychology,* eds. D. Berliner & R.C. Calfee, 62–84. Mahwah, NJ: Erlbaum.

Marks, H. M. 2000. Student engagement in instructional activity: Patterns in the elementary, middle and high school years. *American Educational Research Journal* 37 (1): 153–84.

McDermott, P. A., M. Mordell, & J. C. Stolzfus. 2001. The organization of student performance in American schools: Discipline, motivation, verbal and non-verbal learning. *Journal of Educational Psychology* 93 (1): 65–76.

Roderick, M., & M. Engle. 2001. The grasshopper and the ant: Motivational responses of low-achieving students to high-stakes testing. *Educational Evaluation Policy Analysis* 23 (3): 197–227.

Rossi, R., & A. Montgomery. 1994. *Education reforms and students at risk: A review of the current state of the art.* Washington, DC: U.S. Department of Education.

Schlechty, P. 2001. *Shaking up the school house: How to support and sustain educational innovation:* San Francisco: Jossey-Bass.

Willingham, W. W., J. M. Pollack, & C. Lewis. 2002. Grades and test scores: Accounting for observed differences. *Journal of Educational Measurement* 39 (1): 1–37.

Yair, G. 2000. Reforming motivation: How the structure of instruction affects students' learning experiences. *British Educational Journal* 26 (2): 191–210.

Judy R. Jablon, MS, is a consultant, facilitator, and author who works with teachers and administrators in a variety of settings serving children ages 3 through 11. Books she has coauthored about instruction and assessment include *The Power of Observation* and *Building the Primary Classroom.* **Michael Wilkinson** is managing director of Atlanta-based Leadership Strategies–The Facilitation Company and is a certified master facilitator (CMF). He is author of *The Secrets of Facilitation* and *The Secrets of Masterful Meetings* and has served as a consultant for school systems in Florida, Tennessee, and Georgia.

Meeting the Needs of All Students through Differentiated Instruction: Helping Every Child Reach and Exceed Standards

Students enter classrooms with different abilities, learning styles, and personalities. Educators are mandated to see that all students meet the standards of our district and state. Through the use of differentiated instruction strategies, educators can meet the needs of all students and help them to meet and exceed the established standards. In this article, the author gives practical examples of how to differentiate content, process, and product for your students. Grouping techniques, assessment strategies, and tiered lessons are also addressed.

HOLLI M. LEVY

Mrs. Johnson walks into her fifth-grade classroom on the first day of school to meet the twenty-five children she will teach for the next ten months. She has read their files, examined their standardized test scores, and met with their fourth-grade teachers. However, it is only when she has spent time with her class that she gets to know each of them as a child and learner. One student loves hamsters; another is an avid fisherman. One student is a writer beyond her years; another has trouble stringing two sentences together but can solve complex math problems. One student would like to be invisible and another wants to be noticed every minute of the day. Several students race through their work to be the first one finished, but one child wears out erasers in an effort to make every letter perfect and needs extra time to complete an assignment. Four students receive support for their learning disabilities, three are English-language learners, one child has Asperger's syndrome, and one has attention deficit disorder.

Mrs. Johnson's class is not unusual, and the mountain she has to climb is not insurmountable. Mrs. Johnson's mission is to teach this varied group so each student successfully meets the standards set forth by the state in which she teaches. More important, the greater challenge is to meet each child where he or she is and move each forward in his or her learning as far as possible.

A Focus on Standards: Why Now?

The standards movement evolved in an effort to ensure that all children received an equivalent level of education. The teaching model prior to standards-based reform left a great deal of choice to the individual teachers regarding what was taught, how long it was taught, and how to assess what was learned. Students in different classrooms in the same school would get a different education. One could see an even greater variance in underprivileged schools. This was not because of intellectual differences among the students but rather differences in teacher expectations because of divergent student needs and life experiences. There are other populations of students for whom expectations have been lower. Students with physical, emotional, mental, or learning disabilities have been required to do less in school because less was expected of them. In a standards-based educational system, local school districts, states, and the federal government have each set standards that all students must achieve regardless of the teacher, socioeconomic status, disabilities, or other differences in either the educational institution or the student.

Differentiated Instruction

Differentiated instruction is a term that has been bandied about in the field of education for quite awhile. If we take another look at Mrs. Johnson's class, it is clear that she has an enormous task in front of her. Each of the students in her class must meet a set standard of education. Students will be evaluated through a standardized test, the results of which will be scrutinized by the school district, the state government, and the federal government. What can Mrs. Johnson do for the child who is so far below his or her goal on the first day of school that this task seems impossible? What can she do for the child who comes into class already possessing the skills necessary to achieve his or her goal on the standardized test?

Every teacher who has entered a classroom has differentiated instruction in one way or another. Teachers differentiate when they give a student more time to finish an assignment, allow children choice in what they read, give different types of assessments, and myriad other ways. Although these are all good strategies, as educators, we can make our classrooms more responsive to student needs by being more systematic in our approach to differentiation. Differentiated instruction is a set of strategies that will help teachers meet each child where they are when they enter class and move them forward as far as possible on their educational path.

Content, Process, and Product

The district and state and federal governments have established our standards and handed our curriculum down to us. These standards make up the goals established for all of our students. How we reach these goals may require different paths. The core of differentiated instruction is flexibility in content, process, and product based on student strengths, needs, and learning styles.

Content

Content is what we teach. Each child is taught the same curriculum but the content may be quantitatively or qualitatively different. There are children who read and write well above grade level. Why would we want to limit them to the confines of the curriculum and standards when they can go much further? Students who are well below grade level will be more successful with a smaller amount of content or content at an appropriate level for the learner. The student who has not yet mastered multiplication and division is not ready for equivalent fractions. We must be sure the building blocks are in place for students before we ask them to move on to the next task. Differentiated instruction allows for variation in content without losing sight of the curriculum to which all children are entitled.

Process

Process includes how we teach and how students learn. The activities we provide for student learning must address differing student abilities, learning styles, and interests. Mrs. Johnson might begin a unit on problem-solving strategies in mathematics with a minilesson outlining the analysis of a problem. From there, she might break students into smaller ability-level groups, giving each group a problem that is at an appropriate level for their readiness. As the class progresses through this unit Mrs. Johnson might show different ways students solve the same problem by grouping students based on learning styles. Student learning style can be determined through learning styles questionnaire or inventories given early in the year. By grouping students who are kinesthetic, linguistic, and artistic into separate groups they can demonstrate three distinct ways to solve problems and show how they came to a solution.

Students do not all learn the same way, so we cannot teach them all the same way. We have to adjust our teaching style to reflect the needs of our students. To do this, we must find out where our students are when they come into the process and build on their prior knowledge to advance their learning

(addressed in more detail in the following). Students will need different levels of support that can be determined through formative assessment. Of course, for learning to be meaningful and lasting students must recognize its importance. Mrs. Johnson must include the purpose and application for the learning they are doing in her lessons.

Product

The *product* is the way our students demonstrate what they have learned. I discuss this *summative assessment* in the following; it must reflect student learning styles and abilities.

Assessment Is a Tool More than a Test
Preassessment

If we do not know where we are, how can we get where we are going? Students come to us with greatly varying abilities and experiences. The place to begin is with preassessment. Preassessments can be anything from a KWL (what I Know, what I Want to know, what I Learned) chart to a teacher-prepared test. The idea is to find a tool that gives you a snapshot of where your student is with respect to what you plan to teach. The use of preassessment tools allows Mrs. Johnson to look at her students more objectively. She has to teach long division, but what about the student who has all these skills already? What about the student who should have come into class knowing the basic facts of multiplication and division but is still counting on his fingers and making tally marks on his paper? You cannot build the top floor of a building without the support of the floors below it. To be effective teachers, we must begin at each student's individual level.

Formative Assessment

As we teach, we must periodically check in with our students. Mrs. Johnson ends her direct instruction by asking, "Are there any questions?" She is always amazed when the children assure her they know exactly what she is talking about and then, as she walks around the room, she finds that many students do have questions; they just did not realize it until they started doing the independent work. Formative assessment can be done in many ways and the results will give a teacher direction for further instruction.

Summative Assessment

Summative assessment is used to determine whether the student has successfully learned what was taught. These assessments can look as different from one another as our students do. Summative assessments include standardized tests, as well as teacher-made tests, quizzes, projects, performance assessments, and anything else one can imagine that can be objectively graded and is based on the curriculum. It is not necessary to make the assessment the same for every student. Because students vary in their ability levels, learning styles, and areas of interest, the ways in which they demonstrate what they know should vary as well.

Ability Levels, Learning Styles, and Interest

The days of grouping children randomly as bluebirds, robins, and buzzards are gone. Using the differentiated instruction model, grouping should be based on different criteria regarding the needs of the students and the short-term goals of the teacher in an effort to meet the desired standard.

Grouping for Student Needs

There are times when grouping by ability is the most appropriate action. The teacher has taught the lesson and a small group of students need further instruction. The teacher pulls these students together for additional support. This grouping is based on ongoing, formative assessment. There was also a group who came into class knowing what was taught. The teacher can pull these students together and take the lesson to the next level through more challenging activities. Ability groups are not stagnant; they change each time we assess the children.

Grouping for Learning Styles

How a student learns is as varied as the personalities in class. We can view learning styles through the lens of Gardner's multiple intelligences, Myers-Briggs Type Indicator, Dunn and Dunn learning styles model, or many other theorists' work. Common to all these theories is the idea that different children learn in different ways. Some students only pay attention to what the teacher says (auditory learners) and some pay no attention to what is said but watch the teacher and read everything he or she writes on the board (visual learners). Some students have not learned anything until they can do something with it (kinesthetic learners) and some have to discuss it to truly understand what has been taught (verbal learners). You know the children in your room who need to show you, those who need to tell you, and those who need to write it out. There are times when one of each in a group should work together so they can learn from each other. There are also times the builders should be in one group and the writers in another so they can work together for a common goal. How we choose our groups can be confusing, but when we begin with a focus on the standard to which we are teaching these groups become more obvious.

Grouping for Student Interests

When teaching a unit on nonfiction reading, grouping for student interest is a natural choice. Students of all levels who have an interest in animals can work together and support each other, whereas those who have no interest in the study of animals can chose a topic that is of interest to them.

Heterogeneous Grouping

Sometimes whole-class lessons are appropriate. In this heterogeneous grouping we are teaching on a level that meets the needs of all the children in the classroom with the knowledge that the needs of individual students will be addressed elsewhere. Teaching to a large heterogeneous group can be compared with painting with a broad paintbrush. After whole group lessons are complete and students begin their independent work the teacher can pull smaller groups based on need or learning style. Students with an individualized education program may need the additional support of a special education teacher. This is where the smaller paintbrush fills in the details. As stated earlier, formative and summative assessments are the key to establishing the needs of the students.

Differentiating for All Students: Tiered Lessons

How can Mrs. Johnson possibly differentiate for all the learning styles and abilities in her classroom? Tiered lesson planning is one way to stay focused on the standards and curriculum while maintaining flexibility in content, process, and product. With the standard and curriculum in mind, Mrs. Johnson can tier for readiness (above, at, and below grade level), interest, or learning style. She can tier her lesson for content, process, or product.

Returning to the example of a unit on reading nonfiction, the curriculum focus might determine important information (main idea) of the text. Here, starting with a heterogeneous, whole-group lesson would be appropriate. Smaller groups would then be established based on interest. The unit could be tiered through assignments, homework, readings, materials, or assessments that reflect the student's ability level, learning style, or interest. Teachers can explore many models for tiered lessons.

Differentiating for Student Achievement: Focus on and beyond Standards

The standards movement has many good qualities. It is a way to close the achievement gap by clarifying for teachers what must be taught to each student. The danger is that teachers stop there. If teachers and students are judged on how well children perform on the standardized test, many fear teachers will stop there. Educators have to look at where the bar is set and where the students are when they enter classrooms. Some students will work all year with tutelage and barely make the bar; some can leap over the bar gracefully; and some were already over the bar before they entered class. If we use the standards as our guide, we can teach all students equitably. The risk is our focus will shift to the standards and away from the child. With the tools of differentiated instruction, we can keep the focus where it belongs and take each student as far as he or she can go.

HOLLI M. LEVY, MA, is a fifth-grade teacher at Veterans Park Elementary School, Ridgefield, Connecticut, and a doctoral student in the Instructional Leadership doctoral program, Western Connecticut State University, Danbury. Copyright © 2008 Heldref Publications.

From *The Clearing House*, March/April 2008. Reprinted by permission of the Helen Dwight Reid Educational Foundation. Published by Heldref Publications, 1319 Eighteenth St., NW, Washington, DC 20036-1802. Copyright © 2008. www.heldref.org

What's Right about Looking at What's Wrong?

Both students and teachers gain new mathematical understanding by examining the reasoning behind a student's incorrect answer.

DEBORAH SCHIFTER

To teach mathematics for conceptual understanding, we need to treat it primarily as a realm of ideas to be investigated rather than a set of facts, procedures, and definitions to be used. To implement the former approach, teachers must have a deep understanding of content as well as the skill to implement concept-based pedagogy. And these greater demands on teachers, in turn, require well-thought-out forms of professional development. The following classroom lesson illustrates some of the issues involved.

Going Beyond Procedures

Liz Sweeney's 5th grade students all knew the standard procedure for multiplying multidigit numbers. On the day when a research team from the Education Development Center videotaped her class,[1] however, Ms. Sweeney wanted her students to go beyond the procedure. She asked them to find at least two ways to determine the products of several multidigit multiplication problems.

The students worked on this challenge, meeting in small groups to talk about their strategies. With just a few minutes left at the end of the period to discuss their work as a whole group, Ms. Sweeney asked Thomas to write his strategy for solving one of the problems (36×17) on the board, even though it was incorrect.

Thomas wrote ⟶

$$36 + 4 = 40$$
$$17 + 3 = 20$$

$$\begin{array}{r} 40 \\ \times\ 20 \\ \hline 800 \\ -\ \ 4 \\ \hline 796 \\ -\ \ 3 \\ \hline 793 \end{array}$$

Even Thomas knew his answer was wrong. Other strategies had already determined that the answer was 612.

But he explained his reasoning to the class: To make the problem easier, he rounded up by adding 4 to 36 and 3 to 17; then he multiplied 40×20 to get 800, and subtracted the 4 and the 3 that he had added earlier, getting a final answer of 793.

Ms. Sweeney told the class what she had noticed as Thomas presented this method to his small group:

> So I liked this—I was feeling comfortable with it, and it looked like a good strategy, and it was neat. And then Dima was all antsy in his seat, saying, "That's not what I did and my answer is really different"...
>
> So, tonight for your homework, I want you to copy down Thomas's method in your homework books, and I want you to figure out, What was Thomas thinking? And using the first steps of his strategy, how would you revise his approach to come up with a different answer?

Ms. Sweeney's behavior may puzzle readers whose images of effective teaching derive from the mathematics classrooms of their childhood. For many decades, mathematics has been taught the same way: The teacher demonstrates procedures for getting correct answers and then monitors students as they practice those procedures on a set of similar problems. Why did Ms. Sweeney ask her students, who already knew one efficient way to multiply 36×17, to find alternative strategies to do it? Why, at the end of class, did she ask a student to present a strategy that produced an incorrect result? And why did she ask the rest of the class to examine his strategy for homework?

To do mathematics is to test, debate, and revise or replace ideas about mathematical operations.

When we view Ms. Sweeney's behavior from an alternative perspective, it becomes comprehensible. She acted on the belief that mathematics is much more than a set of discrete facts, definitions, and procedures to memorize and recall on demand. In her view, mathematics is an interconnected body of ideas to explore. To do mathematics is to test, debate, and revise or replace those ideas. Thus, the work of her class went beyond merely finding the answer to 36 × 17; it became an investigation of mathematical relationships.

Where Did Thomas's Error Come From?

This was not the first time Liz Sweeney had asked her students to think about different strategies for calculation. She had been assigning similar exercises for all four of the basic operations. By considering the *action* of the operation, students could develop such strategies independently. For example, when asked to add 18 + 24, students might consider the action of addition as the joining of two sets and devise a variety of methods for decomposing and recombining the addends:

- Decompose 18 into 10 and 8; decompose 24 into 20 and 4; add the tens, 10 + 20 = 30, add the ones, 8 + 4 = 12; add the results, 30 + 12 = 42.
- Take 2 from the 24 and add it to the 18. This becomes 20 + 22, or 42.
- Add 2 to 18 to get 20, 20 + 24 = 44. Then remove the 2 you have added on, 44 − 2 = 42.

The activity of devising calculation strategies and explaining why they work helps students cultivate several important mathematical capacities. Students develop a stronger number sense and become more fluent with calculation. They gain an understanding of place value when they decompose numbers into tens and ones. And they come to expect that mathematics will make sense and that they can solve problems through reasoning.

Students come to expect that mathematics will make sense and that they can solve problems through reasoning.

When Ms. Sweeney asked the class to multiply 36 and 17, Thomas decided to try out a strategy that he had used successfully to *add* two multidigit numbers: round up, perform the operation, and then subtract what had been added when rounding up. Thomas was reasoning by analogy, which is often a fruitful way to approach a problem. In this case, the analogy would not hold. But Thomas *was* reasoning; he was not merely careless.

Thomas's mistake—applying an addition strategy to a multiplication problem—is quite common. When faced with multidigit multiplication, such as 12 × 18, both children and adults frequently try (10 × 10) + (2 × 8). After all, to add 12 and 18, one could operate on the tens, operate on the ones, and then add the total. But multiplication involves a different kind of action, and thus requires a different set of adjustments after the factors have been changed or decomposed.

A Context for Multiplication

To think about the action of multiplication, it is helpful to envision a context in which the calculation might be used. For example, Thomas's classmate James thought of 36 × 17 as 36 bowls, each holding 17 cotton balls. With this context in mind, he could imagine an arrangement of bowls of cotton balls that would lend themselves to calculation.

James explained that first he arranged the bowls into groups of 10. Each group of 10 had 170 cotton balls (10 × 17), and there were three groups of ten (170 + 170 + 170). Besides the groups of 10 bowls, there were another 6 bowls with 17 cotton balls in each (6 × 17). To simplify that calculation, James thought of each bowl as having 10 white and 7 gray cotton balls, which yielded 60 white balls (6 × 10) plus 42 gray balls (6 × 7), for a total of 102 cotton balls in those 6 bowls. Then he added 170 + 170 + 170 + 102, which came out to 612.

A basic mathematical principle underlying James's method is the distributive property of multiplication over addition, which says that (10 + 10 + 10 + 6) × 17 = (10 × 17) + (10 × 17) + (10 × 17) + (6 × 17). The distributive property also says that 6 × (10 + 7) = (6 × 10) + (6 × 7). James knew how to apply the distributive property, but when he worked with an image of cotton balls arranged in bowls, he was not merely manipulating numbers based on a set of rules he had memorized. He was able to perform the calculation as it made sense to him—that is, as it followed from his image of the context.

As Thomas, James, and their classmates developed their strategies in small groups, Ms. Sweeney went from group to group, sometimes asking questions or making suggestions and sometimes just listening. Having observed Thomas's mistaken strategy, she decided that it provided a learning opportunity for the class. When she gave the homework assignment, she was asking her students to go beyond evaluating whether the strategy was correct or not; she was challenging them to determine where it went wrong and how to make it right. To answer that question, students needed to examine closely the difference between addition and multiplication, highlighting the importance of thinking in terms of images like James's. This task also gave them an opportunity to state the distributive property explicitly. This one homework assignment yielded two further days of deep mathematical discussion in Ms. Sweeney's 5th grade class.

Teachers Consider Thomas's Strategy

In a professional development seminar,[2] my colleagues and I explored Ms. Sweeney's approach with a group of teachers. After viewing the video clip, many of the teachers were initially shocked by Ms. Sweeney's behavior. They didn't understand why she would "embarrass a student" by asking him to share his incorrect work. Some were dismayed that she would "punish the class" by assigning homework because one student made an error.

Rather than discuss these issues immediately, the facilitator asked the teachers to examine Thomas's strategy for themselves. After Thomas added 4 to 36 and 3 to 17, what would he need to subtract in order to get the correct result?

The teachers went to work in pairs and threes to examine different ways to approach the problem. The facilitator moved from group to group, listening to teachers, asking them to explain in more detail, and sometimes suggesting an approach. When each group had developed at least one way to think about the problem, the facilitator brought them all together to present their ideas.

Annie volunteered to share her initial thinking, which she realized was not completely correct. She said, "I did something that seems like it should be right, even though I know it's not." She explained that when Thomas added 4 to 36 and 3 to 17 and then multiplied 40 × 20, he wasn't adding 4 units and 3 units, but 4 groups of units and 3 groups of units. She continued,

So I first thought you need to subtract 4 groups of 17 and 3 groups of 36. But when I did the calculation, $800 - (4 \times 17) - (3 \times 36)$, I got 624—not 612, which we already know is the answer.

I didn't take away enough, so I thought maybe I multiplied by the wrong size group. Maybe I need to take away 4 groups of 20 and 3 groups of 40. But when I did this calculation, $800 - (4 \times 20) - (3 \times 40) = 600$, I ended up with an answer that was too small!

I thought that was really strange. Then the facilitator came and suggested that we think of a story context.

A story context would allow the teachers to picture the steps of the problem, as James had done. Ming suggested the following context:

There are 40 children in a class, and they each paid $20 for a field trip. The teacher collected 40 × 20, or $800. But on the day of the field trip, 4 students were absent. That means she needed to give back $20 to each of those children, $800 - (4 \times 20)$. Then the teacher went to the museum with 36 children, but when they got there they realized that the entrance fee was $17 instead of $20. That meant that each of the remaining 36 children got $3 back. So now we have $800 - (4 \times 20) - (36 \times 3)$, which the teacher paid to the museum. And that's $612 – $17 for each of 36 children, or 36 × 17.

Ming added, "If you think about what Thomas did, it's like he gave each of the 4 absent students only $1, and he gave only 1 other student $3."

Chad offered his group's use of an array, or the area of a rectangle, to think through the problem (see Fig. 1). He explained,

The white part of the figures shows 36 × 17, and the gray regions show what gets added on when you change the problem to 40 × 20. In the picture on the right, you can see where Thomas went wrong. Instead of subtracting everything that got added on, he just took away what's shown in black.

You can see Ming's story in the diagram on the left. The gray region at the bottom stands for the money that was returned to the 4 children who were absent. The gray region on the right is the money that was returned to the 36 children who went on the field trip. The white region is the money that was paid to the museum.

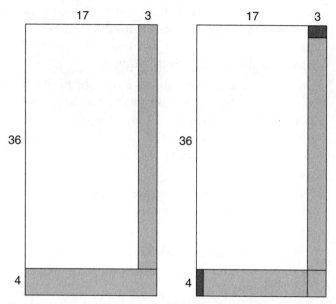

Figure 1 Chad's Diagram. Chad's group used an array, or the area of a rectangle, to explore different methods of finding the product of 36 × 17

Annie pointed out that, when looking at Chad's diagram on the right, she can see more clearly why each of her initial answers was 12 off: "The first way I looked at it, I failed to subtract that little piece in the corner. The second way I looked at it, I subtracted that little piece twice."

Aisha offered a fourth way of viewing the problem:

I wrote out the arithmetic and applied the distributive property: (36 + 4) × (17 + 3) = (36 × 17) + (36 × 3) + (4 × 17) + (4 × 3). So when Thomas multiplied 40 × 20, he needed to subtract those last three terms to get back to 36 × 17. When I was in high school, we called that procedure FOIL—you multiply the First terms, Outer terms, Inner terms, and Last terms. The thing is, I always did that because I was told that's the way to do it. But now that I can see it in the diagram, it really makes sense.

In this professional development session, participants offered four approaches to examine Thomas's strategy and figure out how to correct it. Note that, like Thomas, Annie chose to share her unresolved thinking. Looking together at what seems like it should be right, even though we know it's not, the teachers used several approaches to figure out where Annie's thinking went wrong. By sharing their different approaches, the teachers could compare approaches to see how one representation appeared in another.

The Professional Development Teachers Need

If teachers themselves were taught mathematics as discrete procedures and definitions to be memorized, how can schools prepare them to implement a more challenging, concept-based mathematics pedagogy? As a starting point, professional development needs to challenge teachers' conceptions of mathematics teaching and learning, opening them up to a process of reflection so that new insights can emerge.

Professional development needs to challenge teachers' conceptions of mathematics teaching and learning.

Liz Sweeney's homework assignment provided just such an opportunity to the participants in the professional development seminar. Once the teachers had explored the mathematics in Thomas's error, they returned to their own questions about Sweeney's pedagogical approach. Among their comments were,

Of course all students know that addition and multiplication are different, but they don't always think about that. Our exploration of Thomas's error really highlights how you have to think about multiplication differently.

With these images, the distributive property isn't just a rule to memorize. You can see why it has to work.

I bet Thomas felt proud to have presented something that got his classmates thinking so hard.

Such insights cannot be induced by a series of lectures or workshops on instructional strategies. Instead, professional development programs need to dig deeper, giving their participants opportunities to construct more powerful understandings of learning, teaching, and disciplinary substance.

A first step in helping teachers change their pedagogy is to place them in seminars where they can explore disciplinary content, develop new conceptions of mathematics, and gain a heightened sense of their own mathematical powers. As learners of mathematics, they experience a new kind of classroom. In these seminars, teachers reflect on their own learning processes and consider those features of the classroom that support or hinder them. Through such professional development, we can inspire teachers to envision and implement a new kind of mathematics pedagogy—one in which student understanding and collaborative thinking take center stage.

Notes

1. This classroom episode can be seen in the video component of Schifter, D., Bastable, V, & Russell, S. J. (1999). *Building a system of tens*. Parsippany, NJ: Pearson.

2. The session described here is a composite of several seminar groups that were part of the *Developing Mathematical Ideas* professional development program.

DEBORAH SCHIFTER is Principal Research Scientist at the Education Development Center, Newton, Massachusetts, where she directs Developing Mathematical Ideas and the Mathematics Leadership Program; dschifter@edc.org.

Author's note—This work was supported by the National Science Foundation under Grant No. ESI-0242609. Any opinions, findings, conclusions, or recommendations expressed in this article are those of the author and do not necessarily reflect the views of the National Science Foundation.

UNIT 5

Motivation and Classroom Management

Unit Selections

Key Points to Consider

- Discuss several ways to motivate both at-risk and typical students. What difference is there?

- Why should motivational style be consistent with instructional techniques?

- How are motivation and classroom management related?

- Discuss several ways to discipline both typical students and those with exceptionalities.

- How are classroom management and discipline different? Discuss whether discipline can be developed within students, or whether it must be imposed by teachers, supporting your argument with data derived from your reading.

- In thinking about middle school students and the importance of their social environment, what kinds of environments can you foster in your classroom to support students' need for acceptance and belonging?

- What strategies or interventions would you use if you witnessed one of your students bullying a fellow classmate?

- What unique challenges does student access to technology and use of online communication present to monitoring students' interaction and maintaining a psychologically and emotionally safe environment in school?

- Describe a "typical" student whom you would consider to be at-risk for dropping out. How many of the signals presented in the final article in this unit did you identify? Which ones did you miss or were you surprised by?

Student Web Site
www.mhcls.com

Internet References

I Love Teaching
http://www.iloveteaching.com

The Jigsaw Classroom
http://jigsaw.org

North Central Educational Regional Laboratory
http://www.ncrel.org/sdrs/

Teaching Helping Teachers
http://www.pacificnet.net/ mandel/

Several theories of motivation, each highlighting different reasons for sustained goal-oriented behavior, have been proposed. We will discuss three of them: behavioral, humanistic, and cognitive. The behavioral theory of motivation suggests that an important reason for engaging in behavior is that reinforcement follows the action. When reinforcement is controlled by someone else and is arbitrarily related to the behavior (such as money, a token, or a smile), then the motivation is extrinsic. In contrast, behavior may also be initiated and sustained for intrinsic reasons, such as curiosity or mastery.

Humanistic approaches to motivation are concerned with the social and psychological needs of individuals. Humans are motivated to engage in behavior to meet these needs. Abraham Maslow, a founder of humanistic psychology, proposes that there is a hierarchy of needs that directs behavior, beginning with physiological and safety needs and progressing to self-actualization. Some other important needs that influence motivation are affiliation and belonging with others, love, self-esteem, influence with others, recognition, status, competence, achievement, and autonomy.

The dominant view of motivation in the educational psychology literature is the cognitive approach. This set of theories proposes that our beliefs about our successes and failures affect our expectations and goals concerning future performance. Students who believe that their success is due to their abilities and efforts are motivated toward mastery of skills. Students who blame their failures on inadequate abilities have low self-efficacy and tend to set ability and performance goals that protect their self-image.

In the first article about motivation, Patrick McCabe shows the relationship between learning and self-efficacy. He suggests that the prompts and feedback teachers give to students during tasks play an important role in their self-efficacy and subsequent learning. In "Why We Can't Always Get What We Want," Barbara Bartholomew illustrates the importance of intrinsic motivation as an essential precondition for learning. The next article focuses on fostering student success through engaging students in activities they find meaningful and encouraging self-regulation and goal-setting.

The final three articles on motivation return to a discussion of intrinsic and extrinsic rewards and behaviorist principles. They examine whether extrinsic and intrinsic rewards can be effectively paired to stimulate and maintain students' inherent motivation to learn, how the use of praise can have both positive and negative consequences, and whether reward incentives

© amana images inc./Alamy

based on student performance can be appropriately used in classrooms.

Regardless of how motivated students are to learn, or the teacher's attempts to create lessons that will engage and motivate students, teachers also need to be effective managers of their classrooms. Classroom management is more than controlling the behavior of students or disciplining them following misbehavior. In addition, teachers need to initiate and maintain a classroom environment that supports successful teaching and learning. The skills that effective teachers use include preplanning, deliberate introduction of rules and procedures, assertiveness, continual monitoring, consistent feedback to students, and specific consequences.

The next seven articles address specific classroom management issues facing teachers today. The first article presents proactive strategies for handling the particular dynamics related to classroom management in secondary settings. The second article, "No! I Won't!" presents characteristics of students with Oppositional Defiant Disorder (ODD) and how positive behavior supports and functional behavioral assessment can help teachers understand these students. The next two articles focus on an issue at the forefront in many schools today, the impact of bullying and cyberbullying on students. The final three articles in this section present a variety of issues also related to classroom management including a system for addressing general management problems; a unique look at the social world of adolescents in middle school; and a discussion of warning signs to look for in middle and high school students who might be at risk of dropping out.

Convincing Students They Can Learn to Read
Crafting Self-Efficacy Prompts

Patrick P. McCabe

It is lunchtime at Anytown Middle School, and Ms. Williams, a seventh-grade teacher, is telling Mr. Rodriguez, a sixth-grade teacher, about one of her students. Ms. Williams says:

Maybe you can help me. You know Ezekiel. You had him last year, right? Well, I can't get him to attempt to read words longer than one syllable. He just gives up. He can read small words and syllables in isolation, but those longer words intimidate him. I have tried to teach him word-recognition strategies such as using context clues, breaking up big words into smaller parts, thinking about the topic in which he is reading, and looking at any accompanying pictures and illustrations, but all to no avail. I even bought a book on baseball, and you know he loves baseball. I then gave him a preview of the story and thought he would use this information to make reasonable guesses when he encountered big words in the story. I even previewed two or three of the longer words with him, showing him how to divide them into syllables. He was able to read the words that I broke up for him, but he did not even try others of the same length, even though he could read each syllable when I showed them in isolation to him. I also try to be positive with him. On the rare occasion when he does try and is successful, I tell him that he is doing a great job and give him a high five! Once, after I congratulated him for decoding a three-syllable word, he said, "Aw, that was just luck. I just guessed and it was right! Everyone knows that I am special ed, and that I am dumb. Everyone in my family is like that." With that, he shrugged his shoulders. He has such a self-defeating attitude; it is really starting to bother me. I have tried everything. He is just unreachable. Oh, well! I guess there is nothing else I can do. All I can say is that I have tried my best and must spend my energy where I can really make a difference. I hate doing it, but I do have other students. Maybe Ezekiel will wake up one day!

Discouraged and frustrated with her inability to motivate Ezekiel, Ms. Williams has decided to focus on other students because, in her words, "Ezekiel is unreachable." Ezekiel, convinced of his inability to read multisyllabic words, has decided instead to skip them and thus avoid personal frustration and embarrassment. Although Ms. Williams's words of encouragement were well-intentioned, they apparently did not help Ezekiel recognize his ability to sound out long words. Evident in Ezekiel's comments is a strong belief that he is incapable of learning, and unless his "can't-do" attitude changes, he has doomed himself to fail in school. This is especially unfortunate for Ezekiel because, according to Ms. Williams, he does have the ability to sound out the isolated syllables in multisyllabic words. As May and Rizzardi stated, "Half the battle in teaching is just getting children to take a chance with their self-esteem and try new tasks. If students feel they cannot be successful, the result will typically be what is termed 'work avoidance'" (2002, 331).

Ms. Williams's instruction regarding the use of a repertoire of word-recognition strategies ranging from the use of personal schema and textual context to wordbound strategies was pedagogically sound. However, although her verbal feedback when Ezekiel was successful was encouraging, well-intentioned, and sincere, it failed to help him attribute his success to personal effort and was not as effective as it could have been in developing and maintaining motivation. Her conclusion that Ezekiel was "unreachable" resulted—at least in part—from a lack of understanding of how to affect a learner's motivation. Therefore, the purpose of this article is to explain and provide a research-based rationale for the use of teacher verbal feedback prompts that convince students of their ability to succeed on a task.

Understanding Ezekiel's Behavior

Bandura's (1986) social-cognitive theory of motivation provides a framework for understanding Ezekiel's behavior and attitude, and suggests a practical solution to help Ms. Williams. In this theory, an individual's beliefs about him- or herself are a strong influence on behavior. Thus, if Ezekiel believes he does not have the skills to decode long words, he is not likely to become involved in that task. In Bandura's theory, belief about one's competence on a prospective task is called self-efficacy: it is a perception of one's ability that is not necessarily accurate; self-efficacy and perceived self-efficacy are often used synonymously. "Perceived self-efficacy is defined as people's judgments of their capabilities to organize and execute courses of action required to attain designated types of performances" (Bandura, 391). A self-efficacy belief is task specific, exists prior to attempting a task, predicts how well a person thinks he or she will do, and may vary within the same individual according to the task. Self-efficacy is a relative concept that can be applied generally or specifically. For example, it is possible to have high self-efficacy for math and low self-efficacy for reading, or high self-efficacy for multiplying two-digit numbers and low self-efficacy for multiplying three-digit numbers. Furthermore, self-efficacy differs from self-concept, which is defined as "one's collective self-perceptions" (Schunk 2004, 373); it is possible to have a strong self-concept and simultaneously have low self-efficacy for math, science, or playing golf.

If self-efficacy is positive and strong, and if the goal of a task has value to the individual, he or she will be likely to make the decision to become involved. A student might be able to multiply two-place digits, for example, but not wish to do so because the reward for success may not have value to him or her. However, the same student might quickly become involved in two-digit multiplication to figure out the amount of money he or she might earn from an after-school job in a two-week period.

Self-efficacy beliefs are a powerful influence on motivation. A recent study by Bogner, Raphael, and Pressley (2002) reported a decline in elementary students' motivation to read that correlated with a decline in belief in their ability to read. "People's level of motivation, affective states, and actions are based more on what they believe than on what is objectively the case" (Bandura 1995, 2). Although classroom variables such as appropriate material, tasks, instructional procedures, and teacher affect also influence student motivation and engagement in learning (Alderman 2004; Brophy 1981; Dolezalt et al. 2003; Mastropieri and Scruggs 2004; Pintrich and Schunk 2002; Stipek 2001; Turner 1995), Ezekiel's low self-efficacy for reading multisyllabic words was the critical and most influential factor resulting in his lack of motivation to read.

In describing human fear, Bandura stated, "Persons who judge themselves as lacking coping capabilities, whether the self-appraisal is objectively warranted or not, will perceive all kinds of dangers in situations and exaggerate their potential harmfulness" (1986, 220). Individuals such as Ezekiel, who

feel they cannot read well, will often avoid reading rather than experience failure and frustration. Therefore, Ms. Williams's positive feedback comments to Ezekiel should help him recognize evidence that he does, in fact, have the ability to accomplish the task.

"For learners to evaluate their progress, it is essential that they receive goal progress feedback, especially when they cannot derive reliable information on their own" (Schunk 2003, 164). "These progress indicators convey that students are capable of learning and performing well, which enhances their self-efficacy for further learning" (Pintrich and Schunk 2002, 148). The learner's awareness of indicators of his or her progress is critical to the development of self-efficacy and, thus, to sustaining motivation.

Verbal feedback that makes the learner aware of his or her advancement is one type of progress indicator that, if used correctly, can become a prompt for sustaining learner behavior (Atkinson, Renkl, and Merrill 2003; Ernsbarger 2002; Ormrod 2004). Such prompts "include clues, cues, hints, or reminders that facilitate the occurrence of a particular behavior" (Ernsbarger, 280).

Below I suggest exemplary phrases, consistent with Bandura's framework, that convince students of their ability to learn. (The key word in the previous sentence is "convince" because the words and phrases suggested below are directed toward not just telling but persuading students to have a positive belief about themselves.) Skill level will of course differ among students, so it is important that feedback from teachers is appropriate and credible. Brophy (1981) developed guidelines for effective praise that included being contingent on success and not gratuitous, being specific, demonstrating the value of the task, and attributing success to effort. Telling a student that he or she was successful when that was not the case is disingenuous, unlikely to have value to the learner, and affects the credibility of the teacher. Celebrating student success on a task that was too easy will also have little value to the learner, because he or she may feel the teacher has low expectations of him or her or that he or she is capable of only simple tasks.

What to Say to Ezekiel

Brophy noted that students' interpretation of praise was most valuable when it helped them "make attributions about their abilities and about the linkages between their efforts and the outcomes of those efforts" (1981, 27). While seemingly intuitive, there is also evidence that "teacher feedback can affect self-efficacy. Persuasive statements (e.g., 'I know that you can do this') can raise self-efficacy" (Schunk 2001, 127). Therefore, verbal feedback from the teacher is especially critical and needs to be crafted to convince the learner that he or she possesses the ability to complete a given task. Recently, Brown (2003) and Clark (2004) outlined useful reading instruction prompts to help students decode words. Brown suggested prompts based on developmental stage of reading, and Clark (2004) suggested prompts based on (1) "general cues to prompt thought" (metacognition) and (2) "cues to prompt specific action" (explicit instruction to use word bound and contextual cues). In concluding her article, Brown posed a critical question for teachers: "What kind of prompt should I be using with this reader at this point in development?" (728). To that, I add the following: "What kind of prompt should I be using with this reader at this point in his or her motivational development?"

When prompts such as those suggested by Brown (2003) and Clarke (2004) are used in conjunction with prompts directed toward building self-efficacy, there is an increased probability that students will be successful in reading tasks. Words of encouragement such as "good job," "you can do it," and "fantastic work, keep it up!" are too global and do not address the motivational needs of Ezekiel and students like him because they fail to draw attention to evidence of success. Therefore, they do not adequately convince Ezekiel that he has the ability to sound out multisyllabic words. Just as many students need explicit instruction to learn an academic skill, students like Ezekiel need explicit teacher verbal feedback crafted to enhance their self-efficacy.

In the following paragraphs, I provide a rationale for exemplary words and phrases that can be used to convince students like Ezekiel they have the ability to succeed on a given task. Consistent with Bandura's (1986) theory, the italicized words and phrases embedded within a larger sentence context are critical because they focus learners' attention on important

feedback information about their progress and contribute to enhancing their self-efficacy. Other words and phrases that are consistent with the rationale presented here may be equally effective with students such as Ezekiel.

According to Bandura (1997), there are four sources through which an individual can acquire information about his or her competence and, thus, develop selfefficacy beliefs: enactive mastery, vicarious experiences, verbal persuasion, and physiological/affective state (see Table 1). Each source is explained below, accompanied by relevant exemplary words and phrases. Although these comments are presented below in separate categories according to the sources of self-efficacy, "[a]ny given influence, depending on its form, may operate through one or more of these sources of efficacy information" (Bandura, 79). Therefore, teachers should think of them as complementary and mutually reinforcing.

Enactive Mastery

A student's recognition that he has mastered a task as a result of expending personal effort provides strong feedback that he possesses the ability to succeed. This knowledge, in turn, has a significant effect on the development of self-efficacy. "Enactive mastery experiences are the most influential source of efficacy information because they provide the most authentic evidence of whether one can muster whatever it takes to succeed" (Bandura 1997, 80).

Table 1   Teacher Feedback

Category	Example
Enactive master (accomplishment)	*"You were able to"* *"You got"* *"You now have the idea"* *"Now you have the knack of"* *"You have the skill to"*
Vicarious experience (modeling)	*"Watch me (Oscar) as I (he). . . . You can also do this, just as I (Oscar) did."* *"Did you see what I (Oscar) did? You can do the same thing, just as I (Oscar) did."* *"Notice how I (Oscar). . . . You have the ability to do this, just as I have (Oscar has)."* *"Listen while I (Oscar). . . . You can also do this, just as I (Oscar) can."* *"Try to remember what I am (Oscar is) about to do. You will also be able to do the same thing."*
Verbal persuasion (attribution)	*"Because you"* *"And that helped you"* *"As a result of . . . you were able to"* *"Remembering helped you"*
Physiological/affective state (feeling)	*"You must feel great"* *"Did you realize you smiled to yourself?"* *"Do you know you did not fidget?"* *"How did you feel when?"* *"You must feel proud"*

The following phrases could direct Ezekiel's attention to evidence of success during mastery in decoding multisyllabic words. They specify the particular accomplishment and would make Ezekiel aware of success by explicitly drawing his attention to his accomplishment. These phrases would clearly tell him that he has achieved a noteworthy accomplishment.

> "You were able to sound out all the parts of that long word."
> "You got all the sounds in the word correct."
> "You now have the idea of how to sound out long words."
> "Now you have the knack of sounding out long words."
> "You have the skill to sound out long words."

Vicarious Experiences

"Efficacy appraisals are partly influenced by vicarious experiences mediated through modeled attainments" (Bandura 1997, 86). Being vicarious means taking part in the feeling and experience of another, so vicarious experiences—observations and comparison to others' actions or skills—provide an individual with useful information about his personal competence to the degree that the observer can relate to the model unique to each person. When the observer feels that characteristics of the model, such as age, gender, personal affinity, interests, or ethnicity, are similar to his own characteristics, the vicarious experience of watching a model is an effective learning tool. Such experiences provide a template and help the learner judge the degree to which he can expect to possess a particular skill. The observer might think, "Hey, he is like me, and if he can do it, so can I." Models which the learner cannot relate to are less effective, and peer models can be as effective or more so than adult models. For example, if Ms. Williams used a peer model, she should select someone to whom Ezekiel can easily relate in terms of one or a combination of the characteristics mentioned above. Two categories of models are a mastery model who successfully completes the task, and a coping model who struggles to some degree but eventually implements a strategy or strategies that lead to success.

Expanding on Ezekiel's situation, suppose that Ms. Williams chose Oscar, a classmate of Ezekiel's, as a peer model. Here are some phrases that Oscar could use to increase the probability that Ezekiel will benefit from Oscar's achievement.

> "Watch me (Oscar) as I (he) sound(s) out this word. You can also do this, just as I (Oscar) did."
> "Did you see what I (Oscar) did? You can do the same thing, just as I (Oscar) did. "
> "Notice how I am (Oscar is) dividing the word into parts. You have the ability to do this, just as I have (Oscar has)."
> "Listen while I (Oscar) tell(s) you what I am thinking as I read. You can also do this, just as I (Oscar) can."
> "Try to remember what I am (Oscar is) about to do. You will also be able to do the same thing."

Verbal Persuasion

The goal of verbal persuasion is to convince an individual that success is achieved through his efforts. This is called attribution, "a perceived cause of an outcome" (Pintrich and Schunk 2002, 402). "Research indicates that some students struggle unnecessarily because they incorrectly attribute failure to ability rather than to lack of effort or undirected effort" (Bruning et al. 2004, 125). Students can attribute success on a task to any number of factors; however, students with low self-efficacy tend to attribute their success to luck or happenstance and students with high self-efficacy tend to attribute their success to personal effort (Bruning et al.). Further, Bruning et al. and Pintrich and Schunk reported that students who made attributions in which they recognized themselves as the reason for their success strengthened their self-efficacy and learning. Bruning et al. stated, "For this reason, we believe that teachers should discuss the role of attributions in learning and provide some degree of retraining for students who make inappropriate attributions" (125).

Although there is some evidence that praise for just ability is less motivational than praise for effort (Craven, Marsh, and Debus 1991; Mueller and Dweck 1998), "people who are persuaded verbally that they possess the capabilities to master given activities are likely to mobilize greater sustained effort and sustain it than if they harbor self-doubts and dwell on personal deficiencies when problems arise" (Bandura 1986, 400). Therefore, both effort feedback and ability feedback should be used by teachers in what Burnett (2003) called a "balanced and strategic" (13) manner. Coupled with successful enactive mastery experiences, verbal persuasion that focuses on attribution retraining can bolster feelings of self-efficacy. However, according to Robertson (2000), although attribution training has been advocated for many years, it has not been practiced in the schools. I encourage teachers to use the following words and phrases (and others similar to them) to enhance student self-efficacy by helping students attribute their success to personal effort and ability.

> "You were able to divide the word into parts because you remembered the rule."
> "You remembered the rule and that helped you to divide the word into parts."
> "As a result of studying the rule, you were able to divide the word into parts."
> "Because you studied, you were able to divide the word into parts."
> "Remembering the rule helped you divide the word into parts."

Physiological/Affective State

Physiological and affective reactions can occur concurrently with one or all of the three other sources of efficacy information. For example, success on a new and moderately challenging task is likely to lower anxiety levels and increase positive feelings when confronted with the same or a similar task in the future. However, "by conjuring up aversive thoughts about their ineptitude and stress reactions, people can rouse themselves to elevated levels of distress that produce the very dysfunction they fear" (Bandura 1997, 107). "Bodily symptoms serve as physiological cues. Sweating and trembling may signal that students are not capable of learning. Students who notice they are reacting in a less-agitated fashion to tasks feel more efficacious about learning" (Pintrich and Schunk 2002, 172). Therefore, "parents and teachers can do students a great service by helping them understand their emotional reactions to success and failure" (Bruning et al. 2004, 125). By directing Ezekiel's attention to his physiological or affective state, Ms. Williams can help him recognize such feedback as additional information about his ability to learn. The following direct student attention to physiological and affect reaction.

> "You must feel great that you sounded out that long word."
>
> "Did you realize you smiled to yourself after you sounded out that long word?"
>
> "Do you know you did not fidget so much when you sounded out that long word?"
>
> "How did you feel when you were able to sound out that long word?"
>
> "You must feel proud now that you have sounded out that word."

A Final Few Words

In his discussion of teachers' praise to students, Brophy stated, "rather than just assume its effectiveness, teachers who wish to praise effectively will have to assess how individual students respond to praise" (1981, 27). Therefore, it is important for teachers to monitor students' reactions to self-efficacy comments and make necessary adjustments. Studies have identified a number of situational and personal variables that may individually or in combination affect how students perceive verbal feedback prompts. Teachers should be aware of these variables when assessing the results of their efforts, especially when working with struggling readers with low self-efficacy.

One variable is the difficulty level of the task. Tasks that are too easy or too difficult will likely negate the value of the self-efficacy prompts suggested here; prompts accompanying a task that is perceived by the learner as too easy may engender a counterproductive response in which the learner assigns little or no value to the teacher's comments (Pintrich and Schunk 2002). In such a case, the learner may think, "That was so easy. Why is Ms. Williams telling me how great this was? Is that all she thinks I can do? I must really be dumb!" Assignments that are frustrating to the learner because of the difficulty of material or the nature of the task are equally undesirable because they result in further weakening self-efficacy and motivation and contribute to a reinforced feeling of learned helplessness. A useful concept when designing instructional tasks is Vygotsky's "Zone of Proximal Development," described by

May and Rizzardi as "the difference between what a child can already do alone and what he or she can do with assistance from a more competent person" (2002, 19), and by Pintrich and Schunk as, "the amount of learning possible by a student given proper instructional support" (160). Therefore, prior to assigning a task and providing self-efficacy prompts, the teacher should decide if the student is likely to be successful, and the tasks should be moderately challenging.

Another variable that may affect the impact of self-efficacy prompts is the setting. Some students may be embarrassed when they receive prompts in front of their peers, while others may conclude that they have not received the same feedback from the teacher because they lack the ability or potential (Robertson 2000). Individual and private feedback may be more effective for some children, especially those who struggle with, and have low self-efficacy for, reading but are in a class or group in which the majority of students read better than they do.

Teacher credibility is also a critical variable for self-efficacy prompts to be successful. Such prompts should not be used with all students indiscriminately, but only with those who have both the ability and low self-efficacy for a specific task. The teacher's credibility suffers when he gives these prompts to a student who does not have the ability to successfully complete a given task, and this may result in the student ignoring or doubting the teacher in the future.

Additionally, Pintrich and Schunk (2002) and Alderman (2004) reported a host of personal variables, including age, developmental level, gender, ethnicity, and economic background, that can affect students' perceptions of the cause of success or failure on a task. These variables may interact in various combinations and permutations and affect self-efficacy and motivation in different and unexpected ways. Age and gender may affect strength of influence of verbal self-efficacy feedback prompts because "young children see ability as more modifiable than do older students," and "overall, the attributions of girls reflect a lower expectancy pattern" (Alderman, 41). According to Pintrich and Schunk, the relationship and effect of ethnicity to self-efficacy development has been difficult to determine; this area requires additional research. In many of the studies conducted, economic level may have interacted with ethnicity and confounded the explanation of student attributions as due to effort or ability (Alderman; Pintrich and Schunk). In one study reported by Alderman, fifth and sixth graders of various ethnicities from low economic backgrounds rated ability as the cause of success or failure in math; however, in another study, both middle-class African American and white students attributed failure to lack of effort (Alderman).

Alderman (2004) and Pintrich and Schunk (2004) describe the developmental change in attributions in children at about age ten. At this time, children begin to differentiate between effort and ability as the cause of success, but prior to that age they believe that effort and ability are the same. Therefore, the younger student who has tried but has not succeeded on a task may conclude that she does not have the ability and may no longer attempt that or similar tasks. Teachers of young children should take care to ensure that their students are given tasks on which they can succeed in order to avoid starting a young child on a self-defeating path of self-doubt and learned helplessness regarding school tasks.

The exemplary verbal feedback prompts I have suggested should not be limited to middle school students such as Ezekiel, but should be applied throughout the grades. As children become members of the community of learners and are enculturated into the school society in the early grades, teachers should provide them with positive, informative, and credible feedback about their ability to learn. This is especially true for children whose parents or caretakers may have done little to build, and may even have eroded, the child's self-efficacy and even her self-concept. The result of comments such as, "Your sister could read when she was your age. Why can't you?" or "How many times will it take for you to get it?" are deleterious to the young child's beliefs about himself as a learner, will carry over to the formal school environment and, if not immediately addressed by teachers, will become entrenched within the learner's psyche. Other children may be aware of their abilities thanks to nurturing parents or caretakers, but have learned from the formal school experience they are not as good as others and are not achieving according to school standards. This may result from poor or inconsistent instruction, including inappropriate material and pacing, lack of the teacher's individual attention, or classroom environmental issues such as noise level, lighting, overcrowding, or the seating arrangement. Ezekiel may have experienced either or a combination of these scenarios. When the verbal feedback I have suggested is consistently applied throughout the grades and is part of a schoolwide philosophy for learning, students will be much less likely to develop negative or weak self-efficacy beliefs such as those held by Ezekiel.

Although change in self-efficacy perceptions may occur in a relatively short period of time for some children, it is more likely that the results of these verbal prompts will occur gradually over a longer period of time, especially for children who have a painful history of failure and frustration in school. When the prompts I suggest are combined with the instructional prompts suggested by Brown (2003) and Clark (2004) and used in conjunction with sound literacy development practices that include appropriate tasks, materials, and instructional procedures, teachers will have a much better chance of reaching, and teaching, students such as Ezekiel.

References

Alderman, M. K. 2004. *Motivation for achievement: Possibilities for teaching and learning.* 2nd ed. Mahwah, NJ: Erlbaum.

Atkinson, R. K., A. Renkl, and M. M. Merrill. 2003. Transitioning from studying examples to solving problems: Effects of self-explanation prompts and fading worked-out steps. *Journal of Educational Psychology* 95 (4): 774–84.

Bandura, A. 1986. *Social foundations of thought and action.* Englewood Cliffs, NJ: Prentice-Hall.

———. 1995. Exercise of personal and collective efficacy in changing societies. In *Self-efficacy in changing societies,* ed. A. Bandura, 1–45. New York: Cambridge University Press.

———. 1997. *Self-efficacy: The exercise of control.* New York: Longman.

Bogner, K., L. Raphael, and M. Pressley. 2002. How grade 1 teachers motivate literacy activity by their students. *Scientific Studies of Reading* 6 (2): 135–65.

Brophy, J. 1981. Teacher praise: A functional analysis. *Review of Educational Research*, no. 51:5–32.

Brown, K. J. 2003. What do I say when they get stuck on a word? Aligning teachers' prompts with students' development. *Reading Teacher* 56 (8): 720–33.

Bruning, R. H., G. J. Schraw, M. M. Norby, and R. R. Ronning. 2004. *Cognitive psychology and instruction.* 4th ed. Upper Saddle River, NJ: Pearson.

Burnett, P. C. 2003. The impact of teacher feedback on student self-talk and self-concept in reading and mathematics. *Journal of Classroom Interaction* 38 (1): 11–16.

Clark, K. F. 2004. What can I say besides "sound it out"? Coaching word recognition in beginning reading. *Reading Teacher* 57 (4): 440–49.

Craven, R. G., H. W. Marsh, and R. L. Debus. 1991. Effects of internally focused feedback and attributional feedback on the enhancement of academic self-concept. *Journal of Educational Psychology*, no. 83:17–27.

Dolezal, S. E., L. M. Welsh, M. Pressley, and M. M. Vincent. 2003. How nine third grade teachers motivate student academic engagement. *Elementary School Journal* 103 (3): 240–67.

Ernsbarger, S. C. 2002. Simple, affordable, and effective strategies for prompting reading behavior. *Reading and Writing Quarterly* 18 (3): 279–84.

Mastropieri, M. A., and T. E. Scruggs. 2004. *The inclusive classroom: Strategies for effective instruction.* Upper Saddle River, NJ: Merrill Prentice-Hall.

May, F., and L. Rizzardi. 2002. *Reading as communication.* 6th ed. Upper Saddle River, NJ: Merrill Prentice-Hall.

Mueller, C. M., and C. S. Dweck. 1998. Praise for intelligence can undermine children's motivation and performance. *Journal of Personality and Psychology* 75 (1): 33–52.

Ormrod, J. E. 2004. *Human learning.* Upper Saddle River, NJ: Merrill.

Pintrich P. R., and D. H. Schunk. 2002. *Motivation in education: Theory, research, and applications.* Upper Saddle River, NJ: Merrill.

Robertson, J. S. 2000. Is attribution training a worthwhile classroom intervention for K–12 students with learning difficulties? *Educational Psychology Review* 12 (1): 111–34.

Schunk, D. H. 2001. Social cognitive theory and self-regulated learning. In *Self-regulated learning and academic*

ANNUAL EDITIONS

achievement: *Theoretical perspectives*, 2nd ed., ed. B. Zimmerman, 125–52. Mahwah, NJ: Lawrence Erlbaum.

———. 2003. Self-efficacy for reading and writing: Influence of modeling, goal setting, and self-evaluation. *Reading and Writing Quarterly* 19 (2): 159–72.

———. 2004. *Learning theories: An educational perspective.* 4th ed. New York: Pearson.

Stipek, D. J. 2001. *Motivation to learn: Integrating theory and practice.* Needham Heights, MA: Allyn and Bacon.

PATRICK P. MCCABE is an associate professor of education and reading at St. Johns University in Queens.

From *The Clearing House,* July/August 2006, pp. 252–257. Reprinted by permission of the Helen Dwight Reid Educational Foundation. Published by Heldref Publications, 1319 Eighteenth St., NW, Washington, DC 20036-1802. Copyright © 2006. www.heldref.org

Why We Can't Always Get What We Want

Barbara Bartholomew

He was the new reading teacher's greatest challenge—a sixth-grader reading at roughly the first-grade level. Sometimes he acted out, but mostly he just day-dreamed, talked, or slept while his classmates worked. No one, including his guardian, knew how to motivate him to want to succeed.

As she was leaving the building one afternoon, the teacher happened upon a rambunctious game of basketball. She entered the nearly empty gym, sat in the bleachers, and immediately noticed the boy playing with his team. She returned his frantic wave. As the game drew to a close, he dashed up to her, and they launched into an excited conversation about the game.

After that, she made a point of going to almost every practice for the rest of the season. There, she would often study the coach, focusing on how attentive the team was to him. They responded to his intensity, his knowledge of the game and the players, his planning, and his single-minded commitment to winning.

Taking this cue, she set a small number of attainable short- and long-term classroom goals for the boy, simultaneously adjusting her own demeanor, expectations, and responses to more closely match her colleague's. Progress toward reading goals was measured on a hand-drawn schematic of a basketball court in the boy's folder; each movement toward his "basket" was noted with a ball drawn on the paper court. Soon she and the boy began listening and responding carefully to each other.

The note of exasperation on which the year had begun quietly gave way to a fragile optimism shared by the student and teacher, now learners together. The boy began to believe he could make learning connections off the court, and the teacher began to understand that effective teaching depends a great deal on the efforts of the students themselves. After just five months of uneven yet steady progress, the boy's reading score had risen by more than a grade.

The year was 1995. The teacher was me.

Context First

What I had stumbled on in my first year of teaching would take years to implement consistently as a way to drive instruction. It was, in a word, *motivation*. Motivation involves creating the inspiration *to do* or *to achieve*. Some students arrive at school fully motivated. Often, though, the opposite is the case.

As a new teacher, I had assumed what most in the field of education believe to be true: motivation springs from effective curriculum and instruction. If we have some perfect blend of elements—direct instruction, whole-language instruction, a new trade book or textbook, an intervention, a new set of standards—students will become deeply involved and interested learners. Everything circled back to effective curriculum and instruction. It had been the focus of my college course-work, of every professional development session I had ever attended, and of every piece of advice I had ever received from a principal. But it was clear to me from that first experience that the most vexing issues I faced as a teacher stemmed less from the content that I knew and could control than from the context of things I did not know and could not control.

Chief among these things was what made my students tick. Human thought processes are not directly observable. Because we see others behaving in a way that is consistent with our efforts to influence their actions, we deduce that we have succeeded in our attempts to motivate them. But for every teacher who has run a "token" society, rewarded those who comply with candy, phoned a parent to gain a student's cooperation, changed seating charts in the hope of ending chatter, or flashed classroom lights as a signal for silence, it remains unclear exactly what is motivating the students. It is easy to confuse behavioral cueing with motivational change.

The Star Story

A principal I knew had once been a teacher at an alternative high school. Many of his pupils were returning from stints in jail or in drug treatment programs. Most were in their late teens and quickly bonded with him as a strong and important male presence in their lives. His dream for them was that they would be able to defy the odds of repeated failure and, as he had done, forge independent paths of success for themselves.

He placed a motivational chart in his classroom. As students reached important milestones, he would reward them with a gold star on the chart. One day, with only a few minutes until class was to begin, he realized that it was reward day and that he had run out of gold stars. He dashed across the street to a local grocery, only to find it was sold out of the tiny gold stars. He settled for silver stars instead.

When award time rolled around, he began posting the silver stars that he had purchased as substitutes. Almost immediately furious shouts erupted from his normally quiet group, and within moments the class had dissolved into a chaotic mix of fist fighting and chair throwing. The police were summoned. As the students were being questioned, virtually every one, some in tears, expressed frustration that their teacher had disrespected them by demoting them from the level of gold stars to the lesser status of silver.

With no background in either the power or the shortcomings of behavioral motivation models, he had missed important pieces of the context in which he was working. He failed to account for how much value his students had placed on the public recognition of individual accomplishment played out in front of the entire group. Other contextual issues might have affected their motivation as well. Had fair and equitable rules been set for earning the rewards? Could he have anticipated that an all-male class would see the stars as designations of merit similar to gold and silver medals?

It is well established in the literature of motivation that successful motivational models do not necessarily rely on extrinsically controlled rewards and punishments. Rather, the best motivational models take advantage of those "satisfiers" and "valuations" chosen and controlled by an individual. Without knowing of alternative ways of developing autonomous learners, the teacher had simply resorted to the carrot-and-stick model that was actually least likely to bring him the results he wanted.

Classroom Management or Motivation?

A common confusion of teachers and school leaders alike is that classroom management and motivation are basically one and the same. Teachers continue to focus on tight control of the environment and curriculum in the closely held belief that doing so will eventually create motivated students and positive learning outcomes. Since it sometimes does, they are encouraged to keep trying whatever occasionally successful system brings them the result they seek. Because a quiet classroom where students are busy is equated with good teaching, it is an ideal for which most teachers strive. The paradox, of course, is that such successful behavior management does not create motivation to learn, any more than work completed with little care for learning demonstrates student progress.

What classroom management can provide is the space to create motivating opportunities for students to engage in a level of self-determination about their own learning.[1] But if the chance is not seized, teachers will find themselves very quickly painted into a corner of endlessly distributing rewards and punishments, with little opportunity to focus on mastery in content areas.

A number of studies, including the government's own, have established the correlation between teacher attrition and lack of classroom control.[2] These same data suggest that more than 50% of teachers leave the profession because of poor student behavior.

What we have failed to provide in the professional training of teachers is a realistic understanding that control and compliance will not in themselves create a climate for academic attainment. Indeed, in some cases, they may actually prove to be a disincentive to learning. Causes of disengagement vary, from boredom and frustration to anger and depression. So long as we continue to focus on the symptoms of the uninspired rather than on the problem itself, we will persist in overlooking the root causes of why students fail to thrive.

A Misunderstood Precondition

The education community has not done a good job of articulating the idea that student motivation is a necessary precondition to learning that teachers need to create and foster. And teachers must do this nurturing from their diagnostic and practical knowledge of human behavior, not from a knowledge of subject matter. Not one of the top 10 schools of education in the *U.S. News and World Report* rankings requires students seeking credentials as teachers or pursuing graduate degrees in leadership to complete a dedicated class in educational motivation. Typically, the study of motivation has been located in graduate schools of psychology or in departments of educational psychology. Students in these areas are not very likely to become the professionals who interact with students daily in a school setting.

If motivation is covered at all in most schools of education, it is folded into the subject matter of another class, such as organizational management or learning theory, rather than studied as an essential stand-alone subject. In the endless parsing of "best practices" in training programs for teachers and school leaders—both preservice and inservice—learning to foster student motivation, the most obvious of all best practices, is conspicuously absent.

There exists an entrenched belief in American education that student learning will spring from the right alchemic brew of macro components: firm direction from state and local departments of education, strong district- and school-based leadership, a good teacher, the right curriculum, and appropriate books.[3] However, such matters as the steady increase in the number of students whose families face grave economic stresses and the need for common touchstones in a multicultural society argue that the time is right to examine carefully the framework of human variables involved in teaching and learning.

The best place to start is the field of educational motivation, which encompasses a well-developed and compelling body of knowledge from such fields as psychology, sociology, linguistic and speech studies, and organizational management. In this knowledge base we are sure to find at least part of what we need to help us create classrooms that will appeal to those who teach and those who learn.

Higher up the policy ladder, state and local administrators are beginning to reassess the effect on student achievement of micromanaged schools and scripted curricula. They will need to consider what elements and training will be necessary to create motivational classrooms. It is also essential that they take a hard look at the impact of factory-model educational designs of the kind encouraged by the No Child Left Behind (NCLB) Act on school personnel's morale and, in turn, on student achievement.[4]

As the reauthorization of NCLB looms in 2007, we would be wise to ask ourselves how we can do better at preparing highly qualified professionals for the jobs they will face. It is widely acknowledged that something monumental has shifted beneath our feet, and teachers have been saying for years that they are social workers and psychologists first. Yet we continue to prepare them as content specialists and to evaluate their teaching proficiency on how well they meet subject content standards. What is our plan, then, for the human content standard?

Rethinking Preparation and Practice

One reason schools, offices of education, and even university departments of education have ignored motivational theory and practice is doubtless the difficulty of identifying generalizable and effective courses of action for teachers, given the endless variety of challenging conditions educators face. It is unlikely that there will ever be a single program to address all possibilities, but some relevant universals can be found.

It is in education that behaviorism has probably come closest to achieving mass popularity, and it has done so in part because of the simplicity of its basic stance and its appeal to commonsense ideas about control and reward. However, as the "star story" illustrates, behaviorism is not always an easy tool to use. Nevertheless, it would be foolish and impractical to dismiss thoughtful behavioral reward systems altogether simply because they do not draw on intrinsic motivation or because they violate an ideological ideal. Those programs that provide meaningful, noncontrolling feedback or those in which students themselves determine how they wish to be rewarded are clearly worth examining.[5]

Programs that have proved useful in enhancing student learning should not be dismissed simply because they do not conform to today's trends in practice. What is important is that both instructional and motivational programs demonstrate a justifiable probability of success. Moreover, whatever the theoretical underpinnings of a program, those who would apply it must learn both the theory and the ways it plays out in practice.

Both teacher preparation programs and educational leadership programs should require a minimum of a one-term class dedicated to the topic of motivation. Indeed, a full-year sequence would be best. Such a program should provide its students with broad preparation in the cross-disciplinary cornerstones of motivational theory and in the details of practice. Case study analyses, combined with opportunities for clinical observation, practice, and reflection, would give all educators a far better chance of success.

Motivation in Action

One of the great puzzles of education is how to take a successful innovative program, transfer it to a new setting, and obtain equally good results. Though we don't always like to acknowledge it, classroom and school cultures are created at the local level. Successful instructional motivation programs must therefore be able to take account of the context of individual communities and of the students in specific classrooms. What drives people of all ages to make choices about where to exert themselves is, to some degree at least, relevance to their lives. If we perceive that something is relevant, we will choose to participate in learning it even if it does not interest us or even if we feel we don't have the ability to learn it easily. Following a similar line of thought, psychologist Gordon Paul posed a classic question for clinical researchers: "*What* treatment, by *whom*, is most effective for *this* individual with *that* specific problem, and under *which* set of circumstances?"[6] These are sage words for anyone wondering where to begin a discussion of motivation.

While there is no universal framework to follow, there are a number of fundamentals that apply broadly and can be used as a foundation for building models of classroom excellence. When they are ignored or violated, we decrease our chances of fostering the personally meaningful satisfaction and enrichment of lives that education has always sought.

One such general principle of "satisfaction" could be stated this way: we are drawn to do what gratifies us and avoid doing what pains us—especially when we see no clear benefit from the undesirable experience. Below, I mention briefly several other considerations that would have both broad applicability and individual relevance for creating a classroom where intrinsic motivation rules.

• *Sustainability must be considered.* Good practices get better as routines are established and weaknesses identified and weeded out. No program or component of a program should be kept if it is not working.

• *Age determines course of action.* Opportunities for students to achieve success at every level of schooling are crucial to establishing and maintaining motivation. Younger children are generally more confident that they will succeed in school—probably because their perceptions have not yet been firmly shaped with regard to their abilities and achievement history.[7] From grades 3 through 8, studies have shown that intrinsic motivation falls off steadily.

Older students—like those in the star story—present complex personal histories and problems. Those who have accepted failure and those who have learned helplessness may not believe that they possess the ability to change their learning outcomes. Others seek to avoid failure in a variety of unsatisfactory ways, including not challenging themselves to learn and even lapsing into plagiarism and other forms of cheating.[8]

Standardized assessments may not accurately determine how prepared students are in content areas. And uncovering the strengths students bring to the classroom and the relevance to their lives of classroom learning is key to remediation and engagement, especially for older students.

• *Teachers set expectations and establish routines.* Classroom management will not be the focal point of efforts to increase student motivation. Instead, a well-managed classroom will be the result of good organization, clear expectations, positive teacher communication, and valuing student input and engagement. Teachers must model and enforce the kind of respectful interchange they expect. Praise is an appropriate reward when it is specific and deserved; it should never be used when students have performed work without effort or care. And once again, consistency is essential in establishing an effective classroom and in maintaining a classroom culture of trust and equality.

• *Students, with guidance from teachers, establish goals, strategies, and achievement plans.* Allowing students to set goals is probably the most effective means of having them begin to take charge of their learning. How this process is arranged can vary, but students' plans should incorporate short- and long-term goals and an explicit outline of what will be needed to achieve them. So as not to overwhelm students, the goals can be broken down into smaller units of daily or weekly goals. Some students may wish to work with partners to brainstorm, to gauge their progress, and to obtain feedback on their work. Student-maintained records of individual progress can provide incentives for self-monitoring.

• *Providing students with choices can be motivating.* In general, we should allow students to participate in class decision making and should give them as many choices as possible about the topics and work they will pursue. Class-constructed rubrics can establish group norms for how work will be evaluated. Students will perceive evaluation systems into which they have had input as fairer than those from which they have been excluded.

• *Teachers set class tone; students set their individual tone.* In the classrooms I have observed, minds at rest have a tendency to stay at rest until an outside force acts on them. Once in motion, if they're encouraged and supported, they tend to stay in motion and continue to move forward independently. Building students' intrinsic motivation involves a seemingly contradictory degree of stage setting, coaching, and feedback from the teacher, especially as routines are being set. And even as the students "take over," teachers must still be comfortable with a wide variety of teaching strategies in order to accommodate the range of subjects and the range of student learners.

Two components that help set the tone are likely to play key roles in the degree to which students engage themselves independently as learners. The first is respecting the power of listening. The simple act of listening carefully to others while holding their gaze conveys attentiveness, interest, respect for (though not necessarily agreement with) the speaker's views, and a range of other nonverbal messages. By combining attentive listening with such conversational guidelines as turn-taking, gauging understanding, and conveying empathy, the teacher can both build and help monitor engagement.[9] Creating opportunities to teach and practice listening is a frequently overlooked element in establishing a mutually motivational environment for both teacher and student. Listening is also an important

aspect of relationship building, the most obvious of all motivational strategies.

The second component that helps foster a tone that supports motivation is building and expanding on positives. The expanding field of positive psychology has yielded insights into the phenomenon of "learned optimism," or the theory that positive thinking patterns can be acquired.[10] In one classic experiment, researchers paired animated, happy individuals with nonexpressive partners in a conversational setting. In a short time, the mood of the nonexpressive individuals began to lighten and approached that of the more positive individuals.[11] Such positive emotions as joy, pride, and contentment have been shown to lead to physiological and psychological changes that cause individuals—at least momentarily—to broaden their cognitive perceptions, to become more open to change, and to increase their emotional well-being.

Barbara Fredrickson has proposed a "broaden and build" theory that suggests that positive moments create opportunities for mental expansiveness. Seizing on these moments when the potential for growth is at its peak can lead to greater classroom learning.[12] Humor, celebrations, trips, visual reminders, and games fall under the umbrella of building intrinsic motivation through positive approaches.[13]

The Satisfaction Principle

Educators are not all that different from students. They also thrive in climates where they feel their input is viewed as important, where they can engage in daily curricular and instructional choices, and where they feel valued and respected.[14] Like older students, they will avoid the pain of working in environments over which they have little control and in which they meet daily failure. When they are unable to find satisfaction in their work environment, the data show that they will leave.

One failing that has been noted about standards-based systems is that, when externally mandated goals are not met, blame enters the picture. In such work climates, teachers are unlikely to experiment with any classroom technique that could cause them to be targeted for blame should students fail to achieve.[15] In the present national environment of rigid adherence to lock-step formulas, following standard practice is the equivalent of job insurance. If students fail because of policies made higher up the chain of command, then schools and teachers can say that they did as they were told, and culpability will be pushed back up the ladder. Teachers are a well-educated group and will, when they have had enough, move on. Students, lacking this option, will be the ones who will lose the most.

It is within our power, as a profession, to reshape what exists into what could be. We have misplaced the knowledge that hope and dreams are the mortar of our business. We now define and justify our actions through the accountability sweepstakes, but until we reset our direction, we will remain disappointed, like the students racing for gold stars and inexplicably receiving silver ones. The star chart has replaced the satisfaction principle.

Notes

1. Edward L. Deci and Richard M. Ryan, "The Paradox of Achievement: The Harder You Push, the Worse It Gets," in Joshua Aronson, ed., *Improving Academic Achievement: Contribution of Social Psychology* (New York: Academic Press, 2002), pp. 59–85.

2. "The Condition of Education, 2005, Special Analysis: Mobility in the Teacher Workforce," U.S. Department of Education, http://nces.ed. gov/programs/coe/2005/analysis/index.asp; and New York City Council, "A Staff Report of the New York City Council Division on Teacher Attrition and Retention," Eric Goia, Chair, 2004.

3. Michael J. Feuer, "Better Than Best," *Harvard Education Letter,* May/June, 2006.

4. Barbara Bartholomew, "Transforming New York City's Public Schools," *Educational Leadership,* May 2006, pp. 61–65.

5. Martin V. Covington and Kimberly J. Mueller, "Intrinsic Versus Extrinsic Motivation: An Approach/Avoidance Reformulation," *Educational Psychology Review,* vol 13, 2001, pp. 157–76.

6. Gordon L. Paul, "Strategy of Outcome Research in Psychotherapy," *Journal of Consulting Psychology,* vol. 31, 1967, p. 111.

7. Deborah J. Stipek, *Motivation to Learn* (Boston: Allyn and Bacon, 1993), p. 14.

8. Ibid.; and Covington and Mueller, pp. 169–70.

9. Lyn S. Turkstra, "Looking While Listening and Speaking: Eye-to-Face Gaze in Adolescents with and without Brain Injury," *Journal of Speech, Language, and Hearing Research,* December 2005, pp. 1429–41.

10. Martin E. P. Seligman, *Learned Optimism* (New York: Simon and Schuster, 1998).

11. Howard S. Friedman and Ronald E. Riggio, "Effect of Individual Differences in Nonverbal Expressiveness on Transmission of Emotion," *Journal of Nonverbal Behavior,* December 1981, pp. 96–104.

12. Barbara L. Fredrickson, "The Role of Positive Emotions in Positive Psychology: The Broaden and Build Theory of Positive Emotions," *American Psychologist,* vol. 56, 2001, pp. 218–26.

13. Paula Milligan, "Bringing Fun into Organization," *Teaching Pre-K–8,* August/September 2006, available at www.teaching-k-8.com/archives/articles/bringing_fun_into_organization_by_paula_milligan.html.

14. Catherine Scott, Stephen Dinham, and Robert Brooks, "The Development of Scales to Measure Teacher and School Executive Operational Satisfaction," paper presented at the annual meeting of AARE-NAARE, 1999, Melbourne, Aus.

15. Nona Tollefson, "Classroom Applications of Cognitive Theories of Motivation," *Educational Psychology Review,* March 2000, pp. 63–83.

BARBARA BARTHOLOMEW is an assistant professor of reading and literacy at California State University, Bakersfield.

From *Phi Delta Kappan,* April 2007, pp. 593–598. Copyright © 2007 by Phi Delta Kappan. Reprinted by permission of Phi Delta Kappan and Barbara Bartholomew.

How to Produce a High-Achieving Child

Frantic parents trying to ensure that their children can maintain an edge throughout their school careers have become a fixture of today's society. But Ms, Kuhn suggests that we are focusing on the wrong side of the equation. Instead of dwelling on what students bring with them to school, we should be considering whether school offers children and young adults sufficiently meaningful experiences to engage them.

DEANNA KUHN

Any lingering pleasant associations parents might entertain in connection with their children's schooling are increasingly being edged out by anxiety. Have I done all I can to ensure my child is on the right track? Perhaps even ahead of the pack? Did I arrange the best summer activities? The right social connections? Or have my efforts been too little or, worse, too late? Is my child already in danger of being "left behind"?

Especially poignant is the fact that in many cases the children of parents harboring these anxieties are no more than a few years old. And these anxieties are not particular to the privileged. They lurk in the minds of parents from one end of the socioeconomic continuum to the other. Among parents at the high end, "average" has become a disappointing outcome, and a large proportion of parents—and their children along with them—are destined to find themselves disappointed.

It is worrying, then, that recent research appears to justify this parental angst. The NICHD Early Child Care Research Network offers this summary in a recent report: "The early childhood years are increasingly seen as a crucial period for the growth and consolidation of important . . . skills necessary for successful school transition and later academic functioning. Major individual differences in these skills emerge well before children arrive at school."[1]

A recent study by Angela Duckworth and Martin Seligman, published in a major academic journal and noted in the *Washington Post,* supports this conclusion. Their study claims that the personal trait of "self-discipline" is the most powerful determinant of young adolescents' academic achievement.[2] The authors asked teens to choose between receiving $1 immediately or $2 next week. Better students were more likely to opt for the $2. Even more notable, related studies have suggested that this ability to delay gratification can be identified in preschoolers and remains stable at least into adolescence. Similarly, Stanford psychologist Carol Dweck reports that people show stability from early childhood on in their beliefs about ability (that it is fixed or can be

developed), and she claims that this characteristic significantly affects academic performance.[3]

Is a child's fate determined even before his or her school career has begun? Or are there reasons to doubt that the race to success is won or lost in these earliest years? Among the reasons for doubt is the fact that the formulas for success that focus on traits students bring with them to school leave unexamined the other half of this transaction: what the setting offers the student.

This latter component is critical because it is the student (at any age) who makes what meaning he or she can out of the school experience. We can interpret educational settings only through the lens of how students experience them. And in the end, it is students themselves who select what and when they want to learn. By early adolescence, they begin wanting reasons for investing time and effort in any activity, and they begin to exercise greater autonomy in deciding what is worthwhile.

How I'm Doing versus What I'm Doing

Why do some children come to value the activities they are asked to engage in at school while others do not? The answer seems likely to lie in the meaning they are able to attribute to these activities. How do children go about constructing authentic meaning out of what they do in school? And is such productive meaning-making critical to academic achievement?

The extensive research on psychological factors affecting school performance contains few answers to these questions. The reason is that most research has been focused not on what children think about school activities but rather on what they think about their own abilities and standing with respect to schoolwork. Only as a secondary effect have researchers considered how these self-evaluation factors affect the value students assign to academic activities themselves.

Thus Dweck reports that whether a student has a performance orientation toward school (believing that ability is fixed) or a learning orientation (believing that ability can be developed) does not predict self-esteem in elementary school but does predict self-esteem by the beginning of junior high school.[4] Self-esteem has been found to decline at this time, especially for girls and for those with a performance orientation. So does professed interest in academic subjects.[5] The causal scenario is not hard to imagine. A performance orientation heightens fear that ones incompetence may be exposed, especially once a young person has experienced failure. An unflattering evaluation lowers self-esteem, and as a self-protective mechanism, the value attached to the activity is reduced. "I'm not interested in it" is more protective of self-esteem than "I'm no good at it."

To the extent that a student is ego-involved rather than task-involved, academic activities come to serve primarily as occasions for evaluating one's competence relative to others.[6] In addition to the danger this orientation poses to children's vulnerable self-esteem, it has a further serious downside. With attention focused on evaluating *how* one is doing relative to others, little attention is left to contemplate *what* one is doing. Every occasion becomes an occasion for social comparison, and the results of these comparisons dictate whether one will continue to invest in and value the activity that is the basis for comparison. Highly privileged, pressured children, especially, feel that they can afford to invest time and effort only in those activities at which they excel. Just when children and adolescents might ideally explore and expand their interests, they begin instead to narrow them.

Suppose, instead, we were able to redirect students' attention to the meanings they attach to their schoolwork, rather than to their ability. What do we know about such meanings? Very little, it turns out.[7] Neither parents nor teachers often elicit children's ideas about why it is they study what they study. It's considered enough that the adults in charge have a sound rationale for what they ask children to do and for the goals these activities will meet. But what evidence we do have suggests that students' understanding is not all we might like it to be. When I asked one young teen whether the world history he was studying would be of value to him in the future, he replied, "Only if you were trying to impress somebody in a conversation." Perhaps we shouldn't be surprised, for the value of much of what students do in school is not immediately apparent—least of all to students themselves.

The New York Story

With increasing age, students do become more likely to question what they are asked to do—a fact that New York City Mayor Michael Bloomberg seems to have overlooked. The mayor has declared creation of "a public education system second to none" as a mission of his second term. If he is to fulfill this mission, he and his associates are going to have to think deeply about what makes a school successful.

Following promising improvements in fourth-graders' test scores in response to a tough new no-automatic-promotion policy, Mayor Bloomberg has extended the policy to students in middle schools and high schools. But in so doing, he neglects an important difference between younger and older children. By the preteen years, children have become less pliable and eager to please adults and so less likely to accept parents' and teachers'

admonitions that they must work hard in school or suffer negative consequences. They may become skeptical of the message they've been given that school is the path to success and begin to ask themselves, "What's the point? Why are we doing these things?"

In a society increasingly divided into haves and have-nots, it is the youths in the latter group who most often lack answers. Indeed, they might eventually stop asking questions and simply give up on making sense of much of what their elders ask them to do. Their basic literacy skills are likely to have plateaued at this point, and these young people are sizing up what else it is they're supposed to be getting out of school. Close personal relationships with teachers have largely been sacrificed in the transition from elementary to departmentalized junior high schools, and the students' self-esteem has become even more fragile.[8] If students are going to work any harder, they'll need to find a reason. Complying with the goals adults have for them won't do. For these at-risk youths—who are the primary targets of Mayor Bloomberg's (and many others') effort—the most likely effect of not being promoted is confirmation of a growing sense that "whatever education is about, it's not for me."

Socially advantaged children, in striking contrast, soon develop a ready answer to the "Why are we doing this?" question: to get into a top college. And the competition to do so is stiff enough that they have little time to ponder *why* they're studying what they study ("Will I ever need to know this?"). They've accepted that this is what you need to do to get into college and that getting into college is the path to success. Once there, they'll continue working to fulfill a set of requirements of others' making. And again, the point is to get a degree—and then start a life.

When they do get out into the real world, privileged youths encounter a world in which a markedly different set of norms prevails. All that is done is done for a purpose, most often monetary, and to achieve their purposes people must interact. Both of these characteristics of adult work life—its purposeful and collaborative nature—are largely absent during the school years that precede them. And so, especially in a tight, no-nonsense economy, even the most privileged young people often have a hard time making the transition from school to the working world of adults.

Making School Make Sense

Perhaps one key to the puzzle of academic motivation is to make school make sense, not just to those who structure our school systems or rely on them to educate their children, but to the young people for whom they are designed. Certainly, children's developing self-understanding and the influence of family and community on their development deserve examination, but so does school itself—in particular, the meaning children make of it.

How can we increase the likelihood that school will make sense to students? I suggest two ways. One is to center the curriculum on educational activities whose purpose and value are readily apparent to those who partake in them.[9] This means to a large extent focusing education on intellectual tools—the ones I stress are inquiry and argument—whose purpose and value are easily recognized and whose broad utility and power are evident. Second, and closely related, we need to make schooling more connected to the adult life it is intended to prepare students for.[10] We cannot predict exactly what students will need to know in the

21st century, but we can help them develop the intellectual skills that will enable them to construct this knowledge. Both efforts would serve the haves and have-nots equally well.

Students need to experience for themselves the value of the intellectual activities they engage in and the intellectual tools they acquire. They should become able to make use of them for their own purposes and to see the fruits of their labors, recognizing that intellectual skills, such as inquiry and argument, give them a most productive path for answering questions, solving problems, resolving conflicts, and participating in a democratic society. These are achievements that come about only as the endpoint of a long developmental course, one in which the student is the key player, the meaning-maker. Students do not learn the power of inquiry and argument merely by being told.

Before saying more about how such objectives might be met, I should note that developing sound intellectual motivation depends on students' own intellectual development. This does not mean children are at the mercy of fate, with only some happening to be born to parents who will give them the right recipe to ensure their intellectual development. Rather, the intellectual development of concern here requires only intellectual engagement, and it can take a variety of forms. It is development that is not concentrated in the first few years of life and is within the potential of all children.

Such development encompasses not only the capacity for meaning-making in general, but the ability to make meaning out of ones own life—to find a purpose and to identify goals that can influence actions. We do know that the requisite self-awareness and self-management—what cognitive psychologists are more likely to refer to as self-regulation or "executive control"—do increase in the years between middle childhood and mid-adolescence.[11]

This development is critical because self-regulation is necessary if students are to become active in their own learning and to develop and pursue their own goals.[12] By the time children enter adolescence, they have more discretion than before over how they will spend their time and energy. They are likely to have become more aware of, and highly judgmental about, their own performance. And so their interests will begin to narrow as they make judgments about what they're good at and what they're not good at. And they will have considerable freedom to act on these judgments.

If we want the young people navigating the challenges of this period to decide that the life of the mind is something they are disposed to pursue, we need to consider what they take an intellectual life to be. What is knowledge, and why would one want to invest the effort to acquire it? Researchers studying cognitive development have identified a predictable sequence in students' ideas about the nature of knowledge and knowing, one worth taking into consideration in seeking to understand their academic motivations.[13]

Early in their school lives, children are uniformly naive objectivists. In elementary school, children regard knowledge as something that exists out in the world, independent of the knower. If you and I disagree, it's simply a matter of accessing the information that will determine which of us is right and which wrong. To these young absolutists, there are no shades of gray.

By some time during adolescence, though, fueled by the troubling discovery that reasonable people—even experts—disagree, most young people undergo a dramatic shift and come to embrace, at least for a time, a radical relativism with regard to knowledge and knowing. In a word, everyone is now right. If no one knows for certain, everyone must be accorded the right to believe as he or she chooses. Like pieces of clothing, beliefs are the personal possessions of the believer and not to be questioned. The subjective knower thus enters the equation but eclipses the objective known. Moreover, because everyone has a right to individual beliefs, one belief cannot be said to be any more right than another. Tolerance for multiple views is equated with the impossibility of discriminating among them.

Only some young people will make the transition to the next level of development, one in which the subjective and objective components of knowledge are coordinated. They come to understand that, although all have a right to their own views, some views are nonetheless more right than others, to the extent that they are better supported by evidence. Justification for a belief becomes more than personal preference. The adolescent "whatever" is no longer the automatic response to every assertion. There are now legitimate discriminations and choices to be made.

Until students reach this level of understanding, their motivation for intellectual pursuits remains on shaky ground. If facts can be ascertained with certainty and if they are readily available to anyone who seeks them, as the absolutist conceives, or if any claim is as valid as any other, as the relativist conceives, there is little point in expending the mental effort that intellectual inquiry and the evaluation of claims entail. Only at the third, "evaluativist" level of epistemological understanding are thinking and reason recognized as essential to support beliefs and actions. Thinking enables us to make informed choices between conflicting claims, and understanding this fact leads students to value thinking and to be willing to expend the serious effort it requires.

By the time students reach college, differences in their levels of epistemological understanding correlate with how they process new information and also serve to predict academic achievement.[14] While they are still in high school, students' levels of epistemological understanding predict the degree to which they have identified future academic and career plans and goals. Those who have reached an evaluativist level of understanding are more likely to have specific plans and goals than are those who remain relativists or absolutists.[15]

When looking at the connection between intellectual development and intellectual values, it is interesting to make comparisons across cultural and subcultural groups. Ironically, Asian and Asian American students, despite their reputation for academic achievement, do not show accelerated development of epistemological understanding or intellectual values. My associates and I have asked questions such as the following of middle-schoolers and high-schoolers and their parents in several American communities; in Israel; in Cyprus; and in Japanese, Korean, Korean American, and Taiwanese American communities: "Many social issues, like the death penalty, gun control, or medical care, are pretty much matters of personal opinion, and there is no basis for saying that one person's opinion is any better than another's. So there's not much point in people having discussions about these kinds of issues. Do you strongly agree, sort of agree, or disagree? (If disagree) What do you think?" A majority of American parents and teens disagreed with such statements, claiming that it was worthwhile to discuss these issues. The percentages of those who disagreed among the Asian and Asian American groups ranged from 0% to a high of 38%.[16]

These findings are perhaps not entirely surprising. The Asian distaste for disagreement and desire to maintain harmony are well known—a cultural stereotype almost. Should these values be cause for concern? "To each his own" and "Live and let live" are stances we arguably need more of in every part of the world.

Yet there is a less apparent but real cost. When asked hypothetical questions about two discrepant views (e.g., whether one musical composition could be judged better than another or one scientific theory more correct than another), Asian and Asian American respondents more often espoused the absolutist belief in certain knowledge that would yield a single right answer or the relativist position that one alternative cannot be judged any more right than the other and that disagreeing parties have a right to their respective views. Thus tolerance and indiscriminability are equated.

Asian education experts in high-performing nations like Singapore have begun to ask themselves whether the development of the skills and disposition to engage ideas and examine them critically (and creatively) has been shortchanged in their education systems. Perhaps developing these skills is an important part of what it means to become educated. The best thinking is very often collaborative rather than solitary. But collaborative intellectual engagement comes with what may be a high cost from the Asian perspective—the risk of at least temporarily sacrificing agreement and harmony.

How Do We Help Children Buy into Education?

Parents can push and pull their children to bring home those A's, but in the end, it is the children who need to find sound reasons for wanting to do so. And the most important thing we can do to help them find those reasons may be to make school an endeavor that makes sense. In early adolescence, as children acquire more freedom to choose how to invest their time and energy and as their skills in self-management increase, cognitive support for achievement motivation becomes crucial. Affective factors should not be eliminated from the equation.[17] But it is arguably the cognitive factors—both within the child and within the setting—that have not been given sufficient attention. For too long we have relied on much the same curriculum for secondary schools that these students' parents and grandparents plodded their way through, and we have simply expected today's students to recognize how it meets their needs.

Prominent among such cognitive factors is students' own intellectual development. The intellectual development that occurs in the second decade of life—not just during those early years that receive the lion's share of attention—is enormously important. The die is far from cast in the first years of life. One of the most important things adults can do for older children may be to make

sure that their school experience is the kind that they can readily make sense of instead of having to depend on reassurances from teachers or parents that "this is what you need to know." Such efforts are surely as important in promoting a child's future success as anything a parent does, or fails to do, in the early years.

What makes school experiences easy for students to make meaning of? It's entirely possible to engage secondary students in highly educational activities whose purpose and value become apparent in the process of engaging in them—activities that do not require young people to accept adult pronouncements about the "need to know." As one concrete example, suppose high school students were asked to work together to investigate one of the problems plaguing their city, say, a scarcity of potable water. They would examine causes and potential solutions and in so doing research how other cities, past and present, had dealt with the matter. They would appreciate both what they were doing and why. In the process, they would learn a good deal and learn how to learn—both individually and collaboratively. They would be less likely to ask, "Why do we need to know this?"

They might also escape the norm that prevails in school culture: sit down, be quiet, and wait for instructions. I was struck to learn from my son who graduated this past year from the U.S. Air Force Academy about one bit of educational wisdom that has evolved there. Cadets are being prepared to assume a certain kind of well-delineated leadership role. As part of their education, inside the classroom and out, they are taught not to seek or await instructions (as one might suppose at a military academy), but instead to approach any new situation by identifying the problem and then proceeding to make themselves useful in addressing it. In a word, figure out what needs to be done and get to work doing it.

Problem-based learning is far from new—it can be traced back to John Dewey—and modern evidence for its effectiveness continues to accumulate. The intellectual skills that develop when engaging in problem-based learning aren't tapped by multiple-choice tests. We need new kinds of assessments. Some might lament the diminished command of knowledge measured by conventional tests that students would forgo in pursuing problem-based learning. But if we asked any college to choose between an applicant well versed in biological or historical knowledge and one well versed in analytical thinking, there would be little contest. Colleges are presumptuous enough to believe they can readily impart knowledge. It is students who have learned to use their minds well that they seek. Yet, for now, selective colleges have no choice but to make their increasingly fine admission discriminations primarily on the basis of how well applicants have mastered traditional high school subject matter.

For some time it has been unclear whose needs even well-functioning middle and high schools are serving. And, of course, it's quite possible that they are serving no one's needs very well—not those of young people or those of their future employers or those of institutions of higher learning.

As we continue to pour more effort and resources into schools that aren't working, perhaps the time is finally here to make real change, rather than to simply "get tougher" about what we've already been doing for so long. The "raising standards" approach reflected in Mayor Bloomberg's "no-automatic-promotion" policies and in the myriad regulations of No Child Left Behind represent more of the same. In response to the provocative claim Bill Gates made last year to a coalition of state governors that American high schools were obsolete, the governors responded by pledging to adopt "higher standards, more rigorous courses, and tougher examinations."

We need to be clearer about just where we'd like all the children we're not going to leave behind to be headed. Setting our sights on even one objective might take us a long way. Let's give students in our middle and secondary schools good reasons—ones that readily make sense to them—to invest themselves in school. That means thinking carefully about what we ask them to do there and making sure that it makes sense—to them and to us.

Indeed, if we took the idea of education as an extended meaning-making endeavor seriously, it could change everything. Instead of a contest with winners and losers that is won or lost early in life, school could become a path for development where everyone wins.

Notes

1. NICHD Early Child Care Research Network, "Multiple Pathways to Early Academic Achievement," *Harvard Educational Review,* vol. 74, 2004, pp. 1–29.

2. Angela Duckworth and Martin Seligman, "Self-Discipline Outdoes I.Q. in Predicting Academic Performance of Adolescents," *Psychological Science,* vol. 16, 2005, pp. 939–44.

3. Carol Dweck, "The Development of Ability Conceptions," in Allan Wigfield and Jacquelynne S. Eccles, eds., *Development of Achievement Motivation* (San Diego: Academic Press, 2002), pp. 57–91.

4. Ibid.

5. Allan Wigfield et al., "Development of Achievement Motivation," in Nancy Eisenberg, ed., *Handbook of Child Psychology, Vol. 3: Social Development,* 6th ed. (Hoboken, N.J.: Wiley, 2006), pp. 933–1002; and Allan Wigfield and A. Laurel Wagner, "Competence, Motivation, and Identity Development During Adolescence," in Andrew J. Elliot and Carol S. Dweck, eds., *Handbook of Competence and Motivation* (New York: Guilford Press, 2005), pp. 222–39.

6. John G. Nicholls, *The Competitive Ethos and Democratic Education* (Cambridge, Mass.: Harvard University Press, 1989).

7. Janine Bempechat and Eleanor Drago-Severson, "Cross-National Differences in Academic Achievement: Beyond Etic Conceptions of Children's Understandings," *Review of Educational Research,* vol. 69, 1999, pp. 287–314.

8. Wigfield et al., op. cit.

9. Deanna Kuhn, *Education for Thinking* (Cambridge, Mass.: Harvard University Press, 2005).

10. John Anderson et al., "Perspectives on Learning, Thinking, and Activity," *Educational Researcher,* May 2000, pp. 11–13.

11. Deanna Kuhn, "Do Cognitive Changes Accompany Developments in the Adolescent Brain?," *Perspectives on Psychological Science,* March 2006, pp. 59–67.

12. Barry J. Zimmerman, "A Social Cognitive View of Self-Regulated Learning," *Journal of Educational Psychology,* September 1989, pp. 329–39; and Albert Bandura, *Self-Efficacy: The Exercise of Control* (New York: Freeman, 1994).

13. William Perry, *Forms of Intellectual and Ethical Development in the College Years* (New York: Holt, Rinehart & Winston, 1970); Barbara K. Hofer and Paul R Pintrich, "The Development of Epistemological Theories: Beliefs About Knowledge and Knowing and Their Relation to Learning," *Review of Educational Research,* Spring 1997, pp. 88–140; and Deanna Kuhn and Sam Franklin, "The Second Decade: What Develops (and How)?," in Deanna Kuhn and Robert S. Siegler, eds., *Handbook of Child Psychology, Vol. 2: Cognition, Perception, and Language,* 6th ed. (Hoboken, N.J.: Wiley, 2006), pp. 953–93.

14. Lucia Mason and Pietro Boscolo, "Role of Epistemological Understanding and Interest in Interpreting a Controversy and in Topic-Specific Belief Change," *Contemporary Educational Psychology,* April 2004, pp. 103–28; Michael Weinstock, Yair Neuman, and Amnon Glassner, "Identification of Informal Reasoning Fallacies as a Function of Epistemological Level, Grade Level, and Cognitive Ability," *Journal of Educational Psychology,* vol. 98, 2006, pp. 327–41; and Michelle M. Buehl and Patricia A. Alexander, "Motivation and Performance Differences in Students' Domain-Specific Epistemological Belief Profiles," *American Educational Research Journal,* vol. 42, 2005, pp. 697–726.

15. Sari Locker, "Influences of Adolescents' Developing Epistemological Understanding and Theories of Intelligence on Their Aspirations" (Doctoral dissertation, Teachers College, Columbia University, 2006). Interestingly, high school-aged students who believed ability is fixed were more likely than those who believed it is developed to have made the transition to evaluativist thinking and to have specific future plans. Those who believed that ability develops over time were more likely to remain open with respect to possibilities for their personal futures.

16. Deanna Kuhn and Seung-Ho Park, "Epistemological Understanding and the Development of Intellectual Values," *International Journal of Educational Research,* vol. 43, 2005, pp. 111–24.

17. Suzanne Hidi and Judith M. Harackiewicz, "Motivating the Academically Unmotivated: A Critical Issue for the 21st Century," *Review of Educational Research,* Summer 2000, pp. 151–79.

DEANNA KUHN is a professor of psychology and education at Teachers College, Columbia University, New York, N.Y.

How Can Students Be Motivated: A Misplaced Question?

Great teachers understand the fundamental difference between motivation and inspiration: motivation is self-focused and inspiration is other focused. Exceptional teachers guide students to greatness by inspiring them to discover where their talents and passions intersect. For today's besieged classroom teacher, the desire to motivate students often springs from a place of self-concern: "I want to change your behavior with a reward or incentive, so that, if you meet the targets or goals I set for you, this will help me meet my own needs and goals." Students are highly motivated to perform when they first come to school. The question is not "how can students be motivated?" but rather, "how can educators be deterred from diminishing—even destroying—student motivation and morale through their policies and practices?"

RICHARD F. BOWMAN JR.

Great teachers understand the fundamental difference between motivation and inspiration in the classroom: "Motivation is self-focused; inspiration is other focused" (Secretan 2005, 14). Characteristically, providing motivation is something that a teacher does to a student; inspiration is something that is a result of a trusting, caring, mentoring relationship with a student. Inspiration is something that an extraordinary individual lives, not something that he or she simply does. The image of Lance Armstrong streaking across the French countryside in search of his seventh straight Tour de France title inspired millions of cancer patients by giving new meaning and hope to their lives. In *The 8th Habit,* Covey (2004) argues that the crucial challenge for individuals and organizations in moving from effectiveness to greatness is to discover one's own voice and to inspire others to find their's. For the besieged classroom teacher, however, the desire to motivate students often springs from a place of self-concern: "I want to change your behavior with a reward or incentive, so that, if you meet the targets or goals I set for you, this will help me meet my own needs and goals" (Secretan, 14).

In an era of accountability and high-stakes testing, teachers are becoming adept at manipulating students' personalities through extrinsic rewards and incentives. When students are extrinsically motivated, external forces often determine their emotions and behaviors. When students are inspired, however, forces within determine their emotions and behaviors. Anyone who has worked with a trusted mentor, for example, senses deeply that the mentor is not seeking personal gain but is offering a heartfelt gift of caring and service (Secretan 2005). Relatedly, Schlechty (2002) argues that the primary function of a teacher as a leader is to "inspire others to do things that they

might otherwise not do and encourage others to go in directions they might not otherwise pursue" (xviii).

Exceptional teachers guide students and colleagues to greatness by inspiring them to discover where one's talents and passions intersect. Specifically, teachers inspire students by channeling students' energy and passion toward their strengths. Although students need to be clear about their weaknesses and what makes them afraid, they need to be clearer about those personal strengths that will result "in an increase in performance, service, and life-satisfaction" (Secretan 2005, 14). In a truly productive classroom, a generosity of spirit, a sense of perceived interdependence, and a shared reverence for the gift of learning also inspire—both teacher and student.

Yet, there is a pervasive institutional belief that motivating one's students and colleagues is an essential role of teachers and administrators as leaders. Whether it is merit pay, stickers placed on students' papers, bonus points, or formal recognition ceremonies, considerable energy and organizational resources are expended to execute this perceived leadership task. The refrain, "how can our students and staff be motivated?" punctuates collegial conversations daily in diverse settings, including staff lounges, in-service programs, and parent-teacher conferences.

Thirty years of research related to motivation and performance, however, suggests that there is only one problem with that question: "It is the wrong one" (Sirota, Mischkind, and Meltzer 2005, 24). Although motivation and morale are important to performance in the classroom and the workplace, the query is misplaced because students, faculty, and workers in diverse settings are already highly motivated to perform well when they first come to school or the workplace (Sirota, Mischkind, and Meltzer). Kindergarten children, for example, are typically excited and enthusiastic about going to school each day. Not so, however, for many third and fourth graders. In studies, researchers suggest, "something or someone is decreasing the high levels of motivation" that students and employees bring with them to the classroom and workplace (Sirota, Mischkind, and Meltzer, 25). The pertinent question for educators and parents is not "how can students be motivated?" but rather, "how can educators be deterred from diminishing—even destroying—student motivation and morale through their policies and practices?" (Sirota, Mischkind, and Meltzer).

What can teachers and administrators do to sustain initially high levels of morale, motivation, and performance for students and colleagues alike? First, educators must understand what students and colleagues want; then, they must give it to them (Sirota, Mischkind, and Meltzer 2005). Researchers pinpoint three overarching factors that have the most dramatic and positive impact on classroom and workplace morale: equity, achievement, and camaraderie (Sirota, Mischkind, and Meltzer). Students want to be treated justly and respectfully in their classroom setting. Many educators, for example, mistakenly apply restrictive policies—meant to rein in toxic behaviors of 5 percent of their students—to the 95 percent of students who are motivated to achieve. Not surprisingly, doing so has a negative impact on student morale and intrinsic motivation. Moreover, students want to take pride both in their individual accomplishments and in the achievements of their classmates by engaging collaboratively in a constant reorganizing and reconstructing of meaningful experiences. Dewey (1916) framed the challenge compellingly: "The aim of education is to enable individuals to continue their education and that the object and reward of learning is the continued capacity for growth" (117). Additionally, students want to live out the belief that learning is a relational event by having genuine, interesting, and collaborative relationships with their peers and teachers. Importantly, students sense that any process that enhances learning has two sides: psychological and sociological (Mason 1975). In *Best Practice: New Standards for Teaching and Learning in America's Schools,* Zemelman, Daniels, and Hyde (1998) discovered an unrecognized consensus regarding learners' needs for equity, achievement, and camaraderie: "Virtually all the authoritative voices in each field are calling for schools that are student-centered, active, experiential, democratic, collaborative, and yet rigorous and challenging" (viii).

Katzenbach (2006) argued that pride is what ultimately motivates individuals both in the classroom and the workplace to excel at what they do. Specifically, he contends that more than half a century of clinical and academic research by scholars such as Maslow, Herzberg, and Csikszentmihalyi points the motivational compass in one direction: pride in the work itself is the most powerful agent of change and performance. Moreover, pride is the most easily recognizable descriptor of what motivates artists, musicians, athletes, executives, and students to excel at what they do. Compellingly, Katzenbach asserts, "the peak performers in life are seldom in pursuit of money or formal advancement except as validation of the pride they feel in their workplace achievements" (59).

From that perspective, the real work of teachers as leaders is that of functioning as pride builders in the classroom. Successful teachers, for instance, spontaneously instill pride in students on a daily basis by honoring Csikszentmihalyi's "discovery that people are most highly energized about their work when their mix of skills closely matches their individual and teamwork challenges" (ctd. in Katzenbach 2006, 62). Relatedly, productive teachers are adept at getting students to anticipate how proud they will be when their behavior or achievements ultimately mirror class and societal expectations. U.S. Marine Corps drill instructors, for example, are masters of instilling pride in recruits on a daily basis by making soldiers "anticipate how proud they will feel when their behavior and results conform to the implications of the USMC values" (Katzenbach, 60). The motivational power of anticipation in daily life is hard to overestimate.

A growing number of contemporary educators, nonetheless, are committed to the use of tangible classroom rewards as a motivational strategy. Those rewards, however, can ultimately limit students' ability to unleash their aspirations and excel at what is meaningful to them individually and collectively. Specifically, when teachers and students perceive daily class work as a source of points, grades, and treats—as opposed to a source of learning and deep fulfillment—they are blinded to the other reasons students may want to excel, including an internal desire to create meaning and significance. So, what happens when educators provide both extrinsic and intrinsic rewards in the classroom?

Designing a stimulating and productive learning environment draws on one's beliefs about human nature, the nature of learning, and the passions, interests, and needs of one's students. Ironically, designing a successful video game system draws on the same considerations. Admittedly, analogies fall short because the resemblance between cases is not inexhaustible. Resemblance between the motivational supports in a productive learning environment and a video game system are clearly constrained by differences in mission, resources, and legal statue. Yet, the similarities are striking. In truth, both academically engaging classrooms and video game systems exhibit a common, unmistakable ethos or ambiance:

> Each is steeped in *(a)* clarity of task, *(b)* clear awareness of participant roles and responsibilities, *(c)* choice in the selection and execution of problem-solving strategies, *(d)* potentially-balanced systems of skills and challenges, and *(e)* a progressive hierarchy of challenges to sustain interest. Moreover, each reflects *(a)* unambiguous feedback, *(b)* affirmation of the instructiveness of error, *(c)* seemingly infinite opportunities for self-improvement, *(d)* provision for active involvement in tasks which are rooted in the high probability of success, *(e)* freedom from fear of reprisal, ridicule, or rejection, and *(f)* an overarching recognition of the need for learners to enjoy what they experience in the classrooms of life. (Bowman 1982, 16)

Characteristically, the motivational supports of electronic amusement systems and academically engaging classrooms are both extrinsically and intrinsically rewarding. At the cosmetic level, video games assault the senses with an endless series of kaleidoscopic sights, sounds, and figures. Video games provide players with an undeniable visual and aural sense of momentary triumph and accomplishment. Additionally, video games provide a socially uniting context for displaying one's evolving electronic prowess for friends and family. Yet, these familiar extrinsic motivational supports "fail to account fully for either the intense concentration or the intoxicating sense of power that arcadians experience. A more plausible explanation appears grounded in the domain of intrinsic rewards" (Bowman 1982, 14). Probing the question of what makes a classroom or video activity so enjoyable that it is intrinsically rewarding, Csikzentmihalyi and Larson (1980) propose a balanced state of interaction—a flow state. In this state, students and players find themselves in a peculiar, dynamic experience:

> Flow is described as a condition in which one concentrates on a task at hand to the exclusion of other internal and external stimuli. Action and awareness merge, so that one simply does what is to be done without a critical, dualistic perspective on one's actions. Goals tend to be clear, means are coordinated to the goals, and feedback to one's performance is immediate and unambiguous. In such a situation, a person has a strong feeling of control—or personal causation—yet, paradoxically, ego involvement is low or nonexistent, so that one experiences a sense of transcendence of self, sometimes a feeling of union with the environment. The passage of time appears to be distorted: Some events seem to take a disproportionately long time, but in general, hours seem to pass by in minutes. (64)

Although some researchers argue that intrinsic and extrinsic rewards are negatively related and may impede one another (Deci and Flaste 1995; Deci, Koestner, and Ryan 1999; Kohn 1993), there is arguably room for both intrinsic and extrinsic rewards in a caring, engaged classroom in which students respond productively to a variety of incentives. Admittedly, in many instances, rewards in the classroom have conflicting effects and can be experienced as controlling (undercutting the learner's need for autonomy) or as informational (satisfying the learner's need for competence). In daily practice, however, effective teachers can learn to use both extrinsic and intrinsic rewards in personal, thoughtful, and complementary ways to heighten students' academic engagement.

Researchers in human motivation contrast two motivational states—extrinsic and intrinsic (Deci and Flaste 1995). Students often perform in school, for example, to receive rewards if they succeed or avoid punishment if they fail. Acting a certain way because one feels compelled to by social controls characterizes extrinsic motivation. In contrast, acting a certain way because of an internal desire constitutes intrinsic motivation. Research suggests that "external motivation is more likely to create conditions of compliance or defiance" and that individuals who "are externally controlled are likely to stop trying once the rewards or punishments are removed" (Kouzes and Posner 2002, 112). Researchers also suggest that self-motivated individuals persist in working toward a meaningful goal in diverse activities

involving play, exploration, and challenge seeking, even when little likelihood of an external reward exists. Video game players, for example, typically derive neither material gain nor profit from their activities. Intrinsically motivated students, moreover, tend to have an overarching sense of purpose that is larger than they and goes beyond their classroom teacher. Tellingly, intrinsically motivated students confront the uncertainties of life from the inside out, as they search for what is rewarding rather than what is rewarded.

To be successful in school, students need to feel that they belong there, are accepted and valued, and have the skills and inner resources needed to be productive (Kouzes and Posner 2002). Intrinsic rewards are personal gestures that deepen students' sense of belonging, accomplishment, and efficacy. Intrinsic rewards invite students to develop a deeper awareness of their work and how that work contributes to a larger outcome. More important, intrinsic rewards in the classroom speak to the human thirst for a coherent purpose in daily classroom activities and school events. When students sense that their work is not trivial, they become reenergized in discovering what is worthy of their shared attention (Wheatley 1999).

The art of good teaching, therefore, lies in designing systems and incentives in such a way that students will naturally do the right thing for themselves and for the common good. Admittedly, motivating one's students is as simple as the components of the human body and as complex as the spirit. At issue, then, is how educators can design schools and classrooms so that students are intrinsically motivated to be their best. The classroom-tested approaches that follow represent neither a theoretical framework nor an emergent motivational paradigm. Rather, they represent an exposition of the insights and practices of classroom practitioners in response to the question, "is it possible for effective teachers to use both intrinsic and extrinsic rewards in personal, thoughtful, and complementary ways?"

Say thank you. Emotion deepens learning. Saying thank you reveals a teacher's genuine care and respect for students and their work. Simple, sincere gratitude makes students feel noticed, recognized, and appreciated. For students, a thank you not only serves as a form of encouragement to sustain performance but also deepens trust by shortening the symbolic distance between teacher and student. Research suggests that conveying appreciation for a task well done with an occasional unexpected thank you enhances students' intrinsic motivation and keeps them alert and interested in what the teacher and their peers have to say (Deci, Koestner, and Ryan 1999).

Recognize students' actions. Noticing students' actions that make a difference in attaining class or individual goals helps learners understand how to achieve a high standard. Moreover, providing specific examples helps students build a cognitive map that they can draw on when facing similar challenges or situations in the future. Public recognition or praise signals to other students that their contributions also will be noticed and appreciated.

Research suggests that recognition given informationally has a more positive effect on intrinsic motivation than recognition given in a controlling manner (Deci, Koestner, and Ryan 1999).

Students can interpret classroom rewards as controllers of their behavior or as indicators of their competence. When rewards are given in a controlling manner, those rewards thwart students' needs for autonomy and undermine intrinsic motivation. As much as students value the intrinsic satisfaction of genuine accomplishment, they also value noncontrolling extrinsic symbols of success, such as a choice in how to approach tasks and projects (Deci, Koestner, and Ryan). Choice deepens students' perceived self-determination and competence. The best kind of recognition publicly and informationally celebrates the effort and determination it took for a student to excel in a project or activity and sustains intrinsic motivation. Specifically, informational recognition satisfies the student's need for competence. In short, if educators use tangible rewards in the classroom, they incur a professional obligation to be mindful about the intrinsic motivation and task persistence of the students they reward.

Foster positive expectations. Inviting students to take the lead in setting their own goals develops positive student expectations. It instills a belief in students that they can go beyond what they once thought possible. Efforts to foster that belief show students that their teacher has confidence in their ability to shape their own destiny. For example, teachers who use a Socratic method of leading students through a series of questions allow students "to find their own way to the answers and bolsters their confidence in decision making" (Kouzes and Posner 2002, 343). Research suggests that students act in ways that are consistent with teachers' expectations of them. Adept teachers are aware that reinforcing processes, such as the Pygmalion effect (self-fulfilling prophecy), can amplify small actions into larger consequences for students (Merton 1968). Effective teachers, therefore, purposefully help students shatter belief barriers and self-doubts. In a moment of disarming honesty, if a teacher can genuinely support a student in making a "true commitment not to lead a little life, then most other things will fall into place" (Redmond, Tribbett, and Kasanoff 2004, 13).

Provide precise feedback incrementally. This helps students sense their progress in reaching their goals and lessens stress and anxiety. Purposeful feedback functions as recognition, allowing students to sense that "I can do it" and that "the teacher knew I could do it." Such feedback also shows students that, much like learning to ride a bicycle, trial and error are an inevitable part of a steep learning curve. More important, research shows that teachers' "best opportunity to reinforce or change behavior is very close to the time that the behavior occurs" (Allen and Allen 2004, 32). Timely feedback, therefore, is a natural and necessary part of learning.

Goals without feedback and feedback without goals, however, have only a negligible effect on student motivation (Bandura and Cervone 1983). Oral and written feedback helps students become self-corrective as they pursue goals. It also helps them feel interconnected as they reach out for encouragement and assistance in building their capabilities. In short, "the art of balance is essential to effective feedback" (Allen and Allen 2004, 24). That is, suggestions for improvement must be balanced with compliments. Allen and Allen's 2 + 2 feedback system, for example, has two equally resonant objectives: "First,

recognize successes so that they can be reinforced and repeated, and second, encourage improvement in areas that are most in need of change" (26). The intent in the classroom is to make complimenting and encouraging one another informationally the norm. In contrast, teaching by primarily correcting problems without informationally complimenting successes is not balanced feedback. Moreover, to enhance credibility and trust, teachers' "compliments should not be used simply as a prelude to suggestions for improvement" (Allen and Allen, 26).

Aid students in finding meaning. Getting students to work productively is a key responsibility in a teacher's professional life. Rather than focus on what it is the student is to do or how the student is to do it, the exemplary teacher focuses on why the meaningful work is to be done (Collins 2001). Adept classroom teachers recognize that a student's commitment to learning is a product of confidence, autonomy, and motivation. Self-assured students sense that they have the ability to complete a project without significant supervision. In addition, autonomously motivated students feel driven to do their best in completing a particular task or project. A student could, however, exude confidence in his or her abilities but still lack enthusiasm for tackling an assigned task. Without teacher support, the subsequent disillusionment could undercut a student's committed performance (Zigarmi et al. 2005).

Put a human face on opportunities. Classroom stories create a readiness for responsibility. They put challenges in a real-life context. Stories make achievements visible to others and enable students to share in the lessons learned. When teachers share stories with a class, the stories provide inspiration and direction to students facing complex, challenging situations. A story is "not only easier to remember and recall than a set of facts, it translates more quickly into action" (Kouzes and Posner 2002, 363.) In his research about how individuals make decisions in emergency conditions, Klein (1998) discovered that the rational model of decision making gives way to intuition, metaphors, analogies, and stories. For students, well-told stories reach inside them and pull them along.

Show values as a source of self-motivation. Values are "deep-seated beliefs about the world and how it operates" (Freiberg and Freiberg 1997, 146). Values are the emotional rules that govern students' attitudes, choices, and behavior in the classroom. Contextually, values are the foundation of rules that make a classroom work. Intrinsically motivated behavior is a purposeful action that is intimately connected to one's core beliefs. Encouraging students to rediscover and honor the beliefs that form the basis of their relationships, such as a genuine care and concern for others and for the common good, helps them to focus behavior and energy toward a desired instructional end. Classroom norms are a living expression of individual and collective values. Without clear end values, however, "purposeful action is limited to transitory adaptation to the environment" (Zigarmi et al. 2005, 125).

Provide new perspectives. Diversity produces the healthiest classroom environment. For students in an interconnected world, a diversity of thought, belief, opinion, and cultural perspective is essential to civic success and long-term survival. In a classroom that embraces and cultivates alternative perspectives, students are intrinsically motivated to open up to various points of view in preparation for a world that is endlessly multifaceted. Students who live out the desire and willingness to open themselves to diverse points of view are understandably better prepared to work through the challenges of a multicultural environment. Thus, the student "who embraces diversity is embracing opportunity" (Redmond, Tribbett, and Kasanoff 2004, 179).

In conclusion, parents, teachers, and students sense that the need for autonomy, encouragement, and recognition is a fundamental human drive. Moreover, each senses that success both in the classroom and life is kindled and sustained through intrinsic motivation. To stimulate and motivate students' internal drive, exemplary teachers focus on clear standards, high expectations, acknowledgment of feelings, the provision of choice, and spontaneously instilling pride in their students. Successful teachers recognize that students' values are a source of self-motivation, classroom stories put a human face on opportunities and propel students, balanced feedback, including complimenting and encouraging, is central to self-corrective learning, a diverse perspective is intrinsically motivating in an interconnected world, and developing students' capacity for meaning making and discernment is the motivating force in learning. In his stunning presentation of logotherapy, Frankl (1959) underscored the core challenge confronting teachers and students: "Man's search for meaning is the primary motivation in his life" (105).

Finally, for caring, competent, contemporary educators who are committed to the use of tangible classroom rewards as a motivational strategy, the issue is how to teach and reward in ways that do not discourage capable students. Research has shown that there are conditions in which extrinsic rewards do not necessarily undercut intrinsic motivation: provision of choice, unexpected and task-noncontingent rewards (unrelated to the target activity), rewards given informationally rather than in a controlling manner, and emphasizing the interesting or challenging aspects of a task (Deci, Koestner, and Ryan 1999). Ultimately, great teaching is something that one lives; it is not something that one does through rewards and incentives. By focusing on the talents, passions, and natural curiosities of one's students, teachers inspire students to share with the world the "music that lies inside them" (Secretan 2005, 14).

References

Allen, D. B., and D. W. Allen. 2004. *Formula 2 + 2: The simple solution for successful coaching.* San Francisco: Berrett-Koehler.

Bandura, A., and D. Cervone. 1983. Self-evaluation and self-efficacy mechanisms governing the motivational effects of goal systems. *Journal of Personality and Social Psychology* 45 (5): 1017–28.

Bowman, R. 1982. A "Pac-Man" theory of motivation: Tactical implications for classroom instruction. *Educational Technology* 22 (9): 14–16.

Collins, J. 2001. *Good to great.* New York: Harper Business.

Covey, S. 2004. *The 8th habit.* New York: *Free.*

Csikzentmihalyi, M., and R. Larson. 1980. Intrinsic rewards in school crime. In *Dealing in discipline,* ed. M. Verble, 31. Omaha, NE: University of Mid-America.

Deci, E., and R. Flaste. 1995. *Why we do what we do: Understanding self-motivation.* New York: Putnam.

Deci, E., R. Koestner, and R. Ryan. 1999. A meta-analytic review of experiments examining the effects of extrinsic rewards on intrinsic motivation. *Psychological Bulletin* 125 (6): 627–68.

Dewey, J. 1916. *Democracy and education: An introduction to the philosophy of education.* New York: Macmillan.

Frankl, V. 1959. *Man's search for meaning.* Boston: Beacon.

Freiberg, K., and J. Freiberg. 1997. *Nuts! Southwest Airlines' crazy recipe for business and personal success.* New York: Broadway.

Katzenbach, J. 2006. Motivation beyond money: Learning from peak performers. *Leader to Leader* 41: 59–62.

Klein, G. 1998. *The sources of power: How people make decisions.* Cambridge, MA: MIT Press.

Kohn, A. 1993. *Punished by rewards.* Boston: Houghton Mifflin.

Kouzes, J., and B. Posner. 2002. *The leadership challenge.* San Francisco: Jossey-Bass.

Mason, R. 1975. Dewey's culture, theory, and pedagogy. In *John Dewey: Master educator,* ed. W. W. Brickman and S. Lehrer, 115–25. Westport, CT: Greenwood.

Merton, R. 1968. The self-fulfilling prophesy. In *Social theory and social structure,* ed. R. K. Merton, 475–92. New York: Free.

Redmond, A., C. Tribbett, and B. Kasanoff. 2004. *Business evolves, leadership endures.* Westport, CT: Easton Studio.

Schlechty, P. 2002. *Working on the work.* San Francisco: Jossey-Bass.

Secretan, L. 2005. Inspiring people to their greatness. *Leader to Leader* (36): 11–14.

Sirota, D., L. Mischkind, and M. Meltzer. 2005. Assumptions that kill morale. *Leader to Leader* 38: 24–27.

Wheatley, M. 1999. *Leadership and the new science.* San Francisco: Berrett-Koehler.

Zemelman, S., H. Daniels, and A. Hyde. 1998. *Best practice: New standards for teaching and learning in America's schools.* Portsmouth, NH: Heinemann.

Zigarmi, D., M. O'Connor, K. Blanchard, and C. Edeburn. 2005. *The leader within.* Upper Saddle River, NJ: Prentice Hall.

RICHARD F. BOWMAN JR., PhD, is a professor emeritus in the College of Education at Winona State University, Minnesota. Copyright © 2007 Heldref Publications.

From *The Clearing House,* November/December 2007, pp. 81–86. Reprinted by permission of the Helen Dwight Reid Educational Foundation. Published by Heldref Publications, 1319 Eighteenth St., NW, Washington, DC 20036-1802. Copyright © 2007. www.heldref.org

The Perils and Promises of Praise

The wrong kind of praise creates self-defeating behavior.
The right kind motivates students to learn.

CAROL S. DWECK

W e often hear these days that we've produced a generation of young people who can't get through the day without an award. They expect success because they're special, not because they've worked hard.

Is this true? Have we inadvertently done something to hold back our students?

I think educators commonly hold two beliefs that do just that. Many believe that (1) praising students' intelligence builds their confidence and motivation to learn, and (2) students' inherent intelligence is the major cause of their achievement in school. Our research has shown that the first belief is false and that the second can be harmful—even for the most competent students.

As a psychologist, I have studied student motivation for more than 35 years. My graduate students and I have looked at thousands of children, asking why some enjoy learning, even when it's hard, and why they are resilient in the face of obstacles. We have learned a great deal. Research shows us how to praise students in ways that yield motivation and resilience. In addition, specific interventions can reverse a student's slide into failure during the vulnerable period of adolescence.

Fixed or Malleable?

Praise is intricately connected to how students view their intelligence. Some students believe that their intellectual ability is a fixed trait. They have a certain amount of intelligence, and that's that. Students with this fixed mind-set become excessively concerned with how smart they are, seeking tasks that will prove their intelligence and avoiding ones that might not (Dweck, 1999, 2006). The desire to learn takes a backseat.

Other students believe that their intellectual ability is something they can develop through effort and education. They don't necessarily believe that anyone can become an Einstein or a Mozart, but they do understand that even Einstein and Mozart had to put in years of effort to become who they were. When students believe that they can develop their intelligence, they focus on doing just that. Not worrying about how smart they will appear, they take on challenges and stick to them (Dweck, 1999, 2006).

More and more research in psychology and neuroscience supports the growth mind-set. We are discovering that the brain has more plasticity over time than we ever imagined (Doidge, 2007); that fundamental aspects of intelligence can be enhanced through learning (Sternberg, 2005); and that dedication and persistence in the face of obstacles are key ingredients in outstanding achievement (Ericsson, Charness, Feltovich, & Hoffman, 2006).

Alfred Binet (1909/1973), the inventor of the IQ test, had a strong growth mind-set. He believed that education could transform the basic capacity to learn. Far from intending to measure fixed intelligence, he meant his test to be a tool for identifying students who were not profiting from the public school curriculum so that other courses of study could be devised to foster their intellectual growth.

The Two Faces of Effort

The fixed and growth mind-sets create two different psychological worlds. In the fixed mind-set, students care first and foremost about how they'll be judged: smart or not smart. Repeatedly, students with this mind-set reject opportunities to learn if they might make mistakes (Hong, Chiu, Dweck, Lin, & Wan, 1999; Mueller & Dweck, 1998). When they do make mistakes or reveal deficiencies, rather than correct them, they try to hide them (Nussbaum & Dweck, 2007).

They are also afraid of effort because effort makes them feel dumb. They believe that if you have the ability, you shouldn't need effort (Blackwell, Trzesniewski, & Dweck, 2007), that ability should bring success all by itself. This is one of the worst beliefs that students can hold. It can cause many bright students to stop working in school when the curriculum becomes challenging.

Finally, students in the fixed mind-set don't recover well from setbacks. When they hit a setback in school, they *decrease* their efforts and consider cheating (Blackwell et al., 2007). The idea of fixed intelligence does not offer them viable ways to improve.

Let's get inside the head of a student with a fixed mind-set as he sits in his classroom, confronted with algebra for the first time. Up until then, he has breezed through math. Even when he barely paid attention in class and skimped on his homework, he always got As. But this is different. It's hard. The student feels anxious and thinks, "What if I'm not as good at math as I thought? What if other kids understand it and I don't?" At some level, he realizes that he has two choices: try hard, or turn off. His interest in math begins to wane, and his attention wanders. He tells himself, "Who cares about this stuff? It's for nerds. I could do it if I wanted to, but it's so boring. You don't see CEOs and sports stars solving for *x* and *y*."

By contrast, in the growth mind-set, students care about learning. When they make a mistake or exhibit a deficiency, they correct it (Blackwell et al., 2007; Nussbaum & Dweck, 2007). For them, effort is a *positive* thing: It ignites their intelligence and causes it to grow. In the face of failure, these students escalate their efforts and look for new learning strategies.

Let's look at another student—one who has a growth mind-set—having her first encounter with algebra. She finds it new, hard, and confusing, unlike anything else she has ever learned. But she's determined to understand it. She listens to everything the teacher says, asks the teacher questions after class, and takes her textbook home and reads the chapter over twice. As she begins to get it, she feels exhilarated. A new world of math opens up for her.

It is not surprising, then, that when we have followed students over challenging school transitions or courses, we find that those with growth mind-sets outperform their classmates with fixed mind-sets—even when they entered with equal skills and knowledge. A growth mind-set fosters the growth of ability over time (Blackwell et al., 2007; Mangels, Butterfield, Lamb, Good, & Dweck, 2006; see also Grant & Dweck, 2003).

The Effects of Praise

Many educators have hoped to maximize students' confidence in their abilities, their enjoyment of learning, and their ability to thrive in school by praising their intelligence. We've studied the effects of this kind of praise in children as young as 4 years old and as old as adolescence, in students in inner-city and rural settings, and in students of different ethnicities—and we've consistently found the same thing (Cimpian, Arce, Markman, & Dweck, 2007; Kamins & Dweck, 1999; Mueller & Dweck, 1998): Praising students' intelligence gives them a short burst of pride, followed by a long string of negative consequences.

In many of our studies (see Mueller & Dweck, 1998), 5th grade students worked on a task, and after the first set of problems, the teacher praised some of them for their intelligence ("You must be smart at these problems") and others for their effort ("You must have worked hard at these problems"). We then assessed the students' mind-sets. In one study, we asked students to agree or disagree with mind-set statements, such as, "Your intelligence is something basic about you that you can't really change." Students praised for intelligence agreed with statements like these more than students praised for effort did. In another study, we asked students to define intelligence. Students praised for intelligence made significantly more references to innate, fixed capacity, whereas the students

praised for effort made more references to skills, knowledge, and areas they could change through effort and learning. Thus, we found that praise for intelligence tended to put students in a fixed mind-set (intelligence is fixed, and you have it), whereas praise for effort tended to put them in a growth mind-set (you're developing these skills because you're working hard).

We then offered students a chance to work on either a challenging task that they could learn from or an easy one that ensured error-free performance. Most of those praised for intelligence wanted the easy task, whereas most of those praised for effort wanted the challenging task and the opportunity to learn.

Next, the students worked on some challenging problems. As a group, students who had been praised for their intelligence *lost* their confidence in their ability and their enjoyment of the task as soon as they began to struggle with the problem. If success meant they were smart, then struggling meant they were not. The whole point of intelligence praise is to boost confidence and motivation, but both were gone in a flash. Only the effort-praised kids remained, on the whole, confident and eager.

When the problems were made somewhat easier again, students praised for intelligence did poorly, having lost their confidence and motivation. As a group, they did worse than they had done initially on these same types of problems. The students praised for effort showed excellent performance and continued to improve.

Finally, when asked to report their scores (anonymously), almost 40 percent of the intelligence-praised students lied. Apparently, their egos were so wrapped up in their performance that they couldn't admit mistakes. Only about 10 percent of the effort-praised students saw fit to falsify their results.

Praising students for their intelligence, then, hands them not motivation and resilience but a fixed mind-set with all its vulnerability. In contrast, effort or "process" praise (praise for engagement, perseverance, strategies, improvement, and the like) fosters hardy motivation. It tells students what they've done to be successful and what they need to do to be successful again in the future. Process praise sounds like this:

- You really studied for your English test, and your improvement shows it. You read the material over several times, outlined it, and tested yourself on it. That really worked!
- I like the way you tried all kinds of strategies on that math problem until you finally got it.
- It was a long, hard assignment, but you stuck to it and got it done. You stayed at your desk, kept up your concentration, and kept working. That's great!
- I like that you took on that challenging project for your science class. It will take a lot of work—doing the research, designing the machine, buying the parts, and building it. You're going to learn a lot of great things.

What about a student who gets an *A* without trying? I would say, "All right, that was too easy for you. Let's do something more challenging that you can learn from." We don't want to make something done quickly and easily the basis for our admiration.

What about a student who works hard and *doesn't* do well? I would say, "I liked the effort you put in. Let's work together some more and figure out what you don't understand." Process praise keeps students focused, not on something called ability that they may or may not have and that magically creates success or failure, but on processes they can all engage in to learn.

Motivated to Learn

Finding that a growth mind-set creates motivation and resilience—and leads to higher achievement—we sought to develop an intervention that would teach this mind-set to students. We decided to aim our intervention at students who were making the transition to 7th grade because this is a time of great vulnerability. School often gets more difficult in 7th grade, grading becomes more stringent, and the environment becomes more impersonal. Many students take stock of themselves and their intellectual abilities at this time and decide whether they want to be involved with school. Not surprisingly, it is often a time of disengagement and plunging achievement.

We performed our intervention in a New York City junior high school in which many students were struggling with the transition and were showing plummeting grades. If students learned a growth mind-set, we reasoned, they might be able to meet this challenge with increased, rather than decreased, effort. We therefore developed an eight-session workshop in which both the control group and the growth-mind-set group learned study skills, time management techniques, and memory strategies (Blackwell et al., 2007). However, in the growth-mind-set intervention, students also learned about their brains and what they could do to make their intelligence grow.

They learned that the brain is like a muscle—the more they exercise it, the stronger it becomes. They learned that every time they try hard and learn something new, their brain forms new connections that, over time, make them smarter. They learned that intellectual development is not the natural unfolding of intelligence, but rather the formation of new connections brought about through effort and learning.

Students were riveted by this information. The idea that their intellectual growth was largely in their hands fascinated them. In fact, even the most disruptive students suddenly sat still and took notice, with the most unruly boy of the lot looking up at us and saying, "You mean I don't have to be dumb?"

Indeed, the growth-mind-set message appeared to unleash students' motivation. Although both groups had experienced a steep decline in their math grades during their first months of junior high, those receiving the growth-mind-set intervention showed a significant rebound. Their math grades improved. Those in the control group, despite their excellent study skills intervention, continued their decline.

What's more, the teachers—who were unaware that the intervention workshops differed—singled out three times as many students in the growth-mindset intervention as showing marked changes in motivation. These students had a heightened desire to work hard and learn. One striking example was the boy who thought he was dumb. Before this experience, he had never put in any extra effort and often didn't turn his homework in on time. As a result of the training, he worked for hours one evening to finish an assignment early so that his

teacher could review it and give him a chance to revise it. He earned a B+ on the assignment (he had been getting Cs and lower previously).

Other researchers have obtained similar findings with a growth-mind-set intervention. Working with junior high school students, Good, Aronson, and Inzlicht (2003) found an increase in math and English achievement test scores; working with college students, Aronson, Fried, and Good (2002) found an increase in students' valuing of academics, their enjoyment of schoolwork, and their grade point averages.

To facilitate delivery of the growth-mind-set workshop to students, we developed an interactive computer-based version of the intervention called *Brainology*. Students work through six modules, learning about the brain, visiting virtual brain labs, doing virtual brain experiments, seeing how the brain changes with learning, and learning how they can make their brains work better and grow smarter.

When students believe that they can develop their intelligence, they focus on doing just that.

We tested our initial version in 20 New York City schools, with encouraging results. Almost all students (anonymously polled) reported changes in their study habits and motivation to learn resulting directly from their learning of the growth mindset. One student noted that as a result of the animation she had seen about the brain, she could actually "picture the neurons growing bigger as they make more connections." One student referred to the value of effort: "If you do not give up and you keep studying, you can find your way through."

Adolescents often see school as a place where they perform for teachers who then judge them. The growth mind-set changes that perspective and makes school a place where students vigorously engage in learning for their own benefit.

Going Forward

Our research shows that educators cannot hand students confidence on a silver platter by praising their intelligence. Instead, we can help them gain the tools they need to maintain their confidence in learning by keeping them focused on the *process* of achievement.

Maybe we have produced a generation of students who are more dependent, fragile, and entitled than previous generations. If so, it's time for us to adopt a growth mind-set and learn from our mistakes. It's time to deliver interventions that will truly boost students' motivation, resilience, and learning.

References

Aronson, J., Fried, C., & Good, C. (2002). Reducing the effects of stereotype threat on African American college students by shaping theories of intelligence. *Journal of Experimental Social Psychology, 38:* 113–125.

Binet, A. (1909/1973). *Les idées modernes sur les enfants* [Modern ideas on children]. Paris: Flamarion. (Original work published 1909)

Blackwell, L., Trzesniewski, K., & Dweck, C. S. (2007). Implicit theories of intelligence predict achievement across an adolescent transition: A longitudinal study and an intervention. *Child Development, 78,* 246–263.

Cimpian, A., Arce, H., Markman, E. M., & Dweck, C. S. (2007). Subtle linguistic cues impact children's motivation. *Psychological Science, 18,* 314–316.

Doidge, N. (2007). *The brain that changes itself: Stories of personal triumph from the frontiers of brain science.* New York: Viking.

Dweck, C. S. (1999). *Self-theories: Their role in motivation, personality and development.* Philadelphia: Taylor and Francis/Psychology Press.

Dweck, C. S. (2006). *Mindset: The new psychology of success.* New York: Random House.

Ericsson, K. A., Charness, N., Feltovich, P. J., & Hoffman, R. R. (Eds.). (2006). *The Cambridge handbook of expertise and expert performance.* New York: Cambridge University Press.

Good, C., Aronson, J., & Inzlicht, M. (2003). Improving adolescents' standardized test performance: An intervention to reduce the effects of stereotype threat. *Journal of Applied Developmental Psychology, 24,* 645–662.

Grant, H., & Dweck, C. S. (2003). Clarifying achievement goals and their impact. *Journal of Personality and Social Psychology, 85,* 541–553.

Hong, Y. Y., Chiu, C., Dweck, C. S., Lin, D., & Wan, W. (1999). Implicit theories, attributions, and coping: A meaning system approach. *Journal of Personality and Social Psychology, 77,* 588–599.

Kamins, M., & Dweck, C. S. (1999). Person vs. process praise and criticism: Implications for contingent self-worth and coping. *Developmental Psychology, 35,* 835–847.

Mangels, J. A., Butterfield, B., Lamb, J., Good, C. D., & Dweck, C. S. (2006). Why do beliefs about intelligence influence learning success? A social-cognitive-neuroscience model. *Social, Cognitive, and Affective Neuroscience, 1,* 75–86.

Mueller, C. M., & Dweck, C. S. (1998). Intelligence praise can undermine motivation and performance. *Journal of Personality and Social Psychology, 75,* 33–52.

Nussbaum, A. D., & Dweck, C. S. (2007). Defensiveness vs. remediation: Self-theories and modes of self-esteem maintenance. *Personality and Social Psychology Bulletin.*

Sternberg, R. (2005). Intelligence, competence, and expertise. In A. Elliot & C. S. Dweck (Eds.), *The handbook of competence and motivation* (pp. 15–30). New York: Guilford Press.

CAROL S. DWECK is the Lewis and Virginia Eaton Professor of Psychology at Stanford University and the author of *Mindset: The New Psychology of Success* (Random House, 2006).

Should Learning Be Its Own Reward?

Daniel T. Willingham

How does the mind work—and especially how does it learn? Teachers' instructional decisions are based on a mix of theories learned in teacher education, trial and error, craft knowledge, and gut instinct. Such gut knowledge often serves us well, but is there anything sturdier to rely on?

Cognitive science is an interdisciplinary field of researchers from psychology, neuroscience, linguistics, philosophy, computer science, and anthropology who seek to understand the mind. In this regular American Educator column, we consider findings from this field that are strong and clear enough to merit classroom application.

Question: In recent months, there's been a big uproar about students being paid to take standardized tests—and being paid even more if they do well. Can cognitive science shed any light on this debate? Is it harmful to students to reward them like this? What about more typical rewards like a piece of candy or five extra minutes of recess?

There has been much debate recently about boosting standardized test scores by paying students. Here are a few examples that I read about in the news. In Coshocton, Ohio, third- and sixth-graders are being paid up to $20 for earning high scores on standardized tests. In New York City, fourth-grade students will receive $5 for each standardized test they take throughout the year, and up to $25 for each perfect score. Seventh-graders will get twice those amounts. In Tucson, Ariz., high school juniors selected from low-income areas will be paid up to $25 each week for attendance. These and similar programs affect just a tiny fraction of students nationwide. But rewarding students with things like small gifts, extra recess time, stickers, certificates, class parties and the like is actually pretty common. Most teachers have the option of distributing rewards in the classroom, and many do. For example, in a recent survey of young adults, 70 percent said that their elementary school teachers had used candy as a reward (Davis, Winsler, and Middleton, 2006).

So whether or not your district offers cash rewards for standardized test scores or attendance, you've probably wondered if rewarding your students for their classwork is a good idea. Some authors promise doom if a teacher rewards students, with the predicted negative effects ranging from unmotivated pupils to a teacher's moral bankruptcy (e.g., Kohn, 1993). Others counter that rewards are harmless or even helpful (e.g., Cameron, Banko, and Pierce, 2001; Chance, 1993). Where does the truth lie? In the middle. There is some merit to the arguments on both sides. Concrete rewards can motivate students to attend class, to behave well, or to produce better work. But if you are not careful in choosing what you reward, they can prompt students to produce shoddy work—and worse, they can cause students to actually like school subjects less. The important guidelines are these: Don't use rewards unless you have to, use rewards for a specific reason, and use them for a limited time. Let's take a look at the research behind these guidelines.

> **Concrete rewards can motivate students to attend class, to behave well, or to produce better work. But if you are not careful in choosing what you reward, they can prompt students to produce shoddy work—and worse, they can cause students to actually like school subjects less.**

Do Rewards Work?

Rewarding students is, from one perspective, an obvious idea. People do things because they find them rewarding, the reasoning goes, so if students don't find school naturally rewarding (that is, interesting and fun), make it rewarding by offering them something they do like, be it cash or candy.

In this simple sense, rewards usually work. If you offer students an appealing reward, the targeted behavior will generally increase (for reviews, see O'Leary and Drabman, 1971; Deci, Koestner, and Ryan, 1999). Teachers typically use rewards like candy, stickers, small prizes, or extra recess time. They use them to encourage student behaviors such as completing assignments, producing good work, and so on. In one example

(Hendy, Williams, and Camise, 2005) first-, second-, and fourth-graders were observed in the school cafeteria to see how often they ate fruits and vegetables. Once this baseline measure was taken, they were rewarded for eating one or the other. Students received a token for each day that they ate the assigned food, and tokens could be redeemed for small prizes at the end of the week. Not surprisingly, students ate more of what they were rewarded for eating.

But things don't always go so smoothly. If you mistakenly offer a reward that students don't care for, you'll see little result. Or, if you reward the wrong behavior, you'll see a result you don't care for. When I was in fourth grade, my class was offered a small prize for each book we read. Many of us quickly developed a love for short books with large print, certainly not the teacher's intent. In the same way, if you reward people to come up with ideas, but don't stipulate that they must be good ideas, people will generate lots of ideas in order to gain lots of rewards, but the ideas may not be especially good (Ward, Kogan, and Pankove, 1972). It's often possible to correct mistakes such as these. Unappealing rewards can be replaced by valued rewards. The target behavior can be changed. My fourth-grade teacher stipulated that books had to be grade-appropriate and of some minimum length.

Because rewards are generally effective, people's objection to them in the classroom is seldom that they won't work. The op-ed newspaper articles I have seen about the student payment plans described above don't claim that you can't get students to go to school by paying them (e.g., Carlton, 2007; Schwartz, 2007). They raise other objections.

The common arguments against rewards fall into three categories. Let me state each one in rather extreme terms to give you the idea, and then I'll consider the merits of each in more detail. The first objection is that using rewards is immoral. You might toss your dog a treat when he shakes hands, but that is no way to treat children. Classrooms should be a caring community in which students help one another, not a circus in which the teacher serves as ringmaster. The second objection is that offering rewards is unrealistic. Rewards can't last forever, so what happens when they stop? Those who make this argument think it's better to help students appreciate the subtle, but real rewards that the world offers for things like hard work and politeness. After all, adults don't expect that someone will toss them a candy bar every time they listen politely, push their chair under a table, or complete a report on time. The third objection is that offering rewards can actually decrease motivation. Cognitive science has found that this is true, but only under certain conditions. For example, if you initially enjoy reading and I reward you for each book you finish, the rewards will make you like reading less. Below, I'll explain how and why that happens. Let's consider each of these arguments in turn.

Are Rewards Immoral?

Don't rewards control students? Aren't rewards dehumanizing? Wouldn't it be better to create a classroom atmosphere in which students wanted to learn, rather than one in which they reluctantly slogged through assignments, doing the minimal work they thought would still earn the promised reward? Cognitive science cannot answer moral questions. They are outside its purview. But cognitive science can provide some factual background that may help teachers as they consider these questions.

It is absolutely the case that trying to control students is destructive to their motivation and their performance. People like autonomy, and using rewards to control people definitely reduces motivation. Even if the task is one students generally like, if they sense that you're trying to coerce them, they will be less likely to do it (e.g., Ryan, Mims, and Koestner, 1983). It is worth pointing out, however, that rewards themselves are not inherently controlling. If students are truly offered a choice—do this and get a reward, don't do it and get no reward—then the student maintains control. Within behavioral science, it is accepted that rewards themselves are coercive if they are excessive (e.g., National Commission for the Protection of Human Subjects of Biomedical and Behavioral Research, 1978). In other words, if I offer you $200 to take a brief survey, it's hard to know that you're freely choosing to take the survey.

Rewards in classrooms are typically not excessive, and so are not, themselves, controlling. Rather, rewards might be an occasion for control if the teacher makes it quite clear that the student is expected to do the required work and collect his or her reward. That is, the teacher uses social coercion. So too, we've all known people we would call "manipulative," and those people seldom manipulate us via rewards. They use social means. In sum, the caution against controlling students is well-founded, but rewards are not inherently controlling.

Are rewards dehumanizing? Again, it seems to me that the answer depends on how the student construes the reward. If a teacher dangles stickers before students like fish before a seal, most observers will likely wince. But if a teacher emphasizes that rewards are a gesture of appreciation for a job well done, that probably would not appear dehumanizing to most observers.[1] Even so, rather than offer rewards, shouldn't teachers create classrooms in which students love learning? It is difficult not to respond to this objection by saying "Well, duh." I can't imagine there are many teachers who would rather give out candy than have a classroom full of students who are naturally interested and eager to learn. The question to ask is not "Why would you use rewards instead of making the material interesting?" Rather, it is "After you've wracked your brain for a way to make the material interesting for students and you still can't do it, then what?" Sanctimonious advice on the evils of rewards won't get chronically failing students to have one more go at learning to read. I think it unwise to discourage teachers from using any techniques in the absolute; rather, teachers need to know what research says about the benefits and drawbacks of the techniques, so that they can draw their own conclusions about whether and when to use them. Considering the merits of the two other objections will get us further into that research.

Sanctimonious advice on the evils of rewards won't get chronically failing students to have one more go at learning to read. I think it unwise to discourage teachers from using any techniques in the absolute; rather, teachers need to know what research says about the benefits and drawbacks of the techniques.

What Happens When Rewards Stop?

This objection is easy to appreciate. If I'm working math problems because you're paying me, what's going to happen once you stop paying me? Your intuition probably tells you that I will stop doing problems, and you're right. In the fruits and vegetables study described earlier, students stopped eating fruits and vegetables soon after the reward program stopped.

Although it might seem obvious that this would happen, psychologists initially thought that there was a way around this problem. Many studies were conducted during the 1960s using token economies. A token economy is a system by which rewards are administered in an effort to change behavior. There are many variants but the basic idea is that every time the student exhibits a targeted behavior (e.g., gets ready to work quickly in the morning), he or she gets a token (e.g., a plastic chip). Students accumulate tokens and later trade them for rewards (e.g., small prizes). Token economies have some positive effects, and have been used not only in classrooms, but in clinical settings (e.g., Dickerson, Tenhula, and Green-Paden, 2005).

When the idea of a token economy was developed, the plan was that the rewards would be phased out. Once the desired behavior was occurring frequently, you would not give the reward every time, but give it randomly, averaging 75 percent of the time, then 50 percent of the time, and so on. Thus, the student would slowly learn to do the behavior without the external reward. That works with animals, but normally not with humans. Once the rewards stop, people go back to behaving as they did before (Kazdin, 1982; O'Leary and Drabman, 1971).[2]

Well, one might counter, it may be true that students won't spontaneously work math problems once we stop rewarding them, but at least they will have worked more than they otherwise would have! Unfortunately, there is another, more insidious consequence of rewards that we need to consider: Under certain circumstances, they can actually decrease motivation.

How Can Rewards Decrease Motivation?

The previous section made it sound like rewards boost desired behavior so long as they are present, and when they are removed behavior falls back to where it started. That's true sometimes, but not always. If the task is one that students like, rewards will, as usual, make it more likely they'll do the task. But after the rewards stop, students will actually perform the previously likable task *less* than they did when rewards were first offered.

A classic study on this phenomenon (Lepper, Greene, and Nisbett, 1973) provides a good illustration. Children (aged 3 to 5 years old) were surreptitiously observed in a classroom with lots of different activities available. The experimenters noted how much time each child spent drawing with markers. The markers were then unavailable to students for two weeks. At the end of the two weeks, students were broken into three groups. Each student in the first group was taken to a separate room and was told that he or she could win an attractive "Good Player" certificate by drawing a picture with the markers. Each was eager to get the certificate and drew a picture. One-by-one, students in a second group were also brought to a separate room, encouraged to draw, and then given a certificate, but the certificate came as a surprise; when they started drawing, they didn't know that they would get the certificate. A third group of students served as a control group. They had been observed in the first session, but didn't draw or get a certificate in this second session. After another delay of about two weeks, the markers again appeared in the classroom, and experimenters observed how much children used them. The students in the first group— those who were promised the certificate for drawing—used the markers about half as much as students in the other two groups. Promising and then giving a reward made children like the markers less. But giving the reward as a surprise (as with the second group of students) had no effect.

This has been replicated scores of times with students of different ages, using different types of rewards, and in realistic classroom situations (see Deci et al., 1999 for a review). What is going on? How can getting a reward reduce your motivation to do something? The answer lies in the students' interpretation of why they chose to use the markers. For students who either didn't get a reward or who didn't expect a reward, it's obvious that they weren't drawing for the sake of the reward; they drew pictures because they liked drawing. But for the children who were promised a reward, the reason is less clear. A student might not remember that he drew because he wanted to draw, but rather he remembered really wanting the certificate. So when the markers were available again but no certificate was promised, the student may well have thought "I drew because I wanted that certificate; why should I draw now for nothing?"

The analogy to the classroom is clear. Teachers seek to create lifelong learners. We don't just want children to read, we want children to learn to love reading. So if, in an effort to get children to read more, we promise to reward them for doing so, we might actually make them like reading less! They will read more in order to get the pizza party or the stickers, but once the teacher is no longer there to give out the rewards, the student will say "Why should I read? I'm not getting anything for it."

The key factor to keep in mind is that rewards only decrease motivation for tasks that students initially like. If the task is dull, motivation might drop back down to its original level once the rewards stop, but it will not drop below its original level. Why does the appeal of the task make a difference? As I mentioned, rewards hurt motivation because of the way students construe the situation: "I drew with markers in order to get a certificate," instead of "I drew with markers because I like to draw with markers." But if the task is dull, students won't make that mistaken interpretation. They never liked the task in the first place. That hypothesis has been confirmed in a number of studies showing that once the reward is no longer being offered, having received a reward in the past harms the motivation for an interesting task, but not for a dull task (e.g., Daniel and Esser, 1980; Loveland and Olley, 1979; Newman and Layton, 1984).

The key factor to keep in mind is that rewards only decrease motivation for tasks that students initially like. If the task is dull, motivation might drop back down to its original level once the rewards stop, but it will not drop below its original level.

This finding might make one wonder whether rewards, in the form of grades, are behind students' lack of interest in schoolwork; by issuing grades, we're making students like school less (Kohn, 1993). It is true that students like school less and less as they get older. But it is wise to remember that motivation is a product of many factors. Researchers often distinguish between extrinsic motivators (e.g., concrete rewards or grades that are external to you) and intrinsic motivators (things that are internal to you such as your interest in a task). The effect described above can be succinctly summarized: Extrinsic rewards can decrease intrinsic motivation. We would thus expect that intrinsic and extrinsic motivation would be negatively correlated. That is, if you work mostly for the sake of getting good grades and other rewards, then you aren't very intrinsically motivated, and if you are highly intrinsically motivated, that must mean you don't care much about rewards. That's true to some extent, but the relationship is far from perfect. College students whose intrinsic and extrinsic motivation have been measured usually show a modest negative correlation, around -.25[3] (Lepper, Corpus, and Iyengar, 2005). This seems reasonable since motivation is actually pretty complex—we rarely do things for just one reason.

What Makes Rewards More or Less Effective?

If you decide to use rewards in the classroom, how can you maximize the chances that they will work? Three principles are especially important. Rewards should be desirable, certain, and prompt.

The importance of desirability is obvious. People will work for rewards that appeal to them, and will work less hard or not at all for rewards that are not appealing.[4] That is self-evident, and teachers likely know which rewards would appeal to their students and which would mean little to them.

If you decide to use rewards in the classroom, how can you maximize the chances that they will work? Three principles are especially important. Rewards should be desirable, certain, and prompt.

Less obvious is the importance of the certainty of a reward, by which I mean the probability that a student will get a reward if he or she attempts to do the target behavior. What if you've set a target that seems too difficult to the student, and he won't even try? Or what if the target seems achievable to the student, he makes an attempt and does his best, but still fails? Either reduces the likelihood that the student will try again. Both problems can be avoided if the reward is contingent on the student trying his best, and not on what he achieves. But that has its drawbacks, as well. It means that you must make a judgment call as to whether he tried his best. (And you must make that judgment separately for each student.) It is all too likely that some students will have an inflated view of their efforts, and your differing assessment will lead to mistrust. Ideally, the teacher will select specific behaviors for each student as targets, with the target titrated to each student's current level of ability.

A corollary of rewards being desirable is that they be prompt. A reward that is delayed has less appeal than the same reward delivered immediately. For example, suppose I gave you this choice: "You can have $10 tomorrow, or $10 a week from tomorrow." You'd take the $10 tomorrow, right? Rewards have more "oomph"—that is, more power to motivate—when you are going to get them soon. That's why, when my wife calls me from the grocery store, it's easy for me to say "Don't buy ice cream. I'm trying to lose weight." But when I'm at home it's difficult for me to resist ice cream that's in the freezer. In the first situation, I'm denying myself ice cream sometime in the distant future, but in the second I would be denying myself ice cream right at that moment. The promise of ice cream two minutes from now has higher value for me than the promise of ice cream hours from now.

It is possible to measure how much more desirable a reward is when given sooner rather than later. In one type of experiment, subjects participate in an auction and offer sealed bids for money that will be delivered to them later. Thus, each subject might be asked "What is the maximum you would pay right now for a reward of $10, to be delivered tomorrow?"[5] Subjects are asked to make bids for a variety of rewards to be delivered at delays varying from one to 30 days. Then, researchers use subjects' bids to derive a relationship between the amount of time that the reward is delayed and how much people value the delayed reward. Subjects typically show a steep drop off in how much they value the reward—with a one-day delay, $20 is worth about $18 to most subjects, and with a one-week delay, the value is more like $15 (e.g., Kirby, 1997). In other words, there is a significant cost to the reward value for even a brief delay. Other studies show that the cost

What is the Difference between Rewards and Praise?

You may have noticed that I have limited my discussion to the effects of concrete rewards—candy, cash, and so on. Isn't praise a reward as well? It can be, but praise as it's usually administered has some important differences. The most important is that praise is usually given unpredictably. The student doesn't think to himself, "If I get 90 percent or better on this spelling test, the teacher will say 'Good job, Dan!" Rewards are different. There is usually an explicit bargain in the classroom, with the understanding that a particular behavior (e.g., 90 percent or better on a spelling test) merits a reward. As described in the main article, the decrease in motivation for a task only occurs if the reward was expected (and if the students enjoy the task). Since praise is not expected, it does not lead to an immediate decrement to motivation.

Another important difference between praise and concrete rewards is that the former is often taken as a more personal comment on one's abilities. Rewards typically don't impart information to the student. But praise can carry quite a bit of meaning. For starters, it tells the student that she did something noteworthy enough to merit praise. Then too, the student learns what the teacher considers important by listening to what she praises. A student may be told that she's smart, or that she tried hard, or that she's improving. In the short run, sincere praise will provide a boost to motivation (Deci et al., 1999), but in the long run, the content of praise can have quite different effects on the students' self-concept and on future efforts (e.g., Henderlong and Lepper, 2002; Mueller and Dweck, 1998). The key is in what type of praise is given. When faced with a difficult task, a child who has been praised in the past for her *effort* is likely to believe that intelligence increases as knowledge increases and, therefore, will work harder and seek more experiences from which she can learn. In contrast, a student who has been praised for her *ability* will likely believe that intelligence is fixed (e.g., is genetically determined) and will seek to maintain the "intelligent" label by trying to look good, even if that means sticking to easy tasks rather than more challenging tasks from which more can be learned.

A final difference between praise and rewards lies in students' expectations of encountering either in school. At least in the U.S., praise is part of everyday social interaction. If someone displays unusual skill or determination or kindness, or any other attribute that we esteem, it is not unusual to offer praise. In fact, a teacher who never praised her students might strike them as cold, or uncaring. No such expectation exists for rewards, however. It is hard to imagine teaching students without ever praising them. It is easy to imagine teaching students without ever offering them a concrete reward.

For more on praise and its effects, see "Ask the Cognitive Scientist," *American Educator,* Winter 2005–2006, available at www.aft.org/ pubs-reports/american_ educator/ issues/winter05-06/cogsci.htm.

—D.W.

is greater for elementary school students than college students (e.g., Green, Fry and Myerson, 1994). That finding probably matches your intuition: As we get older, we get better at delaying gratification. Distant rewards become more similar to immediate rewards.

In this section I've summarized data showing that rewards should be desirable, certain, and prompt if they are to be effective. These three factors provide some insight into the extrinsic (but non-tangible) rewards that almost all schools offer: grades and graduation. Grades are not as rewarding as we might guess because they are seldom administered right after the required behavior (studying), and the reward of a diploma is, of course, even more distant. Then too, low-achieving students likely perceive these rewards as highly uncertain. That is, hard work does not guarantee that they will receive the reward.

Putting It All Together: Are Rewards Worth It?

When all is said and done, are rewards worth it? I liken using rewards to taking out a loan. You get an immediate benefit, but you know that you will eventually have to pay up, with interest. As with loans, I suggest three guidelines to the use of rewards: 1) try to find an alternative; 2) use them for a specific reason, not as a general strategy; and 3) plan for the ending.

Try to Find an Alternative

It is very difficult to implement rewards without incurring some cost. If the reward system is the same for all class members, it won't work as well as an individualized approach and you will likely reward some students for tasks they already like. If you tailor the rewards to individual students, you vastly increase your workload, and you increase the risk of students perceiving the program as unfair.

The size of the costs to motivation, although real, should not be overstated. As mentioned earlier, there are many contributors to motivation, and putting a smiley sticker on a spelling test will probably not rank high among them. Still, why incur the cost at all, if an alternative is available? The obvious alternative is to make the material intrinsically interesting. Indeed, if you follow that precept, you will never offer an extrinsic reward for an intrinsically interesting task, which is when the trouble with motivation really starts.

It is also worth considering whether student motivation is the real reason you use rewards. Do you put stickers on test papers in the hopes that students will work harder to earn them, or just for a bit of fun, a colorful diversion? Do you throw a class pizza party to motivate students, or to increase the class's sense of community? You might still distribute stickers and throw the party, but not make them explicitly contingent on performance beforehand. Announce to the class that they have done such a good job on the most recent unit that a party seems in order. Thus, the party is still an acknowledgement of good work and still might contribute to a positive class atmosphere, but it is not offered as a reward contingent on performance.

Use Rewards for a Specific Reason

A wise investor understands that taking out a loan, although it incurs a cost, might be strategic in the long run. So too, although a rewards program may incur some cost to motivation, there are times when the cost might be worth it. One example is when students must learn or practice a task that is rather dull, but that, once mastered, leads to opportunities for greater interest and motivation. For example, learning the times tables might be dull, but if students can get over that hump of boredom, they are ready to take on more interesting work. Rewards might also be useful when a student has lost confidence in himself to the point that he is no longer willing to try. If he'll attempt academic work to gain a desirable extrinsic reward and succeeds, his perception of himself and his abilities may change from self-doubt to recognition that he is capable of academic work (Greene and Lepper, 1974). Thereafter, the student may be motivated by his sense of accomplishment and his expectation that he will continue to do well.

Although a rewards program may incur some cost to motivation, there are times that the cost might be worth it. For example, learning the times tables might be dull, but if students can get over that hump of boredom, they are ready to take on more interesting work.

Use Rewards for a Limited Time

No one wants to live with chronic debt, and no one should make rewards a long-term habit. Although the cost of using rewards may not be large, that cost likely increases as rewards are used for a longer time. In addition, there would seem to be an advantage to the program having a natural ending point. For example, students are rewarded for learning their times tables, and once they are learned, the rewards end. The advantage is that any decrease in motivation might stick to the task. In other words, students will think "times tables are boring, and we need to be rewarded to learn them" rather than "math is boring, and we need to be rewarded to learn it." In addition, if students are told at the start of the program when it will end, there may be fewer complaints when the goodies are no longer available.

Notes

1. Such positive framing of rewards does not reverse the negative impact of rewards on motivation, but telling students that rewards signal acknowledgement of good work, rather than the closing of a bargain, seems more in keeping with the spirit of education.

2. Readers who are familiar with interventions to reduce students' aggressive or antiscoial behavior may be surprised at this finding. such interventions do often use rewards and then phase them out. But keep in mind that the rewards are just one part of a complex intervention and that in order to be effective, such interventions must be implemented in full. To learn more about the use of rewards in such an intervention, see "Heading Off Disruption: How Early Intervention Can Reduce Defiant Behavior—and Win Back Teaching Time," *American Educator,* Winter 2003–2004, available at **www.aft.org/pubs-reports/american_educator/winter03-04/index.html.**

3. A correlation of zero would indicate that they were unrelated, and a correlation of -1.0 would indicate that they were perfectly related.

4. There are exceptions to this generalization, notably in the social realm. People will work hard without reward as part of a social transaction. In such situations a small reward will actually make people less likely to work (e.g., Heyman and Ariely, 2004). For example, if an acquaintance asks you to help her move a sofa, you would assume that she's asking a favor as a friend, and you might well help. But if she offers you $5 to move the sofa you think of the request as a business transaction, and $5 may not seem like enough money. These social concerns could apply to the classroom; some students might work to please the teacher. But such social transactions rest on reciprocity. If your friend with the poorly placed sofa never helps you out, you will get tired of her requests. It would be difficult to set up a classroom relationship that used social reciprocity between teachers and students.

5. The procedure is actually what researchers call a second-bid auction; the highest bidder wins the auction, but pays the price of the second highest bid. This procedure is meant to ensure that people bid exactly what the item is worth to them. The workings of the auction are explained in detail to subjects.

DANIEL T. WILLINGHAM is professor of cognitive psychology at the University of Virginia and author of *Cognition: The Thinking Animal.* His research focuses on the role of consciousness in learning. Readers can pose specific questions to "Ask the Cognitive Scientist," American Educator, 555 New Jersey Ave. N.W., Washington, DC 20001, or to **amered@aft.org.** Future columns will try to address readers' questions.

Strategies for Effective Classroom Management in the Secondary Setting

Over the years, researchers have written many books and articles about the lack of discipline or lack of respect students have toward their teachers. This image is enhanced by the daily accounts in movies, newspapers, television, and radio or in speaking to students, their teachers, or parents. In this article, the author provides working strategies that can be used by new and veteran teachers that will provide educators with procedures to maximize classroom instruction by incorporating effective classroom management techniques into their daily routines.

PAUL PEDOTA

Everyone concedes that there is a severe shortage of qualified teachers in the United States and that one of the most frequent reasons cited in the literature regarding the problem of staffing and retaining qualified individuals is the lack of student discipline (Macdonald 1999; Tye and O'Brien 2002). In speaking to new and veteran teachers who have left the profession primarily due to discipline problems in the classroom, many have commented that although they felt that during the preteaching training period sufficient time was spent on classroom management, they were not truly prepared for the realities of the classroom, which contributed to feelings of frustration, anger, and helplessness (Miech and Elder 1996).

In reviewing the research, one can see that effective teachers—those who have fewer discipline problems in the classroom—spend a good deal of time on planning (Brown 1998); take into account diversity as well as the preference of individual learning styles (Daniels, Bizar, and Zemelman 2001; Dunn and Dunn 1993; Sleeter and Grant 2003); provide activities that get students to begin work immediately and ensure there is a sufficient amount of work that will have students working the entire period (Ornstein and Lasley 2004); and are consistent in classroom management techniques with ". . . a healthy balance between rewards and punishment" (Miller, Ferguson, and Simpson 1998, 56).

Establishing, explaining, reviewing, and modifying (as needed) rules, routines, and procedures that are clearly understood to handle the daily recurring activities as well as developing procedures for unpredictable events that may occur, will help you to devote the maximum amount of time available for instruction and enhance classroom management (Marshall 2001).

The following is based on my beliefs, my personality, and thirty-seven years of experience as an educator. Individuals should use this article as a guide and not as a complete list of strategies or techniques that can be used for effective classroom management. Your personality and philosophy of education will dictate those ideas you will or will not use in dealing with developing, setting up, and using an effective strategy to ensure maximum instruction with few classroom discipline problems.

First Things First

As a teacher, ensuring that all students can learn in a safe environment is your prime objective. Before you can begin to teach, you must devote time to preparing your classroom and developing procedures that will help you maximize instruction in a positive climate, such as the following:

Seating Plans

Permanent seating arrangements will help you to learn students' names quickly, take attendance, and perform any other administrative task while students are involved in some instructional activity. The use of a Delaney book or seating chart can help to make this task a simple one. In addition, you should think about how your seating arrangements can be modified to support different types of instruction, such as whole group instruction, small group instruction, or students working individually.

Physical Surroundings

The room should be arranged to ensure that all students can see well, there are no obstructions, the lighting is adequate, and if and when students move around, they do not interfere with other students. Your desk should be positioned so that you can monitor the activities of all students as well as not interfere with movement within the class.

Housekeeping Procedures

Procedures for the storing of equipment and other material, the distribution and collection of student material, keeping the chalkboard clean, the location of the wastepaper basket, using the pencil sharpener, and so on, must also be developed.

Displays

The classroom should be a showcase for student work, as well as posters, magazine covers, charts, maps, and pictures. It is important to let students know that their work is important as well as let others know what students are learning. Your material, as well as student work, should be changed, at least every month or when you begin a new unit. This will allow for all students to have the opportunity to have their work displayed, which will give them a sense of ownership. School and class rules should also be posted as a reminder to students of the code of behavior.

Instruction

Plan for a variety of instructional experiences and keep students actively involved. You will find that by avoiding the sameness of daily classes, you will help prevent discipline problems. One way that this can be accomplished is by allowing students to be active participants in learning rather than passive listeners.

Setting Classroom Standards for Behavior and Work

Students, just like adults, prefer to be in an environment that is structured and predictable. In school, where students have individual teachers who hold different beliefs as to how to handle certain situations, it is important that you make your expectations perfectly clear. To this end, it is extremely important that procedures are in place that are consistent with schoolwide policy and that both students and their parents know what is expected in terms of behavior and class work. If rules are firm, fair, and followed consistently, you will be able to handle most situations that may infringe on the use of instructional time. Developing a written syllabus or contract that includes the subject material, subject class requirements, and class and individual code of conduct helps all to understand their responsibilities (Brophy 1986; Curwin and Mendler 1988).

The following provides some examples of what should be included in a code of conduct:

Student attendance: The importance of daily class attendance must be emphasized. Students should know what are considered legitimate reasons for being absent, procedures to follow when absent as well as when returning from an absence, and the impact recurring absences will have on grades.

Student lateness and dismissal: Students must understand the importance for being on time for class. Being late causes students to not only interrupt instruction for others, but also causes them to miss work. In addition, procedures for dismissal should be in place at the end of the instructional period and students should be reminded that only you dismiss the class.

Classroom interruptions: Procedures should be developed to handle classroom interruptions—such as intercom announcements, visitors, and fire drills. In all of these situations, students must know that you alone give direction on student actions.

Students leaving classroom: What are the procedures for leaving the room? Are you going to use a sign-out book, issue a pass, write the names of students on the chalkboard, or restrict the pass at certain times?

Student work: You should make students aware of the subject manner to be studied; instructional objectives you hope that students will obtain; skills that will be developed; their responsibility regarding class work, homework, or any other assignments; the number and types of tests; and a review of how you will arrive at a grade for each student.

Recognizing students in class: Students should not shout out questions, answers, or comments without first being recognized by you. Moving around the room as you call on volunteers as well as nonvolunteers will ensure that all students are on task as you build a climate for learning.

Instruction: Policies should also be developed to take into account how students should act and interact with each other during different types of instruction. For example, when working in groups what is the expected behavior of students? How is this behavior different from behavior exhibited during other types of instruction? If during group work students are speaking to one another, how do you control the volume?

Recognition of accomplishments: It is important to see the glass as half full not half empty, that is, try to accentuate the positive over the negative. To establish a positive classroom environment, students must feel that you recognize their accomplishments.

Inappropriate behavior: Ignoring inappropriate behavior until it reaches a point that you have no choice but to give a harsh punishment should be avoided. In deciding on the appropriate course to be taken, you must ensure that you are reacting to what took place and not the individual.

It is imperative to realize that once classroom rules and procedures have been developed, the worst thing that you can do is act hastily, not enforce a rule, or enforce it sporadically. In addition, you may not have thought of everything and may have to revise, modify, add, or disregard a rule. Do not be afraid to talk to a colleague or school official if you are having a problem or to change something if what you had originally planned is not working.

You must model the behavior that you expect from your students. You must avoid the use of insulting, abusive, or threatening language. Although it may be hard at times, you must learn to control your temper. Your words and/or actions can upset others and may even instigate physical actions, which can cause harm to the student, other students, or adults. To get respect, you must earn it, and by setting a good example and by treating others as you would like to be treated, this can be accomplished.

Communication

Communication can be verbal and nonverbal and just as in everyday life, poor communication can cause unnecessary problems. Table 1 displays some simple "Dos" and "Do nots" in using communication efficiently and effectively.

If you must reprimand students, use a normal tone of voice, look at the student, do not use gestures such as pointing your finger, and do not insist on the last word (Kerr and Nelson 2002).

Good communication skills and being a good listener, as well as a good speaker, can help in preventing problems in the classroom. When students feel that they are welcomed into a nonthreatening environment where learning is encouraged, they usually come ready, willing, and able to learn.

Table 1 Dos and Do Nots in Communication

DO	DO NOT
Think before you speak	Say you will do something you cannot do
Speak only when you have everyone's attention	Speak to individuals and not pay attention to the class
Give students the opportunity to ask questions	Be close minded
Be specific in your statements, directions, questions, and so on	Take silence as knowing

Strategies to Help Manage Your Classroom

By now you should be asking yourself, how can I build an environment in my classroom where there is trust and mutual respect among all, as well as have rules that are firm, fair, consistent, and followed? Table 2 outlines ten rules to help manage a classroom.

Combining structure and fairness with clear expectations in a caring, nonthreatening environment are the major elements of good teaching and effective classroom management. Students who believe that you really care about them as individuals, that is, academically, socially, and emotionally, will gain status and recognition and a sense of self-worth and belonging (Dreikurs, Grunwald, and Pepper 1971; Glasser 1990) as well as establish your authority and credibility.

Conclusion

By following these simple strategies, you can have an orderly classroom environment that will improve students' learning outcomes while providing for an atmosphere that is structured and consistent and shows that you are serious about teaching and learning. Motivating, challenging, and engaging students as you strive for high expectations will not only help to improve student behavior in school and academic accomplishments but will also provide the key for students to understand how to act in a moral and ethical way in society.

References

Brophy, J. 1986. Classroom management techniques. *Education and Urban Society* 18 (2): 182–94.

Brown, T. 1998. *Effective school research and student behavior.* Southeast/South Central Educational Cooperative Fourth Retreat Making a difference in student behavior. Lexington, KY.

Curwin, R. L., and A N. Mendler. 1988. *Discipline with dignity.* Alexandria, VA: Association for Supervision and Curriculum Development.

Daniels, H., M. Bizar, and S. Zemelman. 2001. *Rethinking high school: Best practice in teaching, learning and leadership.* Portsmouth, NH: Heinemann.

Dreikurs, R., B. Grunwald, and F. Pepper. 1971. *Maintaining sanity in the classroom: Classroom management techniques.* New York: Harper and Row.

Table 2 Top Ten List for Classroom Management

10. Develop a philosophy of "we" rather than "I" and use a personal approach in working with your students.
9. Class rules should be reasonable, fair, equitable, and used in a consistent manner.
8. Your actions, words, and deeds should model the behavior that you expect from your students.
7. Remember self-esteem is as important for adolescences as it is for you—avoid sarcasm or actions that belittle an individual in front of classmates.
6. Be proactive. Move around the room and keep your eyes moving.
5. Before you speak, get everyone's attention and say what you mean and mean what you say.
4. Keep parents informed. Parent involvement will support your role as a teacher.
3. Always give students hope—make them feel that they can accomplish anything.
2. Treat your students as you yourself would like to be treated.
1. Be yourself. Do not be an imitation of someone else. Success will follow if you allow your own personality to show.

Dunn, R., and K. Dunn. 1993. *Teaching secondary students through their individual learning styles: Practical approaches for grades 7–12.* Boston: Allyn and Bacon.

Glasser, W. 1990. *The quality school: Managing students without coercion.* New York: Harper and Row.

Kerr, M. M., and C. M. Nelson. 2002. *Strategies for managing behavior problems in the classroom.* 4th ed. Upper Saddle River, NJ: Merrill/Prentice Hall.

Macdonald, D. 1999. Teacher attrition: A review of the literature. *Teaching and Teacher Education* 15: 839–48.

Marshall, M. 2001. *Discipline without stress, punishments, or rewards: How teachers and parents promote responsibility and learning.* Los Alamitos, CA: Piper.

Miech, R. J., and G. H. Elder. 1996. The service ethic and teaching. *Sociology of Education* 69: 237–53.

Miller, A., E. Ferguson, and R. Simpson. 1998. The perceived effectiveness of rewards and sanctions in primary schools: Adding in the parental perspective. *Educational Psychology* 18 (1): 55–64.

Ornstein, A., and T. Lasley. 2004. *Strategies for Effective Teaching.* 4th ed. Boston: McGraw Hill.

Sleeter, C, and C. Grant. 2003. *Turning on learning: Five approaches for multicultural teaching plans for race, class, gender, and disability.* 3rd ed. New York: Wiley.

Tye, B. B., and L. O'Brien. 2002. Why are experienced teachers leaving the profession? *Phi Delta Kappan* 84 (1): 24–32.

PAUL PEDOTA is a former principal in a New York City secondary school and is currently the director of alternative certification programs at St. John's University, New York.

From *The Clearing House,* March/April 2007, pp. 163–166. Reprinted by permission of the Helen Dwight Reid Educational Foundation. Published by Heldref Publications, 1319 Eighteenth St., NW, Washington, DC 20036-1802. Copyright © 2007. www.heldref.org

"No! I Won't!"

Understanding and Responding to Student Defiance

ANDREA SMITH AND ELIZABETH BONDY

Ms. Jackson was at her wit's end. For the past two months it was the same routine. Taking a deep breath, she crossed her fingers and hoped that today would be different as she asked the students to join her on the rug for a story. Jon, a wide-eyed 8-year-old, remained motionless.

"Jon, please come join us for a story." Silence. "Jon . . . come on over so you can listen to the story." The small boy's eyes narrowed as his jaw tightened. "No! I won't!"

Student defiance, or resisting the authority of the teacher, is commonplace. In fact, some researchers have reported that the vast majority of discipline referrals are due to defiance (Gregory, 2005; Kohl, 1994). Due to the prevalence of childhood defiance and its potential for bringing instruction to a grinding halt, it is essential for educators to be prepared to understand it and respond to students who exhibit it. The authors will examine defiant behavior and the strategies that can minimize and manage it effectively.

Understanding Defiant Behavior

Defiance ranges from minor, easily defused incidents to highly disruptive and dangerous events. Sometimes a student's defiance is so extreme and persistent that the student is identified as having oppositional defiant disorder (ODD). According to the Diagnostic and Statistical Manual of Mental Disorders, fourth edition (DSM-1V), ODD is characterized by a

pattern of negativistic, hostile, and deviant behavior lasting at least six months, during which four (or more) of the following are present. The student (1) often loses his or her temper (2) often argues with adults (3) often actively defies or refuses to comply with adults' requests or rules (4) often deliberately annoys people (5) often blames others for his or her mistakes or misbehaviors (6) is touchy or easily annoyed by others (7) is often angry and resentful (8) is often spiteful or vindictive. (BehaveNet® Clinical Capsule™)

Students with ODD are at an increased likelihood of having problems with substance abuse or juvenile delinquency, developing a mental disorder, and committing violent crimes (van Lier, Muthen, & van der Sar, 2004). This extreme kind of defiance appears to be caused by a variety of factors, including genetics (Eaves, Rutter, Silberg, & Shillady, 2000), chemical imbalance (Jensen, 2001), either excessively authoritarian or *laissez-faire* parenting (Levy, O'Hanlon, & Goode, 2001), and social factors, such the experience of racial discrimination and poverty that can cause severe social stress in a family (Barkley, 1997). In addition, challenging behavior can be related to the quality of the mother's prenatal care and nutrition; the child's prenatal exposure to alcohol, drugs, and/or lead; poor nutrition; inadequate health care; and maltreatment, in the form of negligence and/or physical and emotional injury (Zirpoli & Melloy, 2001). Although these factors are presented as distinct, it is likely that they intermingle, creating a complex system of causation. Because the prevalence of ODD is less common than milder forms of defiance, we turn our attention to the more moderate and commonly observed forms of defiant behavior in elementary classrooms.

A pattern of defiant behavior, as illustrated by Jon in the vignette to the left, often indicates that a student is trying to accomplish something. The defiance serves a particular function. Researchers who study functional behavior assessment (e.g., Day, Horner, & O'Neill, 1994; Scott & Nelson, 1999) note that behavior tends to serve one of two (and sometimes both!) kinds of functions: to acquire and/or to avoid. Specifically, a student who behaves defiantly might be trying to get something, such as power, autonomy, status, attention, or a sense of belonging. The student also might be trying to avoid something, such as an aversive task or person.

Sometimes teachers and peers can trigger defiant behavior. Zirpoli and Melloy (2001) point out that teachers promote noncompliant behavior when they allow themselves to be lured into power struggles with students, react to inappropriate behavior rather than give students attention for their positive behavior, and respond inconsistently so that students are unsure what teachers expect of them. The strategies of functional behavior assessment, summarized later, provide educators with insights into the functions served by a particular behavior as well as environmental triggers for the behavior and consequences in the environment that could be reinforcing the behavior. With insights into the functions served by the defiant behavior and the conditions that support that behavior, educators can learn to intervene productively.

Some scholars remind us that defiance is not necessarily a "disease" (Diamond, 2003). Instead, it could be viewed as a social behavior that students should learn to use effectively. In fact, Kohl (1994) referred to defiance as a form of "creative maladjustment" that students use to resist adults' negative labels (e.g., "troublemaker," "slow learner"). Nevertheless, patterns of defiance in a classroom indicate that something is amiss. Given these insights into student defiance, what strategies might educators use to intervene productively?

Creating a Psychologically Supportive Environment

The old saying "An ounce of prevention is worth a pound of cure" rings true for many aspects of classroom management, and student defiance is no exception. A fundamental strategy in working with defiant behavior is to establish and maintain a psychologically supportive classroom environment (Patrick, Turner, Meyer, & Midgley, 2003). This kind of classroom features caring relationships between adults and students and among students, clear and high expectations for academic performance and behavior, and opportunities for meaningful participation in learning. In this kind of environment, students can develop social competence, a sense of purpose, problem-solving skills, and autonomy—all of which form a core of resilience in young people (Benard, 2004; Henderson & Milstein, 1996). Classroom Morning Meetings (Bondy & Ketts, 2001; Kriete, 2002), the use of positive behavior supports (U.S. Office of Special Education Programs, 1999), and the avoidance of common classroom management traps (Alderman, 1999) all contribute to the development of a psychologically supportive environment for students.

Conducting Morning Meetings

Morning Meeting, articulated and promoted by the Northeast Foundation for Children (Kriete, 2002), is a structure for beginning the school day. Before coming to the Morning Meeting circle, students read and interact with a message board or chart that will become part of the meeting. They then participate in the four elements of the meeting: Greeting, Sharing, Group Activity, and News and Announcements. The entire meeting can last between 15 and 30 minutes.

The Greeting enables students to say "hello" to one another in any number of traditional and nontraditional ways. After the Greeting, a student will start the Sharing portion of Morning Meeting by stating, in one sentence, something he or she would like to tell the group. Classmates are encouraged to listen during the sharing, then ask a predetermined number of questions in response to the sharer's invitation ("I'm ready for questions and comments"). The third component of Morning Meeting is a Group Activity, which usually involves a game, such as those often played in camps, scouts, and other social groups. The final part of Morning Meeting is News and Announcements. The class's attention is focused once again on the message board.

Students read the board and discuss the interactive portion before transitioning into the school day.

As Kriete (2002) explains, Morning Meeting teaches a variety of skills and makes important contributions to the tone and content of a classroom. She notes that Morning Meeting establishes a climate of trust and helps students to believe that they are valued. In short, Morning Meeting helps to establish a psychologically supportive environment in which students are less likely to behave defiantly.

Using Positive Behavior Supports

Special educators have recognized for years the power of positive behavior supports in enabling students to optimally participate in school (e.g., U.S. Office of Special Education Programs, 1999). Unlike traditional approaches to behavior management, which view the individual student as a "problem" that must be "fixed," a positive behavior support approach views the individual in context to understand why the behavior occurs. Although positive behavior supports can be implemented in response to a student's difficulties, many teachers recognize them as powerful proactive strategies. Like Morning Meeting, positive behavior supports contribute to a psychologically supportive environment in which students feel valued and are able to succeed. In this kind of climate, defiant behavior is less likely to occur.

Ruef, Higgins, Glaeser, and Patnode (1998) summarized five teacher-recommended, proactive, proven positive behavior support strategies: altering the physical environment, maintaining predictability and scheduling, increasing choice making, making curriculum responsive to students, and appreciating positive behaviors. Paying attention to these areas enables all students—not only those prone to defiance—to participate successfully in classroom life.

Altering the Physical Environment. Room arrangement and the use of space can influence student behavior. Teachers can avoid overcrowding students at desks, in workstations, and in high-traffic areas of the classroom. Crowds and noise can trigger problem behavior, as can an over- or under-stimulating physical space. Teachers also may need to consider accommodating individual students' environmental needs. For instance, distractible students can benefit from a well-defined workspace located away from high-traffic areas and an identified spot on the carpet when sitting on the floor.

Maintaining Predictability in the Schedule. Predictable classroom schedules and routines help students feel secure and decrease anxieties, frustration, and challenging behaviors, such as defiance. Students should be made aware of the schedule and be prompted to refer to it throughout the day. When changes occur to the daily schedule, such as a fire drill or absence of a teacher, students should be prepared and informed about what the day will look like. Related to maintaining a predictable schedule is preparing students for transitions during the school day. If teachers make students aware of upcoming transitions, students will have time to finish their work and prepare for a change.

Increasing Choice Making. Many have argued that due to high-stakes accountability, teachers have narrowed curriculum and instruction to focus on test preparation (Abrams, Pedulla, & Madaus, 2003; Barksdale-Ladd & Thomas, 2000). In an attempt to comply with local, state, and national mandates, teachers may have reduced the choices available to students and thereby increased the likelihood of defiance. Ruef et al. (1998) asserted that students need opportunities to make choices in order to believe that they have some control over their environment. Of course, adults can develop lists of acceptable choices, perhaps in conjunction with students.

Making Curriculum Responsive to Students. Teachers who adjust the substance and process of instruction to be responsive to a particular group of students are likely to experience less challenging behavior than those who do not (Ruef et al., 1998). In fact, Ruef and his colleagues noted that tasks reflecting students' interests and developmental levels were associated with positive behavior, whereas tasks that did not reflect these characteristics were associated with challenging behaviors. They also noted that the difficulty level length, and pace of an activity influenced students' behavior. Given these findings, the authors recommended that teachers think carefully about the nature of the task (e.g., High or low interest? Too easy or too difficult?) and the way in which it is presented (e.g., Use of different modalities? Pace? Tight teacher control or more student-centered?). When students believe they can be successful, they feel supported and are less likely to behave defiantly.

Appreciating Positive Behaviors. Although teachers want to avoid bribing and manipulating students through contrived reinforcement systems, making positive comments in the classroom will contribute to a psychologically supportive environment more readily than will negative, punitive comments. In addition, positive, encouraging comments can help students develop behaviors that serve them well in and out of the classroom. Punitive comments, on the other hand, can intensify defiance and trigger other challenging behaviors. Ruef et al. (1998) encourage teachers to use words of encouragement, appreciation, and affection as well as hugs, pats, and smiles to signal to students that they are, indeed, on "the right track." In fact, Walker, Colvin, and Ramsey (1995) encouraged teachers to praise students for exhibiting behaviors that are close to, or necessary for reaching, the desired goal recognizing that it could take a while before students have perfected a new, complex behavior. Students who do not have the social, learning, or behavioral skills that will help them thrive in the classroom require coaching and feedback as they develop those skills. When teachers approach students' behavior proactively, they establish an expectation of success and communicate their confidence in students' ability to succeed.

Avoiding Classroom Management Traps

In the crush of activity and on-the-spot decision making in elementary classrooms, teachers can slip into responses that can exacerbate rather than minimize defiant behavior. Alderman (1999) provided useful warnings to teachers about common classroom management traps. By steering clear of these common pitfalls, teachers can preserve a psychologically supportive environment.

The Too-General Trap. When teachers give instruction or direction to students, they must choose their words carefully. Effective directions are specific and stated once in 10 words or less (Bloomquist, 1996). Ineffective directions include vague directions, question directions, rationale directions, frequent directions, and multiple directions. Vague directions use imprecise language (e.g., "Cut it out") that does not communicate clear expectations. If a student does not know what behavior is desired, he or she will be unable to do it. Question directions are stated as a question, such as, "Would you stop tapping your pencil?" This invites a student to provide an answer, either with or without behavioral compliance. Rationale directions are those that include an explanation as to why the student should follow the directions. For example, Ms. Jackson, from the introductory vignette, asked Jon to join the group so he could "listen to the story." Students can perceive this to be a lecture, and may resist by arguing against the teacher's rationale. A typical response could be, "I don't need to come to the rug because I don't want to listen to the story!" (Bloomquist, 1996). Furthermore, rationale directions sometimes become too lengthy. This technique is ineffective, because students will usually quickly stop listening and then focus on the teacher's body language rather than the words (Alderman, 1999). Another form of ineffective direction is one that is repeated frequently, thereby eliciting a cycle of giving directions and obtaining defiant responses. Finally, one should avoid giving directions that include multiple steps in one statement (Bloomquist, 1996), a format that easily confuses and/or frustrates some students.

The "I Must Win Them Over" Trap. Often, the students who struggle the most inspire teachers to dedicate themselves to helping those strugglers to succeed. Teachers hope to see sweeping changes in student behavior and dream of being the one who visibly turns the child's life around. Visible, sweeping changes, however, are not always common, and many of the greatest changes are not readily observable; for instance, it may not be until many years later that a teacher learns of the impact he or she had on a student. Therefore, Alderman (1999) advises teachers not to expect or demand immediate changes. Instead, he recommends that teachers focus on achieving small steps toward the desired goal and celebrating that progress with students and their families. For example, if Jon, the boy from the introductory vignette, were to say "No! I won't!" but then stomp over to the rug, his behavior could be viewed as improved. Although his language is the same, his actions have shifted toward group participation, and this is better than complete refusal to participate. Ms. Jackson might say, in a matter-of-fact tone, "It's good to have you with us, Jon," and proceed quickly to the story.

The Passionate Discipline Trap. Pleading or getting angry while disciplining students is an easy trap to fall into that can trigger student defiance. Often, with the best intentions, a teacher might say something like "Could you PLEASE, just this once, do as I ask?!" or "My goodness! If you do that ONE MORE TIME I'll . . . " These kinds of responses are likely to elicit further undesirable behaviors from students who enjoy exerting power over adults. Alderman (1999) suggests several strategies for avoiding this trap. First, use a matter-of-fact approach to discipline. This includes controlling facial expressions, vocal intonations, and body language. Next, point to or quote a classroom rule that the student is neglecting to follow. Finally, consider writing on a small piece of paper or a sticky note to clarify for the student what he or she should be doing. Each of these strategies can help the teacher avoid an overly emotional response.

Responding to Defiant Behavior

Despite a supportive classroom climate and impeccable avoidance of management traps, some students will continue defiant behavior. This section covers options for responding to such defiant behavior. Although teachers may understandably prefer to avoid thinking about a student who defies their authority and disrupts lessons, avoiding the problem will not resolve it. Kohn (1996) recommends that teachers think of defiance as an opportunity to teach students something new.

Consider the Function of the Defiance

A Functional Behavior Assessment (FBA) is a systematic, seven-step way of determining the function, or purpose, a behavior serves. The Individuals With Disabilities Education Act Amendments of 1997 require that an FBA be conducted under certain circumstances. However, the less formal use of an FBA by a classroom teacher can help that teacher understand the function of the student's behavior and lead to effective intervention. For example, the appropriate intervention for Jon's defiance will vary, based on what function his behavior serves. If he is defiant because he wants to avoid rug time, the intervention should be different than if he is defiant because he wants attention.

There are seven steps in an FBA (see Figure 1). First, one must observe the student's behavior in context to determine what external factors cause and maintain the behavior. This step entails describing the behaviors in observable terms, noting the antecedents that appear to trigger the behavior, and identifying the consequences that appear to reinforce the behavior. Second, a hypothesis should be formed about the function a behavior serves in a particular context. As stated earlier, many behaviors are directed toward acquiring something, avoiding something, or both. Third, the validity of this hypothesis should be assessed through monitoring the behavior, including when it occurs in both the presence and absence of the predicted antecedents and consequences. Fourth, an intervention should be designed that allows the student to achieve the desired function of the behavior by performing a behavior the teacher finds more desirable. This may require teaching the student a "replacement behavior." The goal is to create a win-win situation wherein both the student

and the teacher get what they want. Fifth, the teacher may need to alter the environment in order to help the student replace the old behavior with the new. For example, if a student's disruptive behavior stems from a particular classmate sitting next to him or her, then the seating arrangement should be modified. Or, if the defiance is related to the student's frustration over assignments he or she finds difficult, the teacher should modify instruction and perhaps assignments so the student can participate more appropriately. Sixth, the effectiveness of the intervention must be considered by monitoring its impact on the student. Finally, if ineffective in supporting behavior change, the intervention should be altered.

Ideally, the functional behavior assessment will provide adequate insight into the student's defiance to enable the teacher to intervene and support positive behavior. Perhaps, for example, Jon's teacher discovers that Jon's defiance is related to his anxiety about the student who sits next to him on the rug. Jon seeks to avoid contact with his peer through his defiance, and the teacher reinforces his behavior by allowing him to remain in his seat. By helping Jon get to know the other student, the teacher may resolve the defiant behavior.

Further Interventions

Although teachers can resolve student defiance and many other troublesome behaviors with insights gained through an FBA, some behaviors are so ingrained that more direct, assertive approaches need to be considered. We review some of them here.

Use the Premack Principle. When applicable, teachers should use the Premack Principle (Warner & Lynch, 2002). As applied to teacher commands, the principle produces a directive followed by an incentive statement, reflecting a "When . . . then . . . " format. For example, the person making the command could say, "When you put away your markers, then we will take a game break," or "Once all chairs are pushed under the desks, we can go to recess." This strategy is beneficial in that it pairs a non- or less-preferred activity with a preferred activity (Warner & Lynch, 2002), thereby encouraging the student to comply with the request.

Observe behavior in context to determine its triggers and reinforcers.
Formulate a hypothesis about the function the behavior serves.
Assess the validity of the hypothesis through further observation.
Plan an intervention that enables student to achieve the same function through a desirable behavior. (Teach a replacement behavior, if necessary.)
Alter the environment to help student replace the old behavior with the new.
Monitor the effectiveness of the intervention by observing and recording its impact on student.
Alter intervention if it has not had the desired impact on student behavior.

Figure 1 Steps in a Functional Behavior Assessment.

Provide Consequences. Teachers may need to provide students with consequences for defiant actions. Consequences should be mild, with the intention of informing the student that the behavior is not appropriate. Consequences can be very effective when used appropriately (Bloomquist, 1996). However, students probably will be unhappy with the consequences, and some might express this displeasure. If students do express their unhappiness, the teacher should listen to the student's point of view and avoid getting into a power struggle. If the teacher is unsure how to respond to the student's displeasure or to an explanation the student provides, the teacher can tell the student that he or she will think about the situation and get back to the student at a designated time. The consequence should still be administered (Evertson, Emmer, & Worsham, 2006) in order to avoid providing reinforcement for the student's behavior.

Teachers may want to consider the two main types of consequences—natural consequences and logical consequences when planning consequences for defiant behavior. Natural consequences are those that occur directly as a result of the action, and include emotional responses. For example, if one falls off a bicycle, one might hurt oneself, or if one trips in front of the whole class, one might feel embarrassed. This form of consequence often proves to be the most effective, but it is difficult to administer. In Jon's case, a natural consequence of his refusal to join the group could be disappointment at missing an exciting group activity. The other main form of consequence, a logical consequence, is imposed by someone. In order to be effective, logical consequences should be "relevant," or directly related to the problem behavior. An effective way to develop relevant consequences is to think about what the student should be doing and design the consequence based on that desired behavior. For example, if Jon refuses to participate in a group activity, perhaps he will have to finish it during another period of the day. When consequences are logically connected to the misbehavior, they are likely to discourage the misbehavior. Still, it is important for teachers to gain insight into the function of the student's defiance in order to know what kind of consequence might be effective. Irrelevant consequences are likely to elicit anger and further defiance.

Use Time-Out. Although some researchers suggest that time-out is not always the ideal consequence, it does have the advantage of giving both the teacher and the student a chance to get away from the situation, think, and calm down (Evertson, Emmer, & Worsham, 2006). It also allows students to test their boundaries for autonomy and control while still remaining in a supportive environment (Charney, 2002). If a teacher decides to use time-out, he or she must have a plan for how it will be used. This includes knowing where time-out will occur and deciding ahead of time what actions will warrant time-out.

Some important things must be considered when planning where time-out will occur. Time-out should occur in a quiet place where there will be little to no mental stimulation. Often, teachers send the student to a desk in the hall, where the student has opportunities to chat with friends who pass by. Under these conditions, time-out can be an experience that reinforces the student's undesirable behavior. A teacher also must consider the purpose of the student's defiant behavior. In order for time-out to

be effective, the teacher must be confident that the student is not exhibiting the defiant behavior to escape an aversive situation, such as an assignment or class activity that he or she dislikes. If avoidance is the function of the student's defiance, putting the student in time-out will only reinforce the defiance by helping the student escape. Students should understand, as part of time-out, that their feelings are never inappropriate; however, the actions used to convey these feelings (the actions that might have elicited their placement in time-out) can be inappropriate (Nelsen, Lott, & Glenn, 2000). Many resources are available to help teachers implement time-out (e.g., Brady, Forton, & Porter, 2003; Charney, 2002; Nelsen, 1999). Teachers considering time-out should research the strategy in order to develop a system likely to help their particular group of students.

Try Behavior Charts. Behavior charts are a management tool that can be used for many different forms of misbehavior, including defiance. They come in many forms. For example, Barkley (1997) suggests the use of a daily report card. The advantage of the daily report card is that it involves the family in teaching the desired behavior. As implied by the name, this process involves the teacher filling out a form each day to record and rate the student's behavior. This form should be reviewed nightly by the student's guardian, who then acknowledges the positive remarks and gives points and rewards for the positive behaviors. Guardians should discuss the positive and negative behaviors with the child each night, along with possible strategies for avoiding the negative behaviors and maintaining positive behaviors in the future. A second form of behavior chart is a contingency contract. This contract should outline the behaviors the student should exhibit and the rewards or punishments that will be implemented if the behavior is or is not displayed. The student and teacher come to an agreement on the behavior, rewards, and punishments. Both the student and teacher sign and date the contract (Blendinger, Devlin, & Elrod, 1995). Levy et al. (2001), however, suggest proceeding with caution when using behavior charts, especially those similar to the daily report card. They argue that charts should be implemented for only three to six weeks; after this time period, the children acclimate to them and do not work as hard to gain the rewards. Therefore, behavior charts are not effective for long-term use. Figure 2 provides an illustration of a behavior contract that teacher and student (and parent) can develop collaboratively to target specific behavioral expectations and rewards. The form encourages teacher and student to identify a time period after which progress can be assessed and decisions can be made about next steps.

Collaborate With Other Adults. Teachers who work with defiant students must use several key resources. The first resource is the parent(s) or guardian(s) of the student who exhibits defiance. It is likely that these adults encounter the same difficult behaviors from the child at home and know of a strategy that works for the child. If not, or if their strategy is ineffective, it might be beneficial to collaboratively create a plan for preventing and responding to the behaviors. A collaborative plan ensures that the adults approach the problem in the same way (Greenspan, 2003). If the student's defiant behavior is frequent and/or severe, the teacher should consult with a professional who

This is an agreement between _____ and _____
Student's name   Teacher's name.

The contract begins on _____ and ends on _____ . At this time, we will assess our progress.

The terms of the contract are as follows:

* Student will demonstrate the following behaviour(s) at the following time(s):

* Teacher will help the student demonstrate the expected behavior(s) by:

* When the student demonstrates the behavior, the teacher will:

_____   _____
Student signature   Teacher signature

Figure 2   Behavior Contract.

specializes in defiance. Colleagues, too, can assist in problem solving and the development and assessment of interventions.

Although the thought of managing students who exhibit defiance can be intimidating, a variety of strategies can help. Building a strong classroom community and avoiding common management traps are important for preventing defiance. When defiance occurs, one must consider the function the defiance serves in order to determine appropriate ways to intervene. The goal of intervention is to enable the student to meet his or her needs in more appropriate ways and to preserve a productive learning environment. With a repertoire of strategies for preventing and responding to defiant behavior, teachers can strive to maintain a psychologically supportive environment in which all students believe they can succeed. Under these conditions, defiant behavior is likely to be minimized.

References

Abrams, L., Pedulla, J., & Madaus, G. (2003). Views from the classroom: Teachers' opinions of statewide testing programs. *Theory Into Practice, 42*(1), 18–29.

Alderman, G. L. (1999). Management traps: Recognizing and staying out of common behavior management traps. *Beyond Behavior, 8,* 23–28.

Barkley, R. (1997). *Defiant children: A clinician's manual for assessment and parent training* (2nd ed.). New York: The Guilford Press.

Barksdale-Ladd, M. A., & Thomas, K. (2000). What's at stake in high-stakes testing. *Journal of Teacher Education, 51*(5), 384–401.

Behavenet® clinical capsule™. (n.d.). DSM-IV & DSM-IV-TR: Oppositional Defiant Disorder. Retrieved Aug. 17, 2004, from BehaveNet Inc Web site: www.behavenet.com/capsules/disorders/odd.htm.

Benard, B. (2004). *Resiliency: What we have learned.* San Francisco: WestEd.

Blendinger, J., Devlin, S., & Elrod, G. (1995). *Controlling aggressive students.* Bloomington, IN: Phi Delta Kappa Educational Foundation.

Bloomquist, M. (1996). *Skills training for children with behavior disorders.* New York: The Guilford Press.

Bondy, E., & Ketts, S. (2001). "Like being at the breakfast table": The power of classroom morning meeting. *Childhood Education, 77,* 144–149.

Brady, K., Forton, M., & Porter, D. (2003). *Rules in school.* Greenfield, MA: Northeast Foundation for Children.

Charney, R. (2002). *Teaching children to care: Classroom management for ethical academic growth, K-8* (2nd ed.). Greenfield, MA: Northeast Foundation for Children.

Day, H. M., Horner, R. H., & O'Neill, R. E. (1994). Multiple functions of problem behaviors: Assessment and intervention. *Journal of Applied Behavior Analysis, 27,* 279–289.

Diamond, N. (2003). Defiance is not a disease. *Rethinking Schools Online, 17*(4). Retrieved from www.rethinkingschools.org/archive/17-04/defi174.shtml

Eaves, L., Rutter, M., Silberg, J. L., & Shillady, L. (2000). Genetic and environmental causes of covariation in interview assessments of disruptive behavior in child and adolescent twins. *Behavior Genetics, 30*(4), 321.

Evertson, C., Emmer, E., & Worsham, M. (2006). *Classroom management for elementary teachers* (7th ed.). Boston: Allyn and Bacon.

Greenspan, S. I. (2003). The oppositional child. *Early Childhood Today, 17*(4), 24.

Gregory, A. (2005, September). *A window on the discipline gap: Cooperation or defiance in high school classrooms.* Paper presented at the Curry School of Education Risk and Prevention Speaker Series, Charlottesville, VA.

Henderson, N., & Milstein, M. M. (1996). *Resiliency in schools.* Thousand Oaks, CA: Corwin Press.

Jensen, E. (2001). Fragile brains. *Educational Leadership, 59*(3), 32.

Kohl, H. (1994). *"I won't learn from you" and other thoughts on creative maladjustment.* New York: New Press.

Kohn, A. (1996). *Beyond discipline: From compliance to community.* Upper Saddle River, NJ: Prentice-Hall.

Kriete, R. (2002). *The morning meeting book.* Greenfield, MA: Northeast Foundation for Children.

Levy, R., O'Hanlon, B., & Goode, T. (2001). *Try and make me! Simple strategies that turn off the tantrums and create cooperation.* New York: Penguin Group.

Nelsen, J. (1999). *Positive time-out.* Rocklin, CA: Prima.

Nelsen, J., Lott, L., & Glenn, H. (2000). *Positive discipline in the classroom: Developing mutual respect, cooperation and responsibility in your classroom* (3rd ed.). Roseville, CA: Prima.

Patrick, H., Turner, J., Meyer, D. K., & Midgley, C. (2003). How teachers establish psychological environments during the first days of school: Associations with avoidance in mathematics. *Teachers College Record, 105,* 1521–1558.

Ruef, M. B., Higgins, C., Glaeser, B. J., & Patnode, M. (1998). Positive behavioral support: Strategies for teachers. *Intervention in School and Clinic, 34*(1), 21–32.

Scott, T. M., & Nelson, C. M. (1999). Using functional behavioral assessment to develop effective intervention plans: Practical classroom applications. *Journal of Positive Behavior Interventions, 1*(4), 242–251.

U.S. Office of Special Education Programs. (1999, Winter). Positive behavioral support: Helping students with challenging behaviors succeed. *Research Connections in Special Education,* (4), 1–5. Retrieved from http://ericec.org/osep/recon4/rc4cov.html

van Lier, P. A., Muthen, B. O., & van der Sar, R. M. (2004). Preventing disruptive behavior in elementary schoolchildren: Impact of a universal classroom-based intervention. *Journal of Consulting & Clinical Psychology, 72*(3), 467–478.

Walker, H., Colvin, G., & Ramsey, E. (1995). *Antisocial behavior in school: Strategies and best practices.* Pacific Grove, CA: Brooks/Cole.

Warner, L., & Lynch, S. (2002). Classroom problems that don't go away. *Childhood Education, 79,* 97–100.

Zirpoli, T. J., & Mellow, K.J. (2001). *Behavior management: Applications for teachers* (3rd ed.). Upper Saddle River, NJ: Merrill/Prentice Hall.

ANDREA SMITH is a 4th-grade teacher, Alachua County Public Schools, Gainesville, Florida. **ELIZABETH BONDY** is Professor, College of Education, University of Florida, Gainesville.

Bullying: Effective Strategies for Its Prevention

Put a halt to the name-calling, teasing, poking, and shoving, and make way for learning.

RICHARD T. SCARPACI

S ome people view bullying as a normal aspect of child-hood; teachers who prevent bullying know that this is not true. Bullying is a deliberate act that hurts young victims, both emotionally and physically. Aside from the victims, bullying affects people around them by distracting, intimidating, and upsetting them. Basically, bullying in the classroom is disruptive and prevents students from learning and teachers from reaching their students. Moreover, research has indicated that adopting programs which target antisocial behavior are likely to boost overall student academic performance (University of Washington 2005; Glew et al. 2005).

Though bullying among school children is hardly a new phenomenon, highly publicized media accounts have brought the topic a great deal of attention recently. In approaching this problem, research has suggested that reduction of bullying is best accomplished through a comprehensive, school-wide effort that involves everyone—especially teachers (Limber 2003).

Specific teacher behaviors may limit or prevent bullying in schools. When teachers respect student autonomy, while maintaining young people's sense of belonging, and teach cause-and-effect thinking that promotes development of a sense of right and wrong, schools are likely to deter bullying (Davis 2005). To accomplish this goal, teachers must confront their own beliefs and misconceptions about bullying, learn skills for recognizing the indicators of bullying, and practice strategies for addressing and deterring bullying.

What Is Bullying?

Bullying can be defined as when a more powerful person hurts, frightens, or intimidates a weaker person on a continual and deliberate basis. This behavior manifests itself in three distinct forms (Ritter 2002): physical (hitting, shoving, poking, tripping, and slapping), verbal (name-calling, insults, derision, racist remarks, and teasing) and social (persuading others to exclude or reject someone). Bullying in schools can be described simply as when a student is exposed repeatedly and over time to negative actions on the part of one or more other students (Olweus 2003).

Regardless of definition, some basic concepts provide insight and characterize bullies and bullying.

- Bullying takes at least two people: bully and victim.
- Bullies like to feel strong and superior.
- Bullies enjoy having power over others.
- Bullies use their power to hurt other people.

Though violent incidents are relatively uncommon, harassment in various physical and verbal forms is widespread. The American Medical Association (AMA) claimed that half of all children in the United States are bullied at some point in their lives, and one in 10 is victimized on a regular basis (Ritter 2002). A National Institute of Child Health and Human Development (2001) study found that 13 percent of children in grades six through ten had taunted, threatened, or acted physically aggressive toward classmates, while 11 percent had been the targets of such behavior. Six percent admitted that they both bullied others and had been bullied themselves. Boys were more likely to be bullies or victims of bullying than girls, who more frequently were the targets of bullying in the form of malicious rumors, electronic bullying, and sexual harassment.

Myths about Bullying

The belief that bullying is some sort of childhood disease is false. Olweus (2003) disputed several common assumptions such as this one, finding that many so-called causes of bullying and profiles of typical victims do not stand up to empirical data. Students who wear glasses, are overweight, or speak differently are not more likely to become victims of bullies. Actually, those who are passive or submissive tend to become victims almost 85 percent of the time. Comprising the other 15 percent are aggressive victims who are targeted because of some provocative feature of their personalities.

Myths have been exposed online by the U.S. Department of Health and Human Services (2003), School Bully OnLine (Field 2005), and For KidSake (2006). Some typical myths about bullying are:

1. Bullying is just teasing. "I was just kidding around!" is a refrain educators often hear from bullies.
2. Some people deserve to be bullied.
3. Only boys are bullies.
4. People who complain about bullies are babies.
5. Bullying is a normal part of growing up.
6. Bullies will go away if you ignore them.
7. All bullies have low self-esteem. That's why they pick on others.
8. It's tattling to tell an adult when you're being bullied.
9. The best way to deal with a bully is by fighting or trying to get even.
10. People who are bullied might hurt for a while, but they'll get over it.

Teachers must learn to recognize the indicators of bullying, in both the victims and the bully.

Though a couple of these—such as numbers 6 and 10—may be true sometimes, all the other statements are false. The challenge, then, is to get past the myths and to identify the true indicators of bullying.

Indicators of Bullying

Awareness is the first step in preventing bullying. Teachers must learn to recognize the indicators of bullying, in both the victims and the bully.

Recognizing the Victims

Teachers should be alert to students who have poor social skills and few friends; they may be victims of bullying. Teachers also should keep an eye on students who are physically smaller and act or look unlike other students; they too are potential victims.

Frankel (1996) described the key indicators for a child at risk:

- A child's grades begin to fall.
- A child shows a decrease in interest for school in general.
- A child feigns illness, such as frequent headaches or stomachaches.
- A child who chooses ubiquitous routes home may be hiding the fact that he or she is a victim of a bully.
- A child claims to have lost books, money, or other belongings without a good explanation.
- A child is caught stealing or asking for extra money.
- A child has unexplained injuries, bruises, or torn clothing; bullying may be the cause for any or all of these indicators.

The AMA warned that bullying can damage a child as much as child abuse (Ritter 2002), and has asked doctors to be vigilant for signs that their young patients might be victims of bullying or be bullies themselves. The psychological trauma of recurring harassment puts victims at risk of suffering from depression or low self-esteem as an adult. The younger the child, the more he or she ultimately will suffer from bullying.

To identify whether a patient is being bullied, the AMA suggested that parents and doctors ask a series of questions (Ritter 2002). The questions also are quite appropriate for teachers who suspect that bullying is going on in their classrooms. Developing the skill of asking the right questions may help deter bullying.

1. Have you ever been teased at school? How long has this been going on?
2. Do you know of other children who have been teased?
3. Have you ever told your teacher about the teasing? What happens?
4. What kinds of things do children tease you about?
5. Do you have nicknames at school?
6. Have you ever been teased because of your illness, disability, or for looking different than other kids?
7. At recess, do you usually play with other children or by yourself?

Though one might not think of a student who attacks others as a victim, that is sometimes the case. Bullies are characterized by hypersensitivity toward criticism—being teased, harassed, or generally picked on by those to whom they were violent. Of the 37 school shootings since 1974, the National Threat Assessment Center found that attackers felt persecuted, bullied, threatened, or had been previously attacked. Bullying is a prime factor in two-thirds of school shooting incidents (Viadero 2003). In more than half of the rampages, revenge was the motivation (Vossekuil et al. 2002).

Charles Andrew Williams, the 15-year-old Santee, California student accused of killing two classmates and wounding 13 others (Reaves 2001), was tormented and bullied. Witnesses said that kids burned him with cigarette lighters and accused him of being a faggot. When he announced that he planned to pull a Columbine, two students called him a wimp and dared him to do it. Early intervention might have been able to prevent this tragedy.

Recognizing the Bully

Bullies may be more difficult to identify than the victims of bullying. While the stereotype is that bullies have low self-esteem, actually they're often self-confident, popular, and make friends easily (Cohen-Posey 1995). If slighted, however, they may take it out on someone who can't fight back. The reasons for this are based somewhere in familiar coping mechanisms that bullies have learned.

Bullies often manifest more violent behavior with age and tend to suffer from depression, suicidal behavior, and alcoholism (Olweus 1998). Many bullies come from homes where they're harassed themselves; they also tend to perform poorly at school; and, by age 24, 60 percent of former bullies have been convicted of a crime (Olweus 1998).

What Teachers Can Do

Teachers have dual roles: teach potential bullies social skills, while developing capacity to avoid intimidation. The next steps are to develop and implement the practices and strategies needed to stop bullying at school while assisting its victims.

Eliminating Harassment

Sexual harassment, when viewed as conflict, can be described as intentional or inadvertent conduct offensive to a reasonable person. A female victim of this type of harassment may appear angry, distrustful of her classmates, or self-conscious about her physical maturation as a result of untoward comments. A male may become passive following incidents of sexual insults, threats, or innuendo.

Teachers should investigate all complaints or rumors of sexual harassment. The best tool for the elimination of harassment is prevention. Affirmatively raise the subject in class. Express strong disapproval for untoward actions, develop sanctions (such as referrals to a higher authority), and inform students of their rights to raise the issue of harassment.

Encouraging Openness

To deter bullying, teachers should encourage and practice openness in class. Bullies tend to work in secret; they depend on the silence of their victims. If open communication is practiced, bullies will find it difficult to operate. Hold them accountable for their actions. Use or develop school antiharassment policies and hold bullies responsible for inappropriate behavior.

Practicing Bullying Prevention

Four basic principles for the prevention of bullying should be practiced by teachers (Olweus 2003):

1. Provide warm, positive interest and involvement from adults.
2. Provide consistent application of nonpunitive, nonphysical sanctions for unacceptable behavior or violations of rules.
3. Establish firm limits on unacceptable behavior.
4. Act as authorities and role models.

A bullying prevention program created by Olweus, Limber, and Mihalic (1999) incorporates having regular class meetings with students while establishing and enforcing class rules against bullying.

Neutralizing a Bully

Teachers should know how to neutralize a bully—to use the skill of acquiring information about incidents and then enforcing consequences if the negative behavior continues (Frankel 1996). Victims also should be taught how to deal with teasing so that they can help neutralize the bully. Teachers should practice being role models and encourage victims to make light of teasing by using statements such as:

- *So what?*
- *Can't you think of anything else to say?*
- *Tell me when you get to the funny part.*
- *And your point is?*

Responses such as these, perhaps surprisingly, generally do not incite bullies to further action.

The National Education Association has developed Quit It and Bullyproof—programs that work to neutralize bullies. These programs consist of interactive materials, including discussions and role-playing aimed at educating children about hurtful behaviors, and advice on how to deal with bullying situations (Froschl, Sprung, and Mullin-Rindler 1998).

Resolving Conflict

Bullying creates conflicts for both the victim and the bully. Conflict should be viewed as normal, and an opportunity to develop constructive practices to prevent bullying. Most bullying prevention programs invite teachers to intervene when children's conflict is about power and control, not negotiation (Craig and Pepler 1997). That is, teacher intervention is appropriate and necessary to prevent or end a physical conflict between students; violence, once started, stops only when someone is hurt. Intervention by a teacher is less necessary when students are involved in a conflict whose outcome can be negotiated.

Briggs (1996) advocated extending social and emotional learning by viewing incidents of conflict as teachable moments for social learning, and practicing skill streaming (social skills training), peer mediation, or conflict resolution. Phillips (1997) described how her high school attempted to alleviate and resolve conflicts by establishing a "conflict wall" (see below) that provided step-by-step guidance. If students cannot resolve a conflict, have them agree to disagree; sometimes that is the best we can do.

Closing Thoughts

Specific teacher behaviors can limit or prevent bullying in school. Reject myths about bullying. Believe that effective teachers manage classrooms with care and understanding, while creating an open, warm, nurturing environment that allows less opportunity or incentive for bullying to occur (Scarpaci 2007). Demonstrate active positive interest in student well-being.

Develop the skill of questioning and respectful listening to assess indications of bullying. By learning and teaching conflict resolution skills, teachers create environments that are less conducive to bullying. Employ the skills necessary to address the psychological needs of students: belonging, power, freedom, and fun (Glasser 1998). Focus on remediating student social-skill deficits by addressing classroom survival skills, friendship-making skills, dealing with feelings, and alternatives to aggression.

Teach students how to deal with behaviors that can be hurtful. Role-play in class to illustrate how to deal with teasing and threats of physical aggression. Bullying, when understood, can be prevented by doing what we do best— teaching! By combining education about bullying and establishing consequences for continued bullying, schools not only will neutralize bullying; they also might prevent it.

References

Briggs, D. 1996. Turning conflicts into learning experiences. *Educational Leadership* 54(1): 60–63.

Cohen-Posey, K. 1995. *How to handle bullies, teasers and other meanlees.* Highland City, FL: Rainbow Books.

Craig, W., and D. J. Pepler. 1997. Observations of bullying and victimization in the schoolyard. *Canadian Journal of School Psychology* 13(2): 41–60.

Davis, S. 2005. Schools *where everyone belongs: Practical strategies for reducing bullying.* Champaign, IL: Research Press. Available at: *www.stopbullyingnow.com.*

Field, T. 2005. Myths and misconceptions about school bullying. *School Bully OnLine.* Available at: *www.bullyonline.org/schoolbully/myths.htm.*

For KidSake. 2006. Breaking through the myths. Available at: *www.forkidsake.net/bully_myths_answer_sheet.htm.*

Frankel, F. 1996. *Good friends are hard to find.* Glendale, CA: Perspective Publishing.

Froschl, M., B. Sprung, and N. Mullin-Rindler. 1998. *Quit it! A teacher's guide on teasing and bullying for use with students in grades K–3.* New York: Educational Equity Concepts.

Glasser, W. 1998. *Choice theory: A new psychology of personal freedom.* New York: HarperCollins.

Glew, G. M., M.-Y. Fan, W. Katon, F. P. Rivara, and M. A. Kernic. 2005. Bullying, psychosocial adjustment, and academic performance in elementary school. *Archives of Pediatrics & Adolescent Medicine* 159(11): 1026–31.

Limber, S. P. 2003. Efforts to address bullying in U.S. Schools. *Journal of Health Educalion* 34(5): S23–S29.

National Institute of Child Health and Human Development. 2001. Bullying widespread in U.S. schools, survey finds, Rockville, MD: NICHD. Available at: *www.nichd.nih.gov/new/releases/bullying.clm.*

Olweus. D. 1998. *Bullying at school.* Malden, *MA:* Blackwell Publishers.

Olweus, D. 2003. A profile of bullying at school. *Educational Leadership* 60(6): 12–17.

Olweus, D., S. Limber, and S. F. Mihalic. 1999. *Bullying prevention program,* Book nine of Blueprints for Violence Prevention. Boulder, CO: Center for the Study and Prevention of Violence.

Phillips, P. 1997. The conflict wall. *Educational Leadership* 54(8): 43–44.

Reaves, J. 2001. Charles 'Andy' Williams. *Time,* March 9. Available at: *www.time.com/time/pow/printout/0,8816,101847,00.html.*

Ritter, J. 2002. AMA puts doctors on lookout for bullying. *Chicago Sun Times,* June 20.

Scarpaci, R. T. 2007. *A case study approach to classroom management.* Boston: Allyn & Bacon.

University of Washington. 2005. School programs targeting antisocial behavior can boost test scores, grades. Seattle, WA: UW. Available at: *www.newswise.com/p/articles/view/516342.*

Conflict Wall: Steps for Resolving Conflicts

1. Cool down. Don't try to resolve a conflict when you are angry. Take time out and attempt to resolve the conflict when cooler heads prevail.
2. Describe the conflict. Each person should be given the opportunity to explain what happened in his or her own words. (Make no judgments!)
3. Describe what caused the conflict. Be specific and insist on exact chronological order. (Don't place blame!)
4. Describe the feelings raised by the conflict.
5. Listen carefully and respectfully while the other person is talking.
6. Brainstorm solutions to the conflict.
7. Try your solutions.
8. If that doesn't work, try another solution.

U.S. Department of Health and Human Services. 2003. *Bullying is not a fact of life.* Washington, DC: Substance Abuse and Mental Health Services Administration. Available at: *www.mentalhealth.samhsa.gov/publications/ allpubs/SVP-0052.*

Viadero, D. 2003. Tormentors. *Education Week,* Jan. 15, 24.

Vossekuil, B., R. Fern, M. Reddy, R. Borum, and W. Modzeleski. 2002. *The final report and findings of the safe school initiative: Implications for the prevention of school attacks in the United States.* Washington, DC: U.S. Secret Service and U.S. Department of Education.

RICHARD T. SCARPACI, a former teacher and principal, currently is an Assistant Professor and Director of Field Experiences at St. John's University, Staten Island campus. He has taught courses in Management and Methods as well as conducted Child Abuse and Violence Prevention Seminars. He is a member of the Alpha Beta Gamma Chapter of Kappa Delta Pi.

Cyberbullying: What School Administrators (and Parents) Can Do

ANDREW V. BEALE, EDD AND KIMBERLY R. HALL, PHD

Technology has transformed the lives of adolescents, including the ways they bully one another. Variously referred to as electronic bullying, online bullying, or cyberbullying, this new method of bullying involves the use of e-mail, instant messaging, Web sites, voting booths, and chat or bash rooms to deliberately pick on and torment others. To combat cyberbullying, educators need to better understand the nature of it and be aware of actions that they can undertake to prevent cyberbullying in the schools.

In recent years, considerable emphasis has been placed on implementing bullying prevention programs in public schools (Colvin et al. 1998; Hernandez and Seem 2004; Pellegrini and Bartini 2000). Researchers and administrators have developed programs, written articles, delivered workshops, and given speeches focusing on the goal and importance of eliminating bullying behavior in schools. The difficulty, however, is that despite the major emphasis on prevention of bullying in schools, the problem persists. According to the results of the first national survey on school bullying, 74 percent of eight- to eleven-year-old students reported that bullying and teasing occurred at their schools (Nansel et al. 2001). To make matters worse, technology has escalated bullying to a new and particularly insidious level. Variously referred to as electronic bullying, online bullying, or cyberbullying, this new method of bullying involves the use of e-mail, instant messaging, Web sites, voting booths, and chat or bash rooms to deliberately antagonize and intimidate others.

Although the Internet allows for unbridled communication, it also seems to encourage a measure of mean-spiritedness. When students think they can remain anonymous, they are less inhibited in saying things they never would say to a person face-to-face (Joinson 1998; Keith and Martin 2005; Sparling 2004). Even if he or she can be identified online, an adolescent can blame someone else for using his or her screen name. Because technology provides a screen behind which young people may hide, they do not have to be accountable for their actions, and if a person cannot be identified with an action, fear of being caught and punished is diminished. This phenomenon is referred to as disinhibition and requires that administrators create a comprehensive *sunlight* plan for bringing cyberbullying out of the shadows and to the attention of teachers, parents, students, and staff (Willard 2005).

Although few studies that have documented students' experiences with cyberbullying exist, the one national study to date (R. Kowalski, pers. comm.) found that cyberbullying was prevalent among middle school students, with 25 percent of girls and 11 percent of boys reporting being cyberbullied at least once in a two-month period. Ironically, online bullying seems to follow a gender pattern that is the opposite of what happens offline. On playgrounds, on school buses, and in school hallways, boys tend to be the primary perpetrators and victims of bullying behavior; online, girls are the major players (Beale and Scott 2001; R. Kowalski, pers. comm.). Additionally, what makes cyberbullying so particularly hurtful is that the anonymity of the act often emboldens the person doing it and increases the fear factor for the victim (Belsey 2004). Because it does not occur face-to-face, bullies are able to mete out pain without witnessing the consequences and victims often cannot stand up for themselves, even if they are so inclined. In large part, it is the secretive nature of electronic bullying that helps to make it so insidious. A tormentor can get into a victims' home, harassing him or her while parents sit comfortably in the next room (Keith and Martin 2005; Willard 2005).

As with traditional bullying, cyberbullying seems to increase through the elementary school years, peak during the middle school years, and decline in high school (Migliore 2003). Although girls generally mock others for their physical appearance, boys tend to make more sexually explicit comments (R. Kowalski, pers. comm.; Worthington 2005). Students who are considered overweight, small in size, learning disabled, or overly sensitive (i-SAFE 2004; Willard 2005) are often targeted. However, all students are potential victims of electronic bullying aimed at inflicting unwarranted hurt and embarrassment on its unsuspecting victims. To assist the victims of cyberbullying and develop interventions aimed at preventing it, educators need to be informed about cyberbullying, the forms it takes, and what strategies or actions they might take to combat it in their schools.

Forms of Cyberbullying

We are becoming an increasingly "wired" society. Although technology offers many exciting possibilities for students to create, connect, and learn from one another, there also exists the inherent potential for some students to exploit technology in ways that deliberately antagonize and intimidate others. Cyberbullying involves the intentional use of information and communication technologies to support intentional, repeated, and hostile behavior directed at an individual or a group (Belsey 2005). Six major forms that cyberbullying might take are the following: e-mail, instant messaging (IM), chat rooms or bash boards, small text messaging (SMS), Web sites, and voting booths.

Cyberbullies use e-mail to send harassing and threatening messages to their targets. Most e-mail programs allow for e-mail filters that will block or automatically delete messages from undesirable senders, but these blocks work only to a limited degree, as most e-mail users know. And although it is possible to trace from which e-mail account the offending message was sent, it is almost impossible to prove who actually used the account to send the offending message.

IM is similar to e-mail, but it allows for much faster communication. Typically, the IM system alerts the user when somebody on his or her private list is online, thus allowing the user to initiate a chat session with that particular individual in real time. IM has become a very large part of the social lives of students. Social relationships formed at school are extended and maintained beyond school hours through IM. Most IM programs allow users to create a list of others from which users may wish to block messages. This exclusion feature is one of the most prevalent forms of cyberbullying, that is, willfully excluding a particular student from contacting the user or being allowed to join online chat room conversations. Because screen names can be switched, IM allows students to hide their identities, thus enhancing the potential for bullying.

Chat rooms or bash boards allow for real-time communication between users via their computers. A "virtual" room affords students the opportunity to write back and forth to one another. Once a chat has been initiated, either user may enter text by typing on the keyboard and the entered text will appear on the other user's monitor. Most networks and online services offer a chat feature. The "bash board" is the nickname for an online bulletin board, or virtual chat room, in which students can anonymously write anything they want, true or false, creating or adding mean-spirited postings for the world to see.

SMS is a service for sending and receiving short text messages via mobile phones. The text can include words, numbers, or an alphanumeric combination. A single message can be up to 160 characters long using default global system mobile communications (GSM) alphabet coding and seventy characters when using two-byte universal character set (UCS2) international coding. Similarly, personal digital assistants (PDAs)—such as Palm Pilot, Blackberry, Sony Clie, iPaq, Handspring Visor/Tree, and Pocket PC—are not only personal information organizers, they can now also connect to and browse the Internet and receive and send e-mail.

Cyberbullies can create Web sites that mock, antagonize, and harass others. Voting or polling booths offer users the opportunity to create Web pages that allow students to vote online for "ugliest," "fattest," "dumbest," and so on, boy or girl at their school. It is easy to understand the devastating effect such a "contest" would have on the hapless student(s) selected for inclusion.

Willard (2005) described cyberbullying as sending or posting harmful or cruel text or images using digital communication devices. She identified the following seven ways in which cyberbullying may occur: (a) *flaming* involves sending angry, rude, or vulgar messages directed at a person or persons privately or to an online group; (b) *harassment* involves repeatedly sending a person offensive messages; (c) *denigration* is sending or posting harmful, untrue, or cruel statements about a person to other people; (d) *cyberstalking* is harassment that includes threats of harm or is highly intimidating; (e) *masquerading* is pretending to be someone else and sending or posting material that makes that person look bad or places that person in potential danger; (f) *outing* and *trickery* involve engaging in tricks to solicit embarrassing information about a person and then making that information public; and (g) *exclusion* describes actions that specifically and intentionally exclude a person from an online group, such as blocking a student from an IM buddies list. Willard speculated that every student who communicates online has played one or more of the roles in the cyberbullying, triad: bully, victim, or bystander. Regrettably, the nature of cyberbullying, with its ease and wide scope of dissemination of harmful information, its virtual anonymity for the perpetuators, and the fact that the victims cannot easily escape serves to make it even more harmful than traditional bullying.

Because cyberbullying occurs so extensively in the schools, teachers and administrators need to address it schoolwide. School administrators must implement a comprehensive prevention plan that has the support and cooperation of parents, the school, and community members if students are to be free from cyberbullying. Combating cyberbullying is a mission that requires administrators, teachers, counselors, parents, and students to work together to ensure that all students are afforded a safe and fear-free learning environment.

Recommended Preventions and Interventions
What School Administrators Can Do

School administrators are responsible for ensuring that all students are provided an opportunity to attend school free from fear and intimidation. This includes ensuring that students are using school network or mobile devices in a manner that does not cause harm to others. One of the first steps to eliminate cyberbullying is to assess the level of electronic bullying occurring both at home and at school. Some ways to determine the prevalence, attitudes toward, and gaps in perception and knowledge of cyberbullying include focus groups, class meetings, and surveys sent to teachers, parents, and students. It is naive to assume that cyberbullying is not taking place. A more realistic approach is to attempt to assess the pervasiveness of the problem, thus allowing school leaders to target specific areas or aspects of the problem (for example, incident rates, times, locations, forms). It is equally important to make certain that teachers, staff, parents, and students clearly understand the scope and seriousness of cyberbullying and the consequences of violating school rules regarding harassment, intimidation, and antagonistic behavior. School administrators can begin by implementing the following prevention-intervention strategies gleaned from cyberbullying literature (Aftab 2005; Belsey 2005; Hernandez and Seem 2004; Keith and Martin 2005; Media Awareness Network 2007; Willard 2005):

- Provide student education. Internet bullying lessons should be integrated into the school's curriculum. School counselors, in particular, could collaborate with classroom teachers for presenting classroom guidance sessions on appropriate Internet etiquette.
- Make certain the school or school board's anti-bullying policy includes harassment perpetrated with mobile and Internet technology.
- The school's acceptable use policy should be updated to specifically prohibit using the Internet for bullying. The policy should spell out what constitutes cyberbullying and specify the anticipated negative consequences. Aftab (2005) recommended that a provision be added to the school's acceptable use policy reserving the right to discipline students for actions conducted away from school if such actions have an adverse effect on a student or if they adversely affect the safety and well-being of the student while in school. This makes cyberbullying a contractual, not a legal, issue.
- Provide parents with education. Encourage parents to discuss Internet bullying with their children and the adverse consequences of such behavior, including school discipline, civil litigation, and criminal prosecution.
- Establish a relationship with the local police department, perhaps inviting "cybercops" to school to speak to parents and students on proper Internet use.
- Conduct professional development seminars so that all faculty and staff are alerted to issues related to cyberbullying, especially detection.
- Create a school climate in which students feel encouraged and comfortable reporting any and all forms of cyberbullying to a responsible adult.
- Coordinate with other schools in the district to provide consistent cyberbullying prevention information as students move through grade levels and among schools.
- Establish a schoolwide cyberbullying task force composed of technologically savvy educators, parents, students, and community members to develop and implement anticyberbullying programs aimed at keeping schools safe and secure.

Because school administrators must walk a tightrope to protect students affected by cyberbullying without trampling the free speech rights of bullies, school districts should petition state legislatures to add an electronic bullying component to existing state laws that prohibit traditional bullying. Under such legislation, cyberbullying would not have to occur on school property, take place during school hours, or be done using school equipment, so long as the activity has an adverse effect on a student or school. Currently, forty-five states have passed legislation prohibiting electronic bullying in its various forms. Virginia, for example, has legislation in place that makes it a misdemeanor for a person to use a computer or computer network to coerce, intimidate, or harass another person (Code of Virginia 18.2–152.7:1 2000).

Because many parents are not as computer savvy as their children, schools should sponsor workshops designed to enlighten parents about the nature and forms of cyberbullying. Unless parents are aware of the scope of cyberbullying and its adverse consequences for children, and know what to look for and how to respond, one of the school's major lines of defense against it is ineffective.

One of the most troubling aspects of electronic bullying is that frequently it occurs away from school, thereby limiting administrators in what they can do to control it in a typical disciplinary manner. Absent a *nexus* or direct connection to the school, administrators are stifled in what direct responses they may take to confront those who engage in cyberbullying. Because it does occur away from school, cyberbullying makes it imperative for school administrators to provide information to parents that will allow them to monitor more closely their children's use of technology.

What Parents Can Do

The best advice for students affected by cyberbullying is to get their parents and school administrators involved as soon as possible and not attempt to handle the situation online or suffer in silence. Parents must stand behind the school's efforts to counter cyberbullying by recognizing that it is a reality and addressing the problem with their children. Although traditional bullying occurs at school, electronic bullying mainly occurs at home, causing those affected to believe there is no safe place (Wollack and Mitchell 2000). Lauren Savage, a school counselor in Richmond, Virginia, noted, "In the past when students were bullied at school they could at least seek the safety of their homes, but with cyberbullying the bully goes home with them" (pers. comm.).

Some schools require that students and their parents sign an "Acceptable Internet Use" policy in which students agree to not use their computers to antagonize or harass other students, and parents agree to be responsible for their children's Internet use outside of school. Parental responsibility for monitoring their children's computer use is tricky. Part of the problem in combating cyberbullying is that parents and young people relate to technology differently (Keith and Martin 2005). Most adults approach computers as practical tools, wheras their children view the Internet as a lifeline to their peer groups (Keith and Martin). Adolescents know there is a gap in the understanding of technology between themselves and their parents (Belsey 2004).

Students can tell their parents they are doing homework, but may actually be engaging in some form of Internet bullying. Additionally, instant messaging, chat rooms, and text messaging are likely to be foreign terms to many parents; they are not unfamiliar terms to most students (i-SAFE 2004). Today's young people, including bullies, are computer savvy. Parents, if they are to be successful in monitoring their children's computer use, must learn what to look for, as well as how to "talk the talk." For example, IM has created a whole new user language. How many parents know the meaning of the following common IM acronyms: PIR (parent in room), NOYB (none of your business), G2G (got to go), POS (parents over shoulder), NBD (no big deal), and ILU (I love you)? How many teenagers know the meaning of the same acronyms (and these are the easy ones)? Parents also need to know that the major Internet service providers, such as AOL, Yahoo!, and Microsoft offer forms of parental controls that allow parents to monitor their children's Internet activities.

Often, school administrators, in an attempt to crack down on electronic bullying and increase parental accountability, require that students present a signed permission slip from their parents before they are allowed to have mobile phones in school. Teachers, in turn, inform students that the use of cell phones during class time is prohibited.

In addition to being reminded to monitor their children's activities on the Internet, parents also require assistance in appropriate intervention strategies if they learn that their children are either engaging in cyberbullying or are being affected by it. Parent-teacher associations have teamed up with local law enforcement agencies to create cyberbullying programs aimed at helping parents and students recognize and deal with the problem of cyberbullying (Slater 2005). Using specially trained police officers (commonly referred to as cybercops) and parent volunteers, these programs emphasize the importance of safe learning environments, while offering factual information regarding the consequences associated with cyberbullying and providing instruction aimed at stopping online harassment and keeping students safe on the Internet (Slater). Parents are encouraged to discuss with their children what is and is not acceptable on the computer.

Today's young Internet users have created an interactive world away from adult knowledge and supervision. A recent study found that only 16 percent of the students surveyed regularly talked with their parents about what they do online (Media Awareness Network 2007). Parents should learn everything they can about the Internet and what their children are doing online (Federal Bureau of Investigation n.d.). At a minimum, parents should develop a family online agreement with their children including where they can go online, what they can do there, how much time they can spend on the Internet, what to do if they receive messages that make them feel uncomfortable, and how to protect their personal information (Keith and Martin 2005).

The students affected by cyberbullying are often embarrassed to approach their parents about the online bullying (Aftab 2005; Barr 2005; Belsey 2004). For this reason, parents should encourage their children to come to them if anybody says or does anything online that makes them feel uncomfortable or threatened. Many cases of Internet bullying go unreported because those being bullied fear they will have their computers taken away or will be barred from using the Internet (Barr). Therefore, rather than overreacting, parents are encouraged to stay calm and keep lines of communication and trust open.

Parents of children who are affected by cyberbullying should notify school officials, even if the bullying is after school. Although there may be little the school administrator can do in terms of direct intervention, there are suggestions they can make to parents. For example, administrators can advise parents to contact the parents of the cyberbully and request that the behavior stop. If this does not stop the harassment, save the harassing messages and forward them to your Internet service provider (e.g., Hotmail or Yahoo!) for action. Most service providers have appropriate use policies that restrict users from harassing others over the Internet. As a last resort, parents may wish to contact an attorney about suing the parents of the bully for defamation, invasion of privacy, and intentional infliction of emotional distress. However, in most instances, cyberbullying does not go that far, although parents often try to pursue criminal charges (WiredKids 2005). Of course, parents should contact the police if there are threats of physical violence, intimidation, extortion, hate crimes, or sexual exploitation. The parents' Internet service provider or cell phone service provider should also be contacted for help in resolving the problem.

Conclusion

Cyberbullying is emerging as one of the most challenging issues facing parents and school personnel as students embrace the Internet and other mobile communication technologies. Believing they are free from attribution, cyberbullies engage in cruel and harmful practices that demean, embarrass, and hurt fellow students without the fear of facing the consequences for their actions. From voting for "The biggest——(add derogatory term) in the school," to sending candid locker room pictures of a person taken with a digital phone camera to others (Willard 2005), electronic bullying has reached a level of seriousness in the schools that demands swift and decisive action. Because the problem occurs in the hidden online world of students and it reaches beyond the school and into the home, it is imperative that school administrators, parents, and community representatives work together to eradicate this twenty-first century form of bullying. By working together to deal with this cruel practice, parents and educators will ensure that all children share a learning environment that is free from harassment and intimidation. School administrators' failure to confront cyberbullying head on is to turn their collective backs on the most insidious aspect of modern technology in the schools.

References

Aftab, P. 2005. Cyberbullying: *A problem that got in under parents' radar.* http://www.aftab.com/cyberbullyingpage.htm (accessed December 6, 2005).

Barr, H. 2005. Online *and out of control: Internet takes teen bullying problem to whole new level.* http://news.newstimes.com/story .php?id=69419&channel=local (accessed March 7, 2005).

Beale, A. V., and P. C. Scott. 2001. "Bullybusters": Using drama to empower students to take a stand against bullying behavior. *Professional School Counseling* 4 (3): 300–5.

Belsey, B. 2005. Cyberbullying.ca. http://www.cyberbullying.ca (accessed September 21, 2005).

Code of Virginia 18.2–152.7:1. 2000. *Harassment by computer: Penalty.* http://legl.state.va.us/cgi-bin/legp504.exe?000+cod+18.2–152.7C1 (accessed October 30, 2005).

Colvin, G., T. Tobin, K. Beard, S. Hagan, and J. Sprague. 1998. The school bully: Assessing the problem, developing interventions, and future research directions. *Journal of Behavioral Education* 8 (3): 292–319.

Federal Bureau of Investigation. n.d. *A parent's guide to Internet safety.* http://www.fbi.gov/publications/pguide/pguidee.htm (accessed February 13, 2006).

Hernandez, T. J., and S. R. Seem. 2004. A safe school climate: A systemic approach and the school counselor. *Professional School Counseling* 7 (4): 256–62.

i-SAFE. 2004. *National i-SAFE survey finds over half of students are being harassed online.* http://www.isafe.org (accessed August 27, 2004).

Joinson, A. N. 1998. Causes and implications of disinhibited behavior on the Internet. In *Psychology and the Internet: Intrapersonal, interpersonal and transpersonal implications,* ed. J. Gackenbach, 43–60. New York: Academic Press.

Keith, S., and M. E. Martin. 2005. Cyber-bullying: Creating a culture of respect in a cyber world. *Reclaiming Children and Youth* 13 (4): 224–28.

Media Awareness Network. 2007. *Challenging cyber bullying.* http://www.mediaawareness.ca/english/resources/special_initiatives/wa_resources/wa_shared/backgrounders/challenge_cyber_bullying.cfm (accessed October 30, 2005).

Migliore, D. 2003. *Bullies torment victims with technology.* http://www.azprevention.org/In_The_News/Newsletters/Newsletters.htm (accessed July 20, 2004).

Nansel, T. R., M. Overpeck, R. S. Pilla, J. Ruan, B. Simons-Morton, and P. Scheidt. 2001. Bullying behaviors among US youth: Prevalence and association with psychosocial adjustment. *Journal of the American Medical Association* 285 (16): 2094–100.

Pellegrini, A. D., and M. Bartini. 2000. A longitudinal study of bullying, victimization, and peer affiliation during the transition from primary school to middle school. *American Educational Research Journal* 37 (3): 699–725.

Slater, S. 2005. *Cyber-bullying targeted.* http://www.clintonnewsrecord.com/story.php?id=141028 (accessed March 7, 2005).

Sparling, P. 2004. Mean machines: New technologies let the neighborhood bully taunt you anywhere, anytime. But you can fight back. *Current Health* 28 (8): 18–20.

Willard, N. 2005. *An educator's guide to cyberbullying and cyberthreats.* http://csriu.org/cyberbullying/pdf (accessed September 24, 2005).

WiredKids. 2005. *A quick guide on the escalating levels of response to a cyberbullying incident.* http://www.stopcyberbullying.org/parents/guide.html (accessed December 6, 2005).

Wollack, J., and K. Mitchell. 2000. *Youth Internet safety survey.* University of New Hampshire, Crimes Against Children Research Center. http://www.unh.edu/ccrc/projects/internet_survey.html (accessed August 27, 2004).

Worthington, M. 2005. *Network of victim assistance.* http://www.novabucks.org/ (accessed September 24, 2005).

ANDREW V. BEALE, EdD, taught counselor education at Virginia Commonwealth University, Richmond, for thirty-seven years before retiring in 2006. He is now teaching there as an emeriti faculty member. Kimberly R. Hall, PhD, is an assistant professor and school counseling program coordinator at Mississippi State University. Copyright © 2007 Heldref Publications

From *The Clearing House,* September/October 2007, pp. 9–12. Reprinted by permission of the Helen Dwight Reid Educational Foundation. Published by Heldref Publications, 1319 Eighteenth St., NW, Washington, DC 20036-1802. Copyright © 2007. www.heldref.org

IOSIE: A Method for Analyzing Student Behavioral Problems

The author argues for a rational method to analyze behavior problems and proposes a method of identifying the problem, the objectives to be achieved, the solution, the implementation, and the evaluation (IOSIE) as a practical approach to assist teachers in resolving most classroom behavior management problems. The approach draws heavily on well-known classroom management strategies and encourages readers to put those into place by using the five-step IOSIE approach. The letters in the term IOSIE represent steps to follow when analyzing acts of classroom misbehavior.

RICHARD T. SCARPACI

A five-step process for looking at and reflecting on solutions for behavioral classroom problems is the method described here. The process requires one to identify causes of misconduct, determine objectives, and propose a solution. Implementation provides an opportunity to evaluate the executed solutions (IOSIE; Figure 1). The first letter of each italicized word indicates the steps to follow when analyzing misbehavior in classrooms. If this procedure is followed, disruption and discipline problems should be lessened in classrooms.

Identifying the Problem

Problem behavior analysis is something all teachers have to master. The procedure is unchanging; one cannot fix what is not recognized as broken. The process is not as simple as it might seem at first. Do not be deceived by appearances or biases when attempting to identify the cause of a problem (Danforth and Boyle 2000). A boy who is arguing with a girl in the classroom may not be the instigator of misbehavior. Children who are talking loudly are not automatically being disruptive; a student who is threatening another student is not necessarily the culprit. Do not jump to false conclusions.

In classrooms a problem only exists if it impinges negatively on learning. If this is the case, the teacher must assess seriousness and weigh the problem's impact on student learning. Acting out behaviors, such as threats, loud talking, arguing, and fighting, are problems that must be addressed immediately, but incomplete assignments, attendance, sloppy work, and lost books, although readily identifiable problems, can wait to be resolved. Another category that must be remedied without delay is incidents such as cheating, slander, theft, safety that involves moral codes, or physical well-being.

Problems concerning withdrawal behaviors such as not paying attention, depression, drugs, and alcohol indicate a desire to flee from reality and must be dealt with expeditiously (Curwin 1997). It should be understood that most misbehavior is caused by frustration, ignorance, conflict, displacement, or misunderstanding rules and procedures. In contrast, the reasons for misbehavior can be identified as a desire to achieve one of four immediate goals: attention, power, revenge, or to avoid failure. In the final analysis the choice as to what constitutes a problem is the teacher's decision (Glasser 1990, 1997; Mager and Piper 1997).

Objectives

Teachers are fortunate when it comes to objectives. In classroom behavioral situations two objectives always remain the same: to facilitate learning and encourage self-discipline (Scarpaci 2007). All other objectives relate directly to identifying problems. Objectives describe, in measurable terms, the behaviors needed to attain the desired results within a specific time frame: for example, Billy will complete all ten incomplete assignments satisfactorily by the end of the semester.

- The "I" represents the first step in the process, to identify and assess the problem.
- The "O" stands for the objectives that you wish to achieve through your intervention.
- The "S" stands for the solution, which should be the result of the plan you put into effect to achieve your objectives.
- The "I" indicates the implementation of your plan and the procedures to be followed by the people who should be involved.
- The acronym concludes with the letter "E" that stands for your evaluation and reflection on results.

Figure 1   IOSIE analysis model.

Objectives are specific statements of a learner's behavior. They are the outcomes one wishes to obtain within a specific time limit. They can also be described as statements that answer two questions: What do I want my students to know? How will I know if my students understand? Good objectives show learners what is expected, how the work will be done, and what the minimum standards are. They are explicit, quantifiable, and achievable; they create an end result that can be met within a specific time frame.

Solutions

One of the keys to the IOSIE process is selection of strategy. The steps are not rigid but should be followed in sequence. The method presumes that there are three generic approaches to solutions for classroom misbehavior: a consequence, group guidance, and a guidance approach. A consequence approach such as assertive discipline (Canter and Canter 1976) implies consequences for improper actions. A group guidance approach such as judicious discipline (Gathercoal 1993) encourages classes to establish rules to prevent inappropriate actions. Finally, in a guidance approach such as reality therapy (Glasser 1999), the teacher counsels the rule offender, encouraging students to take ownership of problems. The purpose of each strategy is to assist students to develop self-discipline and responsibility for their actions. A good strategy must be comprehensive and contain in its design components both preventive and intervention procedures. The ideal is to prevent problems before they occur.

Implementation

The most difficult step is the actual implementation. Putting solutions into action is not simply a "just do it" sequence. Basic questions must be addressed before implementation: Who is to implement the solution? How do you get the cooperation and support of everyone involved? How long do you expect it will take before a positive result is accomplished? What happens if the solution does not work?

The answers to the first two questions are easy when the teacher is the implementer. They only become difficult when support and cooperation of parents, staff, and professionals outside of the school need to be elicited. The answer to the third question depends on the severity of the problem, the objectives set, and the resistance met. The personalities of all involved parties should also be considered. The only way to resolve the final question is to go back to the drawing board and attempt a different approach to the problem. When these four questions are satisfactorily answered a guide to evaluation is created.

Evaluation

Assessment of results is often forgotten, ignored, or done incorrectly by teachers. The easiest way to evaluate is to look at your objectives. Are they specific, measurable, and attainable within a defined time frame? Outcomes are wishes achieved within an explicit period and should be easily recognizable and readily assessable. The basic premise of any evaluation is to determine if you achieved what you set out to achieve. If the success lasts for only a brief time, then the solution was not really appropriate. An example would be a child who no longer fights at lunchtime but fights after school. Obviously something is wrong with this picture. If the results are not positive, the whole process must be reviewed. Was the problem really identified? Were the objectives attainable in the time span anticipated? Was the proposed solution appropriate for the objectives you wished to achieve? Was the implementation done correctly? Are you sure you did not succeed, even partially?

Sample Case Studies

Below are three case studies, one for each of the basic approaches, beginning with a case study that lends itself to a consequence strategy, which might afford positive results if implemented properly.

Consequence Approach

Billy Williams, a seventeen-year-old in your twelfth-grade mathematics class, has been accused in an unsigned note of extorting lunch money from his classmates. Billy has a prior record of supposed misdeeds. One specifically, although never proven, was when he was blamed for the recent rash of drug activity outside the school grounds. Billy's misdeeds have never been proven because no one has stood up and charged Billy with any specific misbehavior. For all intents and purposes, he lives under a cloud of suspicion. There are those who believe that Billy is innocent of any major wrongdoing, but their numbers are few. You have spoken to Billy on numerous occasions with regard to his lack of class work, homework, and general deportment during your class with little or no results. He claims he does not know why everyone thinks he is a criminal, because he has not done anything wrong. When you ask about his homework, he again changes the subject by confiding to you that even the principal has threatened him for no reason. He believes people dislike him because he is African American and therefore make up false rumors.

His classmates as well as most of the student body are in deathly fear of Billy because of his physical size and menacing presence. There is a rumor that he has been in fights after school, yet no one has come forward to point him out for any wrongdoing. A colleague tells you that you also have reason to fear for your own safety. Recently, Ms. Kumar had her tires slashed. Ms. Kumar believes the slashing was retaliation for her failing Billy for the first quarter of the semester. You also had expected to fail Billy before this morning's incident when Billy came to you and explained that he had to pass your class to graduate. He pleaded for you to give him a break and pass him. He said if you did not pass him, his parents would kick him out of their house when he turned eighteen.

IOSIE Analysis Using a Consequence Approach
Identify the Problem

What exactly is the problem in this case? Is it the unsigned note claiming that Billy is extorting money? Is it Billy's prior record of misdeeds? Is it Billy's lack of class work, homework, and poor deportment? Is it Billy's charge of racial bias on the part of those who dislike him? Is it the fights after school or Billy's menacing demeanor? Could it be Ms. Kumar's belief that you are in danger because she thinks Billy slashed her tires for failing him during the first quarter? Or could it be the problem Billy presented to you this morning when he said his parents would throw him out of their house if he did not graduate?

You can see that it is not always easy to determine the problem in any given situation. There are usually a number of problems. Look at the potential problems we identified and place them in some type of priority order to better understand the case. A prior record of unproven misdeeds and unsigned accusations should go to the bottom of any list of potential problems. Rumors regarding one's behavior outside of school are usually just gossip and unconfirmed. Billy's size and someone's unfounded accusation regarding slashed tires are not your problems. Billy's belief that he is the butt of racial prejudice is certainly a concern. It is not necessarily a problem that you face with him, because he has confided in you. Billy's academic performance and poor deportment are the immediate problem that you face. His feelings regarding prejudice should also be addressed as a long-term problem.

Objectives

Once the problem has been identified you have to determine your objectives. What is it exactly that you want Billy to do? Based on your identification of the problem, it would appear that you would expect Billy to improve his academic performance and his general behavior in your class for the remainder of the school term. With regard to his personal feelings with "racial bias," you should refer Billy to the appropriate support personnel within your school. This would usually be the school guidance counselor or school psychologist. If these personnel are not available the principal should be notified and outside assistance could also be sought.

Solutions

The solution to this problem should go back to how you can most easily achieve your objective. It would appear that Billy himself handed the answer to this dilemma to you. He gave you a consequence he did not wish to face. He was fearful of being thrown out of his parents' house. This consequence must be corroborated to implement your solution.

Implementation

Once you have confirmed with his parents that they have spoken to Billy and learned exactly what they had told him, you are than ready to implement your solution for your immediate problem of getting Billy to improve academically and behaviorally. Although the consequence is outside of your control, you should offer to assist Billy in avoiding the consequence. Provide tutorial assistance and counsel him on exactly the way you expect him to behave in your class. You should also arrange with the guidance counselor for Billy to be counseled regarding his feelings of prejudice.

Evaluation

Your self-assessment of the results in this case study should be easy to recognize. Did you achieve what you set out to do in the time frame you set up? Did Billy's academic performance and behavior improve incrementally by the end of the term as a result of the consequence with which he was faced? It is important to remember that there should be interim evaluations prior to the final assessment. This affords you the opportunity to fine-tune your solution or change direction if it is not working. If the answer to the prior question of his academic success was yes, congratulations, your solution worked. If the answer was no, then you should go back to your solution and attempt a different approach.

Sample Case Study
Guidance Approach

Sara Ramirez, a thirteen-year-old girl in your eighth-grade social studies class, places her coat and books wherever she chooses, totally disregarding the comfort of her fellow classmates. Students have complained to you but seem to be fearful of addressing Sara directly. Sara comes from a privileged one-parent family in which she has always been the apple of her father's eye. Sara stays with her elderly grandmother when her father is away on business trips, which seems to be most of the time. Sara boasts that she can come and go as she pleases. Sara's mother is fighting for custody, but she is having a difficult time because of her prior drug and mental health issues.

Sara is an average student with definite adolescent tendencies. She is physically mature for her age, dressing way beyond her years, yet at times she acts like a child. She constantly discards her refuse by placing it on a neighbor's desk when she believes no one is looking or throwing it on the floor when they are looking. She is the first to push her way into the wardrobe at dismissal to retrieve her coat. She likes to push other students' chairs about the room thereby creating obstructions so that her classmates have difficulty finding their seats. Sara constantly laughs at the discomfort she creates for her classmates. She teases the boys, and then complains that they are bothering her. During class she is always calling out and gets angry when she is not called on. As a result her class work has deteriorated. You have spoken to her and warned her that her grade would suffer if she continues being disruptive in class. Sara, in true adolescent fashion, "yeses" you to death and continues to misbehave.

IOSIE Analysis Using a Guidance Approach
Identify the Problem

Is the problem Sara's apparent disregard for her classmates? Is it that she appears to be a physically mature child with less than adequate supervision? Is her grandmother too old and her father too distant? Is she reacting to her mother's attempt to gain custody? Could she just be a mean-spirited child, or are there deeper meanings for her antisocial behavior? Is the real problem the deterioration of her grades?

Again, this case study is overburdened with potential problems. Remember this child's specific actions—throwing papers, pushing, teasing the boys, laughing at others, and calling out—are really not the problem but indications that there is a problem. How do you identify the problems that you wish to address? The key is to prioritize. What is the first role of a teacher? Is it to see that her students are learning? In this case Sara's grades have fallen so her academic needs must be considered. Sara's family life seems to be unstable and uncontrollable. Emotional problems are rampant throughout this case description. Therefore, her immediate problem is to improve her grades. The question is how you attempt to do that while this child is facing so many emotional problems at home that are manifesting themselves in her actions at school.

Objectives

Your objectives are in two interrelated areas: improvement of academic standing and emotional well-being. Your objective should be to have Sara improve her grades before the end of the marking period. A second and concomitant objective should be to help guide Sara through the emotional upheaval in her young life.

Solutions

The objectives are easy to establish, but the resolution for Sara may be much more difficult. A guidance approach on your part requires a caring positive relationship with the child. You may want to have a private heart-to-heart in which you encourage Sara to confide in you. You should also explain to Sara that her grades are a major part of her life and must improve. The reason for this is that if Sara could get guidance she could learn to deal with her family environment, which would allow her to work at improving her grades. Her disruptive behavior and antisocial actions in class should stop of their own accord. Once Sara accepts responsibility for her actions and understands that she cannot necessarily change the actions of others, she will be on the path to understanding her problems. Once she understands that she is responsible for choosing her own behavior, she will be better able to deal with the problems she faces.

Implementation

In this case study the implementation is much more difficult than it was in the previous study. In this situation the teacher is expected to assume the role of guide and mentor. These are roles for whom not all are suited. Even if you were suited, the time needed would take away from your primary classroom duties. You would therefore have to seek the assistance of the guidance counselor and involve the family. Most likely the counselor would suggest family counseling as well as individual sessions with Sara. Your role would remain as guide and mentor, yet your actual functions are lessened.

Evaluation

When using a guidance approach, assessment of objectives should be ongoing. Emotional problems can be easily inflamed, especially when parents are fighting over custody. Your evaluation of success should be focused on her academic studies and classroom behavior. The counselor should keep you informed as to the steps she is taking with the child and family. The same cooperation and communication must be established with any outside counseling that might occur. In this case a positive report card would indicate movement in the proper direction.

Sample Case Study
Group-Guidance Approach

Third-grade student Abdul Hussein cries continually during your class. He complains that everyone is picking on him because of his religious beliefs and because he is Arabic. Abdul's behavior has gone from being cooperative, practically docile, to sulking and at times raging at his classmates. Recently Abdul's class work has gone from exceptional to abysmal. You have never seen any of the incidents even though they have been graphically described by Abdul and just as vocally denied by his classmates. The incidents described consist of stolen or spoiled lunches, torn textbook pages, missing homework, and obscene drawings in Abdul's notebooks. Abdul further claims that the other children claim he is responsible for 9/11. Abdul cries when he tells you that his uncle was killed in the World Trade Center while working. He implies that the children call him a liar and they blaspheme his faith. Abdul's parents have complained to you and request that you do something to stop the harassment of their son.

The president of the parents' association, whose son is also in your class, claims that her child thinks Abdul is a compulsive liar and is just acting the way he does to get your attention. She also claims that someone has been destroying other children's property in the class. She believes it is Abdul. Other parents of children in the class concur with the parents' association president. The situation comes to a head when you see the children fighting in the schoolyard at lunchtime. The children claim that Abdul attacked them when they said they would not play with him. He spit at them and called them dirty names.

IOSIE Analysis Using a Group-Guidance Approach
Identify the Problem

Is the problem Abdul's constant crying and whining during class time? Is it the charges of bias toward Abdul's religion and ethnicity? Is it the multitude of incidents in which Abdul's property has been despoiled? Or is it Abdul's academic performance? In this case study there seems to be a clear link between Abdul's academic performance and the incidents, real or imaginary, that have occurred recently. These incidents appear to have been motivated by group racial bias. In this case there are three distinct and interrelated problems that must be addressed: academic performance, racial and religious issues, and physical incidents of misbehavior.

Objectives

Your first objective is to have Abdul return to doing his superior academic work, while simultaneously educating the class with regard to racial and religious bias as well as eliminating incidents of violence and vandalism. If the first two objectives are achieved, the incidents will also end. The physical episodes are a direct result of the apparent racial intolerance that seems to have infected the class.

Solutions

The solution is based on dealing with the question of group tolerance. Guide the class to solve the problem by using a group guidance exercise. Prepare the class by having them read a children's version of *The Diary of Anne Frank* at home with their parents. Read it aloud to the class during a block of instructional time set aside specifically for this purpose. The project requires dividing the class into two subgroups by drawing straws out of a hat. The groups consist of those with red circles and those with green circles, which the children must prominently display on their clothing. The children with the red circles are to make all of the class rules, which must be obeyed by all green circle children. Focus the class by establishing the first three rules:

1. Green-circle children must never line up before a red-circle child at entrance, dismissal, or lunchtime; they must always walk at the back of the line.
2. Green-circle children must keep their heads lower than red-circle children at all times and never look them in the eyes.
3. In any discussion between circle children, the red-circle children will always be considered correct.

The class at the end of the experiment (no more than two days) will evaluate the impact and the result of creating an intolerant society in which there are rulers and second-class citizens. They will be asked to describe their feelings with regard to injustice and intolerance.

Implementation

To implement a scenario as described above takes the cooperation and support of parents, administration, and various mental health providers. The purpose of the exercise should be explained to parents, and be supported by the school administration. Mental health providers such as the school guidance counselor, school psychologist, and outside defamation organizations should be involved.

Evaluation

Assessments when dealing with mental health problems can only be made by evaluating the end product. What did the children describe as their feelings? Did the class want to continue the project? Have the incidents stopped and has Abdul stopped crying, and been allowed to rejoin the class? If the exercise achieves all of its objectives, it is a success.

It should be noted that a group-guidance approach is froth with potential for manipulation (Landau 2000). It is not necessary to be objective when dealing with a situation as described in this case. One should realize, however, that as human beings we do not see resolutions through the same perspective. Children must be given the opportunity to develop their critical-thinking abilities if we are to truly function as a democratic society. A democratic classroom is the single best precursor for a free and democratic nation.

Conclusion

The IOSIE management model is essentially a common sense way for analyzing student behavioral problems. It is a user-friendly approach that provides a framework for teachers to use in resolving the multitude of management problems faced every day. The mnemonic IOSIE applied properly acts as a rubric for guiding teacher actions needed to resolve student behavioral problems. The method provides teachers a strategy to analyze and resolve common, and some not so common, behavioral problems.

References

Canter, L., and M. Canter. 1976. *Assertive discipline: A take charge approach for today's educator.* Seal Beach, CA: Canter and Associates.

Curwin, R. 1997. Discipline with dignity: Beyond obedience. *Education Digest.* December 11–14.

Danforth, S., and J. R. Boyle. 2000. *Cases in behavior management.* Upper Saddle River, NJ: Merrill/Prentice Hall.

Gathercoal, P. 1993. *Judicious discipline.* 3rd ed. San Francisco: Caddo Gap.

Glasser, W. 1990. *The quality school.* New York: Harper and Row.

———. 1997. A new look at school failure and school success. *Phi Delta Kappan* 78:596-602.

——— 1999. *Choice theory: A new psychology of personnel freedom.* New York: Harper Collins.

Landau, B., and P. Gathercoal. 2000. Creating peaceful classrooms: Judicious discipline and class meetings. *Phi Delta Kappan* 81:450–54.

Mager, F. R., and P. Piper. 1997. *Analyzing performance problems: Or you really oughta wanna.* 3rd ed. Atlanta: Center for Effective Performance.

Scarpaci, R. 2007. *A case study approach to classroom management.* New York: Allyn and Bacon.

RICHARD T. SCARPACI is an assistant professor and director of Field Experiences at St. John's University Staten Island campus, New York. He has taught courses in management and methods as well as conducted Child Abuse and Violence Prevention Seminars.

From *The Clearing House,* January/February 2007, pp. 111–116. Reprinted by permission of the Helen Dwight Reid Educational Foundation. Published by Heldref Publications, 1319 Eighteenth St., NW, Washington, DC 20036-1802. Copyright © 2007. www.heldref.org

Middle School Students Talk about Social Forces in the Classroom

Kathleen Cushman and Laura Rogers

The social world of young adolescents comes into the classroom with them. It can cause kids to sit with blank or glum faces while you present your most fascinating assignments. It can drive them to make inappropriate comments at moments that should elicit serious thought. Although we tend to think of middle schoolers as risk-takers, they do not take risks in classrooms. Instead, they are worrying about where they stand in relation to others.

Adolescence brings with it this new power: One can consider how others think about oneself. This development not only allows for more mature social interactions, but may also produce the intense self-consciousness sometimes referred to as "adolescent egocentrism" (Elkind, 1967). Suddenly, what a child imagines that everyone else is thinking infuses each choice he or she makes in the classroom. At the same time, as Elkind noted, young adolescents do not yet accurately distinguish between their internal imaginary audience and the actual perceptions of their friends. They may swing rapidly from an intense desire for privacy to an equally audacious desire for attention. This tension is just one of many that young adolescents experience, and act out, during this period of rapid physical, cognitive, and psychological change.

The new cognitive competencies of adolescence influence social relationships in myriad ways. Students' motivation to succeed academically may become overshadowed by their desire to succeed socially. They become more alert to their standing—both in relation to other students and in the eyes of their teachers—and they begin to doubt themselves and the whole enterprise of schooling (Kagan, 1972). Adolescents are now increasingly aware of the evaluative attributes that influence their social standing (intelligence, athletic prowess, courage, musical talent, personal flair, and so on). As they become more socially aware, Kagan speculated in his characteristically understated way, those who are not at the top of the class find that their "motivation for geometry may descend in the hierarchy" of motives (p. 100). He urged schools to consider how their practices may undermine young adolescents just as they are ready to meet new challenges.

Studies consistently prove Kagan right. Adolescents tend to lose confidence in their academic abilities in the transition to middle school and find social activities more interesting and more important than academic endeavors, as Wigfield and Eccles (1994) have shown. Because of the way schools are organized, these authors noted, middle grades teachers are also less likely to know their students well and to trust them. Consequently, they expect less of students and are less

likely to create opportunities to listen to them or to offer them choices and opportunities for decision making and social interaction.

Teachers in the middle grades could spend all their time trying to resist these social forces. However, if they can figure out just what concerns their students are dealing with, they might put these currents in their classrooms to good use, rather than working against them. In a single classroom, students in the middle grades will express many points of view reflecting their developmental accomplishments and differences (Kegan, 1982). They tend to be passionate about matters of justice and fairness, and they are acutely sensitive to how their teachers express care for them. They may think about issues of fairness according to a concrete, reciprocal exchange schema, or they may be beginning to shift toward shared social norms and expectations in their assessment of "the right thing to do" (Kohlberg, 1984). In their social relationships, they are learning new strategies for negotiating conflict and agreement. They are becoming adept at reciprocal interaction and cooperation, and they are just learning to collaborate to achieve mutually defined goals (Selman, 1980, 2003). They are seeking opportunities to practice social interactions. In fact, research has consistently shown that when students have the opportunity to collaborate, they are more likely to focus on learning, are more interested in the subject matter, and feel less anxious (Pintrich, Roeser, & DeGroot, 1994; Willis, 2007).

As teachers help students navigate their uncertainties, learners will become more engaged, adventurous, and willing to take risks in their academic experiences. As teachers tune in to the issues of fairness that loom large for students, they are better able to resolve some of the conflicts that keep them from learning. Any subject in the middle grades will be enlivened when you deliberately weave social learning into the curriculum and support students' engagement with each other (Schnuit, 2006).

At the request of the MetLife Foundation, over several months in 2005 we asked students from around the country to describe what might stand in the way of their enthusiastic response to the academic opportunities their teachers set forth for them. After consulting with approximately 20 middle grades teachers working in urban schools who had gathered at a conference on learning in the middle grades, Kathleen Cushman framed 65 questions. The questions centered on academic, social, physical, and emotional matters, probing for issues that young adolescents saw as interfering with a positive school experience and for ways that students thought teachers could help them with such issues.

By calling on the extensive network of the nonprofit organization What Kids Can Do (WKCD), Cushman identified 42 middle grades students in five urban areas, including schools configured as grades K–8, 6–8, and 7–8. Of these students, 38 attended public schools, one went to a parochial school, and three attended independent schools. None came from backgrounds of economic privilege, and 35 were students of color. Most came not via their schools but through youth development settings: a New York City neighborhood organization (two students); a "bridge" program, preparing students for high school (eight Providence students and nine San Francisco students); and an after-school community arts center in Middletown, Connecticut (eight students). Of the 42 students, 15 were new ninth graders from two Indianapolis high schools, interviewed specifically about their recent transition from middle school. Seven were interviewed in the summer after they completed sixth grade, six after they completed seventh grade, seven in the early fall of seventh grade, and three in the early fall of eighth grade.

Interviews took place in small groups of two to eight students, with two or three sessions, each lasting two to three hours. Cushman facilitated these tape-recorded discussions, which were later transcribed in their entirety. As with most collaborators on What Kids Can Do books, students were paid for their time (in this case, $7 per hour). Parents or guardians granted permission for the students to participate and for WKCD to publish their actual first names and photographs in published work resulting from their interviews.

As we pored over their eloquent and sometimes poignant answers to questions about life in the classroom, we heard them making six crucial requests of their teachers:

- Help us find common ground with each other.
- Teach us how to work together in safe, collaborative groups.
- Let us practice working out issues that affect the class.
- Treat us all with the same respect.
- Let us tackle problems that help develop our ideas about what is fair.
- Watch closely what is really going on with us, inside and outside the classroom.

In the following pages, we present the responses of 21 of these students, as they describe what they notice, what they care about, and what their teachers do and do not do that affects how it feels to learn, work, and be in school.

What's Going on with Us?

Many middle school students are aware of the competing expectations of their teachers and their peers in the classroom. They may feel pulled in different directions at different times.

We Don't Want to Act Too Good

Middle school kids do recognize what a good student looks like to the teacher:

> The typical good kids stay in a line when the teacher's walking [with them]. When the teacher's out of the room, they continue doing their work. They're full of ideas, they're always raising their hand instead of just sitting there and waiting for someone to have their hand up. They do pretty good on their work, and they hand in their homework all the time.
>
> —Genesis

But their social norms may make it hard for them to want to adopt that image as their own.

> They don't want to be embarrassed by being goody-goodies in school, and so they try to act up just to get approval from the other kids at school. Sometimes, some kids will go through physical torture, like getting in fights at school, just to fit in with the other kids. It makes no sense at all.
>
> —Daquan

When you ask boys and girls to work with each other in class or help each other out, they may be uncomfortably aware that other kids will start pairing them up romantically.

> In my fourth period class, this girl was sitting a couple of seats behind me. She was in my third period pre-algebra class too, and she came up and started asking me did I remember what we had for homework. So, she sat down, and I started telling her so she could write it down. Her friends, they were calling her, and she was like, "Wait a minute, wait a minute." After, they started yelling things: "Oh, you like him." And she was like, "No, I don't! I'm just asking him what the homework was." And they said, "You don't have to hide it," and all this other stuff. It made me feel, like, nervous and embarrassed.
>
> —Denue

They are often very confused, themselves, about their motives when they interact with the opposite sex.

> I think it's different with girls and boys. Girls sometimes get, like, harassed, or people make judgments about them. Because, I don't know, boys just can't control their hormones or something. So, they make fun of girls, and they start saying inappropriate stuff. Maybe it's because they like the girl. They just like picking on people. And the girls might not like what they hear, but they might not want to go to anyone, because they might not feel safe.
>
> —Kenson

They are counting on teachers to know—even if *they* do not know—when they need help. The way a teacher reacts can send a clear message about what is considered sexual harassment and what is simply exploring how to interact socially.

> The girls, they're always bothering the boys, and the boys are always bothering the girls, and the teacher knows that it's just for fun. But one kid, he was bothering this girl. I saw the teacher knew that she didn't like it, so he told the boy to stop it.
>
> —Jason

Being Different Hurts

In the middle school years, students' appearances and capabilities vary even more widely than at other ages. Young adolescents are painfully aware of this.

> There's this girl at my school, and nobody likes her because she smells like she takes a shower once upon a Christmas. The teachers can't make you be friends with her or any other person. You choose who you want to be friends with. You wouldn't want to be caught hanging around that person, because they would think you took a shower once upon a Christmas.
>
> —Daquan

I'm not saying I'm perfect or anything, but sometimes kids like to hate on people, and I'm one person to hate on—I stutter.
—Eric Q.

Students with limited English or students with disabilities face additional hurdles to being included.

There's this girl at my school, she speaks French. So it's like, people actually think she's stupid in a way—the students use her as a clown. They go, "What? Can you say that again?" The teachers, I think they notice it, but they feel they can't control the kids.
—Amelia

I can't read, and that's not my fault. God made me the way he wanted to make me. Did I ask God to do that? I don't think people should pick on me just "cause I can't read. They come up to me, and they be like, "Read this word for me, I can't read it." I'll be like, "You know I can't read, can you get out of my face please?" They'll be like, "Too bad. I forgot you stupid, and you in that retarded class." And I be getting mad, and I want to punch them and stuff.
—Amanda

It is all too easy for students to maintain a connection to their friends by ostracizing someone who is different. Still, kids do not necessarily want to be heartless. Even when they do not speak out about someone's exclusion, they often sympathize.

I don't think it matters, just the way somebody smells or something. The way they smell doesn't mean the kind of person they are. Maybe you [could] just tell them, in a respectful way, "Maybe you should try showering more." Maybe you should try to be their friend.
—Javier

People think about themselves that they're too fat, too thin, too stupid, and they think that people are going to notice whatever they're insecure about. I think that it's just in their mind. I think people should just think positive about themselves, not think in a negative way, and that might help them a little.
—Daniel

Help Us Find Common Ground

Over the course of a year, a teacher will have plenty of opportunities to help middle grades students grow in confidence and reach out to others in positive ways. Students want to know how to find common ground, without sacrificing their own individuality and emerging style. School provides a context in which they can learn about themselves and their classmates, accepting and respecting their strengths and differences.

Faced with the disparities among students, teachers can offer them ways to bridge their differences and discover what each has to offer.

Teachers can try to find out what the kids have in common, [and have them] discuss what they have in common, [so they can] use that to get closer to each other as friends.
—Daquan

It's good to see how you have something in common with a lot of other kids. Maybe, you all tell about an embarrassing

moment, and then you're recognizing that everybody has gone through an embarrassing moment. Or a fear most kids might have. And afterwards, you're, "Oh, that happened to me once."
—Genesis

At the beginning of this year, the teachers made all of us act silly in front of each other. When we're playing games, we're all acting silly and everyone is laughing at each other. You can see other people doing it—not just one person. We played the game "Zip, Zap." One person stands in the middle and says, "zip." The person he says "zip" to has to duck, and the two people shoot each other and say "zap." And we all start laughing if we duck, or if we miss it and get in the middle.
—Javier

Having broken the ice, kids will keep up the process on their own.

This year, I met this kid, and we were talking about baseball, about the Yankees and the Red Sox, and another kid jumped in and started saying how the Red Sox were going to win. And then we started arguing and playing and from that moment on, we always hanged out.
—Denue

In organizing academic work for your class, you can also encourage these connections to develop.

Instead of just having kids do individual work, do more group activities. Because in my room, there's only some people who talk to some people. There are, like, groups. Everybody grew up together, but still, we don't talk to each other as much as you would think, [even though] we've known each other for years.
—Kenson

There's only a small amount a teacher can do, because it's really up to the kids. But if there's a project, she could try to pair up people who really don't talk to each other, don't respect each other. And they could actually learn to become friends and respect each other, knowing they're both being their selves in a way they both can relate to.
—Javier

As teachers get a clearer picture of what is going on among students socially, they will find opportunities to help their students safely connect to each other.

As teachers get a clearer picture of what is going on among students socially, they will find opportunities to help their students safely connect to each other in new and important ways. Just as students are sorting out the ways they want to behave, teachers will be sorting what kind of responses to make to them.

We Care That You're Fair

In matters of their behavior, middle school students often hold a different perspective about what is fair than their teacher does. You can show students that they have an important part in working things out fairly. As a start, you might ask for their thoughts on what is desirable in the classroom, perhaps with questions like these:

- What does it look like when a student shows respect for another student?
- What does it look like when a teacher shows respect for a student?
- What does it look like when a student shows respect for a teacher?
- What can other people do to make it feel safe to speak up when you disagree with another student in class?
- What makes it feel safe to say you don't know the answer?
- What can other people do to make it safe to speak up when you do know the answer?

Make Us Part of the Conversation

Many teachers of the middle grades start the year by establishing norms of behavior on which everyone agrees. Having students collaborate in setting the expectations can be a powerful process.

> The third week, our teacher decided to let the kids make up their own rules that we would follow by ourselves. It's the whole seventh-grade contract, we did it together as a community, because we didn't want the same old school rules that we had last year. Right now, it's working good. We each get a contract with the rules, to make sure we're following them. We judge ourselves every day, and we are honest; if we really know that we didn't do well, we put a "no." If we do something bad, it comes back on the person who messed up. If we are following it, we put down a "yes" or a check. On Friday, at advisory, they check it.
>
> —Jessica

But not all kids will be ready at once to start putting the group's needs before their individual desires. Simply creating classroom norms, as Jessica notes, does not guarantee compliance. As behavior issues come up, you will need to keep referring back to the classroom norms.

> My history teacher this year in eighth grade, she said some kids were eating in her class. She was like, "Oh, every time somebody breaks the rule, I'm going to refer back to the rules that's on the wall." She kept running down the list, the rules, and then kids stopped.
>
> —Kenson

Even when kids want to cooperate in meeting the needs of the class, they may find it difficult to do so. Their attention naturally goes to other things going on around them, and when the teacher is talking to the whole group, they may not hear you.

> Our teacher tells everybody but me and my friend when our class has to leave from lunch for upstairs. So, we get in trouble when we get back to class, and then we have to walk upstairs every day with her. I try to say, "How come you don't tell us?"
>
> —Katelin

Students want to work with you to find solutions to recurring problems, and they often have ideas that are worth considering. When you agree to try out the things they suggest, you also set the stage for future collaborative problem solving.

> When one person goes to the bathroom, then more people will want to go. After a while, when you ask the teacher,

she's going to say "no," 'cause she thinks that you're going to be playing around. And then it will happen to someone who really needs to go to the bathroom. They should just say, "Everyone go at once and come back."
>
> —Edward

Fairness issues also show up in the academic context. For example, if you ignore what students have to say in class, they feel dismissed.

> My teacher will get us interested in a topic, and we'll all be raising our hands and wanting to say something about it. But he only picks on two people to say something, and then he goes into a different thing. I usually call out, because I'm dying to get this comment out, and then the teacher's like, "You're supposed to raise your hand." How am I supposed to raise my hand, if you're not picking me at all? I feel like he doesn't really care what we have to say. He just wants to get over with the day.
>
> —Genesis

Setting norms together for classroom discourse creates a process that kids can trust when they want their voices heard (See Figure 1 for an exercise that can help a teacher better understand students' ideas of fairness).

> They could write names on the board and go in that order. I was in English class, and I had my hand up for 30 minutes, after the teacher told me I was next. She was picking other kids, and then she looked straight at me and just picked somebody else.
>
> —Javier

> For class discussions, we have a ball you throw to someone, and nobody talks if they don't have the ball. It keeps everybody quiet, because you don't want anybody talking when *you* have the ball.
>
> —Amelia

Treat Us All with the Same Respect

Students are more likely to trust a teacher to be fair if he or she knows who individual students are and what matters most to them.

> Many times, the kids who behave good in school, teachers don't know them that much. You have to do something bad so the teachers will know your name—so the teachers will think you're somebody.
>
> —Amelia

On the other hand, nobody likes it when the teacher picks someone out for special treatment.

> Teachers let that favored student do more, even if it's just like a little thing like moving up in the room, or leaving when you want to. As much as students say, "I don't care," they know deep inside that they care.
>
> —Heather

> The band teacher favored this really good clarinet player. It made me feel angry, like I wasn't important to the band, or they don't need me, and I should just quit. Instead of bringing up one person and leaving behind 61, she could have treated everyone the same.
>
> —Daniel

Students in the middle grades vary widely in their ideas about fairness and social responsibility. Some kids still see a dilemma solely from their own point of view. Others have begun to balance competing claims and perspectives. Still others have reached the point where they appeal to a social norm to decide what's fair to all.

At any point in the school year, you can gain insight into the spectrum of how students in your class think about fairness by presenting a dilemma for them to discuss, then noticing what kinds of answers students give and how they share their ideas about working out agreements.

You can use dilemmas that emerge directly from your class experiences, like this one on eating in the classroom:

—*Should we allow eating in the classroom?*

—*If we do, and some students do not clean up after themselves, what should we do:*

- *Suspend the privilege of eating?*
- *Ask the whole class to clean up their mess?*

—*Who is responsible for keeping the class clean—students, teacher, or janitors?*

You might also use dilemmas from your curriculum. For example, you could present choices made by historical or scientific figures, or by fictional characters, in order to achieve a goal or outcome that had negative consequences for someone else. Ask students:

—*What decision was made?*

—*Was it fair? To whom was it fair?*

—*Who might have thought it wasn't fair? What other decision could that person have made? Would it have been more fair? To whom? Why?*

For every action students suggest, make sure to ask them to explain clearly why it seems fair to them. Make clear to them that no one right answer exists, and encourage them to share their opinions, even when they disagree with others.

At the end of the discussion, ask students to help you summarize the discussion:

What things does the class agree about?

_____

_____

_____

What things does the class disagree about?

_____

_____

_____

After such a discussion, a teacher might reflect on what it reveals about how individual students think about fairness. Answering the questions below could help you later, when other issues of fairness come up in class.

Which students took an individual point of view and had trouble thinking about fairness from multiple perspectives?

_____

_____

_____

Which students thought of fairness in terms of a tit-for-tat reciprocity of benefits and injuries?

_____

_____

_____

Which students appealed to social norms of leadership, generosity, responsibility, promises made or broken, group loyalties?

_____

_____

_____

Now think about the students as a group. Which reasons seemed to sway the class more than others?

_____

_____

_____

Figure 1   What's fair from a student's standpoint? An exercise for teachers.

Students may easily—and sometimes accurately—conclude that teachers discriminate against kids based on their race and ethnicity.

> I had this person in my honors classes, he was the only African-American in our class, and he was really funny, he was a nice person to be around. But he jumped around a lot, I guess, and you could kind of tell that these two teachers hated him. When he raised his hand, they would ignore him. I would say that they were disrespecting him because of his race. I think it was a factor.
>
> —Daniel

> I think my teacher was racist of black people. The whole year she was mean to me, wasn't letting me go to the bathroom. When everybody else asked, she would give them a pass: "Be right back." But if I asked: "No! You can't go!" How's that sound?
>
> —Katelin

> Today at lunch, a white boy was sitting at a table where he wasn't supposed to, "cause we are supposed to sit with our class. And, he said that black people are ignorant. We told the vice principal, and he came over and said, 'Just leave it alone.' If it was us, he would have said what he says to everybody: 'Pick up your tray and come to the office.'"
>
> —Thea

Itai's teacher made it clear to the class that all students mattered to her equally, even though her reactions to them might vary from time to time.

> She cared about everyone. And she didn't stereotype; she always said that she wouldn't be biased towards anyone. When she was grading a test, she would always cover up the names and just mark what they didn't get, because she felt that if she wasn't proud of that student that day, maybe she would give them a lower mark.
>
> —Itai

Guard Our Right to a Fair Decision

Whether students are acting within the limits or outside them, everyone is closely watching how teachers respond. Students will draw their own conclusions as to how fair a teacher is.

> My math teacher, it's like he's trying to please the kids that are bad. There's this girl, she doesn't do any of her work, but he lets her get out of the class at any time. He's afraid of getting cussed. But the good kids, he doesn't let them. It's like he's punishing them for being good.
>
> —Amelia

Middle school students also have a sharp eye for teachers who respond to students on the basis of race, ethnicity, or socioeconomic status.

> Teachers should treat all students the same, no matter what color they are or how they do in school. But some teachers treat black students different. At my school, they say a whole bunch of bad stuff about us. And, when a student goes to tell the principal, the principal believes the teacher over the student, if it's someone who doesn't do that well in school.
>
> —Tatzi

Listening well to any such complaints and talking openly with the group about issues of bias and privilege can help us unearth and address entrenched attitudes that hold back students from the conviction that they can learn and taking advantage of the opportunity to do so.

Hold Us to the Norms We Agreed On

When a teacher needs to make the call about what is fair, it helps to refer back to the behavior norms the class earlier helped to shape. If students also have had input into the consequences when someone departs from those agreements, teacher decisions are less likely to seem arbitrary or unfair to them.

Students appreciate it when teachers find humor in their breaches of good conduct, even as they correct them.

> When people swear, I've heard my gym teacher say, "Do you kiss your mother with that mouth?" People laugh, but it makes people understand how they're acting.
>
> —Kenson

Many issues of fairness require balancing the rights of the individual with the rights of the group. Students pointed out certain key areas in which this particularly matters to them.

Punishing everybody for what one person does. Most middle school kids hate it when the whole class gets blamed for what only some of them have done—no matter how clearly you may try to justify such an approach.

> They're trying to say, "The whole class has to take the punishment, because we're all in this together." Well, for me, it's not fair.
>
> —Genesis

On the other hand, they may not know exactly what's fair when a teacher does not know who is responsible for the unacceptable behavior.

> I guess, obviously, then we all gonna have detention or something like that. But they should ask, or people should tell them, or something. Don't punish the whole class. But if you have to, I guess you're gonna have to do what you gotta do.
>
> —Thea

Cleaning up after other people. In the world of young children, people only have to clean up their own messes. Many middle schoolers may not yet see a shared responsibility to maintain the space their group uses for learning.

> If we made the mess, or we didn't, my Spanish teacher makes us pick up papers before we leave his class. He makes you clean the spot that you are sitting at. So, if someone threw a paper next to your desk, or if anyone threw a paper at your desk, you'll end up cleaning up. I don't think that's fair. We didn't put it there.
>
> —Amelia

> I think that the teacher should make kids clean after every period. It's their mess that they made. Nobody else should be responsible for cleaning it up. If you come into that classroom, and you share that seat, the teacher might think that you made the mess.
>
> —Denue

As teachers create opportunities for students to collaborate in the classroom, they will learn the value of teamwork. With time and practice, their role in the group will start to matter more to them, and this will extend to how they see themselves in the larger school community.

Coming to class on time. Tardiness also challenges teachers to help kids see themselves as members of a group in which their presence matters. Conventional consequences like detention can have some effect, but they reinforce students' perceptions that being late is a personal issue, not a group one.

> I'm not saying you have to threaten kids for them to show up on time for school. But my teacher gave me a detention because I was late three times. And that showed me. I didn't want another detention. I just showed up on time every day.
>
> —Javier

> I think they should give us more time to get to class. Sometimes kids have to use the bathroom, and they don't get out by the time they're supposed to be there. And most teachers don't take excuses. You're trying to explain to them, and they're like: "I don't care. You're late for my class, you get a detention."
>
> —Genesis

Motivating students to show up on time for what is going to happen in class tends to work much better in preventing tardiness.

> Teachers should do something good at the beginning of class to make kids want to come early. My teacher does the boring stuff first, and then he gives kids time to relax. So, most kids don't really care when they come late, and when you give them detention, they don't really care either. [In another class], at the beginning of class, we did this game to warm us up, like, if you answer some question, you get a prize. So, kids came, because you wouldn't want to miss the beginning of class.
>
> —Amelia

Here again, many teachers find that humor works well. Javier and Amelia describe an effective song-and-dance ritual, used at their summer program whenever someone arrives late to the morning meeting.

> They just stop the whole lesson and start singing: "Pop, pop, fizz, fizz, pop, pop, fizz, fizz. Check him out, check-check him out. Check him out, Check-check him out." And then—say I was late—I would have to say, "My name is Alex." And then they would say, "And that's no lie, check." And I would go, "Pop, pop, fizz, fizz," and they say, "Mm-mmm, how sweet it is." It works—you don't want to show up late, because people are going to make you do that dance. Because it is a little embarrassing to shake your booty or something. It doesn't feel *really* bad, it's better than that, but it's something that you don't want to get. And it's good, because the teachers get it too, if they're late. It happens a lot.
>
> —Javier

> It's like they're laughing with you, but they're laughing at you, too. And some people don't want to do it, so they just come early so they don't have to do the dance.
>
> —Amelia

Amelia and Javier's teachers have established this playful embarrassment as a norm of classroom life, which helps students consciously experience a kind of physical metaphor for the disruption they cause to the group when they show up late. Other activities might bring them along to a point where they identify even more with the group's needs and priorities.

> We were separated into groups of, like, sixteen, called "families." We didn't do things individually, we did it together as a family, and the families got into competition, like chair-building. When we get into stuff together and we compete, even if you don't like a person, you have to cheer them on, because they're in the family. And if they lose, that means your family loses.
>
> —Amelia

As more students develop attitudes like this, teachers can eventually turn problems like tardiness into something that the whole class can discuss and work on together.

> I think [talking about the problem] is better with the whole class. It can get chaotic, but if you really want this to happen, then it will work out. Because we realized how bad we've been, and we found the problem, and so we really try to work to become a better class.
>
> —Carmela

Reward Our Efforts with Things We Really Want

The gold stars and stickers of elementary school no longer will motivate middle schoolers. Instead, they want gestures and items that fit with their new, more social sense of self. That might mean actual activities, but it also could come across in little signals that the teacher regards students with increased respect.

> I don't think we should get candy. Candy kind of makes the situation worse, 'cause you end up getting hyper. [A good reward is] that the teacher will ease up on you, give you more chances, or respect you more.
>
> —Gabe

> A better reward is giving us funner activities, like playing games or academic activities that are fun.
>
> —Carmela

Giving students a choice can feel like a reward, as they feel they are earning a teacher's respect.

> I think they should take a survey first, to see what would be a good reward if we finished all our work on time. Maybe some people don't want to do something that other people do, so teachers could switch off, and change it after a certain time. I really like reading, so sometimes I wish we could take a break from school, and we would have time at school where we could just read. Or, if you didn't like reading, you could do something else.
>
> —Itai

Help Us Learn As You Correct Our Behavior

Students do not want to change their behavior when teachers humiliate them in front of others. If they feel a teacher's disappointment too keenly, they are likely to withdraw or retaliate.

197

My science/math teacher always embarrasses kids, in a way. Like, if you forgot your math book, or if your homework is overdue for this amount of time, she'll announce it to the whole class, instead of just telling you privately. I don't think they should do that. It kind of makes me feel embarrassed, I just want to go away and crawl into a hole or something.

—Gabe

Teachers should know, like, when somebody's having a bad day. They sit there and yell at us, and we're going to flip out on them. [One teacher] kept telling me to do this, do that, 'cause I was behind in work. And I was trying to do my work as fast as I can, but I don't write that fast. So, I kept going "Whooo! Hufff!" and sucking my teeth and stuff, just to get on her nerves. She was sitting there saying, like, "Amanda, be quiet, Amanda, stop." I got mad, and I just got up and left. [It would have helped me if she would] talk to me about it—like, just let me sit there for a little bit, in the classroom, and be me.

—Amanda

If teachers let them save face by addressing the matter in a private conversation, students are much more likely to shift toward a more positive action.

The way in which teachers impose consequences can make the difference in whether or not students learn from their mistakes. They need both adult insight and adult firmness.

A lot of times teachers are, like, "Don't make these mistakes." But the reason why I am how I am right now is because I learned from my own mistakes. We're going to learn from the consequences, whether it's a time out for a five-year-old or, like, suspension for a 13-year-old. I think it's necessary for kids, especially our age—not too much, but a little bit, so we know not to do them.

—Alma

And when teachers call home, students still want them to be on their side, even when the call is about a problem with their behavior.

I've noticed that the only reason teachers ever call parents are to tell them their kids are in trouble. And how does that help? I'm sick of it. It's horrible. Yeah, well, "Your child, I found out that he or she stole from my classroom," or something. But it doesn't help. They should say, "I think maybe your kid might be experiencing some issues and that's why maybe they're failing their work. Is there anything . . .?" And they should recommend things to help. Like, maybe recommend a tutor, you know. Actually, like, involve yourself in the child's life, not just in the child's education.

—Alma

Know Everything, See Everything

As middle schoolers experience the confusing pushes and pulls of their daily social interactions, they want and need a teacher's presence and watchful eyes. Students are continually exploring the boundary between what adults see and hear and what they do not.

When the teacher's not watching, then the kids curse at each other or throw things. And then the teacher finds out about it, but she don't know who to blame, so she just blame everybody. So, then everybody get in trouble. The people who did not do it should not get in trouble, but that's how people are. But I tell on people, 'cause I'm not getting in trouble for what I did not do.

—Thea

The teacher should know that, like, when her back is turned, kids are making faces about her or talking about her, or stuff like that. And then when they turn back around, we start acting like we wasn't doin' nothin'. I've done it myself sometimes. And I got caught, but then I said I didn't do it, but the teacher knew I did it, cause she seen me.

—Tatzi

School is a complicated social world for kids, and they want you to recognize its different aspects.

[My friend] found this wallet in the gym and stole it, kind of. And, I guess my teacher loves her still, but she found out how bad my friend really acts. She doesn't see the masks anymore. She's more aware. I'm thankful that there's a teacher like that. But not a lot of teachers are like that.

—Carmela

Teachers think that some people are star students, they're the best, they're really smart, they're just great. They don't know that outside of their classroom, they're swearing, doing other stuff that the teachers think are inappropriate. In my class, there was this one kid who was always smart, well behaved, and then outside the classroom, he was always swearing and doing bad stuff. I think they should know more about that.

—Daniel

They need you to help them sort out the many pressures that may interfere with their focus in the classroom.

In my class we've been going through so much trouble 'cause of peer pressure. We started to have class discussions about problems and about things we see each other doing that we don't like to see each other doing. Even if it takes time off math, this is really important, because teachers are the people who teach the students how to be when they grow up. The children are the future. We don't want our leaders in the future to be hypocrites. We don't want them to be confused. And, if we do have leaders like that, think about how the followers will be!

—Carmela

Students know that a teacher's presence in informal moments is just as important as his or her classroom role. If a teacher knows them already, students count on him to understand and perhaps to help them through some difficult moments in the halls or on the playground.

I just wish that there was a teacher during passing period that would stand outside and watch the hallway, 'cause at my school there's a lot of fights.

—Edward

Kids ask to use the bathroom, and they don't really go to the bathroom, they wander around the hallway.

—Katelin

The teachers should try to interact a little bit with the students, like during recess, even though the students may not like it. Teachers should really observe. Because it really helps. People are getting really touchy at my school, and sometimes people cover up for people so they can make out. And a lot of the boys are really also, like, perverts there. They touch girls, and the girls, well, they're so used to it that they don't do anything about it. And everyone swears now. It's like a habit. After every single frickin' word, they swear. And it's very annoying.

—Carmela

As teachers notice the dynamics among kids outside the classroom, they will not only be keeping students safe from harm, they will also be responding to students' need to have adults see what is really going on with them in their groups.

Bullies don't pick on people bigger than them, they just pick on shrimpy little kids. You can see that they can't do anything back to the bullies. I feel like I should try to stand up for them, but then, if I do, then the bullies might beat me up. There could be, like, a line of bullies, and they try to chase you or beat you up, and you have to try to run away from them. I just walk away, and if I see a teacher or something, tell them.

—Edward

Sometimes it's good for the teachers to step in, sometimes it's not. If a kid gets scared of something—if he's, like, down, and you see him getting bullied—and then he walks over to, like, a group or a teacher, then the teacher might know that he's getting bullied. Most of the kids that get picked on just ignore it. But I don't think it's fun.

—Jason

All too often, the problems students experience outside the classroom will also surface, in little ways, inside the classroom.

When you got a problem with a student [in class], teachers don't want to listen to it. They just be like, "Ignore it, ignore it." But you can't really ignore the problem that you having, and then you [go to] settle the problem, and you all end up fighting.

—Thea

The time teachers take to work out such issues lets students see that the benefits of conflict resolution can carry over into the classroom, too.

On Thursdays, [seventh-grade classes] have this little extra section called "goal time," and we talk about little goals we want to accomplish in the class. And, then my class has time for, like, issues. Like, kids can say, "Oh, I have an issue with this person," and then they try to solve it right there. Everybody else in the class will listen and try to help, instead of just listening to the argument and gossiping or something.

—Genesis

I had a problem with my best friend. She was getting jealous of me hanging out with her other best friend. And so we had a fight, and [the teacher] talked to us, and how he settled it was kind of weird for me. We had to change our shoes and act like we were the other person, and that's how we settled our problems. She put on my shoes. Then we had to pretend like we were the other person and talk about why we might

be mad at each other, and why were we sad, and what were we thinking. I was shy at first, I've never settled something before like that. Then we kind of started being friends again, and I want to be thankful for that.

—Jessica

Jessica is not alone in feeling relieved and grateful. Teachers who hear what students say about the social obstacles that keep them from learning will find a world of effective ideas to address those issues. Along the way, they are likely to see students relax and blossom in the classroom, developing the social habits that support their academic skills and understanding.

References

Elkind, D. (1967). Egocentrism in adolescence. *Child Development, 38,* 1025–1034.

Kagan, J. (1972). A conception of early adolescence. In J. Kagan and R. Coles (Eds.), *Twelve to sixteen: Early adolescence* (pp. 90–105). New York: Norton.

Kegan, R. (1982). *The evolving self: Problem and process in human development.* Cambridge, MA: Harvard University Press.

Kohlberg, L. (1984). *Essays on moral development: The psychology of moral development* (vol. 2). San Francisco: Harper & Row.

Pintrich, P. R., Roeser, R. W., & DeGroot, E. A. M. (1994). Classroom and individual differences in early adolescents' motivation and self-regulated learning. *Journal of Early Adolescence, 14*(2), 139–161.

Schnuit, L. (2006). Using curricular cultures to engage middle school thinkers. *Middle School Journal, 38*(1), 4–12.

Selman, R. (1980). *The growth of interpersonal understanding: Developmental and clinical analyses.* New York: Academic Press.

Selman, R. (2003). *The promotion of social awareness: Powerful lessons from the partnership of developmental theory and classroom practice.* New York: Russell Sage Foundation.

Wigfield, A., & Eccles, J. S. (1994). Children's competence beliefs, achievement values, and general self-esteem: Change across elementary and middle school. *Journal of Early Adolescence, 14*(2), 107–138.

Willis, J. (2007). Cooperative learning is a brain turn-on. *Middle School Journal, 38*(4), 4–13.

KATHLEEN CUSHMAN, author of *Fires in the Bathroom: Advice for Teachers from High School Students* (New Press, 2003) and *First in the Family: Advice about College from First-Generation Students* (Next Generation Press, 2005, 2006), is a co-founder of What Kids Can Do, Inc. E-mail: kathleencushman@mac.com. **LAURA ROGERS,** who with Theodore R. Sizer and others founded the Francis W. Parker Charter Essential School in Massachusetts, teaches at Tufts University, Medford, Massachusetts. E-mail: laura.rogers@tufts.edu.

Author note—This article is adapted from the forthcoming book *Fires in the Middle School Bathroom: Advice for Teachers From Middle Schoolers* (New Press, April 2008). Its research and writing was supported by MetLife Foundation.

An Early Warning System

By promptly reacting to student distress signals, schools can redirect potential dropouts onto the path to graduation.

RUTH CURRAN NEILD, ROBERT BALFANZ, AND LIZA HERZOG

The alarm has sounded. The United States has a high school graduation crisis. The crisis does not stem, however, from any precipitous drop in the percentage of students who graduate. In fact, graduation rates are about as high as they have ever been. What makes current graduation rates alarming is a reality of the new U.S. economy: It is practically impossible for individuals lacking a high school diploma to earn a living or participate meaningfully in civic life. Adding to the urgency is evidence of disproportionately low graduation rates among low-income and minority youth. Recent estimates suggest that between one-third and one-half of minorities do not earn a high school diploma (Education Week, 2007).

Policymakers and educators have tended to view dropping out of high school in two contradictory ways. On the one hand, they view it as predictable, given the high dropout rates in certain demographic categories and geographic locations. At the same time, they view the experiences that precede a specific student's dropping out as mysterious, difficult to predict, and idiosyncratic. Some students unaccountably "become bored with school"; "fall in with the wrong crowd"; or experience a jarring life event, such as a pregnancy or a parent's unemployment, that precipitates their dropping out of school.

Our research suggests that, on the contrary, many students who drop out of high school send strong distress signals for years. These students are metaphorically waving their hands and asking for help. By paying attention, schools and districts can develop interventions that can help keep potential dropouts on track to graduation.

These signals form an early warning system that schools can use to identify students who are at risk of dropping out.

Policymakers and educators face several challenges in devising these early intervention strategies. The first is to figure out which signals to look for and when to look for them. These signals form an early warning system that schools can use to identify students who are at risk of dropping out. The second challenge is to develop a set of structures and practices within schools that enable educators to review data and pinpoint those students who are sending signals. The third challenge is to determine the help that students need, on the basis of the signals they send and their responses to previous interventions.

Early Indicators

During the past 25 years, a great deal of research has focused on why students drop out. This research typically uses data from complex surveys or in-depth interviews with students, none of which are commonly available to schools and school districts. We wondered whether the ordinary data that school districts keep in student records could operate as a crystal ball of sorts to predict which students might drop out.

We began our research in Philadelphia, using data on several cohorts of students that became available to us when we established a number of Talent Development High Schools and Middle Grades Programs in the city. Johns Hopkins developed these school models, and the Philadelphia Education Fund was the local reform partner. Schools implementing the Talent Development model were located in areas with low graduation rates.

The school district data that we examined included test scores, report card grades, behavior marks, attendance records, special education status, English language learner status, and demographic categories. We identified the following indicators using Philadelphia data. However, we have been able to replicate them with slight modifications in other cities, such as Boston and Indianapolis.

Signals in the Middle Grades

A high percentage of dropouts send distress signals in the middle grades, long before they actually drop out of school. We followed an entire cohort of students in Philadelphia who entered the 6th grade in September 1996—approximately 14,000 students—to determine their dropout status six years later. Then, going back to the 6th grade data, we looked for any signals—a poor course grade, a low test score—that would give students *at least a*

75 percent probability of dropping out of high school. We chose the 75 percent threshold because it enables schools and districts to focus their scarce resources on students who are at high risk of dropping out.

In Philadelphia, we found that a 6th grader with even one of the following four signals had at least a three in four chance of dropping out of high school:

- A final grade of *F* in mathematics.
- A final grade of *F* in English.
- Attendance below 80 percent for the year.
- A final "unsatisfactory" behavior mark in at least one class.

Students with more than one signal—for example, failing mathematics *and* missing a lot of school—had an even higher probability of dropping out within six years. But we also found that some students sent just one signal, indicating that various factors can culminate in dropping out. Students with failing course grades may struggle with academic skills and motivation, those with inconsistent attendance may find little support for schooling at home, and those with poor behavior marks may have social and emotional challenges that require attention. The signals that have the greatest predictive power relate to student action or behavior in the classroom, rather than to a particular status, such as receiving special education services.

In a separate analysis, we looked at indicators for a cohort of 8th graders. For these students, too, a failing course grade in mathematics or English or an attendance rate of less than 80 percent during the year were highly predictive of dropping out. In fact, more than 50 percent of the students who ultimately dropped out sent one or more of these signals during 8th grade, meaning that more than half of the dropouts in the cohort could have been identified even before they entered high school.

The earlier a student first sends a signal, the greater the risk that he or she will drop out of school.

Although all distress signals should be taken seriously in the middle grades, schools should pay special attention to students who send a signal in 6th grade. The earlier a student first sends a signal, the greater the risk that he or she will drop out of school.

Signals in High School

Ninth grade is a treacherous year for students, particularly those in large urban districts. Even students who were doing moderately well in the middle grades can be knocked off the path to graduation by the new academic demands and social pressures of high school. Among students who sent their first serious distress signal in 9th grade, those who earned fewer than two credits or attended school less than 70 percent of the time had at least a 75 percent chance of dropping out of school. Most of these students did not drop out immediately but attempted 9th grade courses for another one or two years before finally giving up on school altogether.

Eighty percent of the dropouts we studied in Philadelphia had sent a signal in the middle grades or during the first year of high school. The majority of U.S. high school dropouts are enrolled in such large urban districts (Balfanz & Legters, 2004). Consequently, an effective early warning system could identify— at least by 9th grade—the vast majority of future dropouts nationwide.

What Can Schools Do?

Our experience with urban middle schools and high schools suggests that several strategies can help keep students on the path to graduation.

Intervening in the Middle Grades

Philadelphia is currently piloting a middle grades program— Keeping Middle Grades Students on the Graduation Path—that seeks to develop tools and practices for responding to early indicators that signal potential dropouts. Developed through the joint efforts of the School District of Philadelphia, the Philadelphia Education Fund, and the Johns Hopkins University Center for the Social Organization of Schools, the program is based on two fundamental assumptions: (1) that students' signals are surface indicators of deeper academic problems, behavioral issues, or responses to the home or school environment that schools need to identify and address; and (2) that only a small percentage of students will need the most intensive and costly interventions. For the majority of students, lower-cost schoolwide strategies that seek to prevent the problems will suffice.

Schools can identify strategies for addressing each signal— such as course failure, poor attendance, and behavior issues— using a three-tiered schoolbased model for prevention and intervention. The top tier consists of effective *whole-school preventive measures*. In urban districts that struggle with high dropout rates, these whole-school measures can keep an estimated 70–80 percent of the students on track to graduation during the middle grades. For example, a school might institute a schoolwide attendance program that highlights the importance of attendance; tracks attendance daily at the classroom level; has an adult in the building respond to the first absence of each student; and provides weekly recognition and monthly social rewards (such as pizza parties or field trips) to students with perfect or near-perfect attendance.

The second tier of *targeted interventions* is aimed at the 10–20 percent of students who require additional focused supports. A student who continues to miss school despite a schoolwide attendance program might sign an attendance contract or attend a conference at school with family members; the student may then receive a brief daily check-in from a school staff member. This adult might acknowledge that the student is in school and mention that he or she looks forward to seeing the student the next day and will call home if the student does not show up.

Finally, the third tier of *intensive interventions* is reserved for the 5–10 percent of students who need small-group or one-on-one supports. A student with severe attendance problems might be assigned to a team of adults at the school (including, for example, a counselor, an assistant principal, and a teacher) who will work together to understand the source of the attendance problem and try to solve it. If the problem is too deep-rooted for the school alone to resolve, the team will arrange for the student and his or her family to receive appropriate social service supports.

Using the three-tiered model, schools in the pilot program take a hard look at what they are actually doing to address attendance, behavior, and academic performance. Our experience has shown us that schools are often doing far less in each of these areas than they think.

To help schools identify which students send signals and how they respond to interventions, we developed an on-demand, classroom-level data program. Teachers can use this program to track individual students on a day-to-day basis so they can quickly identify students who need to move to a more intensive level of intervention. Likewise, they can reevaluate students who have responded to intensive interventions. This early indicator tracking tool has proved so useful that Philadelphia plans to make it available to other schools through the districtwide integrated data management system.

Keeping an Eye on 9th Graders

The best thing a high school can do to keep students on track to graduation is to develop a comprehensive set of strategies that includes attention to climate, curriculum, and credit accumulation. At a minimum, high schools need to set the conditions for 9th grade success by making sure that the curriculum and associated supports help fill gaps in mathematics and reading comprehension. Our work with schools in low-income areas across the United States indicates that the majority of students in these schools are two to three years below grade level when they start 9th grade. They need an age-appropriate curriculum that enables them to catch up on the intermediate skills that high school courses assume that students have.

At the same time, schools need to be organized so that they can flag students who are having difficulty early on. Data from urban districts (Roderick & Camburn, 1999) indicate that struggling 9th graders typically send their signals in the first or second marking period—or even during the first few weeks of school. The Talent Development High School model (see www. csos.jhu.edu /tdhs), developed by urban educators and Johns Hopkins researchers, organizes 9th grade teachers into four-person interdisciplinary teams. Each team compares notes about its students' classroom performance and collaboratively decides on strategies for dealing with those who are having trouble.

Finally, schools need to make available to struggling or disengaged students various avenues through which they can experience short-term school success. These include such activities as debates, artistic and performance experiences, and service learning projects, with opportunities to participate linked to good attendance and course effort.

Reengaging Out-of-School Youth

Despite the best efforts of schools to keep students on the path to graduation, some students will always drop out. Some will try to return to school, but the traditional high school format may not serve them well because of their age, lack of credits, or personal responsibilities. In Philadelphia, a group of partners—including the school district, city agencies, nonprofit groups that advocate for children and public education, workforce development organizations, and research universities—has begun to collaborate on a multiple-pathways system that will enable out-of-school youth to earn their diplomas.

This collaboration, known as Project U-Turn (www .projectuturn.net) and led by the Philadelphia Youth Network, envisions a system that offers opportunities for students on the basis of their age, literacy and numeracy levels, and credits earned. By examining district data, the Project U-Turn partners learned that although the largest group of dropouts had earned fewer than eight credits despite being at least 17 years old, they had few opportunities to earn a diploma other than reenrolling in traditional high schools, which were hardly enthused about taking in older students with histories of failure. The partnership is currently working to design and fund new education options for these students. In addition, youth who have dropped out just shy of graduation need opportunities to fast-track their high school diplomas while earning credits from a community college.

The Price of Not Intervening

Data from large urban districts and our work with urban middle schools and high schools have shown us that, for the majority of students who drop out of high school, the major cause is *not* an unanticipated life event or disinterest in receiving a diploma, but rather school failure. Moreover, the vast majority of dropouts stay enrolled in school for an additional year or two after their first experience of course failure. This continuing connection with school, however tenuous, suggests a window of time during which schools can redirect potential dropouts back onto the path to high school graduation.

The majority of students drop out of high school because of school failure.

It also tells us that what schools do matters. Growing numbers of high schools have beaten the odds and kept their students on the path to graduation. Good research-based and practice-validated interventions can improve student attendance, behavior, and effort; academic interventions can improve course performance more directly. The U.S. graduation rate crisis is not fueled by students who lack the potential or desire to graduate, but rather by secondary schools that are not organized to prevent students from falling off the path to graduation or to intervene when they do.

Finally, we need to recognize that some middle schools and high schools are overwhelmed by the number of potential dropouts who walk through their doors. Research shows that approximately 50 percent of the dropouts in the United States are produced by 15 percent of the high schools, all of which serve populations with high poverty rates (Balfanz & Legters, 2004). Further, most of these high schools have two or more feeder middle schools. Dropout rates for an entering cohort can top 50 percent, meaning that hundreds and sometimes thousands of students at each school are in need of comprehensive and sustained supports. These schools need to have in place strong prevention and intervention systems aimed at improving student attendance, behavior, effort, and course performance.

The need for strong programs has significant implications for how we staff and fund the secondary schools that educate economically disadvantaged students. Implementing the whole-school reforms and multitiered prevention and intervention systems that these schools need requires financial and human resources equal to the task, along with high-quality technical assistance. High-poverty schools will also likely benefit from partnerships with external organizations skilled at delivering integrated student supports as well as with community organizations and national service organizations that can provide the necessary people power for mentoring and tutoring on a sufficient scale.

Without question, there are financial costs associated with intervening with students who are on the path to dropping out. But the price of not intervening—in terms of individual lives

that do not reach their potential and the broader social costs of having a class of citizens who lack a basic academic credential—is incalculably greater.

References

Balfanz, R., & Legters, N. (2004). Locating the dropout crisis: Which high schools produce the nation's dropouts? In G. Orfield (Ed.), *Dropouts in America* (pp. 57–84). Cambridge, MA: Harvard Education Press.

Education Week. (2007). *Diplomas Count 2007: Ready for what? Preparing students for college, careers, and life after high school.* Bethesda, MD: Editorial Projects in Education Research Center.

Roderick, M., & Camburn, E. (1999). Risk and recovery from course failure in the early years of high school. *American Educational Research Journal, 36,* 303–343.

RUTH CURRAN NEILD (rneild@csos.jhu.edu) and **ROBERT BALFANZ** (rbalfanz@csos.jhu.edu) are research scientist at Johns Hopkins University and coauthor of *Unfulfilled Promise: The Dimensions and Characteristics of Philadelphia's Dropout Crisis, 2000–2005* (Philadelphia Youth Network, 2006). **LIZA HERZOG** (lherzog@philaedfund.org) is Senior Research Associate at the Philadelphia Education Fund.

UNIT 6
Assessment

Unit Selections

Key Points to Consider

- What fundamental concepts from contemporary learning and motivation theories have specific implications for how teachers assess their students? Are such practices consistent with what is promulgated with standardized tests?

- What principles of assessment should teachers adopt for their own classroom testing? How do we know if the test scores teachers use are reliable and if valid inferences are drawn from the scores? How can teachers make time to involve students in self-assessment?

- Describe some ways you would provide feedback to students about their performance on different types of classroom tasks and assignments. For example, how would the information you provide and how you provide it differ for an in-class group project versus a weekly homework assignment, or paper/report, or unit test?

- What do you think are some of the unintended consequences of the increased focus on high-stakes testing?

- As a teacher, how can you balance effectively preparing students to succeed on high-stakes assessments, while not making them the focus of learning in your classroom?

- If the standards used in different states to determine whether students have performed proficiently on high-stakes tests are defined differently and vary depending on the grade level or content, how can we be sure students have really learned content to expected levels?

Student Web Site
www.mhcls.com

Internet References

Awesome Library for Teachers
   http://www.neat-schoolhouse.org/teacher.html
FairTest
   http://fairtest.org
Kathy Schrocks's Guide for Educators: Assessment
   http://school.discovery.com/schrockguide/assess.html
Phi Delta Kappa International
   http://www.pdkintl.org
Washington (State) Center for the Improvement of Student Learning
   http://www.k12.wa.us/

In which reading group does Jon belong? How do I construct tests? How do I know when my students have mastered the course objectives? How can I explain test results to Mary's parents? Teachers answer these questions, and many more, by applying principles of assessment. Assessment refers to procedures for measuring and recording student performance and constructing grades that communicate to others levels of proficiency or relative standing. Assessment principles constitute a set of concepts that are integral to the teaching-learning process. Indeed, a significant amount of teacher time is spent in assessment activities, and with more accountability there is a greater emphasis on assessment.

Assessment provides a foundation for making sound evaluative judgments about students' learning and achievement. Teachers need to use fair and unbiased criteria in order to assess student learning objectively and accurately and make appropriate decisions about student placement. For example, in assigning Jon to a reading group, the teacher will use his test scores as an indication of his skill level. Are the inferences from the test results valid for the school's reading program? Are his test scores consistent over several months or years? Are they consistent with his performance in class? The teacher should ask and then answer these questions so that he or she can make intelligent decisions about Jon. On the other hand, will knowledge of the test scores affect the teacher's perception of classroom performance and create a self-fulfilling prophesy? Teachers also evaluate students in order to assign grades, and the challenge is to balance "objective" test scores with more subjective, informally gathered information. Both kinds of evaluative information are necessary, but both can be inaccurate and are frequently misused.

The articles in this section focus on two contemporary issues in assessment—standards and the use of high-stakes standardized tests, and classroom assessment that is integrated with teaching.

The first article in this unit provides a review of standards from all 50 states, identifying those that had standards that provided sufficient information regarding what students should learn to allow teachers to develop a core curriculum and a test developer to create aligned assessments. In the second article, Rick

© Getty Images/Digital Vision

Stiggins, an expert in testing, argues that classroom assessment and grading practices should focus on enhancing learning, rather than sorting students. The third article examines the impact of school environments dominated by a focus on high-stakes testing on student motivation. In "Feedback That Fits," Susan Brookhart highlights the importance of formative assessment and reminds us that providing meaningful and appropriate feedback to students is at the heart of its effectiveness. The final article returns to the issue of high-stakes testing, examining the variation across states in how they define "proficiency" and how this might impact students at different levels of schooling.

Mismatch

When state standards and tests don't mesh, schools are left grinding their gears.

Heidi Glidden and Amy M. Hightower

Imagine this: Sylvia and Steve are seventh-graders in different states. They're both eager, hard-working students, and do reasonably well in school. Come springtime, they join most students across the country in taking various state assessments in (at least) reading and mathematics. You know these tests: they're the ones that teachers give to students on behalf of their state to monitor how students are doing in school. They are also used for federal accountability purposes to determine if schools and school districts are doing a good job educating students.

Sylvia and Steve have had different experiences with these assessments. For Sylvia, they're just par for the course. Sure, she'd rather be playing softball, but taking a test of the things she's been taught that year in school has become routine. No huge surprises, no big deal.

But bluntly put, Steve is dreading assessment season this year, based on the state test he had to take last year in math. Last year, he'd worked hard to learn the material he was taught. He always submitted the homework his teacher assigned and listened hard as his teacher explained the concepts of mean, median, and mode. From fractions and ratios to probability and circumference, Steve felt like he was mastering some tough sixth-grade math concepts. His teacher thought so too, giving him As and Bs all year. When springtime testing came around, he'd been ready to strut his stuff. But when he sharpened his #2 pencil and sat down to take the state test, darned if they didn't ask him about the Pythagorean Theorem and three-dimensional objects!

These were things he hadn't studied and his teacher hadn't taught. Wait, wasn't his brother, an eighth-grader, studying some of this stuff? How was he supposed to know the answers now? Had someone given him the wrong test by mistake? No mistake: He just didn't have the knowledge he needed to answer the questions. So he did what anyone in this situation would do—he flipped through the exam and guessed. And he fidgeted. And he watched the clock, waiting for the uncomfortable moment to pass. He remembers the moment like it was yesterday.

What went wrong? Why did both Sylvia and Steve feel ready for the test, but only one of them was actually prepared? Here's a dirty little secret that educators know all too well: State tests and state content standards don't always match up. It's far too often assumed that what's expected, what's taught, and what's

tested are cut from the same cloth. That's the way it should be. It's what advocates of standards-based education assumed. It's certainly rational, and it's something that's never even questioned by the general public once the test results come in—the results that judge students, schools, and sometimes teachers. But as it turns out, this assumption is too often untrue and a lot of things are at play behind the scenes.

As it happens, Steve's state isn't particularly clear about what it expects of students in each grade and in each subject. This puts his teachers in a guessing game about what to teach. It also has test developers guessing about what content to sample from as they design their assessments. Maybe they guess the same, and maybe they don't. But why leave it to chance?

Sylvia's state, in contrast, is more explicit about the grade-by-grade standards students are to meet. Her state doesn't direct teachers in *how* to teach or at what precise moment to introduce a particular concept, but it does set specific, helpful year-end goals for every grade and every subject. These standards are explicit enough for teachers like Sylvia's to build their curriculum around and for testing companies to know what content to draw upon for their tests.

While Steve and Sylvia are fictitious, the problem we've identified is real. Based on our research, just 11 states are like Sylvia's, with all of their reading and math tests clearly aligned to strong standards. The rest, to a greater or lesser extent, are like Steve's. In fact, nine states do not have any of their reading or math tests aligned to strong standards. The consequences are far-reaching since the results of these tests are used to make consequential, high-stakes judgments.

No Child Left Behind (NCLB) has led to the vast expansion of states' testing programs and heightened the stakes associated with testing results. Specifically in reading and math,[1] NCLB requires states to have grade-level standards in grades 3 to 8 and once in high school, and to annually test students in grades 3 to 8 and at least once in high school using assessments that are criterion-referenced/standards-based and aligned with the state's content area standards. The results of these assessments are used to determine if schools and districts are making adequate yearly progress. If not, NCLB imposes a series of escalating sanctions. (To learn more about NCLB, see www.aft.org/topics/nclb/index.htm.)

Given the fact that state standards are often deemed inadequate (see, for example, "The State of State Standards 2006" from the Thomas B. Fordham Institute; "Staying on Course" from Achieve Inc.; and "Making Standards Matter" from the American Federation of Teachers), we wondered how states are doing in developing assessment systems that meet NCLB's requirements and, therefore, can be legitimately used for accountability purposes. So we conducted a study to address two key questions. First, since (as we demonstrate in the next section) it is not possible to align a test to vague standards, are states' content standards in reading and math clear and specific? Second, for those standards that are clear and specific, is there evidence posted on states' Web sites for all to see that the state assessments are aligned with those standards?

For grades 3 to 8 and high school, we looked at all 50 states' and the District of Columbia's reading and math standards, as well as at the test specifications that the states and D.C. provide to their test developers.[2] Of course, we would have preferred to look directly at the actual tests, but they are confidential. Nevertheless, looking at the test specifications is the next best option; it seems highly unlikely that a test could be better aligned to the standards than the specifications upon which the test is based.

Just 11 states have all of their reading and math tests clearly aligned to strong standards. Nine states do not have any of their reading or math tests aligned to strong standards.

Our first step was to examine the strength, clarity, and specificity of the standards themselves. Content standards are at the heart of everything that goes on in a standards-based system, including testing. They define our expectations for what's important for children to learn, and serve as guideposts about what content to teach and assess. These state-developed public documents are the source that teachers, parents, and the general public consult to understand content-matter expectations. Content standards should exist for every single grade, kindergarten through high school, in every subject. Grade-by-grade content standards increase the likelihood that all students are exposed to a rigorous, sequenced curriculum that is consistent across schools and school districts. Grade-specific standards also make it possible to align not only assessments, but also curriculum, textbooks, professional development, and instruction. States that organize their standards grade-by-grade are best able to specify what students should learn and when they should learn it.

We examined each state's content-standards documents to determine whether there was enough information about what students should learn to provide the basis for teachers to develop a common core curriculum and for the test developer to create aligned assessments. There is no perfect formula for this; we made a series of judgments based on a set of criteria. **To be judged "strong," a state's content standards had to:**

- Be detailed, explicit, and firmly rooted in the content of the subject area so as to lead to a common core curriculum;
- Contain particular content:

- Reading standards must cover reading basics (e.g., word attack skills, vocabulary) and reading comprehension (e.g., exposure to a variety of literary genres);
- Math standards must cover number sense and operations, measurement, geometry, data analysis and probability, and algebra and functions;

- Provide attention to both content and skills; and,
- Be articulated without excessive repetition in both math and reading in grades 3, 4, 5, 6, 7, 8, and once in high school.

For any standard we found to be strong, we then examined the extent to which the state's test specifications were aligned with the standard. In our alignment review, each state received a yes/no judgment for each of the NCLB-related tests it administered. **To meet our criteria for alignment, a state must:**

- Have evidence of the alignment of its tests and content standards through documents such as item specifications, test specifications, test blueprints, test development reports, or assessment frameworks; and,
- Post the alignment evidence on its Web site in a transparent manner.

The need for alignment should be obvious, but the need for transparency may not be. Transparency "demystifies" how (or if) the pieces connect to function as a unified *system*. A transparent system is not necessarily an aligned system, but only with transparency can we determine if the tests and content standards are aligned. A transparent testing program provides information to parents, students, teachers, and the public about the development, purpose, and use of state tests. It also brings any problems within the testing program to light so that they can be addressed. This is why, in our review, states could not simply assert that their tests were aligned to their standards. And yet, our alignment criteria were still not as stringent as we believe they should be. A state could receive alignment credit for fairly minimal documentation. For example, if a state had grade-by-grade math standards organized by number sense, algebra, measurement, etc., we gave that state credit for evidence of alignment if it indicated the percentage of items devoted to each of these topics.

Grade-by-grade content standards increase the likelihood that all students are exposed to a rigorous, sequenced curriculum that is consistent across schools and school districts.

As our opening vignette indicates, what we found was not what the average person would assume. There were two basic problems: Standards that were too weak to guide teachers or test developers, and standards that were strong, yet mismatched with tests nonetheless. To explain the problems with the weak standards, in the following section, we provide examples of vague and repetitive standards—and examples that show why tests cannot be aligned with such weak standards. We wrap up that section with data on how widespread weak standards are. Then we turn to the mismatch between strong standards and test specifications. Once again we provide examples of the mismatch as well as data on how widespread this problem is.

Vague Standards Inevitably Lead to Mismatch

The quality of content standards matters greatly to teaching, learning, and testing, so it directly affects the fairness and validity of tests and the accountability systems they support. Despite this obvious and indisputable fact, we found that across the country, many states have failed to write clear and specific standards for every subject and grade. As you read the examples[3] of vague state standards in the table below, consider them from both the teachers' and the test developers' perspectives. None of these standards gives enough information to teachers about what to teach or to test developers about what to test.

Subject	Grade(s)	Examples of Vague Content Standards
Reading	4	Demonstrate the understanding that the purposes of experiencing literary works include personal satisfaction and development of lifelong literature appreciation.
	8	View a variety of visually presented materials for understanding of a specific topic.
Math	4	Students will describe, extend, and create a wide variety of patterns using a wide variety of materials (transfer from concrete to symbols).
	9-12	Model and analyze real-world situations by using patterns and functions.

In contrast, take a look at the following standards; they are clear and specific enough to eliminate the guesswork.

Subject	Grade	Examples of Strong Content Standards
Reading	4	Distinguish between cause and effect and between fact and opinion in informational text. Example: In reading an article about how snowshoe rabbits change color, distinguish facts (such as snowshoe rabbits change color from brown to white in the winter) from opinions (such as snowshoe rabbits are very pretty animals because they can change colors).
Math	4	Subtract units of length that may require renaming of feet to inches or meters to centimeters. Example: The shelf was 2 feet long. Jane shortened it by 8 inches. How long is the shelf now?

These latter examples are particularly strong—most states do not have standards this clear and specific. Instead, most states

occupy a middle ground between these and the terribly vague standards shown previously. But even with middling standards, it's very hard for a teacher to know what to teach and a test developer to know what to test. Teachers may feel like they just have to make do—but test developers often do not. In states with weak standards, additional information is often given to testing companies that further clarifies or elaborates on the standard to be tested. In essence, these states are creating an additional layer or set of "shadow" standards, which are often more specific and detailed than the official standards from which they presumably came. However, it is the test developer who receives these "shadow" standards, not teachers.

Surprised? So were we. Let's look at an example to make this a little easier to understand. Here is a 4th-grade math standard and the corresponding test specification. Clearly, the test developer received much more specific information than teachers—information that would be just as helpful in preparing lessons as it is in preparing tests.

What 4th-Grade Teachers Receive

Describe, model, and classify two- and three-dimensional shapes

What the Test Developer Receives

Students demonstrate understanding of two- and three-dimensional geometric shapes and the relationships among them. In the grade 4 test, understanding is demonstrated with the following indicators as well as by solving problems, reasoning, communicating, representing, and making connections based on indicators—

- Using properties to describe, identify, and sort 2- and 3-dimensional figures [Vocabulary in addition to that for grade 3: polygon; kite; pentagon; hexagon; octagon; line; line segment; parallel, perpendicular, and intersecting lines]
- Recognizing two- and three-dimensional figures irrespective of their orientation
- Recognizing the results of subdividing and combining shapes, e.g., tangrams
- Recognizing congruent figures (having the same size and shape) including shapes that have been rotated

---

Clearly, it is possible for a teacher to believe she has covered a vague standard, and for a test developer to come up with an angle that she hasn't considered. In the example above, a teacher may do several lessons on describing, modeling, and classifying two- and three-dimensional shapes—but she may not think to teach students to recognize them "irrespective of their orientation," as the test specifications state. The only way to avoid such problems is for the teachers and the test developers to receive the same clear, detailed standards.

Some states are creating "shadow" standards, which are often more specific and detailed than the official standards. However, it is the test developer who receives these "shadow" standards, not teachers.

Repetition Makes Standards Vague

Even when states manage to write standards that sound reasonably specific, they sometimes poison the effort by repeating the standard over four or more grades. This problem is especially evident in states' reading standards. For example, one state's reading standards expect eighth-graders to, among other things, "develop a critical stance and cite evidence to support the stance"; "use phonetic, structural, syntactical, and contextual clues to read and understand words"; and "describe how the experiences of a reader influence the interpretation of a text." That may sound reasonable—but the exact same thing is expected of 2nd-graders, 10th-graders, and students in every other grade in between.

Repetition of standards makes it hard, if not impossible, for a teacher to know what content students have mastered in previous grades or to determine the specific differences in student expectations from grade to grade. It certainly isn't enough for a teacher to build his or her lesson plans.

Let's look a little more at that state that expects 2nd- through 10th-graders to develop a critical stance. The vast majority of its reading standards are exactly the same from grade 3 to grade 10 and, shockingly, *more than 40 percent of the 10th-grade standards come from grade 2 standards:*

- 71 percent of the 4th-grade standards are repeated (56 percent come from grade 2)
- 87 percent of the 6th-grade standards are repeated (44 percent come from grade 2)
- 92 percent of the 8th-grade standards are repeated (42 percent come from grade 2)
- 81 percent of the 10th-grade standards are repeated (42 percent come from grade 2)

One can easily imagine how 2nd- and 9th-grade teachers, for example, would develop different lesson plans based on these repetitive standards. But what would prevent 2nd- and 3rd-grade teachers from teaching almost identical lessons? And what happens to the unlucky student who is assigned in 4th, 5th, and 6th grades to use *Charlotte's Web* to "describe how the experiences of a reader influence the interpretation of a text." Or the unlucky student who is never assigned *Charlotte's Web* for any reason? A central purpose of state standards is to avoid such repetition and such gaps—but repetitive standards that do not specify what should be taught at each grade can't serve that purpose and, as a result, they can't be used to develop standards-based tests either.

Unfortunately, the example we've been using is a pretty typical one. Here's an example of reading standards from another state that are even more repetitious from grade to grade:

- 75 percent of the 3rd-grade standards are repeated from K-2
- 98 percent of the 5th-grade standards are repeated from grade 4
- 94 percent of the 7th-grade standards are repeated from grade 4

Repetitious standards are neither clear nor specific enough to guarantee that what's taught in each and every grade and subject is also what's tested. The result? Guesswork on the part of teachers and testing companies. Or, as we saw with the vague standards, sometimes the teachers are left to guess, but the test developers get the extra information they need.

In this example, 3rd- and 4th-grade teachers work from the exact same reading standard, with no indication of what is appropriate for a 3rd-grader versus a 4th-grader. The test developer, however, receives the standard *plus* specific indicators of what is appropriate for a 3rd-grader and what is appropriate for a 4th-grader:

What 3rd- and 4th-Grade Teachers Receive

Determines meaning of words through knowledge of word structure (e.g., compound nouns, contractions, root words, prefixes, suffixes)

What the Test Developer Receives

Determines meaning of words through knowledge of word structure (e.g., compound nouns, contractions, root words, prefixes, suffixes)

Grade 3 Test

Assessment Indicators
Prefixes: *mis-, pre-, pro-, re-, un-*
Suffixes: *-ed, -er, -est, -ing, -ly, -y*
Only test prefixes and suffixes listed above

Grade 4 Test

Assessment Indicators
Prefixes: *anti-, dis-, ex-, non-, under-*
Suffixes: *-en, -ful, -less, -ment, -ness*
Only test prefixes and suffixes listed above

Unlike teachers' information about the reading standard for grades 3 and 4, the test developers receive indicators that are unique to each grade. The indicators add information that would be useful to teachers, but teachers don't receive them—nor do they necessarily know that such an elaboration even exists. An excellent 3rd-grade teacher could, in good conscience and with good reason, deliver highly effective instruction on the prefixes *anti-, dis-,* and *non-,* but because she guessed wrong as to what would be on the 3rd-grade test versus the 4th-grade test, her test results would indicate that her students did not know anything about prefixes. Of course, the 4th-grade teacher is in an equally difficult position—how is she to know which prefixes the students have already learned and which will be tested?

V ague and repetitious standards are clearly a big problem, but just how widespread are they? It depends on the subject. States tend to have fairly good math standards, but weak reading standards. Here is what we found:

- **A majority of states have grade-by-grade reading and math standards in every grade that NCLB requires them to assess.** Six states still have not developed grade-by-grade standards in reading and math despite being required to do so by the guidance written for NCLB: Colorado, Illinois, Montana, Nebraska, Pennsylvania, and Wisconsin. At the high school level, 20 states clustered their reading standards and 22 clustered their math standards.

> **For example, while 3rd- and 4th-grade teachers work from the exact same standard, the test developer receives specific indicators of what is appropriate for a 3rd-grader and what is appropriate for a 4th-grader.**

- **But, grade-by-grade standards do not guarantee clear, specific standards: Only a little more than one-third of states have strong reading and math standards in every grade that NCLB requires them to assess.** Just 18 states and the District of Columbia met our criteria for having strong standards in reading and math in all grades that NCLB requires states to assess: California, Georgia, Indiana, Louisiana, Massachusetts, Michigan, Nevada, New Jersey, New Mexico, New York, North Carolina, North Dakota, Ohio, South Dakota, Tennessee, Virginia, Washington, and West Virginia.

- **Across states and subjects, of all the 714 content standards reviewed, 70 percent met our criteria for being strong.** States had strong standards in mathematics: Eighty-seven percent of the math standards we reviewed met our criteria. In contrast, only about half of the states' reading content standards met our criteria (53 percent).

- **On average, the most vague and repetitious content standards are in reading.** Only 20 states had strong reading standards in grades 3 to 8 and high school; 12 states had weak reading standards in all of these grades. Twenty-one percent of all reading standards reviewed

---

Science Standards and Tests Suffer from Mismatch, Too

No Child Left Behind (NCLB) is somewhat more lenient with science than it is with reading and math. Science standards need not be grade by grade; academic expectations at each of the three grade-level ranges (such as grades 3 to 5, 6 to 9, and 10 to 12) are sufficient. Likewise, starting in the 2007–2008 school year, science must be assessed annually, but just once during elementary, middle/junior high, and high school—and the results are not incorporated into federally required accountability determinations.

Nonetheless, we still wanted to examine states' science standards and the extent to which their standards and test specifications are aligned. Unfortunately, as with reading and math, we found serious problems.

As we explained in the main article, grade-by-grade standards are essential for guiding instruction. And yet, 13 states cluster their science standards at the elementary level, 13 states at the middle-school level, and 21 states at the high-school level. While permitted under NCLB, clustering results in vague standards such as these:

- Grades 5 to 8—Describe the historical and cultural conditions at the time of an invention or discovery, and analyze the societal impacts of that invention;
- Grades 9 to 12—Analyze the impacts of various scientific and technological developments.

Besides getting frustrated, what is a teacher or a test developer to do with such a directive? The teacher can guess what will be tested, and the test developer can guess what will be taught. Or, they can demand more specifics from the state. For the test developers at least, such demands appear to be working.

Take a look at the following example of one 7th-grade science standard and the corresponding test specification—it reveals something we reported on in the main article with reading and math. The test designer gets the same standard that is given to teachers, as well as very specific examples that help clarify the focus of the standard.

What 7th-Grade Teachers Receive:
The student will cite examples of individuals throughout history who made discoveries and contributions in science and technology.

What the Test Developer Receives:
The student will cite examples of individuals throughout history who made discoveries and contributions in science and technology.
- Examples of individuals (and some of their discoveries or contributions) are limited to: Rachel Carson–*Silent Spring;* George Washington Carver–agricultural products, technology; Nicolas Copernicus–Copernican revolution; Charles Darwin–classification, ecology, and natural selection; Galileo Galilei–gravity and telescopes; Jane Goodall–primate research; James Hutton–geology; Anton van Leeuwenhoek and Robert Hooke–microscopy; Johann Gregor Mendel–genetics; Isaac Newton–gravity, mechanics, light, and telescopes; Louis Pasteur–pasteurization; and Alfred Wegener–plate tectonics.

As a teacher, wouldn't you feel like you covered the standard if you taught your students about Thomas Edison's light bulb, Eli Whitney's cotton gin, and Lord Kelvin's Kelvin scale? You might feel good, but you would not have prepared your students for a test that focused on Rachel Carson, George Washington Carver, and Johann Gregor Mendel. Teachers (and their students) would benefit significantly from the additional information provided to the test developers, but that information is not included as a part of the standards. Teachers wouldn't even know to look for this elaboration.

—H.G. and A.H.

were significantly repetitious across the grades (meaning word-by-word repetition across the grades at least 50 percent of the time). Fifteen states had reading standards that repeated the same reading standards in three or more grades.

In some states, the clarity and specificity of the standards are not the problem. The grade level and subject content to be taught are specific enough, but the tests simply cover other things.

Even with Strong Standards, Mismatch Can Happen

In some states, the clarity and specificity of the standards are not the problem; instead, it is the lack of follow-through. The grade level and subject content to be taught are specific enough, but the tests simply cover other things. For example, in one state, the 3rd-grade test pulls content from both the 3rd- and 4th-grade standards:

What 3rd-Grade Teachers Receive

Third-grade student uses a variety of strategies to determine meaning and increase vocabulary (for example, prefixes, suffixes, root words, less common vowel patterns, homophones, compound words, contractions).

What 4th-Grade Teachers Receive

Fourth-grade student uses a variety of strategies to determine meaning and increase vocabulary (for example, multiple meaning words, antonyms, synonyms, word relationships, root words, homonyms).

What the 3rd-Grade Test Developer Receives

Third-grade test content limit—Vocabulary words for prefixes (e.g., *re-, un-, pre-, dis-, mis-, in-, non-*), suffixes (e.g., *-er, -est, -ful, -less, -able, -ly, -or, -ness*), root words, multiple meanings, antonyms, synonyms, homophones, compound words, and contractions should be on grade level.

A 3rd-grade teacher in this state is unlikely to have her students prepared for questions relating to words with multiple meanings, antonyms, or synonyms because, according to the state's content standards, these concepts are not to be addressed until grade 4. As the example above demonstrates, the specific content standards that teachers receive from their state don't always match up with what the state gives test developers to create the tests.

Here's another example (taken from a different state) that reveals a similar problem. In this case, there are 8th-grade math

---

What 8th-Grade Teachers Receive

Under the header "Measurement and Estimation" are the following seven standards:

- Develop formulas and procedures for determining measurements (e.g., area, volume, distance).
- Solve rate problems (e.g., rate × time = distance, principle × interest rate = interest).
- Measure angles in degrees and determine relations of angles.
- Estimate, use and describe measures of distance, rate, perimeter, area, volume, weight, mass, and angles.
- Describe how a change in linear dimension of an object affects its perimeter, area, and volume
- Use scale measurements to interpret maps or drawings.
- Create and use scale models.

What the 8th-Grade Test Developer Receives

Assessment Anchor: Demonstrate an understanding of measurable attributes of objects and figures, and the units, systems, and processes of measurement.
    Convert measurements: Eligible Content
- Convert among all metric measurements (milli, centi, deci, deka, kilo using meter, liter, and gram).
- Convert customary measurements to 2 units above or below the given unit (e.g., inches to yards, pints to gallons).
- Convert time to 2 units above or below a given unit (e.g., seconds to hours).
- Convert from Fahrenheit to Celsius or Celsius to Fahrenheit.

---

standards and test specifications that *almost* match up. Both the standards and test specifications are about measurement, but they diverge in two important ways. First, although the standards say nothing explicitly about converting measurements, the test specification expects students to make several different types of conversions. Second, one of those conversions—moving from Fahrenheit to Celsius—involves content not even included in the 8th-grade standards.

The 8th-grade standards have content that would require students to have, as the assessment anchor requires, "an understanding of measurable attributes of objects and figures, and the units, systems, and processes of measurement." However, since teachers do not receive the specifics that the test developer receives, the 8th-grade teachers do not know to devote extra time to conversions, and the 8th-grade teachers—and their students—end up with the blame when the students perform poorly on the test.

Because of NCLB's testing requirements, states have rushed to establish tests that comply with the law. However, there appears to be very little urgency to align those tests with the content standards or be transparent about which standards are assessed. Here is what we found:

Where and Why Does Mismatch Exist?

Only 11 states met our criteria for having tests transparently aligned to strong standards: Calif., Ind., La., Nev., N.M., N.Y., Ohio, Tenn., Va., Wash., and W.Va. This table shows why the others fell short.

State	Some Test Specifications Not Online	Some Mismatch between Standards and Test Specifications	Percentage of Strong Reading and Math Standards	Percentage of Tests Transparently Aligned to Strong Reading and Math Standards
Alabama		✓	79	64
Alaska			79	79
Arizona			71	71
Arkansas	✓		79	0
Colorado		✓	14	14
Connecticut		✓	50	0
Delaware	✓		50	0
D.C.	✓		100	0
Florida			64	64
Georgia		✓	100	57
Hawaii	✓		50	0
Idaho		✓	57	50
Illinois		✓	0	0
Iowa	✓		0	0
Kansas			50	50
Kentucky			57	57
Maine	✓		50	7
Maryland	✓		57	57
Massachusetts	✓		100	43
Michigan	✓		100	43
Minnesota			50	50
Mississippi		✓	86	79
Missouri	✓	✓	50	0
Montana	✓	✓	0	0
Nebraska	✓	✓	29	29
New Hampshire			50	50
New Jersey	✓	✓	100	43
North Carolina	✓	✓	100	43
North Dakota	✓		100	0
Oklahoma			86	86
Oregon			71	71
Pennsylvania		✓	57	57
Rhode Island			50	50
South Carolina	✓	✓	64	14
South Dakota		✓	100	50
Texas			57	57
Utah		✓	71	50
Vermont	✓		57	57
Wisconsin		✓	21	0
Wyoming		✓	71	0

- **Eleven states met our criteria for having both strong reading and math standards and documenting in a transparent manner that their tests align to them in all NCLB-required grades.** They are: California, Indiana, Louisiana, Nevada, New Mexico, New York, Ohio, Tennessee, Virginia, Washington, and West Virginia. Eleven states is not a lot, but keep in mind that states could fall short for several reasons—having some content standards that are weak, not aligning their strong standards to their tests, and/or not providing evidence of alignment online. Of those who fell short (39 states plus the District of Columbia), 17 did so because at least some of their testing documents were not online, 32 did so because at least some of their standards were weak, and 18 did so because their standards and tests were not aligned.

- **An additional three states had at least 75 percent of their tests aligned to strong content standards.** With a few adjustments in particular grades or in just one subject, these additional three states would fully meet our criteria for alignment to strong content standards: Mississippi (meeting 86 percent of our criteria), Oklahoma (meeting 86 percent), and Alaska (meeting 78 percent).

- **Twice as many states met our criteria for having strong and transparently aligned standards and tests in math than they did in reading.** Twenty-six states have aligned math tests across all grades tested. But, just 13 states have aligned reading tests across all grades tested.

O verall, our results lead us to conclude that states are doing a better job in developing content standards than in using them to drive assessment. Simply put, in too many cases, tests that are not aligned to strong standards are driving many accountability systems. In order to comply with NCLB, states have been under enormous pressure to quickly develop new assessment systems. We hope this research provides some ideas on how they could improve those systems in the near future. For example, state departments of education need to post their content standards on their Web sites, along with information about how their state tests are aligned to these standards—they also need to keep this information current. When test developers or state officials clarify standards in order to write test items that align to them, the clarifications should be made public and should make their way back to the original standards document in the form of clearly marked revisions. This way, educators will be able to skip the guessing game and teach the content that the state believes is most important.

Detailed information about content standards and what will be tested should be readily available to anyone (teachers, students, parents, the general public) at any point, and should not have to be ferreted out. Educators, in particular, need to know that what will be tested draws from the content standards to which they are teaching. Where there's a mismatch, or a fuzzy match, or only an assumed match between the content that's expected and the content that's assessed—and when the results are used to judge students, schools, and teachers—it's no wonder that folks in schools toss up their hands in frustration.

Notes

1. NCLB also requires states to have science standards and, as of the 2007–2008 school year, administer science tests, but the law does not hold states accountable for their science results. Therefore, our main analysis focuses on reading and math, and we deal with science briefly in the box on page 216.

2. For brevity's sake, throughout this document when we refer to the states collectively, we are actually referring to the 50 states and the District of Columbia.

3. When providing examples, we chose not to name the states in the main article because it would unfairly place emphasis on them instead of on the broader problem. The examples are drawn from the following states: 1) vague standards—Arkansas, Connecticut, and Montana; 2) strong standards—Indiana; 3) repetitious standards—Connecticut and Texas; 4) mismatched standards and test specifications—Florida, Kansas, Minnesota, Montana, and Pennsylvania.

HEIDI GLIDDEN, assistant director, and **AMY M. HIGHTOWER,** associate director, are assessment and accountability specialists for the AFT teachers division. This article is based on a research brief they published in July 2006.

Assessment through the Student's Eyes

Rather than sorting students into winners and losers, assessment for learning can put all students on a winning streak.

RICK STIGGINS

H istorically, a major role of assessment has been to detect and highlight differences in student learning in order to rank students according to their achievement. Such assessment experiences have produced winners and losers. Some students succeed early and build on winning streaks to learn more as they grow; others fail early and often, falling farther and farther behind.

We can't let students who have not yet met standards fall into losing streaks, succumb to hopelessness, and stop trying.

As we all know, the mission of schools has changed. Today's schools are less focused on merely sorting students and more focused on helping *all* students succeed in meeting standards. This evolution in the mission of schools means that we can't let students who have not yet met standards fall into losing streaks, succumb to hopelessness, and stop trying.

Our evolving mission compels us to embrace a new vision of assessment that can tap the wellspring of confidence, motivation, and learning potential that resides within every student. First, we need to tune in to the emotional dynamics of the assessment experience from the point of view of students—both assessment winners and assessment losers. These two groups experience assessment practices in vastly different ways, as shown in "The Assessment Experience." To enable all students to experience the productive emotional dynamics of winning, we need to move from exclusive reliance on assessments that verify learning to the use of assessments that support learning—that is, assessments *for* learning.

Assessment *for* Learning

Assessment for learning turns day-to-day assessment into a teaching and learning process that enhances (instead of merely monitoring) student learning. Extensive research conducted around the world shows that by consistently applying the principles of assessment for learning, we can produce impressive gains in student achievement, especially for struggling learners (Black & Wiliam, 1998).

Assessment for learning begins when teachers share achievement targets with students, presenting those expectations in student-friendly language accompanied by examples of exemplary student work. Then, frequent self-assessments provide students (and teachers) with continual access to descriptive feedback in amounts they can manage effectively without being overwhelmed. Thus, students can chart their trajectory toward the transparent achievement targets their teachers have established.

The students' role is to strive to understand what success looks like, to use feedback from each assessment to discover where they are now in relation to where they want to be, and to determine how to do better the next time. As students become increasingly proficient, they learn to generate their own descriptive feedback and set goals for what comes next on their journey.

Teachers and students are partners in the assessment for learning process. For example, teachers might have students study samples of work that vary in quality and collaborate in creating their own student-friendly version of a performance assessment scoring rubric. Or students might create practice versions of multiple-choice tests that parallel the content of an upcoming final exam, which they can then use to analyze their own strengths and weaknesses and to focus their final preparation for that exam. Students can accumulate evidence of their learning in growth portfolios. They can also become partners with teachers in communicating about their own learning successes by leading their parent/teacher conferences.

Assessment for learning provides both students and teachers with understandable information in a form they can use immediately to improve performance. In this context, students become both self-assessors and consumers of assessment information. As they experience and understand their own improvement over time, learners begin to sense that success is within reach if they keep trying. This process can put them on a winning streak and keep them there.

The Assessment Experience

For Students on Winning Streaks	For Students on Losing Streaks
Assessment Results Provide	
Continual evidence of success	Continual evidence of failure
The Student Feels	
Hopeful and optimistic	Hopeless
Empowered to take productive action	Initially panicked, giving way to resignation
The Student Thinks	
It's all good. I'm doing fine.	This hurts. I'm not safe here.
See the trend? I succeed as usual.	I just can't do this . . . again.
I want more success.	I'm confused. I don't like this—help!
School focuses on what I do well.	Why is it always about what I can't do?
I know what to do next.	Nothing I try seems to work.
Feedback helps me.	Feedback is criticism. It hurts.
Public success feels good.	Public failure is embarrassing.
The Student Becomes More Likely To	
Seek challenges.	Seek what's easy.
Seek exciting new ideas.	Avoid new concepts and approaches.
Practice with gusto.	Become confused about what to practice.
Take initiative.	Avoid initiative.
Persist in the face of setbacks.	Give up when things become challenging.
Take risks and stretch—go for it!	Retreat and escape—trying is too dangerous!
These Actions Lead To	
Self-enhancement	Self-defeat, self-destruction
Positive self-fulfilling prophecy	Negative self-fulfilling prophecy
Acceptance of responsibility	Denial of responsibility
Manageable stress	High stress
Feeling that success is its own reward	No feelings of success; no reward
Curiosity, enthusiasm	Boredom, frustration, fear
Continuous adaptation	Inability to adapt
Resilience	Yielding quickly to defeat
Strong foundations for future success	Failure to master prerequisites for future success

When we use assessment for learning, assessment becomes far more than merely a one-time event stuck onto the end of an instructional unit. It becomes a series of interlaced experiences that enhance the learning process by keeping students confident and focused on their progress, even in the face of occasional setbacks.

The goal of assessment for learning is not to eliminate failure, but rather to keep failure from becoming chronic and thus inevitable in the mind of the learner. Duke University basketball coach Mike Krzyzewski has pointed out that the key to winning is to avoid losing twice in a row (Kanter, 2004, p. 251). He meant that if you lose once and fix it, you can remain confident. Losing twice, though, can raise questions, crack that confidence, and make recovery more difficult. So when learners suffer a failure, we must get them back to success as quickly as

possible to restore their confidence in their capabilities. This is the emotional dynamic of assessment for learning.

Scenario 1: Set Students Up for Success

Here is an example of the use of assessment for learning that builds student confidence from the start. Notice who develops and uses the assessment.

A high school English teacher assigns students to read three novels by the same author and develop a thesis statement about a common theme, consistent character development, or social commentary in the novels. They must then defend that thesis in a term paper with references. To set students up for success, the teacher begins by providing them with a sample of an outstanding paper to read and analyze. The next day, the class discusses what made the sample outstanding.

As their next assignment, the teacher gives students a sample paper of poor quality. Again, they analyze and evaluate its features in some detail. Comparing the two papers, students list essential differences. The class then uses this analysis to collaboratively decide on the keys to a high-quality paper.

After identifying and defining those keys, the students share in the process of transforming them into a rubric—a set of rating scales depicting a continuum of quality for each key. The teacher provides examples of student work to illustrate each level on the quality continuum.

Only after these specific understandings are in place do students draft their papers. Then they exchange drafts, analyzing and evaluating one another's work and providing descriptive feedback on how to improve it, always using the language of the rubric. If students want descriptive feedback from their teacher on any particular dimension of quality, they can request and will receive it. The paper is finished when the student says it is finished. In the end, not every paper is outstanding, but most are of high quality, and each student is confident of that fact before submitting his or her work for final evaluation and grading (Stiggins, in press; Scenario 1 adapted by permission).

Scenario 2: Help Students Turn Failure into Success

Here is an illustration of assessment for learning in mathematics used to help a struggling elementary student find the path to recovery from a chronic sense of failure. Notice how the teacher highlights the meaning of success and turns the responsibility over to the student. In addition, notice how the learner has already begun to internalize the keys to her own success.

Gail is a 5th grader who gets her math test back with "60 percent" marked at the top. She knows this means another *F*. So her losing streak continues, she thinks. She's ready to give up on ever connecting with math.

But then her teacher distributes another paper—a worksheet the students will use to learn from their performance on the math test. What's up with this? The worksheet has several columns. Column one lists the 20 test items by number. Column two lists what math proficiency each item tested. The teacher calls the class's attention to the next two columns: *Right* and *Wrong*. She asks the students to fill in those columns with checks for each item to indicate their performance on the test. Gail checks 12 right and 8 wrong.

"During the years prior to school entrance, information that persuades children they are loved becomes critical, and during the school years it is important for children to believe that they can succeed at the tasks they want to master."

—Jerome Kagan

The teacher then asks the students to evaluate as honestly as they can why they got each incorrect item wrong and to check column five if they made a simple mistake and column six if they really don't understand what went wrong. Gail discovers that four of her eight incorrect answers were caused by careless mistakes that she knows how to fix. But four were math problems she really doesn't understand how to solve.

Next, the teacher goes through the list of math concepts covered item by item, enabling Gail and her classmates to determine exactly what concepts they don't understand. Gail discovers that all four of her wrong answers that reflect a true lack of understanding arise from the same gap in her problem-solving ability: subtracting 3-digit numbers with regrouping. If she had just avoided those careless mistakes and had also overcome this one gap in understanding, she might have received 100 percent. Imagine that! If she could just do the test over . . .

She can. Because Gail's teacher has mapped out precisely what each item on the test measures, the teacher and students can work in partnership to group the students according to the math concepts they haven't yet mastered. The teacher then provides differentiated instruction to the groups focused on their conceptual misunderstandings. Together the class also plans strategies that everyone can use to avoid simple mistakes. When that work is complete, the teacher gives students a second form of the same math test. When Gail gets the test back with a grade of 100 percent, she jumps from her seat with arms held high. Her winning streak begins (Stiggins, Arter, Chappuis, & Chappuis, 2004; Scenario 2 adapted by permission).

Redefining Our Assessment Future

We know how to deliver professional development that will give practitioners the tools and technologies they need to use assessment effectively in the service of student success. (Stiggins et al., 2004; Stiggins & Chappuis, 2006). Thus far, however, the immense potential of assessment for learning has gone largely untapped because we have failed to deliver the proper tools into the hands of teachers and school leaders. If we are to fulfill our mission of leaving no child behind, we must adjust our vision of excellence in assessment in at least two important ways that will help us balance assessment *of* and assessment *for* learning.

First, we must expand the criteria by which we evaluate the quality of our assessments at all levels and in all contexts. Traditionally, we have judged quality in terms of the attributes of the resulting scores; these scores must lead to valid and reliable inferences about student achievement. As a result, schools have lavished attention on characteristics of the instruments that produce such scores. In the future, however, we must recognize that assessment is about far more than the test score's dependability—it also must be about the score's effect on the learner. Even the most valid and reliable assessment cannot be regarded as high quality if it causes a student to give up.

We must begin to evaluate our assessments in terms of both the quality of the evidence they yield and the effect they have on future learning. High-quality assessments encourage further learning; low-quality assessments hinder learning.

Understanding the emotional dynamics of the assessment experience from the student's perspective is crucial to the effective use of assessments to improve schools.

Second, we must abandon the limiting belief that adults represent the most important assessment consumers or data-based decision makers in schools. Students' thoughts and actions regarding assessment results are at least as important as those of adults. The students' emotional reaction to results will determine what they do in response. Whether their score is high or low, students respond productively when they say, "I understand. I know what to do next. I can handle this. I choose to keep trying." From here on, the result will be more learning. The counterproductive response is, "I don't know what this means. I have no idea what to do next. I'm probably too dumb to learn this anyway. I give up." Here, the learning stops.

In standards-driven schools, only one of these responses works, especially for students who have yet to meet standards. Assessment *for* learning is about eliciting that productive response to assessment results from students every time. It can produce winning streaks for *all* students.

References

Black, P., & Wiliam, D. (1998). Assessment and classroom learning. *Educational Assessment: Principles, Policy, and Practice, 5*(1), 7–74.

Kanter, R. M. (2004). *Confidence: How winning streaks and losing streaks begin and end.* New York: Crown Business.

Stiggins, R.J. (in press). Conquering the formative assessment frontier. In J. McMillan (Ed.), *Formative assessment: Theory into practice.* New York: Teachers College Press.

Stiggins, R. J., Arter, J. A., Chappuis, J., & Chappuis, S. (2004). *Classroom assessment FOR student learning: Doing it right— using it well.* Portland, OR: ETS Assessment Training Institute.

Stiggins, R. J., & Chappuis, J. (2006). What a difference a word makes: Assessment FOR learning rather than assessment OF learning helps students succeed. *Journal of Staff Development, 27*(1), 10–14.

RICK STIGGINS is Founder and Director of the ETS Assessment Training Institute, 317 SW Alder St., Suite 1200, Portland, OR, 97204; 800-480-3060; www.ets.org/ati.

Testing the Joy out of Learning

School cultures dominated by high-stakes tests are creating more and more reluctant learners.

Sharon L. Nichols and David C. Berliner

Since the passage of No Child Left Behind (NCLB), students have been exposed to an unprecedented number of tests. Every year in grades 3–8 and at least once in high school, virtually all public school students take tests in math and reading (and soon science). Students also take regular benchmark tests—supposedly to predict performance on the mandated tests—and district assessments throughout the school year. The time spent talking about, preparing for, and taking tests has increased exponentially.

What has all this testing achieved? Five years after NCLB was enacted, there is no convincing evidence that student learning has increased in any significant way on tests other than the states' own tests. On measures such as the National Assessment of Educational Progress (NAEP), no reliable increases in scores have occurred, nor have achievement gaps between students of higher and lower socioeconomic classes narrowed.

In contrast, a wealth of documentation indicates that the unintended and largely negative effects of high-stakes testing are pervasive and a cause for concern (see Jones, Jones, & Hargrove, 2003; Orfield & Kornhaber, 2001). In our own research, we have documented hundreds of cases in which high-stakes testing has harmed teaching and learning (Nichols & Berliner, 2007). For example, high-stakes testing has been associated with suspicious forms of data manipulation, as well as outright cheating. The tests undermine teacher-student relationships, lead to a narrowing of the curriculum, demoralize teachers, and bore students.

Research has not fully examined the impact of this test-dominated school environment on students' attitudes and dispositions toward learning. But we suspect that for most students, schooling is less joyful than it was; and for reluctant learners, schooling is worse than ever.

Overvaluing Testing, Undervaluing Learning

From the motivation literature, we know that learners are more likely to enjoy learning when activities are meaningful, fun, or interesting. Yet, again and again, high-stakes testing diminishes the fun and meaning of learning. Under pressure to prepare students to perform well in math and reading, teachers engage in repetitious instruction that boils down content to isolated bits of information, leaving little time to engage in creative interdisciplinary activities or project-based inquiry. One Colorado teacher reports,

Our district told us to focus on reading, writing, and mathematics. . . . In the past I had hatched out baby chicks in the classroom as part of the science unit. I don't have time to do that. . . . We don't do community outreach like we used to, like visiting the nursing home or cleaning up the park that we had adopted. (Taylor, Shepard, Kinner, & Rosenthal, 2003, p. 51)

We also know that students are more hardworking and persistent when they perceive the purpose of learning as self-improvement or achievement of personal goals. Yet a high-stakes testing climate sends a message that the primary purpose of learning is to score well on the test. Sometimes teaching to the test is blatant, as when teachers assign daily worksheets taken from released older versions of the test. Sometimes it is less obvious, as when instruction is based on the specific information that will be on the test. One teacher explains,

I'm teaching more test-taking skills and how to use your time wisely. Also what to look for in a piece of literature and how to underline important details. There is a lot more time spent on teaching those kinds of skills. . . . Read questions, restate the question in your answer, write so the person grading the test can read it, etc. (Taylor et al., 2003, p. 39)

As a result of the overvaluing of test results, the curriculum has narrowed. All across the United States, the time devoted to untested subjects like art, music, and social studies has been reduced or eliminated completely so that schools can teach more math, reading, writing, and now science. For example, in Kansas in 2006, high school freshmen were required to "double dose" their English classes instead of participating in electives. In a California middle school, students were required to take two periods of all core subjects and funding was dropped for music, Spanish, art, and classes in the trades and industrial design (Zastrow & Janc, 2006).

In 2006, the Bill and Melinda Gates Foundation released a report on the reasons students drop out of school (Bridgeland, DiIulio, & Morison, 2006). In this small survey of students who had already dropped out, 47 percent reported that school was "uninteresting." About 70 percent commented that they didn't feel "inspired" at school. For such reluctant learners, the increased test preparation and narrower curriculum resulting from high-stakes testing exacerbates the problem. Faced with an increasingly disjointed, decontextualized curriculum, many become actively disengaged; others simply leave.

I Pledge Allegiance to the Test

A disturbing phenomenon popping up in more and more U.S. schools is the prevalence of schoolwide pep rallies, ice cream socials, and other peculiar events meant to "motivate" students to do well on the state-mandated test. For example, one Texas high school held a rally for parents, teachers, and students during which the principal informed parents of the importance of the Texas Assessment of Knowledge and Skills (TAKS) and compared it to a marathon, in which "students need endurance." He was not subtle when he said, "This is the test of your lives!" This speech was followed by a class pledge in which students promised to "pass the test and take Parker High School to the top and lead us to exemplary" (Foster, 2006).

This is not an isolated incident. In one New York school, every spring just before test time, the principal brings students together to sing songs that will "inspire" them before and during the test. Some songs included "I'm a Believer" and "I've Been Working on My Writing" (Toy, 2006).

Bulletin boards, posters, and daily mantras constitute additional forms of explicit emphasis on the importance of tests. Clichéd slogans often appear on posters and banners throughout the school. Messages like "Take Us to Exemplary" are pervasive in many Texas schools.

When teachers report that most of their time is spent preparing for the test, when we go into schools and find hundreds of posters related to the upcoming test, when we hear of schools with daily announcements about the "test standard of the day," and when students tell us that not a day goes by without mention of the test, we can be pretty sure that the test has become the primary focus for learning.

Marginalizing Youth

High-stakes testing encourages teachers to view students not in terms of their potential, or what unique or new qualities they bring to the learning environment, but rather as test-score increasers or suppressors. Students quickly pick this up and realize they are defined as winners or losers on the basis of their test scores.

Test-score suppressors receive the clear message that they are not valued as highly as their better-performing peers. Sadly, some teachers and principals have done all sorts of unprofessional things to ensure that test-score suppressors either pass (because of rigorous test-prep activities or even more questionable means) or are dropped from testing altogether. For example, more than 500 low-scoring students in Birmingham, Alabama, were administratively "dropped" from school just days before state testing (Orel, 2003). Scores rose, principals received substantial bonuses, and hundreds of students had their lives made infinitely more difficult in the process. Such actions help to transform slow learners into reluctant learners, compounding their problems in school.

Issues associated with test score suppressors are exacerbated in states where high school students have to pass a test to receive a diploma. Hundreds of students are dropping out or opting to take the GED route, mainly because passing the test has become an insurmountable obstacle to them. This is especially true for special education students and English language learners (ELLs). Thousands try as hard as they can but cannot pass the test despite meeting all other graduation requirements. Chronic failure is demeaning, causing many otherwise highly engaged students to give up, drop out, or become increasingly cynical about schooling. The high-stakes testing culture communicates to students that their other abilities are of no value. Outstanding talent in dance, welding, art, knowledge of the U.S. Civil War, computer programming, consensus building in small groups, foreign languages, acting, and so forth count for little.

Even students who score high may become less motivated as a result of the high-stakes testing culture. These test-score increasers often feel "used"—for example, when they are pressured to take the test even when they are sick. As a result, they may adopt cynical attitudes about the purpose of being in school. As one student points out,

> The TAKS is a big joke. . . . *This is the easiest test you could ever take.* . . . I mean, forget logarithms and algebra, forget knowing about government and the Bill of Rights. Instead, we read a two-page story and then answer 11 short questions about it such as, "What was the meaning of the word *futile* in paragraph two? A: generous, B: deceptive, C: useless, and D: applesauce." ("Teen Talk," 2007)

Learners Weigh In

When many students see education as punitive and uninteresting, and when they have their abilities narrowly defined by a single test score, the potential for irreparable and damaging consequences is high. For students who struggle academically, high-stakes testing can diminish their sense of self worth, leading to decreased motivation to do well in school. And for students who see the tests as an easy rite of passage, a school culture formed around high-stakes testing is boring and unconnected. Thus, high-stakes testing cultures build reluctant learners out of even these academically talented students.

How do we know this? The voices of youth are pretty clear. They understand the exaggerated importance of tests in their lives, and it frustrates them. A 12th grader writes,

> Students (teachers as well) focus on only the TAKS. It's almost as if they have been given an ultimatum: Either pass the test and get the ticket out of there, or pass the test months later and live with the disappointment all your life. It's not fair. ("Teen Talk," 2007)

Others find the tests dehumanizing and feel angry about the narrow curriculum being forced on them. They worry that their schooling ignores other aspects of their lives. An 11th grade student writes,

> In Texas many public school districts have found raising their standardized testing averages to be the No. 1 goal of classroom curriculum. Consequently, school is no longer a forum where students can discuss the effects of alcohol, or the best method to achieve a life filled with value and pleasure, or the simple antics of their daily life. ("Teen Talk," 2007)

The pressure to achieve is highest in high-poverty schools because they are most likely to be shut down or reconsolidated under NCLB. There, the score suppressors are often force-fed a daily curriculum that includes bits of information devoid of any connection to their real lives. Foster (2006), talking with Latino students attending a high-poverty high school heard, "We learn in isolation. We learn one skill one day or in a week and then we never see it again until test time." (p. 143). Another Latino student in the same school commented,

> I was written up and sent to the office because I didn't want to do a TAKS assignment. I was told in the office that I had to do it because it was important that I pass this test. I am tired of doing TAKS, TAKS, TAKS. I am not learning anything. (Foster, 2006, p. 144)

Especially revealing are the following excerpts from a transcript of one teacher's attempt to motivate her 16 Latino 11th graders. The teacher had just handed out an essay similar to those that would be on the upcoming state test. Her goal was to motivate and inspire students to perform well on the test. But students were savvy about what was happening.

Teacher: OK, this is last-minute work for TAKS. You can pass the test. You don't want to take it again, right?

Students: *No response.*

Teacher: Please say yes.

Students: *No response.*

Teacher: You are brilliant. . . . The test is not hard. Take your time; in fact take all the time you need.

Students: *No response.*

Teacher: OK, there will be three types of open-ended questions and three types of literary selections. What does "literary" mean?

Students: *No response.*

Teacher: Is it fiction, nonfiction, or biography?

Students: *No response.*

Teacher: Are you going to talk to me or you don't know?

Students: *No response.*

Teacher: (*in an angry voice*) It's fiction, you all. (*pause*) First thing you do is answer the question. It must be insightful and thoughtful. Do not restate the question. You have five lines to fill in. Then you have to support a response. If you summarize in an open-ended question you get a zero. But if you use support for the passage, you get points. Look at this essay. Do you see how this student used textual support?

Students: *No response.*

Teacher: (*in an angry voice*) Come on!

Students: *No response.* (Foster, 2006, pp. 155–158)

And on it goes. Another exciting day at school marked only by passive resistance to what students accurately perceive to be an inferior (and boring) education.

What Can We Do?

High-stakes tests are not likely to go away, but schools can and should try to minimize their harmful effects. Schools should at least refrain from engaging in test-prep rallies, ice cream socials, or social events that focus specifically on the test. Such activities only reinforce the impression that the test is the primary goal of schooling. If schools want to hold such events to create a sense of community, they might simply rename the events to emphasize learning, not testing (for example, a Rally for Learning). Of course, the learning celebrated has to be genuine: completing outstanding science fair projects; presenting classroom projects to the town council; writing poetry, essays, or a play; and so forth. Schools need to reward demonstrations of learning in all its varieties.

Administrators and teachers should work together to reframe the purposes of learning in their school. As a start, eliminate the word "test" from any banner, poster, or encouraging slogan. Instead, use language that focuses on mastering knowledge, improving individual performance, or seeing the value of schooling for enhancing one's future.

In addition, teachers and administrators should strive to create a climate of caring and cooperation, instead of competition. We know that students are more likely to attend school and excel when they feel they belong. Feelings of connection lead to greater effort, greater persistence, and positive attitudes. Feelings of rejection have the opposite effects.

Significant changes in NCLB are unlikely to occur soon. This law has not only exacerbated the problems of reluctant learners already in our schools, but also manufactured additional reluctant learners for the schools to deal with. It is up to administrators and teachers to mitigate the damaging effects of this untenable law on many of our students by proactively working to diminish the importance of high-stakes testing in schools.

References

Bridgeland, J. M., DiIulio, J. J., & Morison, K. B. (2006). *The silent epidemic: Perspectives of high school dropouts.* Washington, DC: Civic Enterprises. Available: www.civicenterprises.net/pdfs/thesilentepidemic3-06.pdf

Foster, S. L. (2006). *How Latino students negotiate the demands of high-stakes testing: A case study of one school in Texas.* Unpublished doctoral dissertation, Arizona State University, Tempe.

Jones, M. G., Jones, B., & Hargrove, T. (2003). *The unintended consequences of high-stakes testing.* Lanham, MD: Rowman and Littlefield.

Nichols, S. L., & Berliner, D. C. (2007). *Collateral damage: How high-stakes testing corrupts America's schools.* Cambridge, MA: Harvard Education Press.

Orel, S. (2003). Left behind in Birmingham: 522 pushed-out students. In R. C. Lent & G. Pipkin, (Eds.), *Silent no more: Voices of courage in American schools* (pp. 1–14). Portsmouth, NH: Heinemann.

Orfield, G., & Kornhaber, M. L. (Eds.). (2001). *Raising standards or raising barriers? Inequality and high stakes testing in public education.* New York: Century Foundation Press.

Teen talk: Tackling TAKS. (2007, March 9). *San Antonio Express-News,* pp. F1, 5. Available: www.mysanantonio.com/salife/teenteam/stories/MYSA030907.01P.TAKS.fbdf0e.html

Taylor, G., Shepard, L., Kinner, F., & Rosenthal, J. (2003). *A survey of teachers' perspectives on high-stakes testing in Colorado: What gets taught, what gets lost* (CSE Technical Report 588). Los Angeles: University of California.

Toy, V. (2006, January 1). Elmont's school success is a lesson to others. *New York Times,* Sec. 14LI, p. 1.

Zastrow, C., & Janc, H. (2006). *The condition of the liberal arts in America's public schools: A report to the Carnegie Corporation of New York.* Washington, DC: Council for Basic Education.

SHARON L. NICHOLS is Assistant Professor, College of Education and Human Development, University of Texas at San Antonio; Sharon.Nichols@utsa.edu. **DAVID C. BERLINER** is Regents Professor, Mary Lou Fulton College of Education, Arizona State University, Tempe; berliner@asu.edu.

Feedback That Fits

To craft teacher feedback that leads to learning, put yourself in the student's shoes.

SUSAN M. BROOKHART

From the student's point of view, the ideal "script" for formative assessment reads something like, "Here is how close you are to the knowledge or skills you are trying to develop, and here's what you need to do next." The feedback teachers give students is at the heart of that script. But feedback is only effective when it translates into a clear, positive message that students can hear.

Student Understanding and Control

The power of formative assessment lies in its double-barreled approach, addressing both cognitive and motivational factors. Good formative assessment gives students information they need to understand where they are in their learning (the cognitive factor) and develops students' feelings of control over their learning (the motivational factor).

The power of formative assessment lies in its double-barreled approach, addressing both cognitive and motivational factors.

Precisely because students' feelings of self-efficacy are involved, however, even well-intentioned feedback can be very destructive if the student reads the script in an unintended way ("See, I knew I was stupid!"). Research on feedback shows its Jekyll-and-Hyde character. Not all studies of feedback show positive effects; the nature of the communication matters a great deal.

Recently, researchers have tried to tease out what makes some feedback effective, some ineffective, and some downright harmful (Butler & Winne, 1995; Hattie & Timperley, 2007; Kluger & DeNisi, 1996). Other researchers have described the characteristics of effective feedback (Johnston, 2004; Tunstall & Gipps, 1996). From parsing this research and reflecting on my own experience as an educational consultant working with elementary and secondary teachers on assessment issues, particularly the difference between formative assessment and grading, I have identified what makes for powerful feedback—in terms of how teachers deliver it and the content it contains.

Good feedback contains information that a student can use. That means, first, that the student has to be able to hear and understand it. A student can't hear something that's beyond his comprehension, nor can a student hear something if she's not listening or if she feels like it's useless to listen. The most useful feedback focuses on the qualities of student work or the processes or strategies used to do the work. Feedback that draws students' attention to their self-regulation strategies or their abilities as learners is potent if students hear it in a way that makes them realize they will get results by expending effort and attention.

Following are suggestions for the most effective ways to deliver feedback and the most effective content of feedback. Notice that all these suggestions are based on knowing your students well. There is no magic bullet that will be just right for all students at all times.

Effective Ways to Deliver Feedback
When to Give Feedback

If a student is studying facts or simple concepts—like basic math—he or she needs immediate information about whether an answer is right or wrong—such as the kind of feedback flash cards give. For learning targets that develop over time, like writing or problem solving, wait until you have observed patterns in student work that provide insights into how they are doing the work, which will help you make suggestions about next steps. A general principle for gauging the timing of feedback is to put yourself in the student's place. When would a student want to hear feedback? When he or she is still thinking about the work, of course. Its also a good idea to give feedback as often as is practical, especially for major assignments.

How Much Feedback?

Probably the hardest decision concerns the *amount* of feedback. A natural inclination is to want to "fix" everything you see. That's the teachers-eye view, where the target is perfect achievement of all learning goals. Try to see things from the student's-eye view. On which aspects of the learning target has the student done good work? Which aspects of the learning goals need improvement and should be addressed next? Are any assignments coming up that would make it wiser to emphasize one point over another? Consider also students' developmental level.

What Mode Is Best?

Some kinds of assignments lend themselves better to written feedback (for example, reviewing written work); some to oral feedback (observing as students do math problems); and some to demonstrations (helping a kindergarten student hold a pencil correctly). Some of the best feedback results from conversations with the student. Peter Johnston's (2004) book *Choice Words* discusses how to ask questions that help students help you provide feedback. For example, rather than telling the student all the things you notice about his or her work, start by asking, "What are you noticing about this? Does anything surprise you?" or "Why did you decide to do it this way?"

You should also decide whether individual or group feedback is best. Individual feedback tells a student that you value his or her learning, whereas group feedback provides opportunities for wider reteaching. These choices are not mutually exclusive. For example, say many students used bland or vague terms in a writing assignment. You might choose to give the whole class feedback on their word choices, with examples of how to use precise or vivid words, and follow up with thought-provoking questions for individual students, such as, "What other words could you use instead of *big*?" or "How could you describe this event so someone else would see how terrible it was for you?"

The Best Content for Feedback

Composing feedback is a skill in itself. The choices you make on *what* you say to a student will, of course, have a big influence on how the student interprets your feedback. Again, the main principle is considering the student's perspective.

Composing feedback is a skill in itself.

Focus on Work and Process

Effective feedback describes the students work, comments on the process the student used to do the work, and makes specific suggestions for what to do next. General praise ("Good job!") or personal comments don't help. The student might be pleased you approve, but not sure what was good about the work, and so unable to replicate its quality. Process-focused comments, on the other hand, give suggestions that move the work closer to the target, such as, "Can you rewrite that sentence so it goes better with the one before it?"

Relate Feedback to the Goal

For feedback to drive the formative assessment cycle, it needs to describe where the student is in relation to the learning goal. In so doing, it helps each student decide what his or her next goal should be. Feedback that helps a student see his or her own progress gives you a chance to point out the processes or methods that successful students use. ("I see you checked your work this time. Your computations were all correct, too! See how well that works?") Self-referenced feedback about the work itself ("Did you notice you have all the names capitalized this time?") is helpful for struggling students, who need to understand that they *can* make progress as much as they need to understand how far they are from the ultimate goal.

Try for Description, Not Judgment

Certain students are less likely to pay attention to descriptive feedback if it is accompanied by a formal judgment, like a grade or an evaluative comment. Some students will even hear judgment where you intend description. Unsuccessful learners have sometimes been so frustrated by their school experiences that they might see every attempt to help them as just another declaration that they are "stupid." For these learners, point out improvements over their previous performance, even if those improvements don't amount to overall success on the assignment. Then select one or two small, doable next steps. After the next round of work, give the student feedback on his or her success with those steps, and so on.

Be Positive and Specific

Being positive doesn't mean being artificially happy or saying work is good when it isn't. It means describing how the strengths in a students work match the criteria for good work and how they show what that student is learning. And it means choosing words that communicate respect for the student and the work. Your tone should indicate that you are making helpful suggestions and giving the student a chance to take the initiative. ("This paper needs more detail. You could add more explanation about the benefits of recycling, or you could add more description of what should be done in your neighborhood. Which suggestion do you plan to try first?") If feedback comes across as a lecture or suggestions come across as orders, students will not understand that they are in charge of their own learning.

Feedback should be specific enough that the student knows what to do next, but not so specific that you do the work. Identifying errors or types of errors is a good idea, but correcting every error doesn't leave the student anything to do.

These feedback principles apply to both simple and complex assignments, and to all subjects and grade levels. The following example of ineffective and, especially, effective feedback on a writing assignment reflects these principles in practice.

A Tale of Two Feedback Choices

As part of a unit on how to write effective paragraphs, a 4th grade teacher assigned her students to write a paragraph answering the question, "Do dogs or cats make better pets?" They were asked to have a clear topic sentence, a clear concluding sentence, and at least three supporting details. Figure 1 shows what a student named Anna wrote and what *ineffective* teacher feedback on Anna's paragraph might look like.

To provide feedback, this teacher decided to make written comments on each student's paper and return the papers to students the day after they turned them in. So far, so good. However, the feedback in Figure 1 is all about the mechanics of writing. This doesn't match the learning target for this assignment, which was to structure a paragraph to make a point and to have that point contained in a topic sentence. Because the mechanical corrections are the only comments, the message seems to be that Anna's next step is to fix those errors. However, this teacher has already fixed the errors for her. All Anna has to do is recopy this paragraph. Moreover, there is no guarantee she would understand why some words and punctuation marks were changed. Recopying by rote could result in a "perfect" paragraph with no learning involved!

This is why I like dogs better than cats. I think dogs are really playful. They can also be strong to pull you or something. They can come in different sizes like a Great Dane or a Wener dog. *Dachshund* They can also be in different colors. Some are just mutts. Others are pedigree. Best of all dogs are cute and cuddly. That is why I like dogs a lot better than cats.

Figure 1   Ineffective Feedback on Anna's Writing Assignment.

The worst part about this feedback, however, is that it doesn't communicate to Anna that she did, in fact, demonstrate the main paragraphing skills that were the learning target. Anna successfully fashioned a topic sentence and a concluding sentence and provided supporting details. She needs to understand that she has accomplished this. Once she knows that, suggestions about how to make her good work even better make sense.

Figure 2 lists *effective* comments a teacher might write on Anna's paper or, preferably (because there is more to say than a teacher might want to write or a 4th grader might want to read), discuss with her in a brief conference. A teacher would probably use a few—but not all—of these comments, depending on circumstances.

Notice that these comments first compare the student's work with the criteria for the assignment, which were aligned with the learning goal. They acknowledge that Anna's paragraph shows that she understands how to produce a topic sentence, supporting details, and a concluding sentence.

The rest of the feedback choices depends on the context. How much time is available to discuss this paper? Which other feedback comments would align with learning targets that have previously been emphasized in class? Which of the possible next steps would be most beneficial for this particular student, given her previous writing? For example, if Anna is a successful writer who likes writing, she probably already knows that describing traits she has observed in her own dog was a good strategy. If she has previously been an unsuccessful writer but has produced a paragraph better than her usual work—because the assignment finally asked a question about which she has

Possible Teacher Comments	What's Best About This Feedback
Your topic sentence and concluding sentence are clear and go together well. You used a lot of details. I count seven different things you like about dogs.	These comments describe achievement in terms of the criteria for the assignment. They show the student that you noticed these specific features and connected them to the criteria for good work.
Your paragraph makes me wonder if you have a dog who is playful, strong, cute, and cuddly. Did you think about your own dog to write your paragraph? When you write about things you know, the writing often sounds real like this.	This comment would be especially useful for a student who had not previously been successful with the writing process. The comment identifies the strategy the student has used for writing and affirms that it was a good one. Note that "the writing often sounds genuine" might be better English, but "real" is probably clearer for this 4th grader.
Your reasons are all about dogs. Readers would already have to know what cats are like. They wouldn't know from your paragraph whether cats are playful, for instance. When you compare two things, write about both of the things you are comparing.	This constructive feedback criticizes a specific feature of the work, explains the reason for the criticism, and suggests what to do about it.
Did you check your spelling? See if you can find two misspelled words. Feedback about making the topic sentence a stronger lead might best be done as a demonstration. In conference, show the student the topic sentence with and without "This is why" and ask which sentence she thinks reads more smoothly and why. Ask whether "This is why" adds anything that the sentence needs. You might point out that these words read better in the concluding sentence.	These comments about style and mechanics do not directly reflect the learning target, which was about paragraphing. However, they concern important writing skills. Their appropriateness would depend on how strongly spelling, style/usage, and word choice figure into the longer-term learning targets.

Figure 2   Examples of Effective Feedback on Anna's Writing Assignment.

something to say—it would be worth communicating to her that you noticed and naming "write about what you know" as a good strategy for future writing.

Feedback Practice Makes Perfect

Feedback choices present themselves continually in teaching. You have opportunities to give feedback as you observe students do their work in class and again as you look at the finished work. Take as many opportunities as you can to give students positive messages about how they are doing relative to the learning targets and what might be useful to do next. Make as many opportunities as you can to talk with your students about their work. As you do, you will develop a repertoire of feedback strategies that work for your subject area and students. The main thing to keep in mind when using any strategy is how students will hear, feel, and understand the feedback.

Make as many opportunities as you can to talk with your students about their work.

References

Butler, D. L., & Winne, P. H. (1995). Feedback and self-regulated learning: A theoretical synthesis. *Review of Educational Research, 65,* 245–281.

Hattie, J., & Timperley, H. (2007). The power of feedback. *Review of Educational Research, 77,* 81–112.

Johnston, R H. (2004). *Choice words. How our language affects children's learning.* Portland, ME: Stenhouse.

Kluger, A. N., & DeNisi, A. (1996). The effects of feedback interventions on performance: A historical review, a metaanalysis, and a preliminary feedback intervention theory. *Psychological Bulletin, 119,* 254–284.

Tunstall, R, & Gipps, C. (1996). Teacher feedback to young children in formative assessment: A typology. *British Educational Research Journal, 22,* 389–404.

SUSAN M. BROOKHART is an educational consultant and Senior Research Associate at the Center for Advancing the Study of Teaching and Learning (CASTL) at Duquesne University in Pittsburgh, Pennsylvania. She is the author of the upcoming (Fall 2008) ASCD book, *How to Give Good Feedback;* susan brookhart@commatbresnan.net.

The Proficiency Illusion

<small>JOHN CRONIN ET AL.</small>

At the heart of NCLB is the call for all children to become "proficient" in reading and math by 2014. Yet that law expects each state to define proficiency as it sees fit and to design its own tests. Serious problems have arisen as a result. We summarize four of them here. For the full results of our study, read *The Proficiency Illusion* online at **http://edexcellence.net/doc/The_Proficiency_Illusion.pdf.**

I. State Tests Vary Greatly in Their Difficulty

To compare how difficult it is to score proficient on states' tests, we needed to convert the states' proficiency cut scores to a single common scale. Our Measures of Academic Progress (MAP), a computerized adaptive test, provided that scale; having done extensive norming studies with MAP, we were able to estimate the percentile scores on MAP corresponding to each state's cut scores. As Figure 1 shows, we found that eighth-grade reading cut scores ranged from the 14th percentile (Colorado[1]) to the 71st percentile (South Carolina).

II. Differences in State Proficiency Cut Scores Can Be Seen in the Rigor of the Assessment Items

The differences in proficiency cut scores are not numerical artifacts. They represent real differences in the assessment items that students are expected to be able to answer. To illustrate this point, we selected several states to represent the range of proficiency cut scores used for grade 4 reading and math. We then extracted questions from the MAP item pool that were equivalent in difficulty to the proficiency cut scores for each of these states. Using the MAP items shown below, we can compare what "proficiency" requires in reading and math in several different states.

To make comparison easier, all the reading items focused on a single skill that is commonly required in all state standards: the ability to distinguish fact from opinion. Almost all reading curricula have introduced this concept prior to fourth grade.

For mathematics, we extracted examples of items from the MAP item bank with difficulty ratings equivalent to five states'

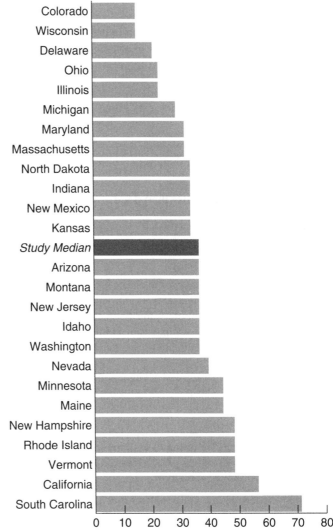

Figure 1 Grade 8 estimated reading proficiency cut scores for 2006. (ranked by MAP percentile)

proficiency cut scores in algebraic concepts. None of the items requires computational abilities that would be beyond the scope of a typical grade 4 curriculum.

Reading Exhibit 1. Grade 4 MAP item with difficulty equivalent to Colorado's proficiency cut score. (scale score 187, 11th percentile)

Alec saw Missy running down the street. Alec saw Paul running after Missy. Paul was yelling, "Missy, stop! Wait for me!"

What do we know for sure?

A. Missy is Paul's big sister, and she is mad at him.
B. Paul is mad at Missy and is chasing her down the street.
C. Alec saw Paul running after Missy and calling for her to wait.
D. Alec tried to stop Missy because Paul wanted to talk to her.

Almost all fourth-graders answer this item correctly. It contains a very simple passage and asks the student to identify the facts in the passage without making an inference. The student does not have to understand terms like "fact" or "opinion" to correctly answer the question.

Reading Exhibit 2. Grade 4 MAP item with difficulty equivalent to Wisconsin's proficiency cut score. (scale score 191, 16th percentile)

Which sentence tells a fact, not an opinion?

A. Cats are better than dogs.
B. Cats climb trees better than dogs.
C. Cats are prettier than dogs.
D. Cats have nicer fur than dogs.

This item is also quite easy for most fourth-graders and does not require reading a passage. It does introduce the terms fact and opinion, however, and some of the distinctions between fact and opinion are subtle. For example, some children may believe that the differences in cat and dog fur are fact.

Reading Exhibit 3. Grade 4 MAP item with difficulty equivalent to North Dakota's proficiency cut score (scale score 199, 29th percentile)

Summer is great! I'm going to visit my uncle's ranch in July. I will be a really good rider by August. This will be the best vacation ever!

Which sentence is a statement of fact?

A. Summer is great!
B. I'm going to visit my uncle's ranch in July.
C. I will be a really good rider by August.
D. This will be the best vacation ever!

Most fourth-graders answer this item correctly. The differences between fact and opinion in this item are considerably more subtle than in the prior item. For example, many fourth-graders are likely to believe that "Summer is great!" is not a matter of opinion.

Reading Exhibit 4. Grade 4 MAP item with difficulty equivalent to California's proficiency cut score. (scale score 204, 43rd percentile)

The entertainment event of the year happens this Friday with the premiere of Grande O. Partie's spectacular film Bonzo in the White House. This movie will make you laugh and cry! The acting and directing are the best you'll see this year. Don't miss the opening night of this landmark film—Bonzo in the White House. It will be a classic.

What is a fact about this movie?

A. It is the best film of the year.
B. You have to see it Friday.
C. It opens this Friday.
D. It has better actors than any other movie.

Just over half of fourth-graders from the MAP norm group answer this item correctly. The question requires the student to navigate a longer passage with more sophisticated vocabulary.

Indeed, the student has to know or infer the meaning of "premiere" to answer the question correctly.

Reading Exhibit 5. Grade 4 MAP item with difficulty equivalent to Massachusetts's proficiency cut score. (scale score 211, 65th percentile)

Read the excerpt from "How Much Land Does a Man Need?" by Leo Tolstoy.

So Pahom was well contented, and everything would have been right if the neighboring peasants would only not have trespassed on his wheatfields and meadows. He appealed to them most civilly, but they still went on: now the herdsmen would let the village cows stray into his meadows, then horses from the night pasture would get among his corn. Pahom turned them out again and again, and forgave their owners, and for a long time he forbore to prosecute anyone. But at last he lost patience and complained to the District Court.

What is a fact from this passage?

A. Pahom owns a vast amount of land.
B. The peasant's intentions are evil.
C. Pahom is a wealthy man.
D. Pahom complained to the District Court.

This item is clearly the most challenging to read (it is Tolstoy after all), and the majority of fourth-graders in the NWEA norm group got it wrong. The passage is long relative to the others and contains very sophisticated vocabulary. At least three of the options identify potential facts in the passage that have to be evaluated.

Math Exhibit 1. Grade 4 MAP item with difficulty equivalent to Colorado's proficiency cut score. (scale score 191, 8th percentile)

> **Tina had some marbles. David gave her 5 more marbles. Now Tina has 15 marbles. How many marbles were in Tina's bag at first?**
>
> **What is this problem asking?**
>
> A. How many marbles does Tina have now?
> B. How many marbles did David give to Tina?
> C. Where did Tina get the marbles?
> **D. How many marbles was Tina holding before David came along?**
> E. How many marbles do Tina and David have together?

This item, which reflects the Colorado NCLB proficiency cut score, is easily answered by most fourth-graders. It requires that students understand the basic concept of addition and find the right question to answer, although students need not actually solve the problem.

Math Exhibit 2. Grade 4 MAP item with difficulty equivalent to Illinois's proficiency cut score. (scale score 197, 15th percentile)

> **Marissa has 3 pieces of candy. Mark gives her some more candy. Now she has 8 pieces of candy. Marissa wants to know how many pieces of candy Mark gave her.**
>
> **Which number sentence would she use?**
>
> A. $3 + 8 = ?$
> **B. $3 + ? = 8$**
> C. $? \times 3 = 8$
> D. $8 + ? = 3$
> E. $? - 3 = 8$

This item, reflecting the Illinois cut score, is slightly more demanding but is also easily answered by most fourth-graders. It requires the student to go beyond understanding the question to setting up the solution to a one-step addition problem.

Math Exhibit 3. Grade 4 MAP item with difficulty equivalent to Texas's proficiency cut score. (scale score 205, 34th percentile)

> **Chia has a collection of seashells. She wants to put her 117 shells into storage boxes. If each storage box holds 9 shells, how many boxes will she use?**
>
> **Which equation best represents how to solve this problem?**
>
> A. $9 - 117 = ?$
> B. $9 \div 117 = ?$
> C. $117 \times 9 = ?$
> D. $117 + 9 = ?$
> **E. $117 \div 9 = ?$**

This item, at a difficulty level equivalent to the Texas cut score, is answered correctly by most fourth-graders but is harder

than the previous two. The student not only must be able to set up the solution to a simple problem, but must also know how to frame a division problem in order to answer the question correctly.

Math Exhibit 4. Grade 4 MAP item with difficulty equivalent to California's proficiency cut score. (scale score 212, 55th percentile)

> **$8 + 9 = 10 + ?$**
>
> A. 6
> B. 9
> C. 17
> **D. 7**
> E. 6

Most fourth-grade students in the MAP norm group do not answer this question correctly. The more advanced concept of balance or equivalency within an equation is introduced in this item. This concept is fundamental to algebra and makes this much more than a simple arithmetic problem. The student must know how to solve a problem by balancing the equation.

Math Exhibit 5. Grade 4 MAP item with difficulty equivalent to Massachusetts's proficiency cut score. (scale score 220, 77th percentile)

> **The rocket car was already going 190 miles per hour when the timer started his watch. How fast, in miles per hour, was the rocket car going seven minutes later if it increased its speed by 15 miles per hour every minute?**
>
> A. 205
> **B. 295**
> C. 900
> D. 1330
> E. 2850

This is obviously the most demanding item of the set and is not answered correctly by most fourth-graders within the MAP norm group. The student must understand how to set up a multiplication problem using either a two-step equation, $190 + (7 \times 15) = ?$, or a multi-step equation, $190 + (15 + 15 + 15 + 15 + 15 + 15 + 15) = ?$

These examples from reading and mathematics make it apparent that the states we studied lack a shared concept of proficiency. Indeed, their expectations are so diverse that they risk undermining a core objective of NCLB—to advance educational equality by ensuring that all students achieve their states' proficiency expectations. When the proficiency expectations in grade 4 mathematics range from setting up simple addition problems to solving complex, multi-step multiplication problems, then meeting these expectations achieves no real equity. The reading examples, too, show that "proficiency" by no means indicates educational equality. A student who can navigate the California or Massachusetts reading requirements has clearly achieved a much different level of competence than has one who just meets the Colorado or Wisconsin proficiency standard.

When the proficiency expectations in grade 4 mathematics range from setting up simple addition problems to solving complex, multi-step multiplication problems, then meeting these expectations achieves no real equity.

The proficiency expectations have a profound effect on the delivery of instruction in many states. Because of the consequences associated with failure to make adequate yearly progress (AYP), there is evidence that instruction in many classrooms and schools is geared toward ensuring that students who perform near the proficiency bar pass the state test (Neal and Whitmore-Schanzenback, 2007). In Illinois, for example, this is apt to mean that some classrooms will place greater emphasis on understanding simple math problems like the one in Math Exhibit 2, while California and Massachusetts students are working with algebraic concepts of much greater sophistication, such as those in Math Exhibits 4 and 5.

III. Standards for Mathematics Are Generally More Difficult to Meet than Those for Reading

Two sample items (Reading Exhibit 6 and Math Exhibit 6) illustrate the difference in difficulty between the reading and math standards.

Reading Exhibit 6. Grade 8 MAP item with difficulty equivalent to Massachusetts's proficiency cut score. (scale score 216, 31st percentile)

Read the passage.

Katya's eyes adjusted to the dimness. She could tell that someone had once inhabited this place. She noticed markings on the walls, and she knew they would be a significant part of her archaeological study. There were jagged lines of lightning and stick figures.

What story element has the author developed within this passage?

A. theme
B. plot
C. conflict
D. setting

This reading item has the same difficulty as the Massachusetts grade 8 reading cut score and is answered correctly by the vast majority of eighth-graders. The passage is not complex, and

students who are familiar with the literary concept of setting will answer it correctly.

Math Exhibit 6 Grade 8 MAP item with difficulty equivalent to Massachusetts's proficiency cut score (scale score 242, 67th percentile)

Maria has \$5.00 more than Joseph. Together they have \$37.50. Which of these equations would you use to find the amount of money Joseph has?

A. $j + (5 \times j) = \$37.50$
B. $j + (j \div 5) = \$37.50$
C. $5 \times j = \$37.50 + j$
D. $2 \times (j + 5) = \$37.50$
E. $j + j + 5 = \$37.50$

This item has the same difficulty as the Massachusetts mathematics proficiency standard and is missed by the majority of eighth-grade students in the NWEA norm group. The question is a multi-step problem and addresses a concept commonly found in Algebra I. Although the items in these two exhibits come from different disciplines, we know that the mathematics item is empirically more difficult than the reading item because far fewer eighth-graders within the NWEA norm group successfully answer the math item than the reading item.

IV. Reading and Math Tests in the Upper Grades Are Generally More Difficult to Pass than Those in Earlier Grades (Even after Taking into Account Obvious Differences in Student Development and Curriculum Content)

The experience of Minnesota illustrates some of the issues that may be encountered when a proficiency standard is not calibrated across grades. Imagine that you are a parent viewing the results of the Minnesota Comprehensive Assessment—series II (MCA-II) in the newspaper. Figure 2 shows the spring 2006 statewide reading results.

A parent interpreting these results would probably assume that third-graders in the state were doing far better than their peers in eighth grade. They might be concerned about the "deteriorating" performance in grades 7 and 8. Indeed, newspaper editorials, talk radio, and online discussions might identify a "crisis in the middle grades" and call for radical changes in the curriculum and organization of middle schools. Gradually, Minnesotans might come to believe that the discrepant results are a product of slumping middle school students and their lackluster teachers; meanwhile, they might believe that all is well in their elementary schools. Yet it is not clear that either inference would be warranted. If we look at Minnesota students' performance on the 2005 NAEP test in reading, shown in Table 1, we see that fourth- and eighth-graders

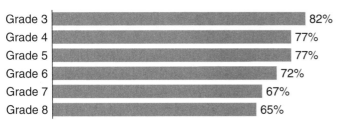

Figure 2 Proportion of students scoring proficient or better on the Minnesota Comprehensive Assessment in reading (MCA-II), 2006.

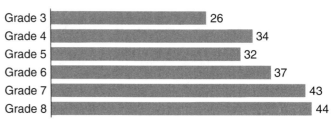

Figure 3 Reading proficiency cut scores by grade in MAP percentiles, 2006.

Table 1 Minnesota's Performance on the 2005 NAEP in Reading

	Grade 4	Grade 8
Percentage performing "proficient" or above	38%	37%

perform about the same on their respective tests (albeit far below state-reported performance). Why then the grade-to-grade gap in performance on the Minnesota state assessment?

The answer lies in understanding that the difference in reported performance is really a function of differences in the difficulty of the cut scores and not actual differences in student performance. If we look at Figure 3, which shows the NWEA percentile ranks associated with the MCA-II proficiency cut scores for reading, we see that the third-grade cut score was estimated at the 26th percentile, meaning that 26 percent of the NWEA norm group would not pass a standard of this difficulty. By extension, 74 percent of NWEA's norm group would pass this standard. The proficiency cut score for eighth-grade, however, was estimated at the 44th percentile. This more difficult standard would be met by only 56 percent of the NWEA norm population.

Now we can see that the difference in reported performance reflects differences in the difficulty of the cut scores rather than any genuine differences in student performance. According to our estimates, because of the difference in difficulty of the standards, about 18 percent fewer students would pass the Minnesota test in eighth grade than passed in third (74% − 56% = 18%). And in fact the Minnesota results show that 17 percent fewer eighth-graders passed the MCA-II than third-graders.

Poorly calibrated standards create misleading perceptions. Younger students who might need help do not get resources because they have passed the state tests, while schools serving older students may make drastic changes in their instructional programs to fix deficiencies that may not actually exist.

These data make the problem obvious. Poorly calibrated standards create misleading perceptions about the performance of schools and children. They can lead parents, educators, and others to conclude that younger pupils are safely on track to meet standards when that is not the case. They can also lead policymakers to conclude that programs serving older students have failed because proficiency rates are lower for these students, when in reality, those students may be performing no worse than their younger peers. And conclusions of this sort can encourage unfortunate misallocations of resources. Younger students who might need help now if they are to reach more difficult standards in the upper grades do not get those resources because they have passed the state tests, while schools serving older students may make drastic changes in their instructional programs in an effort to fix deficiencies that may not actually exist.

Bringing coherence to the standards by setting initial standards that are calibrated to the same level of difficulty can help avoid these problems. If states begin with calibrated standards, then they know that between-grade differences in performance represent changes in the effectiveness of instruction, rather than in the difficulty of the standard. Armed with this knowledge, schools can make better use of resources to address weaknesses in their programs and can build on strengths.

Note

1. Colorado currently reports the state's "partially proficient" level of academic performance on its state test as "proficient" for NCLB purposes, while using the higher "proficient" level for internal state evaluation purposes. In effect, Colorado has two standards: an easier standard for NCLB, and a harder standard for internal state use. For purposes of fairly comparing Colorado to other states, we used its NCLB-reported standard. Consequently, all subsequent references to "proficient" or "proficiency" in Colorado should be understood as referring to the NCLB-reported standard.

JOHN CRONIN is a research specialist with the Northwest Evaluation Association (NWEA), where MICHAEL DAHLIN and DEBORAH ADKINS are both research associates. G. GAGE KINGSBURY is NWEA's chief research and development officer. This sidebar is adapted from the "National Findings" section of *The Proficiency Illusion*, published by the Thomas B. Fordham Institute and the NWEA.

From *American Educator*, Winter 2007–2008, pp. 23–27. Copyright © 2008 by John Cronin, Michael Dahlin, Deborah Adkins, et al. Reprinted with permission of the American Educator, the quarterly journal of the American Federation of Teachers, AFL-CIO, and reprinted with permission of John Cronin, Michael Dahlin, Deborah Adkins, et al.

Test-Your-Knowledge Form

We encourage you to photocopy and use this page as a tool to assess how the articles in *Annual Editions* expand on the information in your textbook. By reflecting on the articles you will gain enhanced text information. You can also access this useful form on a product's book support Web site at *http://www.mhcls.com*.

NAME:

DATE:

_____

TITLE AND NUMBER OF ARTICLE:

_____

BRIEFLY STATE THE MAIN IDEA OF THIS ARTICLE:

_____

LIST THREE IMPORTANT FACTS THAT THE AUTHOR USES TO SUPPORT THE MAIN IDEA:

_____

WHAT INFORMATION OR IDEAS DISCUSSED IN THIS ARTICLE ARE ALSO DISCUSSED IN YOUR TEXTBOOK OR OTHER READINGS THAT YOU HAVE DONE? LIST THE TEXTBOOK CHAPTERS AND PAGE NUMBERS:

_____

LIST ANY EXAMPLES OF BIAS OR FAULTY REASONING THAT YOU FOUND IN THE ARTICLE:

_____

LIST ANY NEW TERMS/CONCEPTS THAT WERE DISCUSSED IN THE ARTICLE, AND WRITE A SHORT DEFINITION:

We Want Your Advice

ANNUAL EDITIONS revisions depend on two major opinion sources: one is our Advisory Board, listed in the front of this volume, which works with us in scanning the thousands of articles published in the public press each year; the other is you—the person actually using the book. Please help us and the users of the next edition by completing the prepaid article rating form on this page and returning it to us. Thank you for your help!

ANNUAL EDITIONS: Educational psychology 09/10

ARTICLE RATING FORM

Here is an opportunity for you to have direct input into the next revision of this volume.
We would like you to rate each of the articles listed below, using the following scale:

1. **Excellent: should definitely be retained**
2. **Above average: should probably be retained**
3. **Below average: should probably be deleted**
4. **Poor: should definitely be deleted**

Your ratings will play a vital part in the next revision.
Please mail this prepaid form to us as soon as possible.
Thanks for your help!

RATING	ARTICLE	RATING	ARTICLE
	1. Character and Academics: What Good Schools Do		21. Improve Your Verbal Questioning
	2. Memories from the 'Other': Lessons in Connecting with Students		22. Designing Learning through Learning to Design
	3. A National Tragedy: Helping Children Cope		23. Using Engagement Strategies to Facilitate Children's Learning and Success
	4. Play: Ten Power Boosts for Children's Early Learning		24. Meeting the Needs of All Students through Differentiated Instruction: Helping Every Child Reach and Exceed Standards
	5. Sustaining Resilient Families for Children in Primary Grades		25. What's Right about Looking at What's Wrong?
	6. The Curriculum Superhighway		26. Convincing Students They Can Learn to Read: Crafting Self-Efficacy Prompts
	7. The Under-Appreciated Role of Humiliation in the Middle School		27. Why We Can't Always Get What We Want
	8. Risk Taking in Adolescence: New Perspectives from Brain and Behavioral Science		28. How to Produce a High-Achieving Child
	9. Thinking Positively: How Some Characteristics of ADHD Can Be Adaptive and Accepted in the Classroom		29. How Can Students Be Motivated: A Misplaced Question?
	10. Universal Design in Elementary and Middle School		30. The Perils and Promises of Praise
	11. Recognizing Gifted Students: A Practical Guide for Teachers		31. Should Learning Be Its Own Reward?
	12. Mélange Cities		32. Strategies for Effective Classroom Management in the Secondary Setting
	13. Nine Powerful Practices: Nine Strategies Help Raise the Achievement of Students Living in Poverty		33. "No! I Won't!"
	14. Becoming Adept at Code-Switching		34. Bullying: Effective Strategies for Its Prevention
	15. Boys and Girls Together: A Case for Creating Gender-Friendly Middle School Classrooms		35. Cyberbullying: What School Adminstrators (and Parents) Can Do
	16. Differentiating for Tweens		36. IOSIE: A Method for Analyzing Student Behavioral Problems
	17. Critical Thinking: Why Is It So Hard to Teach?		37. Middle School Students Talk about Social Forces in the Classroom
	18. Constructing Learning: Using Technology to Support Teaching for Understanding		38. An Early Warning System
	19. Successful Teachers Develop Academic Momentum with Reluctant Students		39. Mismatch: When State Standards and Tests Don't Mesh, Schools Are Left Grinding Their Gears
	20. Teaching for Deep Learning		40. Assessment through the Students' Eyes
			41. Testing the Joy out of Learning
			42. Feedback That Fits
			43. The Proficiency Illusion

BUSINESS REPLY MAIL
FIRST CLASS MAIL PERMIT NO. 551 DUBUQUE IA

POSTAGE WILL BE PAID BY ADDRESSEE

McGraw-Hill Contemporary Learning Series
501 BELL STREET
DUBUQUE, IA 52001

ABOUT YOU

Name   Date

Are you a teacher? ❏ A student? ❏
Your school's name

Department

Address   City   State   Zip

School telephone #

YOUR COMMENTS ARE IMPORTANT TO US!

Please fill in the following information:
For which course did you use this book?

Did you use a text with this ANNUAL EDITION? ❏ yes ❏ no
What was the title of the text?

What are your general reactions to the Annual Editions concept?

Have you read any pertinent articles recently that you think should be included in the next edition? Explain.

Are there any articles that you feel should be replaced in the next edition? Why?

Are there any World Wide Web sites that you feel should be included in the next edition? Please annotate.

May we contact you for editorial input? ❏ yes ❏ no
May we quote your comments? ❏ yes ❏ no